THE
BIGGS MACHINE

OLD TIME POLITICS
IN POLK COUNTY, TENNESSEE

BY
TYLER L. BOYD

Acclaim Press
Your Next Great Book

P.O. Box 238
Morley, MO 63767
(573) 472-9800
www.acclaimpress.com

Book & Cover Design: Rodney Atchley

Copyright © 2023, Tyler L. Boyd
All Rights Reserved.

No part of this book shall be reproduced or transmitted in any form or by any means, electronic or mechanical, including photocopying, recording or by an information or retrieval system, except in the case of brief quotations embodied in articles and reviews, without the prior written consent of the publisher. The scanning, uploading, and distribution of this book via the Internet or via any other means without permission of the publisher is illegal and punishable by law.

First softcover print, 2025
ISBN: 978-1-965370-22-3 | 1-965370-22-5
Library of Congress Control Number: 2023934808

Previously published as hardcover in 2023
ISBN: 978-1-956027-52-5 | 1-956027-52-1

Printed in the United States of America
10 9 8 7 6 5 4 3 2 1

This publication was produced using available information.
The publisher regrets it cannot assume responsibility for errors or omissions.

Cover photos courtesy of the Polk County Historical and Genealogical Society (Burch Biggs) and http://www.courthousephotos.com (Polk County Courthouse).

For Geoffery Suhmer Smith, history buff, soldier, police officer, and my oldest and closest friend.

"What's right is right and what's wrong is wrong, no matter who you are."
- Sheriff Buford Pusser

"Power tends to corrupt and absolute power corrupts absolutely."
- Lord Acton

"If you want to find out what a man is to the bottom, give him power."
- Robert G. Ingersoll

"My father's family moved from Marietta, GA to Cleveland, TN in 1948, and the bus line came up 411 Hwy to Benton. He told me how scared he was as a six-year-old child when he got off the bus and saw the National Guard troops around the Polk County courthouse. This book had me reliving what my dad experienced and helped me understand the divisions I can still see at times in modern day Polk County. I once had a public official tell me 'we've been screwed for years. It's time for us to do the screwing.' I wondered where such hard feelings came from. After reading Tyler's book, I now know."
—Mike Bell (R),
former Tennessee State Senator

"Tyler Boyd has captured the political climate in Polk County, Tennessee in the mid-20th century with this book. This picturesque rural county in East Tennessee with its small population became a must stop for every politician seeking state or federal offices. Burch Biggs was a political strategist that was able to control all local races for years, and grew his influence to affect adjoining counties and state and federal elections as well. His influence in the state legislature was well documented. The Sheriff controlled the county with little oversight in these days. During this same time, several murders occurred, many that were a direct result of political differences and evidences of voter suppression and stuffing the ballot boxes."
—Richard W. Brogan,
retired Tennessee Bureau of Investigation
Special Agent in Charge for East Tennessee

"Tyler Boyd has written not only a well-researched and engaging story but has also written the definitive account of how Polk County politics came to be dominated by the infamous, political-machine boss, Burch Biggs. This is essential reading for anyone interested in the history of Tennessee politics."
—Dr. Warren Doctker,
President and CEO, East Tennessee Historical Society

"Tyler Boyd's extensive research has preserved an important uniquely American story about freedom and what is necessary to preserve it. This book confirms that police brutality, unfair elections and public corruption are nothing new. It also tells us how an independent citizenry overcame tyranny. Furthermore, this story teaches us that freedom can be lost without informed voters, fair, impartial jurors, and ordinary citizens who meet their civic responsibilities in adversity. *The Biggs Machine* should be read by every student of American democracy."

—Jerry Estes,
former District Attorney General for the 10th Judicial District of Tennessee

"*The Biggs Machine* is an engaging, comprehensive, and detailed account of politics in Polk County during the early and mid-twentieth century. Tyler Boyd's research for this book has been painstaking…he carefully leads the reader through the events of Polk County politics, painting a dark, three-dimensional portrait of the Biggs machine and the larger regional and state landscapes in which it operated."

—Dr. Neil Greenwood, Social Science professor,
Cleveland State Community College

"Tyler Boyd is not only a great story teller but also a very good historian. *The Biggs Machine* is a captivating read which is filled with political intrigue. It's been said that 'politics is a contact sport.' This sometimes proved to be true in rural Polk County in southeast Tennessee soon after the turn of the twentieth century. The book is a page turner. I highly recommend it."

—State Representative Dan Howell (R),
Tennessee House District 22

"Once again, Tyler Boyd, takes us on a journey into the life of a historical mover and shaker, Burch Biggs, that transformed both an industry and community. His detailed accounts give us great insight into an era, and cause of journalism that we often miss today. Whether you are a history buff or someone who just simply wants to understand how to be a positive impact on community, this book will shine light into the characteristics, determination and commitment to truth it takes to change a social and political landscape."

—State Senator Adam Lowe (R),
Tennessee Senate District 1

"Meticulously researched, *The Biggs Machine* details the violence and political skullduggery that plagued southeast Tennessee county government in the first half of the 20th century. Tyler Boyd provides us a valuable cautionary tale for the 21st century."

—Ann Toplovich,
former executive director, Tennessee Historical Society

Contents

Preface 14
Acknowledgments 17

Prologue: From Lawman to Politician 20
1. Burch's Big Comeback 33
2. Consolidating Power 38
3. The Road Contractor and the Deputy Sheriff 48
4. Dissent Among the Ranks 53
5. "You Aren't Going to Kill Me Like This, Are You?" 60
6. Taking on the "Rump Democrats" 68
7. "Elected Behind Rifles" 76
8. Sheriff Broughton Biggs 85
9. State vs. Emmett Gaddis 88
10. George Ledford, Complainant 96
11. Hood vs. Green 99
12. "He Knew of the Bad Character of the Deputies" 102
13. The Harmony Ticket 105
14. Living High on the Hog 111
15. "They Wanted to Get Rid of Him" 115
16. Burch The Kingmaker 117
17. The Strike 122
18. The Dynamitings 130
19. The Republicans Give Up 134
20. The Machine Can't Lose Anywhere 139
21. A Triple Murder in Greasy Creek 146
22. "The Biggs Machine Could Teach Crump Tricks" 150
23. "A Small Payment for the Privilege of Voting" 158
24. "Skullduggery" in Bradley County and Copperhill 163
25. A Landmark U.S. Supreme Court Decision 169
26. Bradley County Fights Back 171
27. Shorty Richards Gets a "Raw Deal" 173
28. The Ocoee Speed Trap 176

29. A Summer in the Spotlight 178
30. Biggs vs. Beeler 183
31. Jennings Must Go 187
32. Taking a Swing at Knox County 195
33. Choosing Their Voters 204
34. Sheriff Burch Glen Biggs 207
35. Kefauver's Shift 210
36. Bob Barclay Speaks Out 212
37. A Fatal Knock on the Door 215
38. The Last of the Old Time Democratic Conventions 217
39. A Second Declaration of Independence in Athens..........221
40. The Origins of the Good Government League 226
41. Chairman Barclay 230
42. "The Fee Business was Good for the Sheriff" 233
43. "We Haven't Enjoyed a Clean Election in the Past 16 Years" 237
44. The GGL's First Test 246
45. Repealing the Rippers...252
46. The Polk County Commission Act..................................255
47. The Keys to the Ballot Boxes and the Treasury................258
48. The Crown Prince Passes 266
49. The Draewell Audit..267
50. "A Clean Slate in '48" 273
51. "Mark Your Ballot, Mark it Well, Mark it Straight for the GGL!"..........282
52. "The Most Eventful Day in the History of Polk County" 291
53. Occupied Polk 299
54. Counting the Votes 308
Epilogue: "A Man on the Sunset of Life" 315

About the Author 322
Bibliography...323
Endnotes...328
Index..360

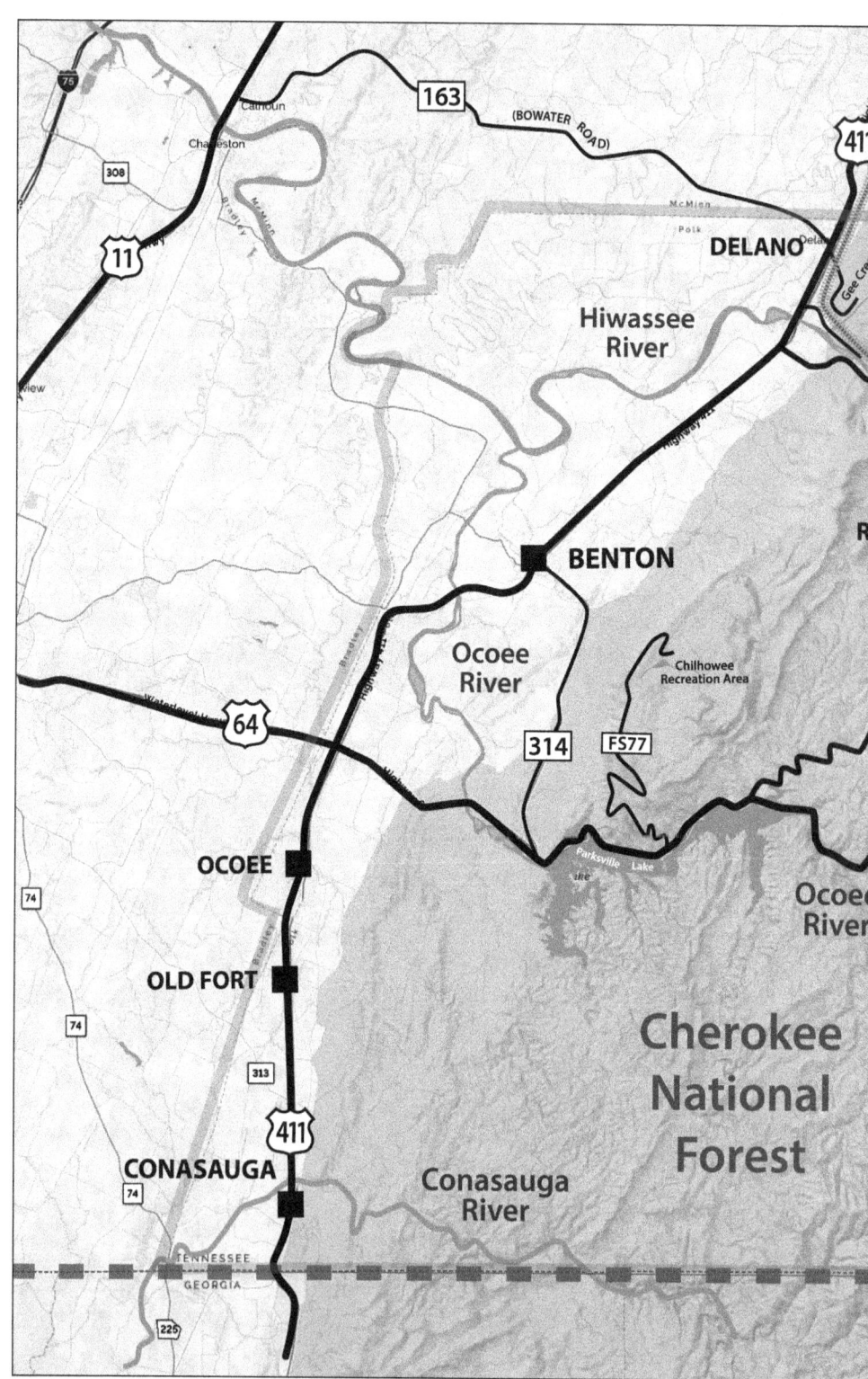

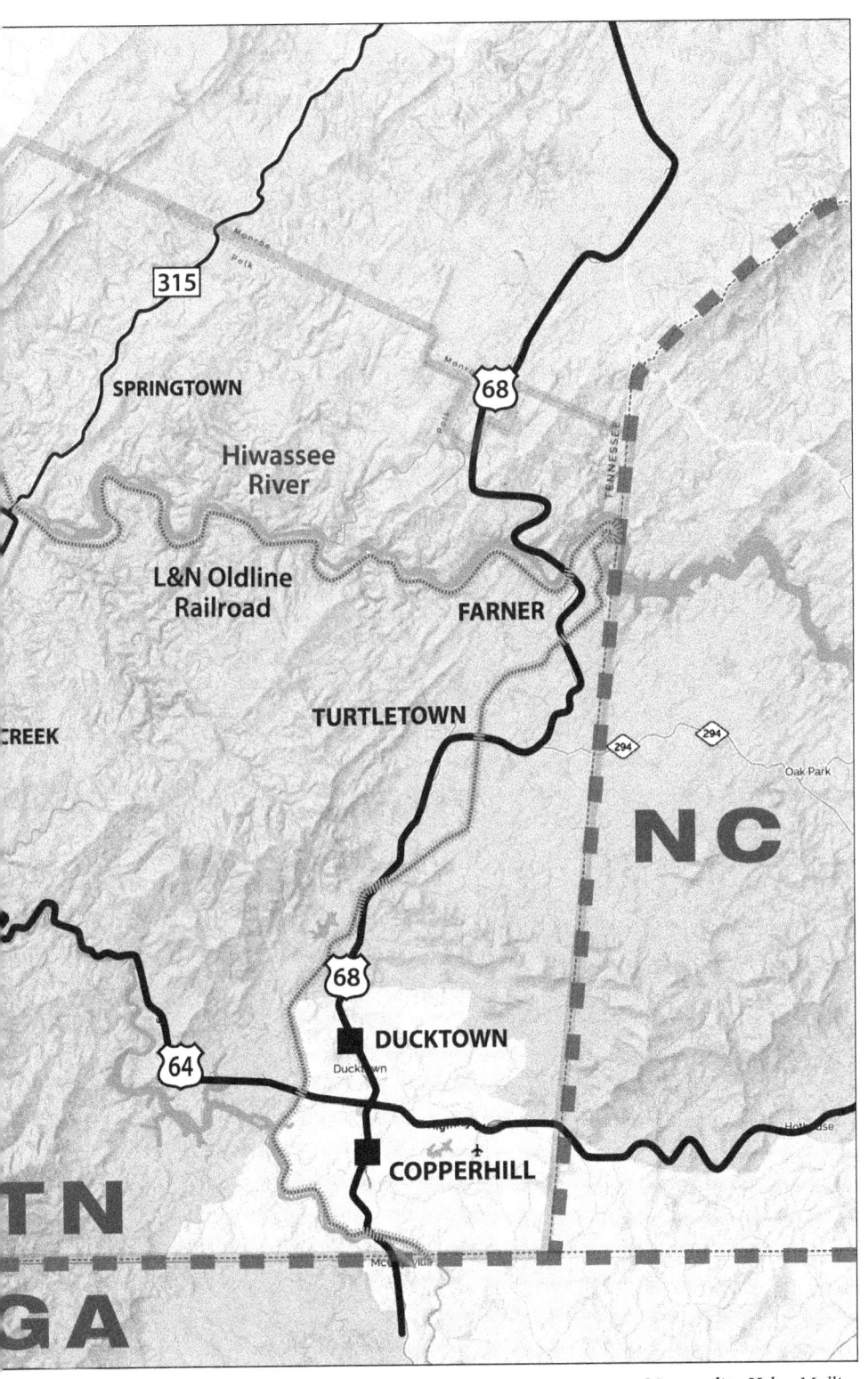

Map credit - Helen Mullins

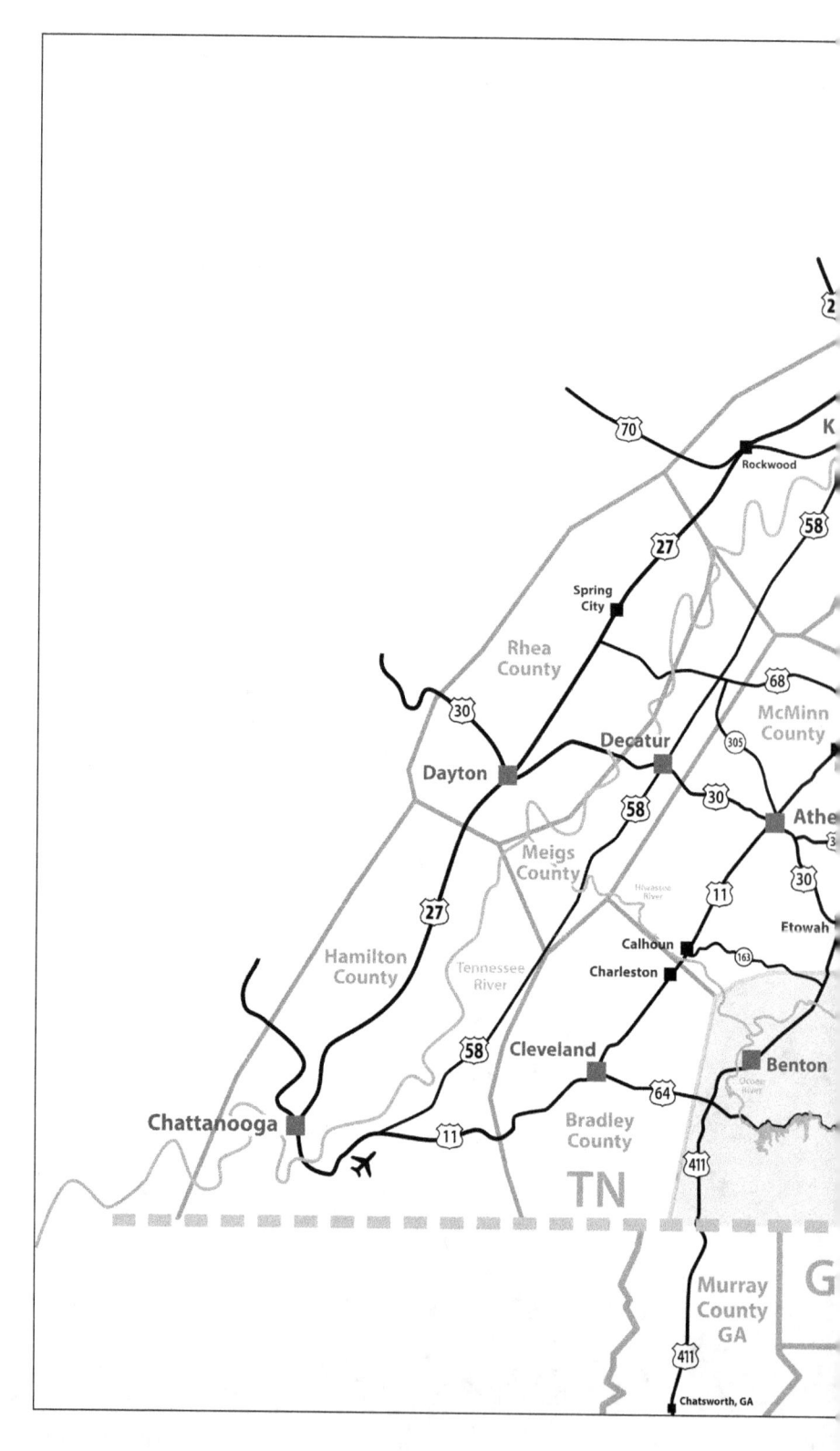

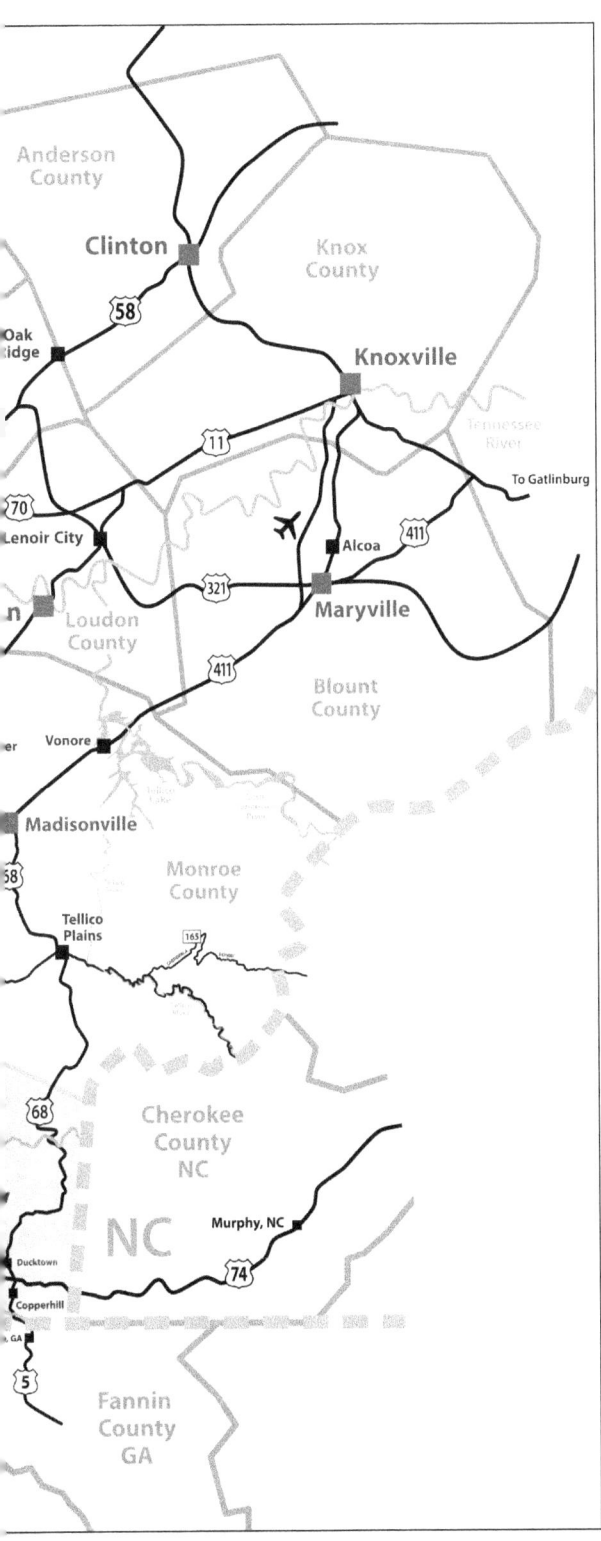

Map credit - Helen Mullins

Aerial view of Benton – Polk County Historical and Genealogical Society

Preface

Many of you are probably wondering why someone who was born and raised in McMinn County is writing a book about Polk County political history. My county is best known for two historic events: Harry T. Burn's deciding vote for the 19th Amendment, and the Battle of Athens. My first book is a biography of Burn, my great-granduncle. I first learned of Polk County's political turmoil while researching Burn's tenure in the state senate. I learned of the connections between Burch Biggs' political machine in Polk County and Paul Cantrell's machine in McMinn County. Cantrell's machine was overthrown in the Battle of Athens on August 1, 1946.

Having always been fascinated by the battle and what precipitated it, I was delighted to learn that *New York Times* best-selling author Chris DeRose was writing a book about it. Unlike several previous publications, his book, *The Fighting Bunch*, told the complete and true story. His vigorous research and willingness to uncover all of the facts paid off, resulting in the definitive book on the topic. Intrigued by Burch Biggs, he suggested I write a book about Polk County politics.

I find Burch Biggs to be an interesting and unexplored figure. I noticed that very little had been written about Polk County's political history, with the most extensive treatments being two master's theses. There are also a handful of nationally-published magazine articles and the occasional local newspaper article that barely scratches the surface. Nothing comprehensive had ever been attempted.

Being from a neighboring county with little to no ties to Polk County, I knew I could approach this project impartially and tell the story without bias. I have two distant connections to the county. One of my great-great-great-grandfathers, William Avery Vaughn, was born in Polk County in 1849. A great-grandfather, Joseph Henry Shell, was born in Polk County in 1898, but he lived his entire adult life in McMinn County. Joseph's father, William Shell, eventually settled in his birthplace of McMinn County after living in Polk County for many years where his father, Benjamin Shell, worked on a farm.

I was not surprised to learn how sensitive this subject still is to many people. The individuals who remained tight-lipped about their role in the Battle of Athens did so mostly out of fear of being implicated in an illegal act. McMinn County's political turmoil was brief, and ended after 1946. Polk County had no such luck. Several families today still feel the pain and stress caused by the county's violent political history. Dozens of people were murdered, with some of them still unsolved. Countless people were assaulted, terrorized, and ostracized by their political opponents. Many lives were ruined. Worst of all, no one in Nashville or Washington seemed to care. Being a small, rural, and somewhat isolated community, Polk County felt ignored for so long.

When the Good Government League (GGL) took control of the county, there were hopes for "the dawn of a new era" of peace and reform. But the political turmoil, while never as bad as the Biggs era, continued for many years. The GGL attracted some who had been pushed for so long and felt they had no choice but to "fight fire with fire." Not surprisingly, the GGL also attracted some who never cared about reform and just wanted their "turn" to wield power.

Like many political machines, the Biggs machine was built upon three pillars: election fraud, police brutality, and graft. While it is true that Biggs was not the first or last sheriff to permit "fee-grabbing," take kickbacks from moonshiners, or buy some votes with "election day whiskey," the duration and brutality of his tenure makes him exceptional. It should come as a surprise to no one that he was defeated in a violent election by a veteran-led reform group. After fighting tyranny overseas, they returned stateside to fight tyranny at home.

Burch Biggs started out as a fearless lawman with good instincts and a commendable temperament. But once he got a taste of the power, he stopped at nothing to hang on to it. The power he wielded in his domain was only rivaled by that of Boss Ed Crump in Memphis, who became a close ally. U.S. Senator Kenneth McKellar, Crump's number one ally and controller of all federal patronage, was another close friend. At his peak, Biggs controlled every elected office in the county. His deputies got away with just about anything. Despite having a legally-capped salary and running a farm during an economic downturn and wartime austerity, his wealth increased exponentially. Election returns became preposterously lopsided, standing out as a glaring anomaly in not just the region, but the entire state. His connections in Nashville and Washington prevented any oversight or accountability. Unsatisfied with absolute power in Polk County, he tried to expand his machine into neighboring counties. His influence on state politics was wildly disproportionate. An amiable and warm person, with an ability to compartmentalize his political activities from his social life, he managed to escape some of the blame for his machine's actions.

Through nearly three years of research, I utilized every primary source imaginable. Dozens of Polk County natives shared their stories with me. Many of these people actually lived through this era, while others relayed stories passed down from parents or grandparents, some of whom left behind diaries and memoirs. I refused to print anything I could not verify in multiple ways. This story needs to be documented in a single-source so people will realize how fortunate they are to live in a time when such political corruption and turmoil is a thing of the past.

I present this story for the first time. In a comprehensive look at Polk County politics in the first half of the 20th century, Burch Biggs stands out as the dominant figure. The impact of his reign is still felt in the county today. Many elders still live with the memories of this era. The county's youth, as well as families who recently moved there, struggle to believe all of this actually happened. But it's all true. This history must be preserved.

Acknowledgments

Since this subject is still controversial, several people who assisted me do not want their name in this book. You all know who you are, and you have my most heartfelt gratitude. The names of my anonymous sources will not be divulged without their or their family's permission after their passing.

My family, especially my parents Michael and Sandra Boyd, were as supportive as ever. Much thanks to Chris DeRose, the *New York Times* bestselling author of *The Fighting Bunch*, for giving me the idea for this book. The enthusiasm, encouragement, assistance, and advice of many good friends, including Patsy Duckworth, Dr. Tyler Forrest, Dr. William Hardy, and Judge Carroll Ross, is much appreciated. My proofreaders and blurb writers helped improve my writing and historical accuracy.

Several organizations in Polk County assisted in many ways, including the Polk County Historical and Genealogical Society, the Ducktown Basin Museum, the Polk County Register of Deeds office, and the *Polk County News*.

Special thanks to the many libraries and archives that helped, including the East and West Polk Public Libraries, the Etowah Carnegie Library, the Chattanooga Public Library's local history department, and Margot Still and the Cleveland-Bradley County Public Library History Branch and Archives. The staff at the E.G. Fisher Public Library processed my numerous ILL requests. In their old building, and later their magnificent new building, the Tennessee State Library and Archives were of great help during my in-person visits and through emails and phone calls. Dr. Ann McCleary, Keri Adams, and Zach Ledbetter at the University of West Georgia's Center for Public History digitized a treasure trove of oral histories. Nikki Patterson Cantrell recorded the oral histories and preserved so much history. Thomas A. Lemond Jr. answered my questions about his graduate thesis. Maureen Hill and the staff at the National Archives at Atlanta shared federal court records.

My alma mater, the University of Tennessee, provided much appreciated assistance. Kris Bronstad pulled several boxes at the Modern Political

Archives as I looked through the papers of public officials from our state's history. The Special Collections staff at the John C. Hodges Library did the same. The Joel A. Katz Law Library permitted convenient access to public and private acts passed by our state legislature.

Photographs and maps always enhance storytelling, especially in the field of history and biography. I am grateful to the many people and organizations that preserved and shared high-resolution images. Helen Mullins created detailed maps for the book.

I am indebted to Ralph Painter, Sally Hutchins Gregory, Mary Lethco Lewis, Lowell Posey, Charlie Guinn, Billy Rice, and many others for sharing their memories of living through this era in Polk County history.

The families of numerous individuals that feature in this story helped in ways I can never repay. Scott Barclay shared memories of his grandfather and gave me a tour of Copperhill. Lura Edwards Ward shared memories of her father and the political climate of her childhood. William Frank Lowery and Lamon Lowery Rose passed down their Uncle Frank's stories. T. Blair Lillard II shared stories passed down in the John M. Lillard family. Buck Sartin's family shared helpful information. Pamela Underhill shared memoirs from her late mother, Patsy Crox Underhill. Rusty Arp recalled stories passed down by his father, Little Buck Arp. LaVance Davis shared thoughtful recollections of her father and the political talk during her childhood. Lori Rosenbloom shared memories of her grandfather, Bill Rose. Leach Park's grandson, J. Franklin Park, Jr. also shared his memories. Bryan Allen gave me closure to one of the book's mysteries.

For the descendants of Burch Biggs who did speak with me, I appreciate your time and kindness. I know it was difficult for you. My objective was to tell this story truthfully and to be as fair to your ancestor as possible.

Wally Avett, Lenora Lillard Barber, Paul Bates, Bill Dalton, Rob Davis, Doug Gregory, Margaret Gregory, Sheriff Joe Guy, Denson Hamby, Mike Harper, Pamela Park Joao, Dr. Will Simson, and Tiffany Stephens connected me with others and shared important resources. Lynne Hurst took me on a historic tour of Ducktown. Mellissa Jarrett-Ball preserved and shared her father's notes from initial work on a book that never came to fruition.

Special thanks to Pamela McFadden King, Rosemary McFadden Sink, Sandy Osborne, Emmett Thompson, Mary Ann Lockaby, Andrea Land Alexander, Angela Land Lorinchak, Danny Shearer, and Cheryl Loudermilk Kear, relatives of the many murder victims in this story.

I must extend my gratitude to four great people who passed away before I completed this book. Wilma Edwards Jones shared wonderful memories of her father and the political talk from her childhood. Durant Tullock, Etowah's historian and biggest champion, shared city records and other resources. David Talley answered several of my questions about growing up in Ducktown and the people he remembered in this story. He was candid and thorough, and was encouraging me to keep working just days before he passed. Larry Wallace, former Athens policeman, McMinn County Sheriff, Tennessee Highway Patrol Colonel, Tennessee Bureau of Investigation Director, and Criminal Justice professor, shared his memories of working in Polk County and was so excited to read this book. I really wish all of you were here to read it.

A big thank you to Randy Baumgardner at Acclaim Press for taking on publication of this book. The team at Acclaim Press are great to work with and have done a fine job preparing this book for publication.

Lastly, I thank my love, Sarah, for her patience during the long and tedious research and writing for this book, my most ambitious one yet. She always helps me when I go on the speaking circuit to sell books. I could not do any of this without her.

Prologue
From Lawman to Politician

Burch Biggs had a distinguished heritage. His Scots-Irish great grandfather, John Biggs, fought in the American Revolution.[1] He settled on the north bank of the Hiwassee River in the southeast corner of Tennessee. On his deathbed, he bequeathed his sword to his son, William McClure Biggs. "Don't ever do anything to disgrace this sword."[2] Through the Treaty of Removal in 1835, the federal government obtained land inhabited by the Cherokee and created the Ocoee District. Polk County was established in 1839, named for Tennessee's then-governor, James K. Polk.

A first-generation American and pioneer settler of Polk County, Col. William M. Biggs served as the first circuit court clerk and was later elected to the state legislature. A Unionist, he represented his county at the East Tennessee Convention. But Polk County became one of only six counties in Unionist East Tennessee to vote for succession. He raised his family on a large river-bottom farm on the Hiwassee River. One of his sons, Thomas Temple Biggs, was known as "Uncle Tom" Biggs.

"He was a man of open-handed generosity to his friends and those in distress," Burch later said of his father, Tom Biggs.[3] A civic-minded man, Tom served on federal grand juries and as chairman of the Polk County Democratic Party. He raised his family in Wetmore, in the northwest corner of the county. He had seven children with his second wife, Eunice Attaline "Attie" Kimbrough, including a son named Burch Euclid, born in 1874.

Benton, the Polk County seat, was established in northwestern Polk County. Once called "Four-Mile Stand," it is situated less than two miles from the junction of the Ocoee and Hiwassee Rivers. Surrounded by rich and fertile farmland, Benton enjoys two "never failing" springs in the center of town. The Chilhowee Mountains to the east overlook the city.

Burch was introduced to Tennessee politics at a young age. Brothers Alf and Bob Taylor opposed each other for governor in 1886, playing their fiddles and engaging in civil debates across the state. Then twelve years old, Burch joined a crowd of thousands to watch the brothers outside the courthouse in Benton.

The Biggs family's association with law enforcement began with Burch's older brothers. Temp Biggs was a deputy sheriff and Coop Biggs was a deputy U.S. Marshal. "Polk County furnishes the largest number of bootleggers each year," the *Chattanooga Times* later wrote. Burch accompanied his brothers raiding moonshine stills in "the wilds of Polk County" as a teenager. The fearless and aspiring lawman was tall and lean with dark hair and piercing blue-gray eyes. A memorable family photo showed young Burch wearing his hat over one eye "at a jaunty angle."[4] Burch would gain invaluable experience at a young age enforcing the law "above the mountain" in eastern Polk County's Copper Basin region.

Polk Countians had no idea just how valuable the Copper Basin, also known as the Ducktown Basin, would become until the discovery of copper in a branch of the Potato Creek in 1843. Mining began in 1850, making Polk one of the state's wealthiest counties. Ducktown, situated in the heart of the basin, was for a time more prominent than Knoxville or Chattanooga. Julius E. Raht, a German immigrant, began work as a mine captain. He advanced to become chief operator of all mines and smelting works in Ducktown, owned commissaries, and started a bank in Cleveland. He was once known as "The Richest Man in Tennessee."[5]

The Copper Basin's booming industry attracted some of the brightest minds, aggressive investors, and hardest workers from around the globe. But not all of them were easy-going. "Many who came to Ducktown were rough and tough. They expected to work for a living and fight and carouse for a pastime," historian R.E. Barclay later wrote.[6] The county needed exceptionally tough lawmen to maintain law and order "above the mountain."

It was a 30-mile trip along the "Old Copper Road" through the Ocoee River Gorge past the Frog Mountains to reach Benton. The road was completed in 1853, and copper haulers had to travel for two days using oxen, horses, and mules to transport wagons full of the valuable element to the nearest depot in Cleveland. The mines closed in 1878, but later reopened when the railroad came to Ducktown in 1890.

The mountain range split Polk County into two sections. The county's fertile farmland is "below the mountain" to the west, home to the communities of Delano, Benton, Ocoee, Parksville, Old Fort, and Conasauga, all in the First Civil District. Also "below the mountain" are the mountain com-

A view of the Copper Basin from an overlook in the Cherokee National Forest. - Cleveland-Bradley County Public Library History Branch and Archives, Ridley Wills Collection

Before the railroad came to Ducktown in 1890, the Old Copper Road was the only east-west route through the county. - Cleveland-Bradley County Public Library History Branch and Archives

munities of Servilla (Springtown), Reliance, and Archville (Greasy Creek). These are all in the Second Civil District, also known as the "Mountain District," and are part of the Cherokee National Forest. The county's rich mineral deposits are "above the mountain" to the east in the Copper Basin, where the communities of Farner, Turtletown, Ducktown, Isabella, and Copperhill were established in the Third Civil District (additional districts have been added and removed through the years, but there are three at present). Such a massive natural barrier led to tensions between the two sides of the county that still lasts to this day. Although a law court would be established in Ducktown, political power still resided in the county seat of Benton.

Tom Biggs proved to be a fine role model for his children, but they sadly failed to learn from his example. They had an edge, even at an early age. Coop once instigated an all-out melee at a store in Benton. Burch always had an edge. He and his younger brother, Duke, were expelled from the Taylor's School in Sagetown for "drawing their knives on the teacher."[7] Burch worked on his father's farm, and was later appointed as a deputy sheriff by Sheriff Charlie Campbell in 1898. That same year, he married Della Lillard, granddaughter of pioneer settler Abraham Lillard. The marriage made Burch related to thousands of people in the county. They welcomed a daughter, Della Etholeen, in 1899.

In his first campaign for sheriff, Burch rode all over the county on horseback, and was often gone from home for several days at a time. He loved the mountain folks, many of whom invited him inside their homes for supper and offered him lodging for the night. "You always know where the mountain folks stand," he later told his family.[8]

Burch became the new sheriff at age thirty after defeating William Hamilton in August 1904. He and Della welcomed a son, Broughton Euclid, two months later. Burch's margin of victory was 135 votes. At this time, Polk County was what would now be described as a purple county, almost evenly divided between Democrats and Republicans. This political split originated in the Civil War when the farming communities "below the mountain" supported the Confederacy and became solidly Democratic while the industrial-based Copper Basin communities "above the mountain" supported the United States and became solidly Republican. The

Democrats held most county offices after the Civil War and managed the county's finances remarkably well. The Republicans took control in 1894. The two parties split in Polk's presidential elections between Reconstruction and the turn of the century, but the Democrats carried the county in seven of eleven gubernatorial contests. Landslides were rare, especially in local races. Intra-party disputes were mostly personal, and sometimes led to split-ticket voting, making the county even more mixed politically.

Burch was unintimidated and had good instincts. He made a good sheriff for Polk County. T.J. Addington, Joe Williams, and E.A. Clark were among his first deputies. The new county jail opened in 1905, complete with a third-floor apartment for the sheriff's family.

One of the jail's first guests was Bill Cody, a yeggman who had terrorized the region for years. With a "record like that of a Western bandit," Cody was near impossible to contain.[9] He once sawed his way out of jail in Benton. In another escape, he jumped from a moving train into the Mississippi River. He even managed to abscond unscathed after three Bradley County deputies surrounded a house where he was hiding. Burch transported Cody from the Chattanooga jail back to Benton where he was convicted of felonious assault and sent to Brushy Mountain State Penitentiary in Morgan County. But he was not there for long.

In 1906, Burch now had his own farm, 90 acres near his father, but not on the river.[10] He joined with seven others to incorporate The Benton Banking Company. That same year, he won reelection by 123 votes (53 percent of the vote), a close but comfortable margin, over Charles Barnes. There was little controversy in this election. The Democratic candidate for circuit court clerk filed an election contest after losing by twelve votes.

On the night of December, 6, 1906, W.A. Guinn, a prominent attorney in McCays (later renamed Copperhill) was shot in front of his home. Before he died, he said he had no clue who had shot him or why. Much of the evidence pointed to a miner named James Allen. His shoes matched the footprints in Guinn's garden. Several people had seen Allen with a rifle the day of the murder and he had allegedly confessed to a friend who later led the police to where the rifle was buried. There was speculation he had been hired by Guinn's widow, Abbie McCay Guinn, to commit the murder, and they had recently been seen together. Abbie's father, Harbert T. McCay, was the namesake of McCaysville, Georgia. "I know what you want me for, but I am not guilty," Allen said as Burch arrested him.[11]

Allen's mother was a sister of the infamous Hedden Brothers, known for moonshine and violence in the mountains of Polk County. The jury returned a guilty verdict, but added "with mitigating circumstances," a shocking and unprecedented outcome. The judge ordered a new trial, resulting in the same verdict. The jurors were seemingly unsure of his guilt

Burch, third from left, is pictured with other county officials in 1906. - Polk County Historical and Genealogical Society

Burch was first elected sheriff shortly after the turn of the century when Benton still had dirt roads around the courthouse square. - Polk County Historical and Genealogical Society

and wanted to save him from the gallows. But the judge sentenced him to death by hanging. Two days before the scheduled execution, Allen's father sent a petition to Governor Malcom Patterson, managing to get his son's sentenced commuted to a life term.

Never in doubt of Allen's guilt, an angry Burch criticized the governor's "grievous mistake" and said he was convinced that Allen is "as guilty a man as was ever arraigned before the bar of justice."[12] Allen's attorney responded with serious accusations against the sheriff. Allen had been induced to testify before a grand jury prior to obtaining legal counsel. During his stay in the county jail, Allen had allegedly been fed poorly and denied a private conversation with his attorney and his family. Burch supposedly sent his sister, Sue Biggs Lillard, to see Allen for "spiritual advice" in a disguised attempt to offer him a reduced sentence if he confessed and implicated Guinn's widow in the plot.

According to the Allen family, he was indeed guilty. Having previously rejected Allen's marriage proposal, Abbie Guinn later found herself in an unhappy marriage. Allen confronted W.A. Guinn about his mistreatment of Abbie. Guinn threatened to go to the police about the Hedden family's ill-gotten moonshine fortune. Burch may have violated the law to convict Allen, but he was right about his guilt. Abbie later married Charles Barnes, Burch's opponent in the 1906 election.

As the new century progressed, a culture of violence plagued Polk County. Many people viewed politics like a religion and engaged in what seemed like never-ending personal disputes. Conflicts were often "solved" through violence, and cooler heads rarely prevailed. Sadly for Burch, his elderly father fell victim to one of the county's many hotheads.

In 1907, one of Tom Biggs' horses got loose and trampled into tenant farmer Tom Carter's cornfield. Carter's confrontation with Tom became so heated the two started fighting. The sheriff's father struck Carter with his garden hoe. Carter pulled out his gun and shot Tom in the head, killing him instantly.

Upon hearing the news, Burch rushed to his father's farm, meeting his mother on the way. She was kneeling in prayer. "Son, protect Mr. Carter and let the law take its course." Burch suppressed his anger and arrested his father's killer.[13]

Late that night, an angry mob surrounded the jail and awakened the sheriff. "Burch, we don't ask you to do anything. Just leave the keys and go away somewhere." But Burch refused to let the mob lynch Carter. "No, he's going to stand trial."[14] Carter was later acquitted, a common outcome in Polk County murder trials.

Even in the twenty-first century, it is said that visiting Reliance is like traveling back through time. "We call it Reliance that it has a reliable sound," Sarah Vaughn (the town's first postmaster) once said.[15] Located in a small, fertile valley on the Hiwassee River deep within mountains rising thousands of feet high, Reliance was relatively untouched by the Civil War. The railroad that finally connected the Copper Basin to the west passed through the peaceful, scenic community in the late 19th century. Historic homes, churches, and a general store still stand today. But up in the mountains in Lost Creek, where the Hedden Brothers lived, it was anything but peaceful.

Previous sheriffs were terrified of Garrett Hedden, the meanest of the brothers. Garrett had killed his own brother. Dubbed a "walking arsenal" and a "deadshot," he could walk into town without anyone bothering him.[16] "Murder, incest, criminal assault, and many other crimes have bathed in blood and depravity the moonshine trail trod by this hot-tempered, ruthless, God-scorning clan of the hills," wrote the *Chattanooga Times*. Burch had already arrested Riley Hedden, and was not intimidated by Garrett. Charged with nine murders, he threatened to make Burch the tenth. The sheriff was ready to take on Garrett Hedden once and for all.

Burch led a posse, including Chief Deputy Gus Barclay and Monroe County Sheriff Pryor Watson, in a raid on Garrett's still up near Lost Creek. The newspapers claimed Burch saw Garrett standing outside the still house before yelling "Throw your hands up! You're under arrest!" and only shooting after Garrett reached for his gun. But some dispute this story, alleging that Burch and his posse could not see anything but blurry figures amongst the early morning mountain fog and just started shooting at anything that moved, without warning. The successful raid made Burch, who fired the shot that killed Garrett, a local hero. Although, he later said he was unsure if it was his shot that killed the notorious outlaw.[17]

A third term should have been a foregone conclusion, but the voters gave Republican challenger George Hood about 100 more votes than Burch in

The Lost Creek recreation area is not far from the site of Garrett Hedden's moonshine still that Burch and his posse raided in 1908. - Author's photo

Burch with his first chief deputy, Gus Barclay, in the 1900s. - Robert E. Barclay Jr.

the 1908 election. The election was peaceful, but two dozen Republicans in Copperhill claimed Democratic election judges refused to let them cast a ballot. Disappointed, Burch returned to work on his farm, now spanning 300 acres (with much inherited from his father).[18] He and a business partner, Walter Harrison, built a successful livestock trading business and shipped cattle as far as Atlanta and Cincinnati.

The new city of Etowah in southeastern McMinn County was a railroad boomtown. Located fifteen miles north of Benton, they hired Burch as their first police chief in 1909. He resigned after 16 months, and the city commission thanked him for his "good service."[19] Health problems had led to his resignation, and he took to his sick bed. Some thought he might never recover.[20] He could not have been encouraged when James Allen received a full pardon from Governor Patterson after serving only four years in prison. In 1913, things went from bad to worse when Burch lost $700 after a bad investment, but some others in the community lost even more.[21]

At the turn of the century, the Tennessee Copper Company (TCC) established its headquarters in McCays, Tennessee, a community also named for Harbert T. McCay. The TCC built company houses, shops, and a commissary. The city was situated alongside a steep hill rising just above the Georgia line by the Ocoee River. Having suffered a massive flood and devastating fire in its first decade, the city that came to be known as Copperhill proved resilient. Historian and TCC executive R.E. Barclay later wrote that it "was indeed a hastily drawn-up mining town that was endeavoring to find a footing in a fertile river bottom and on steep, rough hills."[22]

In a lot of ways, the Copper Basin had the look and feel of an Old West town. Having spent decades chopping down trees to fuel copper smelting, combined with the release of sulfur gas causing acid rain, industrial activities killed most of the region's vegetation. It was like living in a desert. The Basin became known for its "red hills" that looked like the surface of Mars, and was for a time visible from space. The TCC was sued for damages multiple times, but little was done to address the environmental damage. It could not have been more different than the green, fertile farmland "below the mountain" in western Polk County, yet both regions were in the same county.

Incorporated in 1913, Copperhill already had four banks and was building a high school. The city of nearly one thousand residents inside boundaries smaller than a square mile was growing fast. They hired their first police chief—Gus Barclay, Burch's former chief deputy. There had been "longstanding political trouble" between former sheriff George Hood and Chief Barclay.[23] To make matters worse, Hood was a heavy drinker, and Barclay had a short fuse.

On Christmas Eve 1913, Barclay, who had recently arrested Hood in a brutal beating, saw Hood on the street near the post office and the First National Bank. "Hello, George," Barclay said in a "tantalizing voice." Hood turned around at Barclay. "There is no hello for you, you son of a bitch." A furious Barclay responded: "Don't you call me that!" The chief tried to take Hood by the arm. "Get your hands off me!" Hood shouted. Barclay pulled out his pistol and fired at Hood, striking him in the hip. Hood staggered, but remained on his feet. Barclay shot Hood again, this time in the chest. Hood fell, but returned fire at Barclay. By the time they had emptied their six-shooters, they were both on the ground. Barclay crawled over to beat Hood in the head with the butt of his pistol, but Hood drove the hammer of his pistol into Barclay's skull, killing him.[24] Another conflict resolved with violence, between two lawmen no less.

Hood barely survived the duel. He pled self-defense and was acquitted in a trial that "never lagged from start to finish."[25] Chief Barclay was survived by several children, including R.E. "Bob" Barclay. Hood went on to own and operate the Colonial Hotel in Copperhill. Upon his death in 1922 at age 42, his family suspected he might have been poisoned.

After his health improved, Burch worked as a policeman for the TCC, but it was not long before he decided to make another run for sheriff. In 1914, the voters returned him to office by 100 votes (52 percent of the vote), over Sheriff Albert Crumley. He appointed F.D. "Dyke" Higgins, George Harbison, Herman Fetzer, and Will Duffy as deputies. In the spirit of his civic-minded father, he donated five acres of land at Taylor's to be used for a new school.

During this term, Burch first met Ed Crump, a Mississippi native who was quickly rising through Memphis politics. Burch learned all about "ripper" bills, taking advantage of the archaic state constitution that allowed the legislature to redraw civil district lines, remove duly elected local officials, and handpick their replacements. Elected local officials could literally be "ripped" out of office via state legislation. The Republicans had controlled the county court for two decades. Burch wanted that to end, so he secured passage of a ripper bill during the 1915 legislative session that redistricted the county's civil districts to advantage the Democrats.

Introduced by a Monroe County legislator, the bill violated "local courtesy." Legislators from Polk County fought the bill, claiming their constituents opposed it. Speaker of the House William Prentice Cooper, father of future governor Prentice Cooper, supported the bill, which became law. Polk County Democrats never forgot this. Over two decades later, Polk County clerk and master William F. Russell wrote to Governor Prentice Cooper thanking him for his father's role in helping the Democrats gain power in Polk County.[26] W.H. Williamson, a staunch Democrat, did not trust Burch or Russell when it came to politics. "They are out to make something out of it for themselves," Williamson wrote to a friend.[27]

1915 proved to be a devastating year. The first homicide by a deputy under the Biggs administration occurred when Deputy Hugh Burris fatally shot James Spurling after an argument. Burris was convicted and given a long sentence, a rare instance of justice in the county. Polk County's law enforcement officers were still held accountable, at least for now. But Spurling's mother sued Burch for $30,000 in damages.[28]

Etholeen Biggs was preparing for her final year at Polk County High School. She loved to play piano. Tragically, she came down with typhoid fever. Burch rushed to her side before she passed away, aged sixteen. "A sacred and solemn stillness" settled over the entire city of Benton.[29] They laid her to rest next to her slain grandfather.

Still in mourning, Burch was rejected by the voters a year later when his wife's cousin, Abraham "Abe" Lillard III, won by 140 votes (53 percent of the vote). The grandsons of two pioneer settlers of Polk County faced off three-quarters of a century after the county was established. The ripper bill had done Burch no favors as the Republicans swept all county offices. He and Della pressed on, welcoming another son, Burch Glen, in 1917. But he was not out of politics completely. The county court later elected him to the school board.

The City of Etowah asked Burch to return as their police chief in 1922, the same year he and Della welcomed another daughter, Gwendolyn L'Ene.

The family rented a home on South Washington Avenue, but Burch still owned his river-bottom farm on the Hiwassee River. Although he had sold some of the farmland, he still had 288 acres assessed at $10,000.[30] Burch took special care of his mother, Attie Biggs, who had several other children that could have cared for her. She spent her final years in Burch's home before she passed away in 1925.

The *Knoxville Journal and Tribune* described Burch as "a terror to law violators" and "fearless in the performance of duty." He befriended McMinn County's new sheriff, Burkett Ivins, and Paul Cantrell, a businessman who later built a political machine of his own. After Ivins lost his bid for a third term in 1926, he and Burch were indicted for issuing counterfeit poll tax receipts. In the first of many lucky breaks for Burch, the indictments were quashed. Burch was indicted a year later for felonious assault after shooting Bill Moore, but that was also quashed. "Lack of evidence" or lack of a prosecutor were cited as reasons.[31]

The worst episode in Burch's second stint in Etowah involved the arrest of James Hugh Moss. Allegedly matching the description of one of three suspects wanted for the murder of Coleman Osborn in Chatsworth, Georgia, Moss was arrested by one of Burch's officers. Moss was carrying a package, which the officer did not open before placing it under the passenger seat. Burch later took Moss to the home of a justice of the peace (JP) for his hearing. The arresting officer brought the package to Burch, who found a gun inside. "Chief, you know it wasn't my pistol," Moss said.[32]

Along with Clifford and Eula Thompson, Moss was tried for murder in Murray County, Georgia. Being a black man in the South at this time, Moss had little chance to survive the accusations against him. The trio was found guilty, and Moss and Clifford Thompson were executed. Eula Thompson was given a life sentence and later pardoned.

The evidence against the accused trio was circumstantial, and there existed far too much reasonable doubt for a just conviction. Their fate was set by the Etowah Police Department determining their guilt upon their arrest. Even though his department was not initially investigating the murder, Burch was most likely wrong about this one. He worked in Etowah for the remainder of the decade.

Chapter 1
Burch's Big Comeback

Even though he lived in Etowah, Burch was still involved in the Polk County Democratic Party but he was always in the background, once serving on a nominating committee. He was well aware of the political disfunction in his home county.

Polk County had never experienced a decade as tumultuous as the 1920s. Democrats and Republicans fought each other with ouster suits. Justices of the peace (JP), school board members, and even the county court chairman were all removed from office at different points during this time. The two parties constantly swapped the state representative seat for the Floterial District representing Polk and Bradley Counties, sending their man to Nashville to pass favorable legislation. If a party wanted to add county court seats for their benefit, they secured legislation to incorporate a town, and if they wanted to remove a JP from the opposing party, they passed laws to unincorporate. Despite this back-and-forth, no one party or figure ever had control for long. But that was about to change.

Local elections were always down to the wire. Vance Davis, a Democratic JP, defeated William Oliver "Ol" Harrison for sheriff in 1926 by about two dozen votes in an otherwise strong year for the Democrats. The Democrats accused the Republicans of distributing dozens of forged voter registration certificates. The Republicans cried disenfranchisement. As a result, a group of Democratic election workers, including Leach Park, W.A. Kerr, G.E. Stephenson, and L.B. Lanning, were among those charged with "preventing legal voters from casting ballots." Harrison unsuccessfully contested the election.

Also victorious in 1926 were Circuit Judges John J. Blair and Pat Quinn, elected in the judicial cycle. One Democrat claimed that "for the next eight years, with two Democrats as judges in this circuit for the first time in history, the courts will not be used to harass Polk Democrats who are elected."[33] This prescient statement would prove to be true for much longer than just the next eight years.

In 1928, Ol Harrison won the rematch with Sheriff Vance Davis by eleven votes. Over 200 people crowded into the courthouse to watch the election commission count the votes. One citizen called it "the last free election for twenty years."[34] McMinn County Democrats considered nominating Burch for sheriff that same year.

In state and federal elections, Polk County had begun trending red at the turn of the century. The Republicans carried the county in every presidential election since 1892, usually winning comfortably, with 1928 being one of the few blowouts when Herbert Hoover defeated Al Smith by 27 points. The Republicans won twelve of the fifteen gubernatorial contests with the largest margin of victory being 22 points. Republicans did well in congressional elections for the first decade, but starting in the 1910s, voters increasingly supported their Democratic Congressman John A. Moon and later Samuel D. McReynolds. Except elections where they faced token opposition, incumbent congressmen never won Polk County in a landslide.

Taking advantage of the county's political instability, Burch staged his comeback for 1930. As the Great Depression worsened, the Democrats found themselves back in the good graces of the voters. Burch claimed "certain Polk County people" asked him to come back home and run for sheriff. He won his party's nomination and was set to face off against Ol Harrison, who Burch alleged was "not pleasing to a good many people."[35] But there was just one problem with Burch's candidacy: he did not live in Polk County.

Although he still owned his river-bottom farm on the Hiwassee, he had "laid his head" in Etowah for the past eight years. Multiple newspapers, including the *Polk County News*, reported on his residency in Etowah as late as February, and he was not even nominated until April. The state constitution required all voters, and therefore candidates, to reside in the county for at least six months before the election. This dashed all hopes for a non-controversial election. So did the news of former Democratic trustee George Williams being caught with forged poll tax receipts.

The two parties basically tied in the 1930 county election. Burch tallied 131 more votes than Harrison for 51.4 percent of the vote. R.E. "Bob" Barclay, a son of Burch's late chief deputy Gus Barclay, lost the trustee's race to Republican incumbent G.W. Passmore. Vance Davis was elected county judge (the equivalent of today's county mayor or commission chairman) over James M. "Jim" Shearer. Democratic circuit court clerk George L. Gilliland and Republican county court clerk Alfred R. "Buck" Arp were reelected. Porter Campbell won the register of deeds office for the Democrats. Most candidates won comfortably, but nobody won in a landslide.

The county's third courthouse stood from 1897 to 1935. - courthousephotos.com

Burch and Harrison each won around two-thirds of the vote in their respective strongholds of Delano and Linsdale. Burch tallied nearly 60 percent of the vote in Benton and Ocoee, while Harrison performed similarly in Ducktown and Copperhill. Old Fort and Turtletown were nearly 50-50 splits. However, the results at the Conasauga precinct stood out in comparison. Every Democrat on the ticket won in Conasauga, with the entire ticket averaging 81 percent of the vote. Burch tallied 112 more votes there than Harrison. If Burch did have the ballot box stuffed at Conasauga, it gave him a major advantage over Harrison, but he made sure not to make his margin too high lest there be too much skepticism of the election being fair.

Burch did not yet have control of the election commission or the sheriff's office, so stealing this election would not have been easy, and the result was always going to be fairly close. The results of the Conasauga precinct in 1930 lend credence to the oft-repeated story of how Burch allegedly stole the election: One of Burch's supporters invited the Conasauga poll workers over for lunch. While the Republican workers were facing away from her at the table, she allegedly swapped the ballot box under the quilt she was knitting with one stuffed with votes for the Democrats.[36]

Ol Harrison won an injunction from Chancellor Oscar Yarnell of Chattanooga restraining the election commission from certifying Burch's victory. He collected affidavits of voters claiming their votes were not counted and charged irregularities in mail-in ballots. A large crowd gathered inside the courthouse, but only seven representatives from both parties were allowed to watch as election commissioners Marvin Lowery, Flint Copeland, and Burch's nephew Hoyt Lillard, counted the votes. During the canvassing, a pack of armed men, allegedly Harrison's deputies, stormed in demanding their defeated Republican JP candidate, Jim Pike, be issued a certificate of election. "Now sign them, damn you!" The commissioners complied, but the certificate's authenticity would inevitably be litigated. Harrison denied any knowledge of the incident.[37]

A riot almost broke out on the courthouse square. The "mob-like spirit" made Democratic leaders consider asking the governor for help. Two Benton ministers wrote to the governor requesting National Guard assistance. Harrison won another injunction, this time restraining the new county judge, Vance Davis, from swearing Burch into office since he was not a legal resident at the time of the election. But Burch quickly obtained an injunction superseding Harrison's and was sworn in for his fourth term as sheriff on September 3. He appointed Abraham B. "Abie" Green as chief deputy, Herman Wright as jailer, and George Crawford and Charles Bates as new deputies.

The Democrats did well in the November election, winning the state and federal races by comfortable margins. C.L. "Roxy" Campbell, a Great War veteran, bus liner operator, and son of former sheriff Charlie Campbell, won a special election for JP in Copperhill. The Republicans alleged illegal voting and claimed that Burch and multiple deputies stood guard to intimidate voters at the Copperhill precinct.[38] But Campbell's election was certified and gave the Democrats control of the county court. After making "sensational" charges of corruption, the county court proceeded to remove the entire school board, comprised mostly of Republicans. All but one of the new board members were Democrats. One of them was Hoyt Lillard. Having lost his father at a very young age, Lillard was close with his Uncle Burch.

Circuit Judge Pat Quinn heard Harrison's election contest in March 1931. Harrison testified to the alleged lunchtime vote switch in Conasauga, and claimed Burch did not move all of his belongings and take up residence in Polk County until May 1930. Burch insisted that he moved some of his furniture to a rental property in January. Despite the evidence in Harrison's favor, Judge Quinn ruled Burch eligible and certified his election. Harrison appealed to the state supreme court, where Burch again emerged victorious. The 1930 sheriff's election was finally settled, fifteen months after the polls closed.[39]

Chapter 2

CONSOLIDATING POWER

During the 1931 legislative session, State Rep. Marvin Lowery authored a successful bill creating the office of chief deputy sheriff with an $1,800 annual salary.[40] Another bill abolished the fourth civil district, legislating two Republican JPs out of office.[41] Such bills were nothing new in either political party, but things were about to get a lot worse.

Charles Guinn, a Republican attorney and good friend of Burch, wrote an article in the *Copper City Advance* concerning the recent audit of the sheriff's office and expressing concern over the county's expenditures. The Democrats blasted the article as purely political, emphasizing that Guinn made no accusations of illegality. But Guinn had legitimate reason for concern.

Many sheriffs in this era, from both parties, were guilty of "fee-grabbing" and pocketing some of the money without depositing it all in the county treasury. After being arrested for questionable reasons, several people had to pay a fine to a JP at a hearing (this matter is handled by today's General Sessions Courts). But the "fee-grabbing" would soon get out of control in Polk County on Burch's watch.

In August 1932, Burch defeated Frank Tate for reelection by 371 votes (54 percent of the vote), a comfortable margin. Trustee G.W. Passmore lost to Roxy Campbell by a similar margin, and Republican tax assessor Boyd Mason lost a close race to R.G. Hood. The only Republican officer left at the courthouse was county court clerk Buck Arp. J. Creed Brock, former deputy under Vance Davis, was elected as a First District JP.

James Lucius "Red" Passmore remembered election fraud as early as the 1932 election, which was the second term for election commissioner Hoyt Lillard, Burch's nephew. Then seventeen, Passmore saw boys his age lined up outside Lillard's office accepting $2 to vote. "They'd give you a ballot, already marked, and you'd take it to where they had the election and give it to the returning officer and he'd put it in the ballot box." John K. "Chet"

Gilliland, also aged seventeen and a nephew of George L. Gilliland, cast a ballot that year. He later said his father, Bill Gilliland, helped steal the election. Passmore even recalled someone casting a ballot for their newborn son.[42] Not everyone who was paid to vote wanted money. Some were happy to receive some "election whiskey."

Voters did not even get to drop their ballots in the box. That was the returning officer's job. "They would take the ones they did not want in there out, remark them, or put new ones in there…They did that after the polls closed," Red Passmore remembered about Burch's handpicked election workers. The scroll sheet at each precinct listed the name of every person who cast a ballot. In a violation of the secret ballot, it also listed each candidate they voted for. "They took the election boxes to somebody's house and rewrote the scroll sheets and put in whatever they wanted to," Passmore said.[43] Patsy Crox Underhill recalled how Burch would vote the dead, also known as "voting the cemetery."[44]

Others had similar recollections, including those who lived above the mountain. North Carolina native and future TCC employee Earl Oliver remembered ineligible voters casting ballots. "Biggs would just take elections," Oliver said.[45] Lowell Posey, son of a longtime TCC employee, remembered dead people voting and people voting multiple times under different names.[46] David Talley, son of sometime deputy sheriff Arthur Harold "Chuck" Talley, recalled that the Biggs machine "definitely" stuffed the ballot boxes.[47]

E.A. Clark, Grover Park, Ernest McGee, M.N. Waldrop, Wes Pierce, Leslie Rogers, P.R. Bates, Jim Hawkins, Flavis Bates, and P.R. Hutchins (son of former sheriff John S. Hutchins) were among Burch's new deputies in 1932. In 1929, Flavis Bates had shot and killed Deputy Sheriff Raymond Prince. Then a constable, Bates alleged Prince threatened to shoot him. He was tried for murder four times, with every trial resulting in a hung jury. District Attorney R. Beecher Witt dismissed the case in 1932. Despite this, Burch saw it fit to hire Bates as a deputy. He later hired his brother, Temp Biggs.

Upon taking office in 1930, the county court did not inherit an ideal financial situation. The county had been running $100,000 deficits for years and was $1,000,000 in debt. The depression showed no signs of slowing down. Unable to agree on a tax increase, the county court cut the high

The Polk County Sheriff's Department in 1932. L-R: P.R. Hutchins, P.R. Bates, George Crawford, Broughton Biggs, E.A. Clark, M.N. Waldrop, Wes Pierce, Burch E. Biggs, J.E. Williams, Grover Park, Abie Green, Ernest McGee, Herman Wright, Leslie Rogers. - Polk County News

school teacher's salaries by 15 percent in fall 1932 and reduced the school budget. But the court did approve paying Burch .75 cents per day for boarding prisoners and appointed his older son, Broughton, as coroner.

In the November presidential election, Franklin D. Roosevelt won handily and carried Polk County by a high but not unbelievable 21-point margin. Presidents Harding and Hoover had won the county by similar margins. Hill McAlister became the new governor, winning Polk County by 14 points.

State Rep. Marvin Lowery fell out with Burch during the 1933 legislative session, but it was not all bad for the sheriff. While Lowery authored successful bills reducing Burch and Abie Green's salaries, he pushed through a bill to benefit Hoyt Lillard.[48] The bill created the office of school board chairman to be elected by the board. The chairman was to "devote their entire time to the duties of said office."[49] The board appointed Lillard, who owned and operated his own business, to the position, paying him a hefty $2,400 per year. This was not a bill the voters wanted to pass. Lillard was the most disliked member of Burch's organization. "He was derogatory and always talked down to people," one citizen remembered.[50]

In 1933, three Republican taxpayers represented by Democratic attorney Winston Prince obtained an injunction preventing Vance Davis and Roxy Campbell from paying Burch and Abie Green excess fees. Prince cited the 1921 general salary law that capped salaries for county officials and instructed said officials to deposit all fees in excess of their salary into the county treasury. A "third class" county due to its population, Burch could not legally make more than $5,000 annually. The general salary law also made filing false financial reports a felony.[51]

The injunction claimed that Burch, through an unconstitutional 1931 private act, had "drawn in salaries with his ex-officio fees more than $10,000" while only reporting $50 in fees collected since taking office in 1930. The 1931 act permitted him to collect board, turnkey, and court fees. Less than 60 people had been jailed since he took office, but the injunction claimed Burch was "making a profit of $750 to $900 per month on board alone." Claiming that the illegal fees "seriously hampers the proper handling of the county's affairs," the injunction asked that the illegal acts be declared unconstitutional. The key to such a graft was to overcharge the county for expenses and pocket the profits rather than depositing it into the county treasury.[52]

Just like Charles Guinn, Prince considered the Biggs family his friends, but he had legitimate concerns about the county's finances under Burch's control. Inspired by the actions of neighboring counties, he suggested a "non-political" taxpayer's meeting to discuss cuts in taxes and spending. "During these days of depression, every individual, firm, and corporation have been cutting expenses."[53] The county owed $1.5 million in bonds and outstanding warrants. Prince worried that many people would not be able to pay their property taxes and preserve their life savings.

The county court did not share Prince's concerns. Burch had the Wood-Higgins Audit Company, co-owned by Broughton's future father-in-law Jake Higgins, audit the county's books. The audit alleged that, due to "errors in jail reports" between 1931 and 1933, the county owed Burch $862.20. The county court voted unanimously to pay Burch the full amount.[54]

In 1934, the Democrats set their sights on the county court clerk's office, held by Buck Arp since 1918. Arp worked as a railroader for many years until he was forced to change careers. Caught between two rail cars, he lost an arm and a leg in a freak accident. Undeterred, he used his "strong right hand" and remained in the work force, learning telegraphy and entering public service.[55]

The Democratic JPs accused Arp of a $6,000 deficit in his accounts. Arp vehemently denied the charges, calling it "political bunk" and challenged anyone to prove them. "Sheriff Biggs wants to be Kaiser of Polk County and has decided the best way to get full control is to destroy me." Arp alleged Burch was getting $20,000 to $30,000 a year in fees.[56]

Arp was not Burch's only target. County judge Vance Davis, his biggest inter-party rival, was accused of overdrawing almost $8,000 from the gas tax fund. The county court voted to take control of the gas tax fund away from Davis and gave it to former trustee George Williams, who had been caught with forged poll tax receipts.

Burch's sudden reversal of fortune raised several eyebrows. Certainly, his livestock trading company was successful, but he had quickly become one of the county's wealthiest individuals. His farm was now 315 acres and was assessed at $12,000. He had also recently acquired another 106 acres of farmland in the same area assessed at $5,100. In early 1932 he had paid off one of his mortgages in the amount of $7,200.[57] He did all of this despite his legally-capped salary and running a farm as the depression worsened.

The Republicans did not nominate a full ticket in 1934. Henry Crox, a dairy farmer and son of former Bradley County sheriff William H. Crox, was nominated for sheriff. William, who refused to run for a third term, once had to shoot a man attempting to escape custody, something he always regretted. One citizen said Henry Crox was "too nice to be sheriff."[58]

Crox's daughter, Patsy Crox Underhill, remembered how often her father's farm hands were "fee-grabbed" as they went into town. "The deputies would get them whether they got a bottle or even drank it." Crox had to go pay their fines for "public drunkenness." A JP was "always ready to pass judgement on them." It was quite an elaborate and lucrative racket, especially if there is no turnover in the sheriff's office.[59]

Burch easily won his party's nomination for sheriff, but his support was waning. John Harbison, aligned with Vance Davis, garnered nearly 40 percent of the vote at the convention. Leach Park, a car salesman and veteran of the Great War, was nominated for county court clerk. Marvin Lowery's time in Nashville was over, as Burch saw to it that Maj. James F. Corn of Cleveland was nominated for state representative. Corn later called Burch "a great fellow and a friend worth having in East Tennessee."[60]

The Democrats had a mixed record to defend. The county's finances were in a deplorable state, but Burch was still keeping his deputies in line. Deputy Fred Styles beat Burton Brown so badly he caused a concussion. Only sixteen years old, Brown was resisting arrest, but they had not seen the last of him. Burch arrested Styles for assault and fired him. He would not tolerate police brutality, at least for now.

Burch had lost two deputies during this term. In March 1933, Deputy Leslie Rogers was shot and killed at the home of Fannie Price in Cherokee

Charles Guinn, an attorney and staunch Republican, was a friend of Burch despite their many disagreements. - Tennessee State Library and Archives

Henry Crox, a successful dairy farmer and Republican stalwart, was a longtime critic of Burch. - Polk County Historical and Genealogical Society

County, North Carolina. Felix Hill, who had long feuded with Rogers, was alleged to have shot the young deputy through a window. Ernest McGee witnessed the shooting. Hill denied the charges, and was later acquitted by a Cherokee County jury. Just days after Hill's acquittal, Deputy Grover Park, brother of Leach Park, was killed while responding to a domestic dispute at his son's girlfriend's house. John Headrick, the girl's father, shot Park in the head with a shotgun. A grand jury returned a "no true bill" against Headrick, indicating that he may have acted in self-defense.

In a purple county, with a near equal number of Democrats and Republicans, a few dozen illegal ballots here or there might swing a countywide election in one candidate's favor, but wholesale election fraud is not possible without control of the ballot boxes. The August 1934 election marked the first time Burch had control of the county election commission. Hoyt Lillard was now chairman of the commission, handpicking precinct workers. Broughton Biggs ran the Benton precinct with a coterie of Democrat loyalists including Deputies Herman Wright and Ben Smith, Traynor Witt, Jess Rymer, and future deputy G.E. Stephenson. At the Ocoee precinct, Deputy Flavis Bates was a judge and future deputy Louis Wright was a Democratic watcher. Deputy Frank Clayton was a judge in Old Fort. Other officers of election were JP

Benson Hammons, Servilla; Temp Biggs, Greasy Creek; Emmett Gaddis, Ducktown. Democrat Elias Runion, and his Republican brother, John, were officer of election and watcher respectively in Turtletown.

In his largest margin of victory yet, Burch defeated Henry Crox by almost 900 votes out of nearly 5,400 votes cast for 58 percent of the vote. The Democratic incumbents were all reelected, but county court clerk Buck Arp lost to Leach Park by almost 1,000 votes. The Democrats now controlled every office in the courthouse for the first time in decades. The *Copper City Advance* called Park's victory "one of the biggest surprises."

The only area of strength for the Republicans was Copperhill. Numerous arguments during the counting at several precincts above the mountain delayed the final results until Friday morning. A scrappy bunch of Republican election workers in Copperhill, including J.E. Adams, Amos Ballew, Julius Turner, and W.C. Dalton, ensured a fair count at their precinct. In the state races, Governor Hill McAlister won the primary in Polk County by one vote. Judges Pat Quinn and John J. Blair, and District Attorney Beecher Witt, were all reelected in the judicial cycle, dominating in Polk County.

Henry Crox told his daughter the Democrats fixed the election. "Daddy told the story often that they left the ballot boxes out in the hall of the courthouse. Daddy opened one and they had even left the false bottom in the box. He said you could tell the false ballots, for they were all marked with the same pencil and in the same manner." Matt Witt, stepson of Deputy Herman Wright, recalled how Burch "usually won elections by stuffing ballot boxes after taking them over for 'safekeeping.'"[61]

Crox and the Republicans did not contest the election. But, at their next meeting, the Republicans demanded that Jim Shearer resign as the Republican election commissioner. Upset at his refusal to appoint "honest, God-fearing Republicans" to work the election, they accused him of appointing election workers sympathetic to the Democratic candidates.[62]

Burch's new deputies included Frank Clayton, Emmett Gaddis, Wes Pierce, John Deal, John Blackwell, Dud White, E.J. Vann, and George Williams. While some got new jobs after the election, others lost theirs. Ruth Crox and R.W. McClary were fired from their teaching positions. Some of Patsy Crox Underhill's classmates teased her for her father's election loss and her mother's firing, and some in the Crox and McClary families left the county.

Grace Lillard, wife of Hoyt Lillard, maintained a close relationship with her childhood friend Ruth Crox despite their husbands being bitter political foes. Crox worked to ensure her daughters had happy childhood. "Our

A.R. "Buck" Arp, a Republican, served four terms as county court clerk from 1918-1934. He later operated an Esso station on Highway 411 across from the courthouse. - Buck Arp family

Leach Park became the new county court clerk in 1934, giving the Democrats control of every office in the courthouse for the first time in decades. - J. Franklin Park Jr.

mothers made the difference for they were determined that the politics that the men were into was not going to ruin the lives of the children and that we children had a good life," Underhill fondly recalled.[63] Many Polk County natives who lived through this era recall a happy childhood where everyone played together, regardless of their family's politics. The women and children had no involvement in the politics. Many of the men, especially Burch, had a remarkable ability to compartmentalize their political life from their family and community life.

But not everyone was able to avoid the strife: "Politics were so important to many people that they could not even have friends who were of the opposing party, especially at election time," one citizen recalled.[64] Sally Hutchins Gregory, granddaughter of Deputy P.R. Hutchins, observed how Burch's conduct contrasted inside and outside of the political realm. "Burch was a good man in a lot of ways," Gregory recalled, "but he could be harsh."[65]

By this time, Ed Crump had become "Boss Crump," and had complete control of Memphis and Shelby County politics. He was the most powerful man in Tennessee, and his closest ally was U.S. Senator Kenneth McKellar. Crump controlled at least 60,000 votes in Shelby County, more than enough to tip statewide elections in his favor. McKellar controlled all federal patronage in the state, down to the postmasters in the backwoods districts. For the next fifteen years, the two handpicked the governor and junior senator, and Burch supported them unwaveringly. McKellar paid Burch a visit nearly every time he traveled to southeast Tennessee.

In November 1934, Governor Hill McAlister won Polk County by an almost two-to-one margin, high for the county's historical trends, but not unbelievable. Congressman Sam McReynolds' 80 percent vote share, however, was almost unheard of, with only one congressional candidate winning by such a margin since 1900. The historically Republican McMinn, Bradley, and Loudon Counties did not give their congressman near as high a vote share, and neither did purple Monroe County or blue Meigs County.

Through his handpicked State Rep. James F. Corn, Burch went after Vance Davis even more aggressively in the 1935 legislative session. Corn authored successful legislation abolishing the county judge position. Practically half the courthouse, including Burch, went to Nashville to lobby for Corn's bills. Aligned with Davis, Winston Prince fought the bills. Another bill created the office of county court chairman, naming Dr. W.A. Trevena, a JP, to the position. Davis ignored the new law at the April county court meeting and obtained an injunction to stop the county court from "interfering with his right to continue in office."[66] The matter would be litigated in the chancery court.

Corn's next bill targeted the Fourth Fractional Township in Ducktown, wresting control away from the commission that always cared for it. An 1841 law preserved the township's 657 acres for school land. Lawsuits ensued after the discovery of copper in the area, but the township commissioners ensured the revenue from leasing the land to mining companies went to the schools. Corn's bill removed the three commissioners, including Dr. L.E. Kimsey, replacing them with Burch's handpicked men.

Undesirous of power, Dr. Kimsey was one of the county's greatest civic-minded individuals. He spearheaded the Kimsey Highway, a long, winding mountain road connecting Harbuck to Reliance. Before the Old Copper Road was rebuilt and became part of U.S. Highway 64 in the early 1930s, the Kimsey Highway was the only east-west road connecting the two sides

The Kimsey Junior College building was never used for higher education, eventually operating as a county school in Ducktown. - Tennessee State Library and Archives

of the county. Working with the other commissioners, Kimsey built a junior college building for the Copper Basin. The $200,000 structure, complete with 27 classrooms, a gymnasium, library, cafeteria, and auditorium, opened in 1933 and was named in his honor.

Dr. Kimsey filed suit, and Chancellor T.L. Stewart ruled Corn's bill unconstitutional. But the state supreme court overturned Stewart's decision. The school sat empty for three years before its conversion into a county school. Dr. Kimsey's dream of a junior college for students above the mountain was never realized.

In a win for Vance Davis, Stewart struck down the bill abolishing the county judge position. This left Corn's legislative accomplishments near non-existent. His experience in Nashville had not turned out well, and it was not far enough away to escape Polk County's style of conflict resolution. During a meeting with constituents, a fight broke out in his hotel room. Someone broke a chair over his head. He did not run for reelection in 1936.

Chapter 3

THE ROAD CONTRACTOR AND THE DEPUTY SHERIFF

On November 27, 1935, the day before Thanksgiving, David W. McFadden was leading a road crew grading a section of what is now U.S. Highway 64 in Isabella. The middle-aged father of three worked as a foreman with the Knoxville-based Crippen Construction Company, employing 120 local workers on a Works Progress Administration (WPA) relief project.[67]

Dozens of Polk County laborers disrupted the worksite. "Fire them foreign workers and hire men from our own ranks," an unemployed laborer shouted.[68] D.A. Crippen arrived to help McFadden reason with the mob. "Only one of your truck drivers is a local boy." Polk Countians comprised the entirety of Crippen's work force, with 80 percent from the relief list. Some of the men amongst the angry mob had worked the day before. "McFadden's been abusing us and threatening to fire us."[69] Given the project's location, it could very well have been laborers from Fannin County, Georgia or Cherokee County, North Carolina wanting a job.

The mob, like all mobs, could not be reasoned with. They started throwing rocks at the road crew. It was not long before the shooting started, and there was no telling who fired the first shot. Crippen was struck in the mouth with a pistol and punched repeatedly.

Deputy Emmett Gaddis and Constable Ernest McGee, two of Burch's roughest men above the mountain, arrived on the scene. McGee approached McFadden, who was engaged in a fight with Lloyd Cardon. Before McGee attempted to arrest them, McFadden pulled out a pistol and fired a shot in the air, with the gunpowder burning McGee's eye in the process. Merely trying to scare away his attackers, McFadden's shot hit no one. A split second later, McFadden was shot in the mouth, with the bullet passing through his shoulder.

The authorities managed to quell the riot, and McFadden and Crippen were taken to the Kimsey-Guinn Hospital in Ducktown. McFadden was in serious condition, but eventually pulled through. Local doctors treated six oth-

David McFadden was leading a road construction crew grading and paving what would later become U.S. Highway 64 through the Copper Basin. - Tennessee State Library and Archives

er men for severe bruises, including P.C. Simpson, a foreman. "I don't know what complaint the men had who attacked us," Crippen said. "We must have protection if we are to continue on the job."[70] Deputy Gaddis blamed the mob for starting the fight. According to Crippen, none of the men in the mob had the required relief card. McFadden told the authorities that Gaddis shot him.

McFadden hired Chattanooga attorney John S. Wrinkle, who asked Governor McAlister to ensure protection for his client. The governor replied that Burch was his "personal friend" and agreed to meet with him to discuss the matter. McAlister said that Burch did not show the "slightest reluctance" in his assurance to furnish the "necessary protection" for McFadden.[71]

Early in the morning on Christmas Eve, Deputy Gaddis heard a knock on the front door of his Isabella home. "Emmett, Emmett, Emmett, come here!" a man shouted.[72] It was 5:00 o'clock in the morning, and his two young children were asleep. Before he could look to see who was there, a .45 round blasted through the front door, hitting him in the shoulder. Another shot hit the door frame. "It was McFadden! I recognized him," Gaddis later told Burch. The assailant hastily escaped in a getaway car.[73]

The bullet went through Gaddis' shoulder and lodged in his side. Doctors at the TCC hospital had to take X-Rays to find it. He was released after a couple of weeks. "I focused a flashlight into his face while he was shooting," Gaddis said. "There was nothing to keep me from identifying him…I worked with McFadden and would know him as good as anybody."[74]

Based on Gaddis' version of the events, Burch swore out a warrant for David McFadden. Charged with felonious assault and attempted murder, McFadden denied the allegation, claiming he was in Chattanooga that night. John Wrinkle had witnesses ready to corroborate his client's claims. "He hasn't been in Polk County since the trouble there nearly a month ago," Wrinkle said, recalling the day McFadden was shot in the mouth.[75]

Burch ordered an all-out manhunt for the man alleged to have shot his deputy. He even asked Bradley County Sheriff O.J. Lawson for help. Lawson found that McFadden had checked into the Cherokee Hotel in Cleveland on December 20 and was driving a new Plymouth. "No other trace of McFadden was found here."[76] On New Year's Eve, McFadden issued a statement proclaiming his innocence:

> "I was with my family in Chattanooga at the time of the alleged assault on Gaddis. The last time I saw him was the morning of November 27, at 6:30 a.m. when he assaulted me, while surrounded by about 35 or 40 of his henchmen. I was being held when Gaddis shot me. In addition to Gaddis, there were others shooting at me. The trouble arose over the fact that I would not work men selected by Biggs, Gaddis, and others, who did not have government 'work' cards, as I was under contract to work men only with cards issued by the National Reemployment Service."[77]

McFadden was indicted on January 22, 1936 and arrested a few days later in Asheville. He made bond of $2,500 and fought Governor McAlister's attempt to extradite him back to Tennessee. Burch planned to travel to Asheville and bring him to Benton. "My client will not waive extradition," said McFadden's Asheville attorney. "He can prove that he was asleep in Chattanooga…when Gaddis was shot."[78] McFadden alleged Gaddis was trying to frame him.[79]

On Valentine's Day in downtown Chattanooga, two Hamilton County detectives arrested McFadden. He had made an unwise decision to go there, especially as his extradition hearing in Raleigh was scheduled for the next day. McFadden's signed statement read:

> "McFadden and Crippen (holding the sub-contract) had been on this United States work program highway project only a few days before demand for $500 graft money was made on us by a Biggs deputy. Of

David W. McFadden, a road contractor from Asheville, NC. - Polk County News

Emmett Gaddis, a native of Cherokee County, NC, was first hired as a deputy sheriff in the early 1930s. - Chattanooga Times-Free Press

course, this was refused. There was no labor trouble whatever...Early on the morning of Nov. 27 a well-organized mob, led by Biggs' chief deputy in the copper basin and his henchmen, appeared on this federal project and feloniously assaulted us. I was beaten over the head and face and shot by a Biggs deputy and his henchmen, and when they thought they had killed me they ceased their assault on me and pursued other workmen.[80]

McFadden's statement called the attack on him and his road crew an assault on Tennessee, the federal government, and President Roosevelt. He lamented the damage sustained on the road that the people of Chattanooga, Cleveland, Polk County, and North Carolina have wanted so long to see completed. "I was asleep in the Read House in Chattanooga at the time the shooting occurred," he claimed. "I have never seen better engineers and finer men than are in the state highway department and I have been treated splendidly by all of the people of Tennessee, except the sheriff's office of Polk County."[81]

Even the *Chattanooga News* reported that the labor riot occurred after McFadden refused to pay the $500 to Burch's deputies. "Government representatives made a thorough investigation of the affair." Several copies of the report were made, including one sent to the U.S. Attorney General.[82]

McFadden made bond, but only after Burch tried to prevent his release. "I do not want to come into the hands of Sheriff Biggs or any of his deputies... For they have not only attempted to assassinate me, but they have attempted also to assassinate my partner and my men." He asked the state courts to keep him out of Burch's hands. "Two days after the attempt to assassinate us Sheriff Biggs made this statement in a meeting held in Copperhill in the highway office before several highway officials and other reputable men: 'I have no protection in Polk County for McFadden.'"[83]

On February 17, two Hamilton County detectives accompanied McFadden and John Wrinkle across Bradley County to the Polk County line. Burch refused to accept McFadden's bond outside of his jurisdiction, forcing McFadden to enter Polk County. Judge L.D. Miller forced Burch to accept the bond after Wrinkle filed a writ of habeas corpus to protect his client from being taken into custody. "It is not safe for my client to return to Polk County under any circumstances...I fear for his life if he were sent back to Benton... Sheriff Biggs is highly prejudiced against McFadden and seeks to do him bodily harm."[84] McFadden's trial was set for May.

Chapter 4

DISSENT AMONG THE RANKS

The courthouse caught fire in December 1935, resulting in a total loss. Some suspected arson in an attempt to destroy certain county records. Leach Park moved the county clerk's office into the Benton Banking Company, where he served on the board, while Vance Davis moved into the Prince Building.

The county court passed a resolution to rebuild the courthouse and voted to rent out the Clemmer Building to use as office space for elected officials, including trustee Roxy Campbell. Hoyt Lillard would receive another stream of revenue from county taxpayers. He had recently bought the Clemmer Building for $2,000. The *Polk County News* described it as "one of the best business buildings in town."[85]

Through a decree from Chancellor Stewart, Burch became part owner of the Alpha Spinning Mills in Delano. Formerly the Prendergast Cotton Mills, Hoyt Lillard and Polk County Schools Superintendent J.C. McAmis joined Burch in the purchase. The property consisted of a hotel, barber shop, restaurant, store, other business houses, and eighty residences. They planned to operate the mill on a smaller scale. The county court released the new owners from all the back taxes on the property. The venture only lasted a few years before closing.

On February 10, 1936, a group of taxpayers filed five bills in chancery court against several county officials, charging them with "collecting salaries under unconstitutional legislation and accepting illegal fees." John Wrinkle, counsel for David McFadden, and Chattanooga attorney Estes Kefauver, Burch's cousin, represented the plaintiffs. The defendants were Burch, Abie Green, Leach Park, W.F. Russell, Roxy Campbell, Charles Williams, and Hoyt Lillard. Only George Gilliland and Porter Campbell were not charged.[86] Chancellor J. Lon Foust of Hamilton County signed an injunction restraining Vance Davis from issuing any further warrants for the payment of salaries which the officials were receiving on the basis of "obviously unconstitutional legislation." George H. Ledford led fourteen other complainants, all Democrats, in filing the bills.[87]

The *Polk County News* barely covered the story, while other papers, especially the *Chattanooga Times*, went into great detail. The bills charged Burch with violating a 1921 public act.

> "*Sheriff Biggs has constantly violated these requirements in that he has not at any time kept accounts of the fees collected by him as required by the act and has not filed itemized statements thereof monthly, and has not paid over to the county trustee the amounts collected by him in excess of his salary and the expenses to which he is entitled under the provisions of the act…In open defiance of the act, Sheriff Biggs has appropriated all fees collected by him and in addition has continuously drawn a salary from the county treasurer. The result is that Biggs has received compensation as aforesaid far in excess of the amount to which he is legally entitled.*"[88]

The five bills targeted other legislation, authored by former state legislator Marvin Lowery, that created new offices for Burch's friends. Abie Green became chief deputy through a 1931 legislative act. Charles Williams, son of George Williams, became Roxy Campbell's deputy trustee, receiving $150 per month. Through another act, Leach Park appointed his wife, Bertha, as deputy court clerk, paying her $100 per month.

Hoyt Lillard benefited the most from recent legislation, drawing $2,400 per year as school board chairman, a position that previously paid far less. The bills charged trustee Roxy Campbell with signing warrants to pay Lillard without the approval of Vance Davis. Burch and Lillard claimed the taxpayers had no right to bring the suits and that some of them paid a small portion of the county's taxes, as if such a fact diminished their right to file suit.

The complainants argued that the act creating the position of school board chairman violated the state constitution in multiple ways. Article XI Section 17 reads: "No county office created by the legislature shall be filled otherwise than by the people or the county court." The defendants argued that Lillard was elected by the school board who was in turn elected by the county court. But the complainants emphasized that the act purported to create a new position which put Lillard in office via a private act, not through election by the county court or the people. If the act did not create a new position, then Lillard's extra salary was illegal. The defense lacked a sound argument either way. The act, the complainants argued, unconstitutionally benefited Lillard. Article XI Section 8 of the state constitution reads:

"The Legislature shall have no power to suspend any general law for the benefit of any particular individual, nor to pass any law for the benefit of individuals inconsistent with the general laws of the land; nor to pass any law granting to any individual or individuals, rights, privileges, immunitie [immunities], or exemptions other than such as may be, by the same law extended to any member of the community, who may be able to bring himself within the provisions of such law."

Hoyt Lillard, Burch's nephew and right-hand man. - Polk County Historical and Genealogical Society

The complainants also argued that the act created a discrimination in favor of Lillard's position against other school board chairmen in the state and imposed a burden on the county's taxpayers "which is not imposed on any other county in the state." They cited a 1925 law prescribing the duties of chairmen of boards of education, arguing Lillard's duties under the private act were no different. The complainants cited precedent where the courts struck down illegal acts written to benefit individuals. They concluded their argument:

> "...The act under attack in this case is one in a series of private acts, the general scope and purpose of which is to take a number of the public officials of Polk County entirely out of the control of the general laws and provide a separate system for the compensation of such officials applicable to Polk County alone."[89]

Lillard attempted to justify his position and salary. Explaining why he, a "large taxpayer" active in the county's business affairs, was induced to accept the position, he said he hoped to "remedy the conditions" plaguing the school system. He also claimed he had eliminated the deficit and saved the county money. He described the "wide mountain range" separating the county's two population centers and the "numerous and widely separated" schools. Therefore, the position had "required far more of his time than either he or the taxpayers had anticipated," necessitating his high salary. Never mind the fact that several other county officials performed their duties traveling above and below the mountain while receiving no extra salary. He said the act imposed "substantial and extensive duties, obligations, and responsibilities" not imposed on other school board chairmen in the state. Both sides awaited Chancellor Stewart's ruling.[90]

By the middle of the decade, several of Burch's deputies were abusing their power, growing increasingly violent. Sally Hutchins Gregory recalled that some of the deputies were "pretty bad."[91] People in the Copper Basin received the worst treatment of all, even those who were just passing through. In March 1935, a carnival came to Copperhill, led by California showman Jack Quinn. According to Quinn, Deputies Emmett Gaddis, Windom Gaddis, Wes Pierce, and Constable Ernest McGee confronted him outside of his hotel one evening. "Throw up your hands," one of the lawmen allegedly shouted. Initially thinking he was being robbed, they told him he was under arrest for "public drunkenness." Having only drunk one beer that night, Quinn protested his arrest, so they upped the charges and took him to the Copperhill jail.

While standing in the men's washroom with another prisoner, McGee and Pierce allegedly beat Quinn nearly to death, striking him on the head and kicking him until he was unconscious. They dragged him back to his cell and finally called for a doctor the next morning. Unable to pay the $21.25 fine, Quinn was transported to the jail in Benton, costing him another $8.25. They fed him an egg sandwich and a cup of coffee, adding a little more to his total bill. Dr. W.A. Trevena, also a JP, finally gave Quinn proper medical treatment. But Quinn soon took a turn for the worse, and was taken to a hospital in Chattanooga.[92]

Deputy Emmett Gaddis denied any involvement with Quinn's arrest, and claimed Quinn was beaten because he tried to flee from the jail. Deputy Pierce alleged Quinn knocked him down and made a run for the exit. Gaddis and Burch both disputed the location of Quinn's arrest, claiming it was outside a beer parlor and that the deputies were responding to a disturbance call. Burch claimed that a JP in Georgia wrote to him warning that Quinn's carnival operated gambling machines that "took money away from children." After he was asked why Quinn was sent to a Chattanooga hospital, Burch said "He fell and hurt his head in a cell." When Quinn was discharged from the hospital, he had two black eyes, broken ribs, and a concussion.[93] Whether he was a drunken swindler of children or not, there was no justification for such brutality.

Another episode involved near-fatal gunplay. In March 1936, Deputies George Crawford and James McMillan, and their friend James Carver, escorted three ladies to a dance. The ladies said they were "frightened" during the date and asked a local CCC crew to take them home in their ambulance. This enraged the deputies, who chased the ambulance for seven miles along a mountain road, shooting a few holes into the side of the vehicle. The chase ended after they shot out the ambulance's tires in Fannin County. No one was injured.[94]

Represented by Copperhill attorney R.P. Taylor, the deputies pled guilty in federal court of damaging government property and were sentenced to thirty days in jail and a $15 fine. "I think it is extraordinary that a peace officer should stop a government vehicle and shoot at it under such circumstances," said Federal District Judge E. Marvin Underwood of the Northern District of Georgia.[95]

Some of Burch's deputies, however, did have a conscience. The child of a deputy once asked their father why he always went along with the sheriff. He replied that he felt he had to follow his boss's orders. "He had a lot of control over his men," this citizen said of Burch.[96]

John A. Harbison, a Benton automobile dealer who challenged Burch for the sheriff's nomination in 1934, announced another run. He pledged to "faithfully perform all lawful duties" and to reduce the expenses of the sheriff's department.[97] He and his wife, Hattie Crowe Harbison, owned and operated the Harbison Hotel, located catty- corner to the courthouse on Highway 411.

The Republicans elected Charles Guinn as chairman and endorsed Dutch Woody of Reliance for state representative. Woody had previously served on the school board and as circuit court clerk. The party drafted the following statement:

> "We deplore the waste and extravagance that has been practiced by our present county officials as a result of which our county has been plunged into debt to the amount of a million and a half dollars and as Republicans and citizens of Polk County we pledge our full support and strength to any and all citizens who are now trying or expecting to try a thorough cleanup of the county government."[98]

Chancellor Stewart overruled Burch and Hoyt Lillard's demurrers hoping to dissolve the injunction that prevented them from drawing their extra salaries. Burch also lost the support of the county's Democratic Executive Committee. Led by R.P. Taylor, F.P. Singleton, and Roy Stillwell, the committee called a convention to nominate their candidates. Over 1,000 Democrats attended, including Vance and Claude Davis, Marvin Lowery, and Winston Prince. This group became known as the "Anti-Biggs" faction of the Polk County Democratic Party. Claude Davis resented the *Chattanooga Times'* designation of the meeting as a "rump" convention.[99]

Rev. Kirby Park nominated Harbison for sheriff, who won the nomination by acclamation. Robert E. "Bob" McClary was nominated for trustee and R. G. Hood was nominated for tax assessor. George Ledford, who had led the group challenging the legislation that paid Burch and his friends extra salaries, was nominated for First District JP. The convention noticeably declined to endorse Congressman Sam McReynolds, Burch's close friend. Burch's most recent term had been terrible, and a significant number of Democrats were eager to support the "Rump Democrats." Lifelong Democrat Dave Haskins openly criticized Burch's "regime."[100]

The "regular" Democrats, the anti-Biggs Democrats, and the Republicans all scheduled meetings on Saturday afternoon, May 16, 1936. Two thousand Democrats attended the regular Democratic meeting at the Benton grammar school. According to the *Chattanooga Times*, "buses, trucks, automobiles, and wagons brought a crowd to Benton from every part of the county. They came from the Savannahs to the Copper Basin; from the mountains to the state line, and included young and old, men, women, and children alike."[101]

"It was the greatest political gathering ever held in Polk County," Burch claimed.[102] Sandy Summers and his sixteen-piece orchestra came up from Chattanooga to entertain while Burch served free sandwiches and soda. Summers passed through Copperhill earlier that day, parading the streets in an effort to increase turnout.

Party chairman George Williams called the meeting to order. Burch's 31-year-old son Broughton was nominated for sheriff, Roxy Campbell was re-nominated for trustee, and chief deputy Abie Green was nominated for tax assessor. Broughton promised to carry on in the "same manner" of his father's administration. The state constitution prohibited sheriffs from serving more than six years in an eight-year period, forcing Burch to step away from the position, at least officially. "I'm satisfied that my party's leadership has been placed in young and safe hands," said Burch, now 62 years old. He expressed no worries over the party split and the Republicans plans for a full ticket. "The regular Democratic ticket will win by a 1,500-vote majority in August," he said with confidence.[103]

The *Polk County News* provided in-depth coverage of the regular Democratic meeting, while the Vance Davis faction and the Republicans received limited coverage. The Republicans nominated Arthur L. Dalton of Copperhill for sheriff, Boyd Mason of Ocoee for trustee, and Melvin Ledford for tax assessor. Burch's faction looked poised to win a plurality of votes, but they did not have majority support in the county.

Chapter 5

"You Aren't Going to Kill Me Like This, Are You?"

David McFadden had a business meeting in Murphy, North Carolina on May 18, 1936, just days before his trial. John Wrinkle advised him not to travel through Polk County, especially at night. To avoid Burch's territory, McFadden would have to take a detour through Knoxville, adding 100 extra miles to his trip. But he foolishly drove through Polk County.[104] "I am an American citizen and I am going to use the public roads."[105]

On Sunday May 17, McFadden left the Cherokee Hotel in Cleveland and drove to Ducktown, where he attended a baseball game. He appeared happy and "unconcerned about the threats he said had been made against him in the county."[106] After the game, he drove in his Dodge sedan toward North Carolina. Three men recognized him and immediately pursued him on the very highway he had been grading when he was shot in the mouth. Just past Isabella, less than a mile from the state line near the site of the original Mt. Harmony Church building, the car passed McFadden and pulled over on a detour road overlooking the highway.

There was dead end up ahead, so McFadden had to take the detour road. At approximately 5:50 PM, ten machine gun slugs pierced his car, including three fired from behind. Some of the bullets passed through the front and rear windshields. McFadden was struck five times: once in the left arm, shoulder, stomach, and twice near the heart.[107] The bullets reportedly struck in a straight line, starting above his left eye and ending in his abdomen.[108]

McFadden exited the car with his hands in the air. Two men dragged him thirty feet to a mound beside the highway, with a third man holding a rifle overlooking the mound. "You aren't going to kill me like this, are you?" McFadden asked the rifleman. "I certainly am," the man replied, just before shooting McFadden several times, including shots in the chest and head. McFadden was allegedly armed, but his pistol had not been fired.[109]

A small crowd approached the crime scene shortly afterward. They found McFadden dead beside his car, full of bullet holes. A bloody trail led to a small pool of blood thirty feet from the car. Most of the blood had been covered with dirt. Deputy Wes Pierce was first on the scene. McFadden's body lay at the scene about forty-five minutes before being removed to an undertaker. Pierce thought a machine gun was used, but Burch disagreed. "It looks to me as if he has been shot with a .44." The undertaker concurred with the sheriff. "There are not any machine guns up here," Burch insisted.¹¹⁰

Initial reports erroneously stated there were no witnesses to the killing, including a statement from Deputy George Crawford. But the *Chattanooga News* spoke to a witness claiming McFadden was "shot down in cold blood" as he exited his car "with his hands in the air." Two witnesses told the *Chattanooga Times* the same thing. Burch vehemently denied this story. "That's not true! There's nothing to it!" He claimed he had three witnesses who "saw the whole thing" and could prove McFadden fired first. He refused to name the witness, but said they were not deputies.¹¹¹ J.P. Robert Frye of Copperhill called together a coroner's jury that quickly determined that McFadden "came to his death at the hands of parties unknown."¹¹²

Shortly after McFadden's body was discovered, a man checked into the TCC Hospital. He had pistol wounds in his thigh and foot. His name was Emmett Gaddis. The doctors said his thigh had only a flesh wound while his foot suffered four fractured bones.¹¹³ Burch stationed two deputies outside Gaddis' room for protection.

"This is their third shooting scrape," Burch said, still assuming McFadden shot Gaddis on Christmas Eve. "There will be no arrests unless a warrant is sworn out." The next day, Gaddis returned home from the hospital, and a grand jury began an investigation.¹¹⁴

John Wrinkle released his correspondences with Governor McAlister concerning his slain client's safety. The day before Gaddis was shot on Christmas Eve, Wrinkle wrote to McAlister requesting National Guard protection so McFadden could resume work on the road from Ducktown to Murphy. McAlister replied that he could not send troops to build roads, but claimed Burch had assured him he "would do everything possible to protect the workers." The contractors later cancelled their contract for the road job. "I don't recall any talk that McFadden would not be safe in Polk County," McAlister wrote.¹¹⁵

Rozelle McFadden buried her husband in Asheville. They had a six-year-old daughter, Thelma, named for McFadden's late first wife. McFadden was

Bullet holes can be seen in the front windshield of David McFadden's car. - Chattanooga Times-Free Press

David McFadden was killed in an ambush while driving through the Copper Basin's "red hills" on the way to North Carolina. - Ducktown Basin Museum

also survived by his mother, three siblings, and two young adult sons, David S. and Frank W. McFadden. His parents were Chattanooga natives, and he had been staying with family there after the Thanksgiving shooting. "We are going to see that justice is done," Frank McFadden said.[116]

Federal agents arrived in the Copper Basin to investigate McFadden's death. Normally, the federal government would not insert itself into a state crime. However, given the origins of the McFadden-Gaddis feud going back to the labor riot on the federal road project, the agents suspected a conspiracy. They spoke with several people, including Copperhill Police Chief Oliver Hood, son of late sheriff George Hood.

The grand jury discovered that more people witnessed the killing than previously thought. Multiple witnesses told the *Chattanooga Times* that McFadden was "forced out of his car after being halted by gunfire" at the Mt. Harmony Baptist Church just outside Isabella. They saw two men with Gaddis, including a deputy.[117] "The proof is positive and absolute as shown by every eye witness that the killing was unwarranted, premeditated, and shocking in its brutality," District Attorney Beecher Witt said. He would not divulge the names of the witnesses.[118]

Emmett Gaddis finally made a statement, admitting he shot McFadden and claiming self-defense. "I've heard the ugly rumors…My political enemies have been spreading them."[119] Two deputies, Lloyd Parton and Clarence Brooks, were with Gaddis when McFadden was killed. Burch confirmed this, but denied that Brooks was a deputy.

A reporter asked Burch, who had just returned from the state Democratic convention in Nashville, if Gaddis would be retained as a deputy pending the grand jury investigation. "It's none of your business," he snapped. "Who wants to know? Does John Wrinkle have anything to do with it?"[120]

The sheriff then exploded into a rant. He called the story of two Hamilton County deputies escorting Wrinkle and McFadden to the Polk County line to pay McFadden's bond a lie. "I blame Wrinkle for stirring up all this…Everything was all right in this county until John Wrinkle came over here!"[121] Burch repeated his claim of having three civilian witnesses that saw McFadden shoot first.[122] "My only interest is to see that justice is done…We have nothing to hide."[123]

Although the *Chattanooga Times* had closely covered Burch's organization with great scrutiny, it was the *Chattanooga News* that published a scathing editorial on May 22 titled "A Reign of Terror in Polk County." Burch was branded as the longtime "dictator" of Polk County. "Sheriff Biggs is said to be an affable man who does not drink, 'chew,' or swear. But he has controlled all patronage out of Polk County." The *News* accused him of "not pursuing the investigation" as he should. "The evidence all points to the fact that McFadden was waylaid, pursued, shot to death in cold blood – that he was in fact 'ganged' by officers who were supposed to uphold the majesty of the law." The *News* lamented "our placidly contemplating the iron rule of petty Hitlers and Mussolinis in our politically-ridden South."

In response to threats made against Chief Hood, Copperhill hired four additional police officers. According to a "reliable source," the *Chattanooga Times* reported that one of Burch's deputies told Chief Hood: "Keep out of the McFadden case or else you'll find your back full of bullets." Burch stationed twelve deputies in the Copper Basin, far more than usual.[124] "All quiet was reported" in Copperhill the next day, with only two deputies seen in town. One of them, Floyd "Bad Eye" Dalton, was arrested for drunkenness. After conducting a personal investigation, Burch concluded there was "nothing to the threats" made against Chief Hood. He said he would serve any paper that may come of the investigation of McFadden's death. "That's what I'm here for."[125] Burch denied that Bad Eye Dalton was his deputy. Several Copperhill citizens disputed the sheriff, claiming they had recently seen an armed Dalton making arrests.

Rozelle McFadden, her stepson David, and John Wrinkle met Beecher Witt and U.S. Attorney James B. Frazier on May 22. "All we are going to do is demand justice," David said with his eyes "glistening."[126] Witt said that he had a "plain, positive case of first-degree murder" and claimed to have seven eyewitnesses prepared to testify that they saw a murder, not a killing in self-defense.[127]

On May 23, before J.P. Robert L. Frye, McFadden's son swore out a warrant for Emmett Gaddis. Charles Guinn delivered the warrant to Burch on May 25, over a week after the killing. The next day, Burch and Deputy Herman Wright arrested Gaddis at his home. The accused deputy did not resist, voluntarily handing over his badge. The county physician said Gaddis was not recovered enough to travel. Burch ordered Deputy John Blackwell to guard Gaddis at home.

Hundreds of people crowded inside the county building in Copperhill, with dozens more waiting outside, during Gaddis' preliminary hearing before J.P. Robert Frye on May 30. The state presented testimony from five witnesses. Represented by Russell R. Kramer of Maryville, Gaddis intended to plead not guilty if indicted.

Bob Payne testified that he was driving with his family back home from North Carolina when Deputy Clarence Brooks flagged him down and made him stop his car. Payne saw McFadden's car below a small hill. Gaddis, Payne alleged, stood atop the hill beside his car holding a "long gun," aiming it at McFadden. "Get out of the car!" Payne heard Gaddis yell to McFadden before firing shots into the road contractor's car. Payne claimed McFadden exited the car with his hands in the air, asking, "Are you going to kill me?" Gaddis replied, "Yes, I am," before shooting McFadden three times. Deputy Brooks then waived for Payne to drive on through. Payne got a good look at McFadden's corpse and his car, and saw no gun anywhere in the vicinity. Payne also claimed he saw blood dripping from Gaddis' leg.[128]

George Headrick lived in Bell Hill, a small neighborhood between Isabella and the state line. Headrick testified that he heard shooting and someone screaming "Get out of the car, damn you!" He looked out the window and saw Gaddis firing a rifle. He also claimed to have seen Deputy Brooks fire in McFadden's direction, and that he saw no gun near McFadden. Dr. H.P. Hyde, who examined McFadden's body, also testified.[129]

Despite Burch's previous claims, the defense presented no witnesses and insisted Gaddis' wounds proved self-defense. Frye ordered Gaddis held for murder and set his bond at $10,000. With help from his father, A.J. Gaddis, and Hoyt Lillard, the accused deputy made bail.

Determined to secure a more thorough federal investigation into McFadden's death, John Wrinkle released more correspondences with elected officials, including U.S. House Majority Leader William Bankhead, Tennessee's U.S. Senators and governor, and U.S. Senator Robert Reynolds of North Carolina. Wrinkle, a staunch Democrat and Roosevelt supporter, also wrote to Congressman Sam McReynolds.

Wrinkle had challenged McReynolds in the congressional primary in 1934, even lambasting him in a campaign speech in Benton. But Burch was a close friend, first having met McReynolds, then a judge, while transporting a prisoner to Chattanooga. Later serving as the chairman of the foreign affairs committee, McReynolds was elected as a U.S. delegate to the London Eco-

Congressman Samuel D. McReynolds spoke to the Chattanooga Automobile Club in Parksville shortly after Gaddis shot and killed McFadden on the same highway less than twenty-five miles to the east. - Cleveland-Bradley County Public Library History Branch and Archives

Third District Congressman Samuel D. McReynolds, a close friend of Burch, took no action in the aftermath of David McFadden's death at the hands of Deputy Emmett Gaddis. - Library of Congress

nomic Conference in 1933. After the conference, where he and his daughter met King George V and Queen Mary, he returned home and had lunch with Burch at the jail in Benton. The two were nearly inseparable.

Wrinkle received mixed responses in his pleas for assistance. "It is practically impossible for the local authorities who are in sympathy with the prosecution to cope with this political machine in Polk County, Tennessee," Wrinkle wrote.[130] Governor McAlister responded that he had spoken to Judge John J. Blair to ensure an impartial grand jury investigation. Senator Reynolds succeeded in persuading the justice department to "give a study" to Wrinkle's request. Unfortunately, Congress was preparing to adjourn for the year and would only pass special legislation to assist him if evidence is found that a federal statute was violated.[131]

Speaker Bankhead replied that he would cooperate with McReynolds "in any way possible," but said it was not a matter "for my personal intervention." House Minority Leader Bertrand Snell said the matter deserved a "careful and prompt investigation." However, Snell doubted he could help since the Democrats controlled Congress. Snell said that McReynolds was "the closest man to the Speaker in the house" and that any investigation would have to start with his initiative. When asked about Wrinkle's letters, McReynolds told the *Chattanooga Times* he had no comment.[132]

After some study, U.S. Attorney General Homer Cummings informed Wrinkle that violent crimes against contractors working on federal projects do not "come within the scope" of federal prosecutors. "This is a matter for the state courts to handle."[133]

At a speech in Parksville, McReynolds boasted of the progress made on federal road projects, especially the road from Cleveland to North Carolina that McFadden had worked on. "I am sorry that Polk County has received criticism in connection with things that have arisen," he said. Claiming to know "nothing" about the McFadden-Gaddis case, he praised Burch as a "moral man" incapable of immoral thought. "He is my friend and I do not care if the world knows it."[134]

On June 29, the grand jury at Ducktown deliberated for an hour before indicting Emmett Gaddis for murder. Clarence Brooks and Lloyd Parton were also indicted. Burch requested that Gaddis be permitted to remain at home under guard. Beecher Witt and Charles Guinn lost their fight with Judge Blair over bond for the accused. Blair granted them freedom under bond, with Gaddis' bond set at $15,000. Hoyt Lillard, who had just returned from serving as a delegate at the Democratic National Convention in Philadelphia, once again helped Gaddis make bond.

David S. McFadden reached out to U.S. Senator Robert Reynolds, asking for a federal investigation into labor conditions in Polk County. Reynolds contacted U.S. Senator Nathan Bachman of Tennessee. David worked in his slain father's profession, supervising road work near Tazewell. "I am bidding myself for a Polk County road job," he said. Although I have been told that some say I will be killed if I come to Polk. I've even heard that they'll get me if I appear at the trial of the men bound over in daddy's slaying – but I'll sure be there."[135] The trial would not be held until after the election.

Chapter 6
Taking on the "Rump Democrats"

In another blow to Burch's organization, Chancellor Stewart struck down the legislative acts paying him and his friends excessive salaries. He also ruled that the taxpayers had the right to bring suit. To avoid the press, Burch met with his attorney, Judge Joe V. Williams, at his home instead of his Chattanooga office, where a throng of reporters awaited the sheriff.

Burch denied that the legislative acts were unconstitutional. "Polk County is different from any other county in the state in that it has a large mountain between Benton and the towns of Ducktown and Copperhill." He claimed traveling the long distance over the mountain required him to "perform extra duties" and "incur extra expenses not common to any other sheriff in Tennessee." The county court had been paying him .75 cents per prisoner, and he claimed that this allowance did not have to be included in all of his fees and emoluments. He also said no one had ever required him to keep an account of the cost of feeding and housing the county's prisoners. He blamed county judge Vance Davis for "never questioning" his right to retain all of the money appropriated by the county court for feeding and housing the prisoners. "I have vigorously performed my duty as sheriff and enforced the laws and have incurred the enmity of the criminal element of this county along with the enmity of the partisans of one of the dominant political parties."[136]

As if he did not have enough to deal with, Burch learned that the Republicans had agreed to a fusion ticket with the Vance Davis Democrats. Arthur Dalton, Republican nominee for sheriff, withdrew from the race. John Harbison would lead the ticket as the candidate for sheriff, with Dalton promised the position of chief deputy. R.G. Hood would challenge Abie Green for tax assessor, while Boyd Mason, Republican candidate for trustee, stayed in the race, taking on Roxy Campbell. A "high-ranking Republican leader," who refused to be quoted, told the press that a fusion ticket could "wrest control of the county from the sheriff in an honest election."[137]

The Vance Davis Democrats had also sent delegates to the state convention. Winston Prince served as attorney for the Davis faction, and James F. Corn represented the Biggs faction. After the "most spirited contest at the convention," the Biggs delegates were seated, and would travel to Philadelphia to re-nominate President Franklin Roosevelt. "That's the last time that bunch will ever be here," Burch said of the Davis delegates.[138] Both factions also appointed their own primary boards. As usual, Burch got his way in Nashville when the state primary board selected his slate.

The same day the fusion ticket was finalized to take on Burch's Democratic ticket, Deputy August Lewis, new to the force, shot a man inside a Springtown store. G. Scott Runion, a deputy under former sheriff Ol Harrison, suffered gunshot wounds in both thighs after Lewis alleged Runion threatened to stab him. According to Runion, he was talking to a friend about the upcoming election when Lewis walked in and said, "You're both drunk. Consider yourselves under arrest." Runion denied the accusation and claimed he was whittling, not threatening to stab Lewis. As he approached Lewis and submitted to arrest, his knife was closed. Burch believed Lewis' story.[139]

In response to trustee Roxy Campbell's policies, the TCC was rumored to be closing on Thursday June 4. This rare occurrence was to give more time to its 450 employees to travel below the mountain to pay their poll tax before the state-mandated deadline of June 8. Campbell had recently announced a break with a longtime tradition of permitting a representative to pay the poll tax for several men at one time. A sixty-mile round trip from the Copper Basin to Benton and back took nearly three hours. With the trustee's office in the courthouse operating during normal business hours every weekday, this placed a great burden on voters above the mountain, home to several registered Republicans. Charles Guinn called Campbell's new policy a "hardship" on voters.[140]

According to Arthur Dalton, tacks were "liberally scattered" along the winding mountain road to impede carloads of miners traveling to Benton. The tacks caused punctures in at least three cars full of miners hoping to pay their poll tax. "We'll take 'em on to Benton in flatcars if we have to," one of the fusionist leaders said. "If an honest election is permitted, we will defeat the Biggs faction by 1,000 to 1,500 votes."[141]

Campbell branded the allegations against him "absolutely false," blaming the reports on an "unsigned document" circulated by his political opponents. He discussed various state voter registration and poll tax laws, emphasizing the illegality of a person purchasing the poll tax receipt of another person "for the purpose of directly or indirectly influencing his vote." He denied imposing any unnecessary hardship on voters above the mountain, and told stories of the many poll tax receipts his office had mailed out and how he permitted family members to pay polls for someone.[142]

The TCC decided to close on June 4, giving hundreds of miners the day off to pay their poll tax. The miners would have to work on Saturday though. "It was our lightest day yet," Campbell said as 400 miners paid their poll tax. "We expect to qualify 4,500 voters this year." He continued, "We are still civilized in Polk County…It is not dangerous for anyone to come through here. We will treat them right."[143]

For political parties, their "get out the vote" campaign was just as important as ensuring their voters paid their poll tax. Burch's organization always got their people to the polls, especially in the Second District, also known as the Mountain District. Burch was popular in the mountain communities of Archville (Greasy Creek) and Servilla, and he started an election day tradition of casting his ballot at the Springtown precinct. One citizen remembered how the mountain folks took their politics very seriously:

> "Some people looked at election day as a social event. People would hang out around the school house precincts all day, chatting, arguing, and talking politics. Sometimes arguments resulted in fisticuffs. These groups might consist of two or three Democrats here and there, and other groups of two or three Republicans. They didn't intermingle much, if any, on election day. For many that was not a day you could overlook your neighbor's political affiliation."[144]

With accusations of graft via special legislation increasing their salaries, two deputies charged with shooting a federal vehicle, another deputy shooting an innocent man in a store, another deputy charged with murder, and an intra-party split, the Biggs organization faced its biggest challenge yet in the 1936 general election. This would also be the year that both Chattanooga newspapers, the *News* and the *Times*, first referred to Burch as the "dictator"

of Polk County. If the Biggs organization was not a machine before 1936, it certainly was now. The *Chattanooga Times* wrote that the fusion ticket "is giving the Polk dictator his first real opponent in years."

The 1936 election also marked the election for JPs. Since 1930, the county tax rate had fluctuated between $1.60 and $1.86 under Democratic control of the county court. The increases were fairly steady, but the rates did not reach the $2.00 highs of the late 1910s. Many citizens were unsure if the services they received justified the tax rates. The court did request relief work projects to repair the courthouse and schools in Ducktown. The *Polk County News* criticized the court for building "political roads" that wasted funds, inflated the tax bill, and blocked "needed feeder roads" connecting small farming areas and communities with main highways. The roads and sidewalks around the courthouse square were in a "disgraceful condition."

Under the Democratic administration, including school board chairman Hoyt Lillard, their record on education was mixed. The county court approved the school board's reduced budget in 1933, including a pay cut for Superintendent J.C. McAmis. But the budget remained steady for 1934 and 1935. With the help of free labor and $5,000 from the Civil Works Administration, the county court voted to build a new grammar school in Benton. Located north of the Nancy Ward Grammar School, the new school would serve students from the rural schools of Taylor's, Oak Grove, Parksville, and Zion.

Broughton Biggs campaigned intensively throughout the summer, telling voters he had "never aspired" to hold political office until recently. An educated man with a well-rounded resumé, he attended Tennessee Wesleyan College and the East Tennessee State Teacher's College (now East Tennessee State University) before working for the L&N Railroad. He gained experience in a high-risk field as deputy fire marshal for the state. Congressman Sam McReynolds and Circuit Judge Pat Quinn had even recommended him for the warden position at the infamous Brushy Mountain State Penitentiary in Morgan County. "He presents himself on his own merits," the *Chattanooga News* wrote. Many of the anti-Biggs Democrats liked Broughton, but feared he would be controlled by his father if elected sheriff.[145] "It is being said that if I am elected my father will still run the sheriff's office, but one thing is sure, if I am elected, I will be sheriff of Polk County."[146]

John Harbison said if elected he would "go into office without being charged to any interests, and I will do my duty to enforce the law without favor."[147] He claimed the general public wanted change. "I have been in every precinct of the county and there is hardly a handful supporting my opponent outside of those on the county and state payrolls who believe they owe their jobs to Sheriff Biggs." A confident Harbison predicted a 1,500-vote victory over Broughton.[148]

The Biggs machine had control of the election machinery in the county, their biggest advantage over the fusionist ticket. Burch's deputies were assigned to work "all but one" of the precincts. John Standridge, a young teacher and road work supervisor for the WPA, had replaced Hoyt Lillard as chairman of the county election commission. Lillard had recently resigned from the commission after several affidavits were filed in Nashville accusing him of misconduct. Still, Standridge and Thomas N. Harbison met in Lillard's office to appoint election workers. Fount L. Love, the Republican election commissioner, did not attend the meeting, and appointed the Republican election workers on his own.

The election workers included Deputy Herman Wright in Benton, Louis Wright and John Kimbrough in Ocoee, Deputy Frank Clayton in Conasauga, Temp Biggs in Greasy Creek, Deputy August Lewis (who shot Scott Runion) in Springtown, Deputy Frank Crawford (a brother of Deputy George Crawford who shot at the CCC ambulance) in Ducktown, and Windom Gaddis (cousin of Emmett Gaddis) and William C. "Bill" Rose in Copperhill. A young man named Manuel D. Price was a poll watcher in Delano. Republican election commissioner Fount Love struggled to get poll watchers and clerks appointed. "The Biggs group ignored the men I appointed when they reported to the polls," he later said.[149]

The county lost another election commissioner in late July when Thomas N. Harbison resigned after several citizens petitioned for his removal. The state election commission replaced him with Leon Howell, a Copperhill automobile dealer. Well liked in the community, Howell had previously worked for Hoyt Lillard at Lillard Auto in Benton. "It is every man's inherit right to vote as he sees fit in any election," Howell said. "I have too many friends on both sides…to be unduly influenced."[150]

One week before the election, a subforeman named John Q. Jett claimed he was fired from his WPA job over politics. Roxy Campbell allegedly approached Jett asking him to "line up his workers" to support the Biggs ticket at the polls. "I told him I won't vote for the Biggs faction because I consider them wrong." A few days later, Daniel B. O'Neal, the county WPA administrator and Campbell's cousin, sent Jett a letter informing him of his "discharge" from WPA work.[151]

Jett wrote to the WPA district director in Chattanooga, demanding a federal investigation into his firing. "I have never been criticized in any manner for the way in which I conducted my work…It is a stench in the nostrils of all honest people to make politics out of poor, unfortunate relief workers." The WPA vowed to "investigate fully."[152] O'Neal denied he fired Jett over politics. "I fired him because he was an agitator and wouldn't obey orders." Two federal investigators were sent to Benton the next day, but nothing came of their investigation.[153]

On Monday August 3 around 10:30 PM, Bill Haddock was awoken by the sound of six gunshots and a loud car speeding by. Haddock lived less than a hundred yards from the Conasauga schoolhouse, under construction to convert the second floor into a voting precinct. Deputies Frank Clayton and B.W. Fite had been guarding the school. Multiple newspapers wrote that the area had been "surrounded with a good deal of mystery."[154]

"What's all the shooting about?" the 69-year-old Haddock asked the deputies as he approached the school. "We're trying to find our night watchman," Clayton answered. "You're making a lot of noise for a civilized country. What do you want with a night watchman?" Haddock asked. "None of your damned business!" Clayton snapped at him. "That's no way to talk to an officer!" Fite threatened to arrest Haddock if he did not "keep his mouth shut." Haddock made another remark, after which Fite slammed the unarmed, elderly man against the car. "You're under arrest!"[155]

"Come on over, dad!" Haddock's son, Walter, shouted from the house next door. Bill made a break towards the house. Clayton fired his 25-20 rifle in the air and three shots at the house. One of the bullets struck Walter's teenage son, Jack, who had just run out on the back porch. The bullet passed through the boy's hip and into the house, striking Walter's wife, Mattie, in her side. Four other children in the house slept through the ruckus. Upon hearing the "cries of the wounded," Clayton took off through a cornfield, leaving his car behind.[156]

The *Cleveland Daily Banner* reported that "the first political shooting of this season" had taken place in Polk County.[157] Haddock's grandson and daughter-in-law did not suffer serious wounds. He tried to get a warrant for Clayton's arrest, but was talked into waiting until after the election due to the "high feeling" in Polk County politics.[158]

Clayton, suffering from a wounded shoulder, told a completely different story. The deputy claimed he was guarding the schoolhouse after hearing threats of arson. "I heard a noise behind the schoolhouse and went to investigate. I saw someone run away, so I fired two shots in the air to frighten the intruders." According to Clayton, Bill Haddock came over asking what the trouble was. "As we were talking, Walter Haddock opened his back door and yelled at his father: 'Get away, I'll take care of the deputy.'" Clayton alleged Walter hit him in the back with a shotgun blast.[159] However, multiple witnesses said Clayton ran away and cut himself on a barbed-wire fence. Clayton faced no consequences for his actions.

To replace the old precinct recently destroyed by fire, the election commission built a new precinct in Turtletown. In a violation of state law, voters in the new building could not see the ballot boxes in full sight. The *Chattanooga Times* reported that the architect "perhaps had the best of intentions" when constructing the precinct. The *Times* described the new building:

> "The voting place is a rough frame structure with booths along the walls. In the center of the floor, near the rear, is a booth about four feet square, walled up solidly to the ceiling on three sides. The fourth side is walled up shoulder high and a pigeon hole is cut in one side, through which, it is presumed, the voter is to hand his ballot for the returning officer to put in the box."

Vance Davis claimed it was "in the interest of economy and good government" for the Biggs machine to be voted out. "The people are anxious to defeat Sheriff Biggs' county court, which the latter has dominated for the past six years, as they are in defeating his son, Broughton Biggs, for sheriff." Davis explained how the county court, chaired by Dr. W.A. Trevena, ran on an economy platform in 1930, and how he had done the same. He blamed Burch and Dr. Trevena for the increasing budget deficits and debt. "$3,500 each year is paid to non-resident teachers by the Polk County board of education," Davis noted, lamenting that Polk natives were passed over for teaching positions. "When Dr. Trevena took charge in 1930, the tax rate was $1.65 and it has jumped to $1.90."[160]

Some questioned Vance Davis' motive. He spoke openly in favor of reform and warned of Burch's increasing power, but not everyone opposed to Burch believed Davis was genuine, worried he just wanted power for himself. Henry Watson, a Democrat from Fannin County, alleged that Claude Davis, who had very small hands, helped her husband by sticking her hand into ballot boxes to remove ballots and replace them with marked ballots.[161] If this happened at all, whether she did it before or after her husband broke with Burch is unclear.

Polk County native T. Sherman Crump, now living in Rome, Georgia, visited his parents two days before the election. While speaking with Noah Blackwell, Crump was asked if he planned to vote in Tennessee. "No, I don't have a poll tax receipt and I live in Georgia now," he replied. "All of that can be handled. I can get you and your wife poll tax receipts," Blackwell said. He asked Crump to "find some more voters to come in and vote." Crump had read in the papers about the way elections were conducted in Polk County and wanted to see what could happen. He agreed to the offer.[162]

Vance Davis was Burch's primary rival in the Polk County Democratic Party for many years. - LaVance Davis

The day before the election, Republican election commissioner Fount Love obtained an injunction from Judge Nat Eldridge of Bradley County prohibiting Polk County election commissioners, judges, and clerks "from interfering with or intimidating voters." The injunction also prohibited deputies from "having arms on them while serving as officers" at the polls or removing ballot boxes "before the counting is completed." John Prince, a Republican attorney and brother of Democratic attorney Winston Prince, obtained the injunction for Love.[163]

"Heretofore the election, officers representing the Burch Biggs faction have carried the ballot boxes anywhere they desired before they began the count," Prince wrote in the injunction request. Such charges had been made against former election commissioners Hoyt Lillard and Thomas N. Harbison. "They resigned in the face of these charges without making denials," Prince noted. He noted that twice the usual number of mail-in ballots had been cast since Burch's faction took over the election commission, with 400 mail-in ballots cast in the November 1934 election. "The intent of this action is to avoid bloodshed and violence and to have an honest election."[164]

After a "quiet" campaign featuring mostly handshaking and door-to-door canvassing instead of the "fanfare of rallies and speakings," Polk County voters went to the polls on August 6. Both the Biggs and Davis factions claimed that "attempts will be made to steal the election."[165] The result would be the most contentious election day in the county's history up to that point.

Chapter 7

"Elected Behind Rifles"

On August 6, 1936, Deputy Frank Clayton, officer of election in Conasauga, arrived at the schoolhouse to open the precinct. He brought some "election day" deputies, including Floyd "Bad Eye" Dalton, B.W. Fite, Euclid Kelley, Ted Kemp, G.C. Lewis, Lake Grady, and John Hall. They were wearing their pistols, a blatant violation of the injunction. Vance Davis and his "posse," including his father, W.I. Davis; brother, Eldon Lee "El" Davis; two sons "Little Vance" and W.I. "Buster" Davis, and supporters Charles Jenkins, Carl Moore, and Newman Watters, arrived with rifles and shotguns to disarm the deputies.[166]

Frank Clayton was carrying the ballot box. "Throw your hands up!" one of the Davis brothers shouted. "I'll blow your head off," El allegedly said. Clayton put the ballot box down and the posse took three pistols off of him. "All we want is a fair and honest election," Vance said. El read the injunction prohibiting election workers from bringing weapons to the precincts. The posse found a school bus near the precinct stashed with shotguns and rifles.[167]

Jake Higgins, Broughton's father-in-law, tried to make a speech on the schoolhouse steps. El Davis kicked him right in his ass, knocking him off the steps. "Damn you, Jake Higgins, get off this platform," El said.[168] The posse held Clayton and the rest of the Biggs men inside one of the classrooms for several hours. The ballot box was left locked on the schoolhouse steps.

Hoping to conduct some sort of election, some of the remaining election workers opened the ballot box. About a hundred voters came throughout the day to cast their ballot. Some tried to vote at Ocoee, including W.G. Ellis, but were turned away. Rev. Kirby Park found marked ballots sealed in an envelope inside the Conasauga ballot box. He found others, but left them unopened and sent them to Benton.[169]

According to the *Chattanooga Times*, State Rep. James F. Corn, also a major in the National Guard, prepared to move his company into Polk County after reports of trouble at Conasauga. But this never materialized. Burch was "indignant" upon learning that Davis supporters disarmed his deputies. "They went and got an injunction prohibiting weapons, and then they used

The 1936 election at the Conasauga Schoolhouse almost turned deadly. - Polk County Historical and Genealogical Society

them themselves." A *Times* reporter pointed out to Burch that his deputies had arrived with their weapons in violation of the injunction. "I know, but they did exactly what the injunction prohibited."[170] But, did Burch stop to think that the injunction did not apply to the armed Davis supporters since they were not deputies or election workers?

Noah Blackwell gave Sherman Crump and his wife poll tax receipts before they went to vote in Benton. "If you found any more people to vote, send them to Leach Park to mark their ticket for Biggs and then George Williams will pay them $5 to vote," Blackwell said. This was not George Williams' first rodeo. The Crumps cast their vote. He told Williams that he saw two boys down on the street that would vote the Biggs ticket for $5 each. One of them was an Adams, and the other was Crump's underage brother. Williams gave Crump $10, which Crump kept, although he did have to ask the boys to vote.[171]

Garfield Lillard, brother of former sheriff Abe Lillard III, objected to Herman Wright marking a ballot for a Benton voter who was clearly not disabled. Deputy P.R. Hutchins allegedly pointed his gun at Lillard and forced him to leave the precinct.[172]

In an all-too common example of politics dividing families in Polk County, Democrat election official Elias Runion prohibited his brother, John, from entering the Turtletown precinct to serve as Republican poll watcher. According to John, Elias was marking ballots for several people, including his underage daughter. Esco Black, another Republican watcher, was also turned away. Pearl Verner saw Jim Rose, a North Carolina resident, carrying a gun. According to John Runion, three other North Carolina men were also there, brandishing firearms. "I am over here for what money I get out of it, and I am paid well," Rose said.[173]

In Ducktown, Frank Crawford refused to let Republican poll watchers Henry McDonald and Dayo Taylor do their jobs and escorted them outside. They told Crawford he was violating the injunction. "I disregard it," he said. Crawford appointed Burl Padgett, who lived in North Carolina, and Clarence Culbertson, a relative of Democratic JP candidate Jim Shearer, to replace McDonald and Taylor.[174] Before going in to vote, Lucian Lockaby saw men loading shotguns and rifles onto a bus outside the precinct. Election worker Wilburn Holder watched as Crawford marked 128 ballots before 10:30 AM. Luther Craig, a minor who had $2.00 allegedly from John Standridge in his pocket, dropped a marked ballot into the box. When Bessie Verner came in to vote she was told "Here's a ballot that's already marked. It's the only one we have. Take this or nothing."[175] Emmett Gaddis walked in after the polls closed. According to election clerk John Massengill, Gaddis said "You'd better get that damned ballot box out of here if you want Jim Shearer elected." Massengill watched as they took the ballot box to a car outside.[176]

Julius Turner, Amos Ballew, and Dr. A.W. Lewis were Republican election workers in Copperhill. Turner saw a Knoxville resident cast a ballot. According to Lewis, Windom Gaddis was marking several ballots. They witnessed a "truckload of strangers" come in to vote. When the polls closed, the Republican poll watchers were chased out of the precinct. Election officer Bill Rose claimed the watchers did not have "written commissions" from the election commission. Turner tried to watch the vote count through a window. Constable Ernest McGee slapped Turner in the face with his pistol. Turner was hospitalized with lacerations over his right eye.[177]

Jim Pike, whose overzealous supporters tried to forcibly certify him as JP in 1930, worked the Springtown precinct. He was turned away before the polls even opened. Republican poll watcher Traynor Chastain counted the absentee ballots, noticing the names of several people who had not lived in the county for many years. Some lived as far away as Detroit, Chicago, and St. Louis. Deputy August Lewis, also working the election, noticed the names, too, including the daughter of former J.P. Hamby who had moved to St. Louis a few years prior. Election judges overruled poll watcher Horace Burchfield when he objected to longtime Georgia residents casting absentee ballots. When the Republican poll watchers tried to watch the counting, the officer of election told them to "sit down or get out!" J.W. Chastain, a candidate for JP, tried to go inside and watch the counting. Burch was allegedly standing outside and made a pass under his left arm, refusing to let Chastain enter.[178] In Delano, Gus Swan saw several men with guns around the precinct, including Dud White.[179]

Several witnesses outside the Benton precinct watched as the ballot boxes were carried upstairs through the "carefully guarded" doors of Hoyt Lillard's building.[180] Many of the county's toughest deputies stood guard on the front porch, including Temp Biggs, Frank and George Crawford, Flavis Bates, Bad Eye Dalton, Frank Clayton, and Elias Runion (brother of John and Scott Runion). A young bootlegger named B.F. "Banjo" Presswood was also there. Despite his indictment for murder, Emmett Gaddis was there as well.

Burch's deputies refused to allow reporters from the *Chattanooga Times* to photograph the counting. They could not even get an update on the vote count. "Reporters, especially *Chattanooga Times* reporters, are not wanted inside here," Deputy P.R. Hutchins said. Ernest McGee approached two re-

Arrows point out the deputy sheriffs that warned newspaper reporters to leave after they tried to photograph the vote counting at Hoyt Lillard's building on the courthouse square in 1936. - Chattanooga Times-Free Press

porters in their car as they attempted to snap a quick photo. "You had better get on out of here!" McGee said as a *Times* reporter stationed across the street snapped a photo. According to *Times* reporter Travis Headrick, the deputies used abusive language. A group of reporters went to ask Burch if he could get them in to see the count. "I have nothing to do with the election board," he said. "I don't know what my men are doing over there."[181]

Although all candidates had been "invited" to watch the count, only John Harbison attended, but did not stay long.[182] Only one Republican poll watcher was permitted entry: former sheriff Ol Harrison. He claimed the election officers would hold five ballots in their hands and refused to let him check them. "The room where the votes were being counted was fully supplied with rifles, shotguns, and plenty of ammunition," he said.[183]

Benton poll watcher J.M. "Jim" Park, brother of Leach Park, discovered a false bottom in the ballot box after counting about 800 votes. Stashed under the bottom were 200 ballots marked for four candidates in the Democratic primary, including gubernatorial candidate Burgin Dossett and Congressman Sam McReynolds, both endorsed by Burch.[184] Park described the false bottoms as "tailor made" and warned that it was possible "all the boxes in the county were prepared in this manner."[185] He said election commissioner John Standridge was in charge of the ballot box with the false bottom, a charge that Standridge angrily denied.[186] Park also said that M.B. Wimberly, officer of election at Ocoee, placed ballots in the box without tearing off the perforation. Two Ocoee poll watchers, Sam Lowery and Homer Davis, also claimed they saw a false bottom. They found fifty marked ballots under it, which they ripped up and threw out.[187]

The election commission finished counting the next morning. They announced that Broughton had defeated John Harbison in the sheriff's race by over 800 votes (58.7 percent of the vote). A 17-point margin of victory in the sheriff's contest was high, but not unbelievable, at least from a historical standpoint. They claimed Roxy Campbell was reelected as trustee, receiving nearly twice the votes as Republican Boyd Mason. Abie Green, former chief deputy, supposedly defeated Davis faction Democrat R.G. Hood by a 2-1 margin for tax assessor. Five Biggs Democrats won seats on the county court. Arthur Dalton was also elected JP for Copperhill. In the gubernatorial contest, Dossett won Polk County by 19 points over Gordon Browning, but

Browning won the nomination. Paul Cantrell, Burch's friend from Etowah, was elected McMinn County sheriff in a close race against Republican incumbent D.C. Duggan.

The Democratic election commissioners defended the secret count and armed guards in Benton after "the trouble at the Conasauga precinct." According to the *Chattanooga News*, the counting of ballots outside of public view "has been a custom in Polk County for years."[188] When told again that his armed deputies were guarding the secret count, Burch said, "That's all hot air. That's why we beat 'em."[189] *Nashville Tennessean* political columnist Joe Hatcher wrote that the replacement of two election commissioners in Polk County "didn't seem to alter the fact that the same old crowd controlled" and that they had carried out their duties "by stuffing the boxes."

With the Republicans endorsing John Harbison, who had significant support among Democrats, bad publicity from the death of David McFadden, incessant litigation over extralegal salaries, multiple deputies shooting at civilians, reports of county employees being fired for not supporting the Biggs ticket, a poll watcher being assaulted, and the votes counted in secret, there was no denying the election was stolen.

Two days after the election, under the cover of darkness, Copperhill Police Chief Oliver Hood left town. "As long as there was any reason to stay and fight, I will remain and do my duty. But there's no point in staying and kill somebody or be killed," he told his mother. As to why he left in the middle of the night unexpectedly, he said he "hated to have his friends think he was yellow." Hood certainly had reason to be scared when he was threatened with "lead in the back" if he did not stop investigating the McFadden-Gaddis feud.[190]

The same day Chief Hood left town, Burch suffered his first jailbreak in six years. After their arrest for the robbing and attempted drowning of an Atlanta man, Bill Dean and Burton Brown sawed their way out of captivity. They had tied the man up and pushed his car down a hill into Parksville Lake. The man managed to exit the car before it hit the water. Brown was not seen again for years, but he would be back.

The atmosphere was tense in Copperhill in the aftermath of the McFadden killing and the 1936 county election. - Cleveland-Bradley County Public Library History Branch and Archives, Ridley Wills Collection

Winston Prince represented John Harbison and over a dozen of the defeated fusionist candidates in contesting the election. Among those filing suit was George Ledford, a candidate for JP who had led the group of taxpayers challenging the legality of legislation paying Burch and his friends extralegal salaries.

The next day, the *Chattanooga News* printed an editorial titled "Who Keeps Biggs in Power?"

> For years, Biggs has been in control of Polk politics. His word has been law, his smile or frown has meant life or death to aspiring politicians…Last week's elections in Polk County were marked by disorder, armed threats, and even the driving off of election officers at one precinct. False bottoms were reported in some ballot boxes…None of this sounds like good democracy."[191]

The editorial referenced the late journalist Lincoln Steffens, known for his exposés of American cities ruled by political machines. "Mr. Steffens gave it as his judgment that no political boss could long stand without the support of the economic interests of the community." The editorial asked "what corporations or economic interests find it profitable to maintain Burch Biggs in his position of political power?"[192]

Sherman Crump told the press that he and his wife voted in Polk County. "I have in my possession now the three $5 bills that George Williams gave me to pay those two boys and my wife to vote for the Biggs ticket." Crump swore that he made the affidavit "in the interest of good citizenship" and not as a favor for anyone. "I was reared in Polk County and I cannot approve of this kind of government that is letting this kind of people pick juries to try issues wherein myself or my people or friends might be involved in court."[193]

Frank Hood, nephew of R.G. Hood, wrote a letter to the *Chattanooga Times*, referring to Burch as the "Kaiser" of Polk County. "It is high time the people were aware of some of the things which are actually happening in this section, where the rights of man are supposed to be equal." Hood witnessed Burch's "lieutenants" toting guns at his precinct, in direction violation of the injunction. "They were present to see that the opposing faction was not represented in any way."

"As the honest taxpayers looked on, they saw their money spent for votes as if at a public livestock auction," Hood wrote. He told the story of an "illiterate" 17-year-old girl who was paid to vote for the Biggs ticket. Despite several objections, election officials let her cast a vote. "This was only one of many illegal votes which are known to have been cast."

The *Chattanooga Times* also wrote an editorial about how the "oil of patronage" enabled political machines to run smoothly. Burch had close relationships with Governor McAlister, giving him access to state patronage, and Senator McKellar and Congressman McReynolds, keys to the highly coveted federal patronage. "Whenever his friends in Polk County need votes, Sheriff Biggs delivers them." In exchange, Burch was granted the power to make political appointments in Polk County, and sometimes outside the county. He had even secured the job of warden at the Brushy Mountain State Penitentiary for Herbert Russell, son of Polk County clerk and master William F. Russell.[194]

The editorial detailed Burch's vigorous campaign for Dossett, the gubernatorial candidate backed by outgoing Governor McAlister. Burch ensured Dossett won Polk County. However, Gordon Browning, supported by Boss Crump, won the primary. Burch sent a congratulatory telegram to Browning. "This situation demanded a change to the winning horse," the *Chattanooga Times* wrote. Frank Hood had written to the *Times* about Burch's patronage power: "The honest taxpayers of Polk County have little chance to obtain good government under present conditions."[195] Matt Witt later remembered: "Everybody below the mountains were looking for patronage jobs. Many farmers had one pay day per year if the crops were good. A county job was a "cash crop" to supplement their farm."[196] Burch had several tenant farmers on his land, and since his handpicked election workers could see how everyone voted, the farmers had two choices: vote the Democratic ticket, or be evicted.[197]

Stolen elections or not, Burch had many ways to remain formidable electorally. He liked to do non-political favors for his political opponents. "The best way to get milk from the cow is to pet the calf, he once said."[198] During the depression's darkest days, he slaughtered some of his beef cows and gave the meat to the county's poorest families.[199] Whenever someone of lesser means took ill or suffered an injury, he "passed the hat around" to help. Sally Hutchins Gregory remembered Burch's involvement in church and charities.[200] His defenders praised his compassion, while his opponents claimed he was just buying votes. One citizen, whose father was a deputy, had nothing but disdain for Burch, calling him "crooked."[201]

One thing was for certain, Burch was an affable man, and some people could not help but like him personally, even if they disliked his politics. A member of the Benton Masonic Lodge and the Benton Lions Club, he counted many people as his friends. Charlie Guinn remembered several farmers tipping their hat to Burch whenever they saw him.[202] He was great with kids. Billy Rice recalled the time Burch gave him a silver dollar when he was about 5 years old.[203]

One week after the election, David S. McFadden was outside his Asheville home when he heard a noise in an adjoining field. He walked over to get a closer look, and saw the "shadowy figures" of three or four men about fifty yards away. He and his brother Frank shouted at them. They responded by firing eight shots towards the McFadden brothers, all of which missed.[204]

Local authorities made a "vigorous" search, but found no clues. "I saw an automobile with a Tennessee license plate around the farm last night," David said. The *Chattanooga News* reported that five men from the Copper Basin "whose identities could not be learned" were seen in Murphy. Burch claimed he had not heard about the assassination attempt on David S. McFadden. "We have no further plans to investigate his father's death," he said.[205] David said he believed the attempt on his life was "an aftermath of difficulties which led to the fatal shooting of my father."[206] His father's killers would be tried in January.

Chapter 8

SHERIFF BROUGHTON BIGGS

R.G. Hood, the incumbent tax assessor who lost to Abie Green, obtained a temporary injunction from Judge L.D. Miller of Chattanooga preventing Green from being sworn into office. The injunction ensured Hood would continue to be paid. Hood also filed a nineteen-page petition alleging "wholesale fraud, vote-buying, and intimidation by gunmen."[207] The election contest would be heard in Judge Pat Quinn's court.

On September 1, 1936, county court clerk Leach Park administered the oath of office to Broughton, who succeeded his father as sheriff. Retaining many of Burch's men, Broughton appointed Herman Wright as his chief deputy, Frank Clayton as jailer, George Crawford as deputy in Ducktown, Frank Crawford as deputy in Isabella, and John Blackwell as a deputy in Farner. He later appointed Earl Gardener, C.A. Ingle, and Manuel D. Price. Broughton planned to "make some changes" in the sheriff's department. The same day, John Harbison said he would start proceedings in his election contest against the new sheriff.[208]

Dr. W.A. Trevena, J.J. Taylor, W.A. Kerr, Benson Hammons, Andrew Bates, Grayson Davis, Jim Shearer (formerly a Republican), and Arthur Dalton also took the oath of office as JPs. Burch's faction had almost total control of the county's legislative body. They would all be facing election contests from the defeated candidates in the Davis faction.

Justice Alexander Chambliss of the state supreme court overruled Judge Miller's injunction, allowing Abie Green to take the oath of office as the new tax assessor. Chambliss cited the issuance of certificates of election to Green and the other winning candidates as "prima facie" evidence of their election.

Broughton and Louise moved into the Lillard cottage with their two-year-old daughter, Joann, shortly after he took office. In one of his first acts as sheriff, he gave an ultimatum to all gambling establishments: get rid of your slot and pinball machines by October 15. "I don't wish to take any drastic measures," he said about giving them time to comply. When a friend claimed removing his slot machines would hurt his business, the new sheriff said he could not break his campaign promise to enforce the law.[209]

Burch's opponents accused him and his deputies, like many sheriffs at this time, of busting a few gambling houses and moonshine stills for show. But the rest of the moonshiners, especially in the Mountain District, cut Burch in on a portion of their earnings. One citizen told his son that most still operators were handpicked and that much of the product was exported out of the county. A native of the Mountain District later showed his grandchildren where all the stills were and said Burch knew all about them.[210] "Everyone knew who sold whiskey, but they were never raided," Patsy Crox Underhill recalled.[211] Matt Witt listed protection money among Burch's sources of revenue.[212] What distinguished Burch from previous sheriffs on the moonshine issue was his long tenure in office and his coordination with the shiners. The moonshine trade thrived like never before under the Biggs machine. Burch knew all about it, and profited greatly from it.

Broughton E. Biggs first became sheriff in 1936 after serving as a deputy under his father. - Tennessee State Library and Archives

According to the *Polk County News*, slot machines "have been run openly in Polk County for the past year or so."[213] The boss of the county's criminal underworld was a young man in Ducktown named B.F. "Banjo" Presswood (pronounced "Ban-jer"). As a boy, Banjo carried around a shoeshine box that he also used to dispense whiskey. He later owned poker-and-crap-game emporiums. He eventually had enough money to buy a Ford dealership in town. Deputy Frank Clayton was a man of many vices, and quite the ladies' man. He was a close friend of Banjo, who could not have maintained his illicit enterprise without cutting Burch in on some of his earnings. "I was told that with the blessing of Sheriff Biggs, Banjo had illegal slot machines in several places throughout Polk County," David Talley remembered.[214] In contrast to most of his peers in the criminal underworld, Banjo is remembered by many for his "heart of gold." Chuck Talley, his son, David, and Don Jones witnessed Banjo's many "good deeds" in the community. But others condemned him as a "gangster."[215]

As the general election approached, and despite his faction's loss in the August election, Vance Davis maneuvered to wrest control of the Polk County Democratic Party from Burch. The state executive committee appointed Davis campaign manager for the Democratic ticket in Polk County. Both the Biggs and Davis factions supported the entire Democratic ticket, including Gordon Browning for governor and Sam McReynolds for Congress.

Now dominated by Democrats aligned with Burch, the county court voted to pay new deputy sheriff Herman Wright a $100 per month salary. Claiming the need for a night jailer, they also voted to pay a night jailer a $50 per month salary. Arthur Dalton, a Republican, was the only JP at the October court meeting whose election was not challenged.

Jim Park was appointed to replace John Standridge on the election commission after Standridge resigned to take a job out of town. Jim Park, a Democrat who was also affiliated with the Benton Banking Company, would serve as election commission chairman. The Biggs machine learned that Jim Park would run things much differently than they expected. Burch complained that Park did not keep his word when he refused to appoint election workers recommended by the state bosses, including Congressman McReynolds.

"The election in Polk County on Tuesday was one of the quietest in years in contrast to the disorders that marked the primary ballots," the *Polk County News* reported on November 5, 1936. Dutch Woody, a Republican, defeated Cleveland Democrat Jess Rymer for state representative. Gordon Browning was elected governor, tallying 73 percent of the vote in Polk County, by far the highest margin of victory in the county for a gubernatorial candidate not facing an Independent since at least 1900. Browning was Crump's man, so Burch made sure he won big.

Congressman McReynolds easily defeated an independent challenger. President Roosevelt won reelection in a landslide nationwide against Alf Landon, and carried Polk County by 13 points, another high but not unbelievable margin. The president won Monroe and Meigs Counties by a similar margin and achieved close victories in the Republican strongholds of Bradley and Cherokee Counties. McMinn, Loudon, and Fannin Counties, reliably Republican, voted for Landon by small margins.

Although he was now "retired," 62-year-old Burch had more time for state politics. He traveled to Nashville with Hoyt Lillard and Leach Park during the 1937 legislative session. Broughton was making his mark as sheriff, but several people maintained that Burch was still in charge. "It was very clear that Burch E. Biggs ran almost everything in the county," David Talley remembered.[216]

Chapter 9
STATE VS. EMMETT GADDIS

Legend has it that the Johnny Cash song "A Boy Named Sue" was inspired by Madisonville attorney Sue K. Hicks. In 1936, Sue Hicks became Judge Sue Hicks of the Fourth Judicial Circuit, succeeding the late Judge John J. Blair. He would be presiding over the trial of Emmett Gaddis for the murder of David McFadden. He set Gaddis' trial for Tuesday January 19, 1937.[217]

Gaddis would be tried alongside Clarence Brooks and Lloyd Parton, the men who were with him when McFadden was killed. Instead of Benton, the trial would be held at the Ducktown Law Court, a two-story frame building. Judge Hicks ordered the Polk County jury commission to summon a panel of 300 potential jurors. The *Knoxville News-Sentinel* reported that McFadden's murder "had aroused so much interest in the county that prosecuting attorneys doubted if 12 'disinterested' jurors could be selected from the 300."[218]

Anticipating a huge crowd, Broughton permitted limited spectators at the trial. The Ducktown Hotel had no vacancies the night before the trial, and even the New York Hotel in Copperhill was booked almost to capacity. Broughton also requested assistance from the state highway patrol for additional security.

Judge Hicks banged his gavel on Tuesday morning to begin what would prove to be sensational trial. Beecher Witt led the prosecution, with Frank Bratton, Charles Guinn, and John Wrinkle assisting. Copperhill attorney Ed Adams, Ducktown attorney G. Parks Hyatt, Maryville attorney Russell Kramer, and Murphy attorney Harry Cooper represented Gaddis and his codefendants. Seats filled up quickly, forcing many spectators to stand in the aisles and "three deep" in the rear. Judge Hicks then ordered everyone who did not have a seat to leave. A carpenter said the building could not support such weight. Burch took a seat next to Broughton.

Emmett Gaddis entered the courtroom on crutches and followed the proceedings "intently." 20-year-old Clarence Brooks, the youngest of the defendants, wore a "worried" look on his face, while Lloyd Parton slouched in his chair.[219] The prosecution announced the imminent testimony of "surprise witnesses" from Georgia. Jury selection lasted nearly all day, with several prospective jurors telling Judge Hicks they had already formed an opinion on the case after reading pre-trial witness testimony. Other dismissed jurors said they opposed capital punishment.

Bill Rose, a Copperhill automobile dealer who lived in Bradley County, admitted he did not live in Polk County and was dismissed. He had also sold a car to Gaddis. The defense objected to his removal. As if all of this weren't enough to disqualify him, he had also worked the Copperhill precinct in the August 1936 election. John Edwards, a CCC worker, confessed he had spoken to Parton, but not about the trial. "I've read about the case in the *Chattanooga Times*, your honor, and I've formed an opinion. But I will be able to return a fair and unbiased verdict." The defense protested Edwards, so Judge Hicks dismissed him. C.R. Webb, T.N. Harbison, C.C. Rymer, Tom W. Hitener, Wayne Johnson, Noah Bates, Jerry Jones, Marion Talley, Noah J. Rymer, Jim Rymer, Arthur Merrill, and Charles Stone comprised the jury.[220]

The defendants pled not guilty to the charge of first-degree murder. On day two, crowds gathered outside the building as a light drizzle turned into a "steady downpour." The prosecution called Rozelle McFadden as the first witness. Dr. H.P. Hyde and undertaker J.P. Chastain also testified. Isabella grocer Alfred Geisler claimed he saw the codefendants get in Gaddis' car where they waited until McFadden's car passed by, at which point they followed him. "Twenty-five minutes later, I heard McFadden had been killed."[221]

On cross-examination, Russell Kramer learned that Gaddis had once arrested Geisler. Kramer accused Geisler of bias, a charge that Witt vehemently denied.[222] Kramer also insinuated that McFadden might have had liquor in the car.[223] Witt introduced into evidence a pen and ink sketch of the murder scene. Luther and Claude McDonald, who lived on the Isabella road, and Arthur Bandy all alleged they saw Gaddis' car pass McFadden's car going 50 MPH.[224] All three witnesses claimed they heard gunshots a few minutes later.

The most devastating testimony came from Dorothy Syfan of Decatur, Georgia, one of the surprise witnesses. Syfan was traveling with her husband, Manning Syfan, and father, Arthur Bearden, on an "afternoon excursion to the mountains" when they found two automobiles blocking the road. "I saw Gaddis get out of the back seat of the car and run toward the other car, the McFadden car, and McFadden had gotten out of the car. He was shaking. He must have been wounded." Syfan alleged that Gaddis walked over to McFadden and shot him with a pistol. "After he fell, he shot him again." McFadden, she said, had his hands up when he exited the car and that she saw "no pistol or weapon on or near McFadden's body."[225]

The Ducktown Law Court was established to hold court and provide county services to residents of the Copper Basin, saving them frequent trips to Benton. The murder trial of Gaddis, Parton, and Brooks was held here in January 1937. - Polk County Historical and Genealogical Society

Judge Sue K. Hicks presided over one his first criminal trials in Ducktown in January 1937. - Dean Wilson

In a blow to the self-defense plea, Syfan also testified she saw Parton shoot Gaddis in the leg with a rifle. "Then he (Parton) came to the left side of our car and told us to drive on. He couldn't get by on account of our car." As a safety precaution, the Syfans were escorted by a state highway patrolman from their hotel in Blue Ridge, Georgia to Ducktown. Arthur Bearden gave nearly identical testimony as his daughter. "I didn't think it was safe to come over here (to Ducktown)," Bearden told Kramer during cross-examination. Kramer proceeded to praise the sheriff's department under the Biggs family.[226]

On the third day, spectators reacted with shock as Gaddis' seventeen-year-old son from a previous relationship testified for the prosecution. Olen Gaddis, estranged from his father, testified that he was riding in a car with friends when he saw his father's car and McFadden's car pass by about a minute apart.[227]

Olen alleged that he approached the scene of the shooting and exited his car. "I saw Emmett fire at McFadden's car several times." His testimony matched those of several other witnesses, that McFadden had his hands in the air when Gaddis shot him. The young Gaddis also claimed McFadden lied on his back as his father fired the fatal shots into the unarmed McFadden.[228] Kramer cross-examined Olen, asking him about his recent incarceration in Bradley County. Like others in the Gaddis family, Olen had a few run-ins with the law.[229]

George Headrick testified that he heard gunshots during supper. He alleged that Brooks fired at McFadden's car and that Gaddis yelled, "Come out, damn you, come out of there." Charlie Elrod, another local, also claimed he heard Gaddis. Newman Bridges, a truck driver, saw McFadden's body loaded onto an ambulance. He observed a couple of two-inch deep bullet holes where McFadden had been fatally shot, and picked up a bullet that he later gave to prosecutors.[230]

The prosecution's final witness, a high school girl named Inez Payne, also testified that Gaddis shot an unarmed McFadden with his hands in the air. She swore she heard McFadden ask, "Are you going to kill me this way?" Gaddis answered, "Certainly, I am." Rozelle McFadden "wept silently" during Payne's testimony, after which the state rested its case.[231]

Dressed in a blue suit as he sat with his arms folded, Emmett Gaddis took to the stand as the defense's first witness. He began his testimony in a "low, clear voice." He claimed he had lived in Polk County since he was twelve and that he served in the Great War.[232] "I had been working as a deputy under former sheriff Burch Biggs for a little more than three years at the time of the trouble," Gaddis said referring to the November 1935 incident. He claimed he approached McFadden about complaints made against him by some of his crew. "He became hostile and said he 'didn't want anything to do with god damn deputy sheriffs or anything to do with them.'" Gaddis alleged he had to confront McFadden the day before the incident because a WPA man told him there would be "some trouble" at the work site.[233]

"I went with Constable Ernest McGee and Deputy Windom Gaddis and found a bunch of men there," Gaddis said referring to the labor riot. He claimed he saw commotion around McFadden's car and that Lloyd Parton and McFadden were grappling over a gun. "McFadden fired the pistol and it looked like he had hit Parton." Then, Gaddis alleged, McFadden looked at him and said "God damn you, I'll shoot the hell out of you!" Gaddis admitted he shot McFadden in the mouth as an act of self-defense. "I took him to the hospital where he told me 'I'll kill you, even if I have to crawl on my belly to do it.'"[234]

Gaddis recounted the Christmas Eve 1935 incident when McFadden allegedly called him to his door at home and shot him in the shoulder through the door. He again swore he used a flashlight to identify McFadden standing outside "with his hands behind his back." Jim Hughes, a friend of Gaddis, had allegedly seen McFadden close to Harbuck Roller Mountain, Gaddis' favorite hunting spot, in April. McFadden had allegedly used an alias and was asking about Gaddis.[235]

On the day of McFadden's death, Gaddis claimed he was on a family outing to Stansbury Gap. After they returned home around 3:00 PM, two men allegedly came asking if Gaddis had seen any drunks pass by. "I got Clarence Brooks, then Lloyd Parton, and drove to the golf course (now the Copper Basin Golf Course) to find the drunks. "I saw a car pass by, but didn't know it was McFadden's."[236] Gaddis said he then pulled over to fix a punctured tire. "As I examined the tires on the back of my car, a bullet struck at my feet and ricocheted into the ball of my foot." He looked back and saw a man holding a rifle.[237]

"Did you see who the man was," Kramer asked. "He was leaning out the left door…It was D.W. McFadden." Gaddis claimed McFadden fired again, hitting his thigh. "I reached my car and got my 250-300 rifle…I commenced shooting." Gaddis said he shot his rifle empty. "Why did you do that," Kramer asked. "Because I knew he'd shoot me if he got the chance." Gaddis denied that he yelled at McFadden to "come out of that car" and if McFadden asked "You aren't going to kill me like this, are you?" Gaddis continued: "I pulled my pistol out of my holster as he came out of his car door and fired two or three shots…I don't remember him falling…I was hurting." He claimed he became "semi-conscious" and had difficulty remembering what happened next. "I was getting weak…I had bled quite a lot." He said he walked down to McFadden's car where Parton and another man, Mote Anderson, took him to the hospital. Gaddis' testimony lasted 45 minutes.[238]

Witt cross-examined Gaddis, receiving several "I don't remember" answers. Gaddis said he never demanded $500 in protection money from McFadden. Witt asked why Gaddis had a high-powered rifle in his car and how he was able to walk down to McFadden's car despite his injuries. He also asked how many men Gaddis had shot in the Basin, which met with fierce objection, sustained by Judge Hicks. After Gaddis denied having pressured his son to not testify against him, he left the witness stand.[239]

Parton testified next, describing his time working for McFadden. He claimed the slain road contractor often overworked and refused to pay them. Gaddis and Parton told similar stories about the November 1935 incident. The defense called other witnesses who testified that McFadden tried to shoot McGee before Gaddis shot McFadden. Multiple witnesses alleged McFadden was seen driving around the area shortly before Gaddis was shot on Christmas Eve 1935, with a rifle in his car, asking about Gaddis and Deputy George Crawford. Witt criticized their testimonies, inquiring about their criminal past and relationship with Gaddis.

Rumors of jury tampering started to spread around the Copper Basin. On day four, Judge Hicks addressed the rumors. "If anyone has approached any of you jurymen and tried to talk to you, I ask you to hold up your hand." None of the twelve men raised their hand. "The court is investigating these rumors." Hicks addressed the entire courtroom, reminding everyone of their duty to report any knowledge of a "fixed" jury or any tampering.[240]

The defense called Dr. H.H. Hyatt to the stand to testify about Gaddis' wounds from Christmas Eve 1935. But it would be Anna Gaddis who took the stand as the final defense witness. The couple's three-year-old daughter sat in Emmett's lap as her mother testified, corroborating her husband's entire testimony.[241] When asked about her husband's rifle in the car, she claimed he brings it with him "practically all the time." With her testimony concluded, the defense rested.[242]

Deputy DA Frank Bratton began the state's closing arguments, emphasizing the "disinterested" Syfan family's testimony. Wrinkle alleged a conspiracy to murder McFadden. "Murder-murder-murder in the first degree, with malice aforethought!" he told the jury. Guinn complimented the Biggs family as his close friends, but asked the jury "not to turn loose" the defendants. "Gaddis shot McFadden down like a dog while he was begging for his life."[243]

Ed Adams opened a strong closing argument for the defense, calling Mrs. Syfan "a little dewdrop" that was "eager to testify." He pointed out that no

Lloyd Parton, Clarence Brooks, and Emmett Gaddis were tried for the murder of David McFadden. - Chattanooga Times-Free Press

other state witness testified to seeing the Syfans and that it was "unbelievable" that Gaddis would take his family on a Sunday ride with intent to commit murder. Parks Hyatt criticized the "sweet-smelling Atlanta witnesses" for wearing silk stockings and perfume. "They aren't our kind of people." Harry Cooper asked if Gaddis "would have so little sense as to have committed a cold-blooded murder on a public highway in broad daylight?" He belittled Mrs. Syfan's testimony. "Women are just women; they always have vivid imaginations." He implored the jury to accept the testimony of the "people you know – your people – not those from Georgia…Forget not, I beg of you, your friend, fellow townsman, and fellow man."[244]

On Saturday, the fifth and final day of the trial, the lead attorneys made their closing arguments. "I do not believe that any jury from the red hills of Polk County or the land below the mountain will 'guess' three men into eternity," Kramer said. He eviscerated the Syfans, and asked why they did not ask the "fine stalwart" Sheriff Broughton Biggs for protection if they were scared to come to Ducktown. Olen Gaddis, Kramer insisted, tried to send his father to the electric chair "without a quiver of emotion." Heaping praise upon the Polk Sheriff's department, he insisted that Burch and his deputies would not stoop to taking graft money. Gaddis' five-year-old son, Andrew Jackson Gaddis, wept while sitting on his father's knee after Kramer asked the jury for a not-guilty verdict.[245]

Witt, in his eleventh year as district attorney, closed with a fiery speech. "Attorneys here have sought to play upon your heartstrings." He referenced the jury tampering rumors, and reminded the jurors to keep their oaths to be fair and impartial. "This is one of the most viscous killings I've ever known in the county of Polk," he said before complimenting Broughton and warning to not judge sheriffs or their deputies by the actions of one law-breaking deputy.[246]

"McFadden was not looking for trouble," Witt insisted before pillorying Gaddis' version of the killing and calling him a "coward." To the charge that the state relied too heavily on outside witnesses, Witt pointed out that the defense did not put one man from the Basin to testify on behalf of the defendants. "Why would Gaddis turn his back on McFadden, who was firing at him, to get a rifle from his trunk when he had a pistol in his holster?" he asked. "These defendants created their own destiny…I ask you to return a verdict of guilty.[247]

Judge Hicks instructed the jury to return with one of four verdicts: first-degree murder, second-degree murder, voluntary manslaughter, or not guilty. He charged the jury at noon. They only deliberated for a few hours. The defendants awaited the verdict: Parton; Gaddis sitting with his wife and kids; and Brooks with his parents. Rozelle McFadden and her seven-year-old daughter, Thelma, did not attend the reading of the verdict, opting to stay in their Ducktown hotel room.

"We find the defendants not guilty," said the foreman. Gaddis cracked a big smile, as did Parton and Brooks. They shook hands with and patted their attorneys on the back. They thanked each juror personally with "clasped hands." Mrs. Gaddis "wept for joy" as she squeezed her young daughter. Witt had no comment, and neither did any of the prosecutors. Kramer praised Judge Hicks and Witt. Hicks dismissed the jury and adjourned court.[248] "The most sensational trial in Polk County's history," according to the *Copper City Advance*, was over.

Upon receiving news of the acquittal, Rozelle McFadden fainted. She lay on the floor prostrated, with her daughter looking on. After she came to, she thanked Witt for his efforts and left for her Asheville home.[249] But Burch would hear from her again.

Both Chattanooga newspapers criticized the verdict. In their editorial titled "A Bad Verdict," the *News* assailed the defense's "poking fun" at the Atlanta witnesses. They called the verdict "one of the worst miscarriages of justice in the state's history." The verdict came as no surprise to the *Times*, who wrote of the defense's portrayal of the Atlanta witnesses as "foreigners." Potential jury tampering was "unimportant," according to the *Times*, compared to the "local prejudice" of the jury that the defense masterfully played upon.

Chapter 10

GEORGE LEDFORD, COMPLAINANT

On March 17, 1937, George Ledford, a barber, anti-Biggs Democrat, and defeated candidate for JP, was "leisurely" driving home to Old Fort. Unbeknownst to him, Deputy Manuel Price had been following him. Troy, Ledford's seventeen-year-old son, saw Price speed by as he was walking home from school around 4:30 PM.[250]

Only 150 yards from the house, Troy saw Price pull into the driveway. As Troy got closer, he saw Price get out of the car carrying a gun. "Come out of there and go with me!" Price ordered Ledford. The two got into a scuffle. "Leave me alone!" Ledford said. Ledford's wife, Cornelia, and two young daughters were standing in the doorway.

Price shot Ledford three times, right in front of his family, in broad daylight. Ledford had recently removed a shotgun he kept just inside the front door because Cornelia worried for their children's safety. According to Ledford's family, had the shotgun been near at hand, Cornelia would have shot Price dead on the spot.

As Price fled the scene, Anna Lee Ledford rushed over to her father. He could hardly speak with the blood gushing from his mouth. He passed away in his thirteen-year-old daughter's arms, moments before Troy arrived home. Cornelia Ledford, a homemaker, was left to raise four children.[251]

Less than two months after one deputy had been acquitted for killing an unarmed man, another deputy had done the same. Ledford's family swore out a warrant for Price, charging him with murder. Broughton, acting much differently than his father had done with Emmett Gaddis, moved quickly and arrested Price himself at the deputy's home.

Price was a new deputy, having been appointed in September. "When I appointed him, he was married and had a good reputation," Broughton said.[252] But Price had no prior law enforcement experience, having worked at a mill in Delano. The *Polk County News* reported on Ledford's previous conflict with Burch. So did the *Chattanooga Times*:

> "The slain man was one of the taxpayers who instituted the suit against former Sheriff Burch Biggs on the Polk County salary act."[253]

Price claimed self-defense and insisted Ledford was armed. Others alleged Ledford was sober and unarmed, which Broughton denied. Claude Davis had seen Ledford at her Conasauga store just before his death and said he had not been drinking. According to the *Chattanooga Times*, "few people cared to discuss the case."[254] William Oscar Scarbrough, father of renown poet George Scarbrough, moved his family to McMinn County after the Ledford killing. "There is no place for us here anymore," he told his family. In the eyes of many, this was not just a murder, it was an assassination.

George Ledford, a Democrat, was a barber originally from Murray County, GA. - George Ledford family

One year later, Price was tried for murder. Judge Pat Quinn, filling in for Judge Sue Hicks, presided over the trial in Benton on March 23, 1938. District Attorney Beecher Witt would once again try a Polk County deputy for murder. Russell Kramer and Charles Guinn defended Price. Will Bishop, Clifford Paris, J.H. Hammons, Tommie Smith, Jim Shelton, Claude Nichols, Riley Brookshire, John Stewart, W.L. Reece, Sam Doogan, John Barker, and Howard Lillard comprised the jury.[255]

Cornelia Ledford and her four children testified that George had just arrived home and "had not had time to get out of the car" before Price drove up behind him and ordered him to get out of the car. "My husband told Price he had done nothing and that he had no cause to be ordered around." She said Price jerked Ledford out of the car, pointed a gun at him, and took Ledford's gun from his pocket. "As my husband was backing away, Price shot him to death and drove away in a hurry."[256]

Price invoked the universal Polk County excuse: self-defense. He claimed Ledford was resisting arrest when he knocked Price's gun from his hand. Then, Price alleged, Ledford reached for Price's gun, but before he could pick it up Price grabbed Ledford's gun and shot him. The defense called two witnesses: Charles Culpepper and Constable Bill Hedden. They had allegedly heard Ledford say he would kill Price if he ever tried to arrest him.[257] Hedden's credibility would soon be heavily tainted, but not before this testimony.

The trial was brief, and Judge Quinn charged the jury that afternoon. They returned two hours later and said they could not agree. Judge Quinn told them to keep deliberating and report back in the morning. They brought back a verdict at 9:00 AM: not guilty.[258] Two deputies working for the Biggs machine had taken a man's life with zero justification.

The message was now loud and clear: no one could stand up to Burch without suffering the consequences. "If you got on his bad side, you were liable to get killed," Sally Hutchins Gregory recalled. She described the way some of the old-time sheriffs and their deputies rationalized their actions and believed they had the right to kill someone if they wanted to. "It was a different time and different way of living."[259]

A few years later, Manuel Price was indicted along with T.W. Dalton and Jack Hedden for the attempted murder of W.D. Simpson. They were not convicted.[260] According to Ledford's daughter, Anna Lee Ledford Avery, a remorseful Price later contacted her to apologize for taking her father's life.[261]

Chapter 11
HOOD VS. GREEN

Two months after Emmett Gaddis' acquittal, and just weeks after George Ledford's murder, the election contest filed by the Vance Davis Democrats went to trial. It was agreed that the evidence in R.G. Hood's suit against Abie Green would be used in the subsequent cases. The only exception was John Harbison, who filed a separate suit against Broughton. Burch's personal attorney Joe V. Williams joined the attorneys who successfully defended Emmett Gaddis to represent the winning candidates, while Winston Prince and Cleveland attorney Charles S. Mayfield Sr. represented the defeated candidates.[262]

Ninety-eight witnesses testified over five days in March 1937. When asked if he knew he was breaking the law by taking money to vote, Sherman Crump said he "just wanted to see what the county would allow."[263] It was revealed that Roxy Campbell's office had issued duplicate poll tax receipts. Multiple Bradley County residents claimed to have received an unsolicited absentee ballot from Polk County. Deputy August Lewis testified to the several out-of-state names he saw on absentee ballots at Springtown. The election judge there claimed several of the absentee voters had recently left the county after marrying or taking a new job. Numerous witnesses recounted seeing armed deputies guard Hoyt Lillard's building as the votes were counted.

The "Battle of Conasauga" was practically given an oral reenactment during testimony. Four key witnesses admitted that Clayton and the election workers had guns but said there was not an "arsenal." El Davis denied telling Frank Clayton he would "blow his head off," but confessed to kicking Jake Higgins off the steps. Higgins dubbed politics in Conasauga "sad and deplorable" and claimed he was unaware of the injunction forbidding election workers from bringing guns to the precinct.[264]

Broughton disputed J.W. Chastain's claim that Burch reached for his gun when Chastain approached the Springtown precinct. "I worked hard to be elected," the new sheriff said. "I can't say my opponent worked hard." He denied telling Wayne Higgins he would be elected "even if I only get three votes" and claimed he turned down a deal to make Wayne a deputy in exchange for his vote.[265]

When asked why the Ducktown ballot box was transported to Benton via Blue Ridge and Ellijay, Deputy Frank Crawford said that "it was my understanding that armed men were on the Benton highway ready to take the box." Compared to other precincts, the Ducktown election was "quiet and without disorderly conduct."

Julius Turner testified to the injuries he suffered at the Copperhill precinct when Ernest McGee struck him in the head for trying to watch the count. Russell Kramer claimed Turner was drunk. So did Dr. H.P. Hyde, whose office was opposite the precinct. Burch's county court had appointed Hyde as county physician, so the good doctor was not going to bite the hand that helped feed him. Turner was enraged at the allegations.

Judge Quinn dismissed Hood's case against Green, ignoring a plethora of evidence. He found that the plaintiffs failed to demonstrate sufficient proof of "fraud and conspiracy" and that there was insufficient proof that enough fraudulent ballots were cast to change the election outcome. John Harbison eventually dropped his case against Broughton.[266]

Broughton and Louise became parents for the second time when Tom Henry Biggs was born on May 30, 1937. Broughton named his son for the grandfather he barely knew, shot down when he was only three years old. Burch must have been delighted to have a grandson named for his father. "Mother and son are doing nicely. So is Grandpa Burch!" the *Copper City Advance* wrote.

While the Biggs machine emerged victorious in the election fraud case, they lost the case challenging recent legislative acts paying them extra salaries. Chancellor T.L. Stewart ruled the acts unconstitutional and ordered Burch, Hoyt Lillard, and Leach Park to pay the county $7,500. George Ledford was not alive to see the result of the lawsuit that he helped initiate. No longer would the county have to pay Burch and his associates extra salaries.

Stewart's ruling would save the county $9,000 per year. But this ruling would not stop the Biggs machine from finding other revenue streams. Current and former county officials George Gilliland, Porter Campbell, and R.G. Hood also faced accusations of drawing excessive salaries. The county court was eager to investigate the accusations against these men who were not really part of the machine.

During the state legislature's three sessions in 1937, most of State Rep. Dutch Woody's bills failed to become law, including a bill creating a budget commission intended to weaken the control Burch's county court had over county finances. Supported by the Vance Davis Democrats, Woody also proposed a bill creating a three-person county commission. The bill had an "anti-nepotism" clause and would prove an inspiration for future reformers in the county.

Woody told county officials to "get their spending straightened out" or else he would not pass any more bills to increase their enormous debts. In addition to building a new courthouse, the county also needed to repair several school buildings.[267] The new courthouse was completed in October and the county court finally voted to repair the crumbling sidewalks and roads on the square. Broughton had the honor of opening the first civil and criminal court to convene in the new building.

Chapter 12

"HE KNEW OF THE BAD CHARACTER OF THE DEPUTIES"

Shortly after her husband's killer escaped conviction, Rozelle McFadden filed suit for $100,000 in damages in federal court, naming Emmett Gaddis, Clarence Brooks, Lloyd Parton, and Burch Biggs as defendants. She charged that Burch had "conspired" with the others to kill her husband.[268]

Rozelle McFadden's suit was not solely about money. She had good reason to believe that her husband's murder was just one ugly episode in a corrupt sheriff's department under Burch's leadership. The widow charged that Brooks and Parton were "what is commonly known as 'sheriffing' or 'fee-grabbing,' and all…should have been known to the defendant, B.E. Biggs." She alleged that Gaddis, Parton, and Brooks had a "well-known, open and notorious record for violence, ill-treatment, and oppression of other people," all while serving under Burch. It was the "statutory duty," she insisted, of Burch and his deputies to ensure her husband's safety. Her attorneys cited five sections of Williams Tennessee Code, including Section 11416: "Public offenses may be prevented by the intervention of the officers of justice by requiring security to keep the peace…"[269]

When the case was heard in January 1938, Clarence Brooks could not be there. A few months prior, his body was found in the Hiwassee River in an apparent drowning accident while fishing. Doctors could not determine what caused the cuts and bruises on his head. They arrested Tom Brock, the man who was fishing with him, but the investigation went nowhere.

Judge Robert Nevin heard the case in Chattanooga. John Wrinkle continued his tireless representation of the McFadden family while Joe V. Williams and Russell Kramer returned to defend Burch. Etowah attorney Reuel Webb represented Gaddis and Parton. Burch's quote, "I have no protection for McFadden in Polk County," was among the widow's strongest evidence. "He knew of the bad character of the deputies," she charged. Burch denied that his deputies practiced "sheriffing" or "fee-grabbing." He also claimed that McFadden, in the only time they ever spoke, thanked him for treating him well.[270]

Seventy-five witnesses testified for over a week. Several witnesses discredited Gaddis' claim that he approached McFadden at the bridge in November 1935 to quell a labor riot. "There had been no labor trouble there." Another allegedly overheard Gaddis in a café threatening to "blow up" the equipment if they don't "work our men." John Haskell "Cap" Lillard, son of John M. Lillard and nephew of former sheriff Abe Lillard III, brought records from the family's hardware store in Benton to discuss Gaddis' recent firearm and ammunition purchases.[271]

The plaintiff summoned several witnesses from the criminal trial. But, two new witnesses testified that Burch had made a long-distance phone call to Gaddis shortly before McFadden was killed. Mrs. Fenton Grubb, a telephone company employee in Benton, said a Mr. Biggs from Benton Station called a Mr. Gaddis at Ducktown. The phone company manager brought records proving the county paid for the call.

"When Sheriff Biggs promised us protection, I told him I thought it a shame that his deputies should lead a mob on my men while they were working," road contractor J.D. Crippen said. After Crippen told Burch that he ought to fire Gaddis, Burch allegedly replied that he "wouldn't fire him for $10,000." Burch said his men "will kill McFadden with the feeling like it is up there."[272]

Shovel operator Herbert Spradling described the shakedowns. "There was no trouble before November 1935. Several days before that, Gaddis came to me in the New York Hotel and told me, 'You are going to have some labor trouble. I can keep that down, but it will take some money – $500.'" Spradling claimed he saw Constable Ernest McGee strike a truck driver on the head and say "We've just shot your goddamn boss. You'll be next if you don't get out."[273]

In her testimony, Rozelle McFadden said she came to the New York Hotel in Ducktown after the November 1935 incident. She allegedly overheard Burch say to another man, "I have no protection in Polk County for McFadden and the sooner he gets out the better."[274] Brownell Humphries testified that he saw Burch driving "in the direction of the killing" an hour before McFadden was killed.[275]

Burch's attorneys asked Judge Nevin to direct the jury to dismiss the charges against their client, citing "insufficient proof" that he was a conspirator in McFadden's death. Kramer insisted that Burch had not neglected his duty, to which Wrinkle and Sizer replied that Burch's prior knowledge that McFadden was in danger made him liable. But Nevin ruled in favor of Burch, saying that there was no substantial evidence that he conspired.[276]

Rozelle McFadden denied allegations that her slain husband shot Gaddis on Christmas Eve 1935. Their story remained consistent: they were sleeping at the Read House in Chattanooga the night Gaddis was shot and John

John Wrinkle, the McFadden family's attorney, sits with Rozelle McFadden and her stepson, David S. McFadden. - Chattanooga Times-Free Press

Wrinkle was to meet them the next morning. Spradling, who stayed with the McFaddens that night, corroborated her testimony. Read House employee Eddie James testified that McFadden's car was parked at the hotel from December 22 to December 24 and that it looked like it had not been moved.

Gaddis again testified that he approached the road workers to "quell a labor disturbance" and that he fired on McFadden only to protect Constable McGee. In an attempt to prove he held no "ill will" toward McFadden, he claimed he helped take McFadden to the hospital.[277] When asked about the phone call he received from "Mr. Biggs" in Benton shortly before McFadden's death, Gaddis alleged that Burch Glen Biggs, then eighteen years old, called asking about a prisoner. Copperhill residents Owen Sparks and W.G. Benson testified to Gaddis' character and reputation. Parton alleged that McFadden threatened both he and Gaddis in November 1935. "You are a God damn son of a bitch! I will shoot and kill every one of you," McFadden allegedly said."[278]

John Wrinkle objected to the alleged statements made by plaintiff's intestate, but was overruled. By admitting this testimony, Judge Nevin violated Section 9780 of the Code of Tennessee. Testimony of such a prejudicial nature, according to Wrinkle, misled the jury to a dead man's character and should never have been permitted.[279]

The jury began deliberations on February 3. After a few hours, the foreman told Judge Nevin that they were hung at ten to two on finding Gaddis and Parton liable. Nevin told them to keep deliberating. They returned an hour later with a verdict that held only Gaddis liable. Gaddis would have to pay Rozelle McFadden $25,000 in damages, only a quarter of what she wanted. Nevin denied the plaintiff a new trial, which was good for Burch, because he was facing another intra-party split.

Chapter 13

THE HARMONY TICKET

On April 30, 1938, the Vance Davis Faction of the Polk County Democratic Party nominated a full ticket for county offices. John Harbison was again nominated for sheriff, Bob McClary for trustee, Traynor Chastain for register of deeds, George Gilliland for circuit court clerk, and M.T. Styles for county court clerk. The convention elected former state representative Marvin Lowery as chairman.

The two factions had been fighting for recognition in Nashville. Former trustee G.W. Passmore sent a petition to Governor Browning requesting "at least two honest commissioners" for the county.[280] Burch was appointed to the election commission along with Parks Kimsey, the Republican, and Bob McClary of the Davis faction. McClary's appointment signaled that the Browning administration would oppose Burch's faction, which came as a surprise since Browning had previously pledged support for the Biggs faction. But after Browning's falling out with Boss Crump, he dropped his support for Burch. Congressman Sam McReynolds tried to get a Biggs man on the commission, and also came out against Browning in the Democratic primary.

Ready to take on the fractured Democrats, the Republicans nominated a full ticket. Bill Poston was elected party chairman and Henry Crox was nominated for sheriff. John M. Lillard for trustee, Clyde Harper for circuit court clerk, Dutch Woody for county court clerk, and Charles Dalton for register of deeds completed the ticket. They also nominated former county court clerk Buck Arp for state representative.

Foregoing their originally scheduled convention for May 7, the Biggs faction called for a new convention and invited all Democrats. "Harmony has been restored," said George Williams, Biggs faction chairman. With the Republicans organized and ready with a full ticket, Burch knew he had to broker a deal to unite the party. The convention was set for May 28, with well over one thousand people expected to attend.[281] "It will be the biggest convention ever held in Polk County," Burch said. "We are together here and everybody is happy."[282]

With Burch and Vance Davis each directing their forces, a "harmony ticket" was nominated. "There was not one murmur of discord," the *Chattanooga Times* reported. The two factions agreed to a 50-50 split of the county offices. Davis nominated Broughton for a second term as sheriff. Burch nominated George Gilliland for a fifth term as circuit court clerk. R.L. Kirkpatrick nominated Leach Park for a second term as county court clerk. Hoyt Lillard nominated John Harbison for register of deeds, replacing Porter Campbell.

Roxy Campbell nominated Bob McClary to replace him as the nominee for trustee. Campbell boasted that he was leaving the county with "one of the cleanest and best kept set of books ever left by any trustee." He also praised his deputy trustee, Charles Williams, claiming there has never been a "cleaner and better man." Charles Williams would remain deputy trustee and was elected party chairman, succeeding his father.[283] After years of loyalty to Burch, Roxy Campbell and his family lost a lot of respect for Burch after Roxy was cast aside for McClary.[284]

"It's of no use fighting here all summer long," Burch said. The two factions avoided all "controversial matters" and did not endorse any candidates for the state or federal primary. They also nominated two separate tickets for the state primary board, choosing to let the state executive committee "fight it out." Control of election machinery depended on which ticket was selected in Nashville, with the Browning faction allied with Davis and the Crump/McKellar faction allied with Burch.[285]

Just as the Democrats hoped, the harmony ticket inspired all but one Republican candidate to withdraw from the race. Republican morale was plummeting. The trustee's office reported that the Republicans had qualified less than 300 voters with the poll tax deadline fast approaching, compared with well over 1,000 Democrats qualified. Only trustee candidate John M. Lillard, brother of former sheriff Abe Lillard III, stayed in the race.

Not long after the harmony convention, Burch had to appear in court as a defendant for the second time in six months as Scott Runion had filed suit against him and Deputy August Lewis. It had been nearly two years since Lewis shot Runion in a Springtown store after Runion allegedly walked toward him with a knife when Lewis tried to arrest him for "drunkenness." John Wrinkle represented Runion and argued before the jury. Unable to prove his case or unwilling to continue, Runion asked that his suit be dismissed.[286]

Broughton would be in court soon as well. Bill, Johnnie, and Ralph Grooms were arrested for manufacturing whiskey. On July 18, 1938, they pled guilty and were sentenced to 90 days in prison and a $250.00 fine. Unable to pay the fine, they had to serve an additional month. But Broughton refused to release them in November, a violation of a court order and a 1937 Public Act. Represented by Charles Guinn, the Grooms' filed a petition for a writ of habeas corpus.[287] While still a minor, Johnnie Grooms had been convicted of voluntary manslaughter and given a light sentence. Conasauga native Ralph Painter remembered the Grooms' were as "mean as a snake."[288] Broughton understandably did not want them back on the street, but had denied them due process.

Winston Prince represented Broughton, who argued that the act did not apply to Polk County since the county court voted to exempt itself from the "unconstitutional act." But the county court had no such power. Guinn pointed to the prisoners' oath of insolvency and that, unless the state can prove otherwise, the oath "shall entitle the prisoner to a release from prison." Judge Pat Quinn denied the writ of habeas corpus. The Grooms' appealed and were finally released from prison in April after the state supreme court ruled in their favor.[289]

Frank Hood wrote another letter to the editor of the *Chattanooga Times*. He disputed Burch's claims that Polk County Democrats "unanimously" supported him and the harmony ticket. "It has not added to his popularity with the voters of this county one iota." Hood insisted he only compromised with the Davis faction to increase his chances of winning. "This is what we shall call Biggs-McReynolds democracy."

Hood blasted Congressman McReynolds for his approval of Burch's "way of doing things" in Polk County, insinuating that he pressured Governor Browning into appointing a "Biggs man" to the election commission to ensure victory. "It is a fact which cannot be denied," Hood said, "that in a fair election the Biggs machine would suffer an overwhelming defeat." He claimed that Republican voters had a majority in the county and that 50 percent of the Democrats "prefer the old type of democracy over the one-man rule" of Burch Biggs. He lamented that Polk Countians would continue "to be forced to live under a dictatorship" until "reliable and unselfish men" are appointed to the election commission.

C.L. "Roxy" Campbell became county trustee in 1932, but had to give up the position at the 1938 "harmony convention." His father, former sheriff Charlie Campbell, first deputized Burch in 1898. - Tennessee State Library and Archives

Winston H. Prince, an attorney and staunch Democrat, set aside his many disagreements with Burch and supported the "harmony ticket" in 1938. But he would soon leave Polk County for good. - Tennessee State Library and Archives

By the deadline, over 2,800 Democrats had paid their poll tax compared to just 334 Republicans. Roxy Campbell reported that over 1,000 fewer people qualified to vote than in 1936. Midterms typically see lower turnout than presidential elections, but it was also a sign of decreased voter morale. Campbell announced his campaign for state representative, facing Winston Prince in the primary. Six weeks before the election, Broughton learned he would have an opponent after all when Democrat Roy Stillwell jumped in the race for sheriff. The 30-year-old former JP called his supporters the "Independent Taxpayers" group, which included former Davis supporters. "I promise law enforcement, decency in office, and the appointment of honest deputies," Stillwell said.[290]

Despite their lack of any meaningful opposition, the Democrats held campaign rallies throughout the county. Hundreds of supporters attended rallies in Ducktown and Turtletown. Bob Barclay, TCC paymaster, praised the county's "good leaders" and approved of the harmony ticket. Winston Prince, a longtime critic of Burch, complimented Broughton. "For two years,

I have been looking for something to criticize Broughton Biggs about, but have seen nothing wrong. He has made you a good sheriff. Give him a second term." Burch thanked the voters for their confidence in his son. On July 30, Burch hosted one of his legendary barbecues at Quinn Springs.[291]

Polk County held its quietest and lowest turnout election in over a decade on August 4, 1938. The *Copper City Advance* reported that less than half the qualified voters above the mountain were expected to vote. The only "hot" election was for Third District Constable. Chuck Talley, Bob Rymer, and Mark Greene all challenged Ernest McGee, known for his role in the initial Gaddis-McFadden incident in 1935.

The Democrats easily defeated their challengers by over one thousand votes. Broughton crushed Roy Stillwell to win a second term as sheriff. John Harbison finally found himself in the winning column, defeating Buck Arp, who decided to reenter the race, for register of deeds. Bob McClary won the trustee's race over John M. Lillard. George Gilliland and Leach Park, both unopposed, won their races for circuit court clerk and county court clerk respectively. Ernest McGee easily won the Third District Constable race. Roxy Campbell defeated Winston Prince to win the nomination for state representative. Judge Sue K. Hicks won the race for criminal court judge over J. Tom Taylor of Athens, performing well in Polk County.

As a result of his fallout with Boss Crump, Governor Browning lost the state primary to Prentice Cooper. Burch had delivered 73 percent of the Polk County vote for Browning in the 1936 general election, but Browning only tallied 36 percent in the 1938 primary. Could Polk voters have really turned against Browning so dramatically and so quickly? The Cantrell machine made sure Cooper also won McMinn County by a large margin. In the unbossed neighboring counties, the results differed little from 1936. Cooper won 54 percent of the Monroe County vote and 62 percent of the vote in Bradley County. In Loudon County, where Browning had not performed well in the 1936 primary against Dossett, Cooper won 65 percent of the vote.

George Scarbrough shared his thoughts on the election in a letter to the editor of the *Chattanooga Times*.

> "Here in Polk County no changes were instituted in the political setup...there being little opposition to the Democratic clique which has

held sway for the past several years. The reason for the general apathy on the part of the Republicans here is that a fair deal is never obtained at the polls. Various arrangements which should make old Machiavelli turn over in his grave for shame, have been employed to ensnare and coerce voters to uphold the miniature dictators in power."

Henry Crox's blood boiled every time he read the election returns. The name of his maternal grandfather, Ben Franklin McClary, appeared on the list of those who paid a poll tax and cast a vote. But it would not be the last time a deceased relative of Henry Crox cast a ballot. After his father's death in 1941, his name appeared on the list of voters in 1942, prompting him to give Leach Park "a piece of his mind."[292] The election fraud would only get worse from here.

Chapter 14

LIVING HIGH ON THE HOG

During Broughton's first term, Burch became known as "The Old Sheriff" to differentiate him from his son, frequently referred to as "B.E. Biggs Jr." in the press. For his second term, Broughton appointed Roxy Campbell as chief deputy, replacing Herman Wright. Campbell's son-in-law, Ralph Painter, suspects Campbell's nomination for state representative and appointment as chief deputy was compensation for having to relinquish the trustee's office to Bob McClary. Broughton, to his credit, did not reappoint Emmett Gaddis. He kept Ben Smith and Burch Maynor on the force as guards.

The depression lingered through the decade, with many Polk County citizens struggling to hold onto jobs and make ends meet. In 1935, fifteen percent of the county was on relief. Seven hundred forty-nine people were unemployed by 1937. New Deal programs, including the Works Progress Administration, Civil Works Administration, National Youth Administration, and the Civilian Conservation Corps provided temporary employment for hundreds of people, but it was not a lasting solution. The Tennessee Valley Authority (TVA) benefited the county the most, providing several good jobs. A few local industries permitted employees to continue living in company housing rent-free.[293] Hundreds of families, especially out in the country, still lived in homes without running water or electricity, and many still had to use an outhouse.

Meanwhile, if you were in with the Biggs machine, you were doing very well for yourself, enjoying a secure job in local government. Many of them lived on Benton Station Road. Leach Park lived in a nice home on a hill just outside of town, and owned a rental house next door. Hoyt Lillard lived on a spacious lot overlooking the Benton Banking Company and the courthouse. Lillard also had the means to purchase a home in Miami, where his family spent many winter holidays. "He always had the best of everything," one citizen recalled.[294] Lillard even managed to purchase the Savannah Farm, one of the most valuable farms in the region. He later sold it for $120,000.[295] "He was a cheat," one citizen said of Lillard.[296] Broughton was preparing to buy a nice lot on Benton Station Road close to the courthouse square. Construction of a nice brick home, next door to Jake Higgins, would soon begin. Roxy Campbell lived in a nice home not far down the road.

Burch and Della formerly lived in the Love residence and later the Clayton residence on the Benton to Cleveland Pike. They purchased the George Norton home at the corner of Main Street and Clemmer Ferry Road in 1937 and had a "nice rock wall" constructed out front.[297] The home was catty-cornered to the jail, a convenient location for Burch. Also convenient was the water supply he received, courtesy of the county, from the pipeline that supplied the courthouse and the jail.[298] The home still stands on Main Street in Benton. "He loved money," Sally Hutchins Gregory said remembering Burch. "They kept it in the organization."[299]

Burch owned property up on the mountain in Benton Springs and even had a few rental properties, including a home in Benton he rented to G.W. Bishop Sr. His beloved Hiwassee River farm now spanned 421 acres, and he had recently acquired an additional 378 acres throughout the northwest corner of the county, including several acres at the confluence of the Ocoee and Hiwassee Rivers.[300] The average farmer in Polk County had only 90 acres.[301]

There were several explanations for the Biggs family's sudden explosion in wealth. "Biggs made considerable money from controlling the county," Matt Witt later recalled. Like many sheriffs of this time period, Burch was accused of extorting protection money from local bootlegging and gambling interests.[302] Some previous sheriffs were likely guilty of the same, but honest elections ensured they were never in office long enough to build up such an elaborate and lucrative racket.

But some accused Burch of even harsher methods, including utilizing convict labor to work his farm, as opposed to public works. Ralph Painter remembered when the Conasauga River Lumber Company, one of the state's largest such industries, paid their employees in scrip and coin. They could use this currency at the company store. Burch often sent his deputies to arrest several employees on pay day. They were charged with the usual stuff, like "drunk and disorderly conduct." Since they had little to no actual cash, they could not afford to pay their fines or make bail. Burch brought them over to his farm to work off their fines or bail, which made running a profitable farm during the depression an easy task. Copperhill native Lowell Posey recalled that Burch's use of convict labor on his farm was "common knowledge." When walking past the jail, Ralph Painter would often talk to prisoners looking out the second-floor window, complaining about how they were about to go work on Burch's farm to pay off their fines.[303]

Burch and Della bought this home at the corner of Main Street and Clemmer Ferry Road in 1937. The home still stands today. - Polk County Historical and Genealogical Society

Burch's river bottom farm, encompassing several hundred acres, is now the site of the Chilhowee Gliderport and Super Sod on Highway 411 north of Benton. - Author's photo

Others claimed that Burch colluded with the Benton Banking Company, whose directors included Hoyt Lillard, Leach Park, and Charles Williams, to acquire several delinquent properties. Matt Witt recalled Burch's numerous purchases of delinquent properties.[304] One citizen lamented that their father could never get a loan for his farm because he was a Republican.[305] "You had to have the right credentials and political persuasion to get a loan," one citizen remembered their father say.[306]

Some had it even worse. If they were even one day late making a house payment to the bank, they were foreclosed on. Burch or one of his associates would then buy the property, make improvements, and sell or rent it. According to Hubert C. "Buck" Sartin, if someone did not keep their road tax receipts or maintain their portion of the road, the Biggs machine would seize their property through a forced deed transfer.[307]

"If you were on the wrong side politically, the bank would not do business with you," one citizen told his nephew.[308] Sally Hutchins Gregory remembered how the Benton Banking Company worked with the Biggs machine to issue scrip, in lieu of cash, to the teachers and courthouse employees.[309] The scrip, of course, was only accepted at business establishments owned by those in the machine, giving them an advantage over their competition.

Burch's county court did eventually spend some money for public benefit. They voted for the most extensive school improvements in many years at their October 1938 meeting. Although the tax rate increased to $1.97, they agreed to use bonds and WPA money to build a new school building in Benton, new gymnasium for the Copperhill High School, and a new grammar school building in Copperhill. But this would prove to be the county's last significant expenditure on education for some time.

Chapter 15
"They Wanted to Get Rid of Him"

No longer on the force, Emmett Gaddis operated a gas station near Isabella. At approximately 6:20 PM on September 14, 1938, Gaddis got in his car and left Mrs. McReynolds' restaurant in Ducktown when Deputies Frank Clayton and Frank Crawford started pursuing him. The high-speed chase ended when Gaddis stopped his car on Main Street across from Carl Center's Furniture Store.[310]

Clayton's marksmanship was legendary. His friends claimed he could drive a car at 50 MPH and "empty his revolver into a telephone poll without missing a shot."[311]

As Gaddis exited his car, Clayton and Crawford yelled, "You're under arrest." According to the *Polk County News*, Gaddis had been told by the sheriff's department to stop carrying a pistol. Refusing to surrender, Gaddis allegedly reached for his pistol.[312] Clayton and Crawford riddled Gaddis with 18 bullets in the head and chest, killing him instantly. The two deputies fled the scene.[313] The man who killed David McFadden was dead.

Several witnesses reported hearing something like firecrackers at the time of the shooting. Chuck Talley was shopping for school supplies with his daughter. They left the store and made their way through the crowd, only to see Gaddis' body lying in a pool of blood. His daughter was visibly upset, so Talley took her home. "I couldn't walk down that side of the street for a long time," she later said.[314]

Broughton came up to Ducktown right away to investigate. Clayton and Crawford later surrendered at the jail. They told Broughton they had killed their former fellow deputy in self-defense and that he was carrying two pistols.[315] Drs. Hyatt, Hicks, and A.J. Guinn examined Gaddis' body and said some of the bullets passed through him. Witnesses said they saw the two deputies trying to disarm Gaddis before shooting him.[316] Constable Ernest McGee told Broughton that he heard Gaddis call Clayton and Crawford "scabs" before they shot him. In the aftermath of a recent dynamiting of the Tennessee Power Company's tower near Parksville, the two deputies had been guarding power lines in the Copper Basin, likely upsetting the labor-sympathetic Gaddis.

The 39-year-old former deputy and Marine was survived by his wife, four kids, two brothers, and his father, who swore out a murder warrant against Clayton and Crawford. They were each held under a $10,000 bond. The next day, the grand jury returned a "no true bill" in their favor.

Chuck Talley remarked that he thought Gaddis knew something that the Biggs men "did not want to get out."[317] Earl Oliver later said "They wanted to get rid of him."[318] Henry Watson alleged Burch paid Clayton and Crawford to kill Gaddis.[319] "They just wanted an excuse to kill him" said David Talley, son of Chuck Talley.[320] Gaddis was no longer a problem for the Polk County Sheriff's Department, and the men who killed him, justifiably or not, still had a badge and a gun.

Deputy Frank Clayton, right, joined with Deputy Frank Crawford to shoot and kill their former fellow deputy Emmett Gaddis. - David Talley

Emmett Gaddis was gunned down on Main Street in Ducktown. - Cleveland-Bradley County Public Library History Branch and Archives, Ridley Wills Collection

Chapter 16

BURCH THE KINGMAKER

In November 1938, Roxy Campbell took back the state representative seat for the Democrats, defeating Dutch Woody. Prentice Cooper and Tom Stewart, backed by Boss Crump and Senator McKellar, became Tennessee's new governor and junior senator respectively. Hobart Carey won the race for state senator. Congressman Sam McReynolds easily won a ninth term.

Although the Democratic Party was still popular across the nation, the Democratic candidates won by unusually high margins in the normally purple Polk County. Cooper, Stewart, and McReynolds all won over 2,500 votes while none of their opponents tallied more than 300 votes. McReynolds' 90 percent vote share was the highest for a congressional candidate against a Republican in the county since at least 1900. McReynolds only tallied 80 percent in his home county of Hamilton, and 73 percent of the vote in the district. Republican Congressman J. Will Taylor won McMinn, Monroe, and Loudon Counties by much smaller margins against an independent candidate in a staunchly Republican district. In the gubernatorial contest, Cooper tallied 88 percent of the Polk vote compared with 53 percent in purple Monroe County, 62 percent in blue Meigs County, and 71 percent in the state primary. McMinn and Bradley Counties went for Cooper by razor-thin margins, but Cooper only won 45 percent of the vote in Loudon County. In the state senate race, Hobart Carey lost the solidly Republican Knox and Loudon Counties and barely won Monroe County. But his 2,222 to 555 margin of victory in Polk County ensured a 423-vote victory in the district.

Campbell's victory over Woody, an incumbent, was by a vote of 2,724 to 424. Only two years prior, Woody had won handily. In the past, his fellow citizens elected him circuit court clerk. He had also served on the school board. What had he done to cause so many Polk voters to turn on him, and so hastily? By ensuring such a high margin in Polk, Burch now controlled the state representative seat for Polk and Bradley Counties, offsetting his much larger Republican neighbor to the west. Accusations of election fraud fell on deaf ears, and since Burch had never lost an election contest in court, there was no reason to waste time and money by filing a lawsuit.

Burch accompanied Roxy Campbell to Nashville for the opening of the 1939 legislative session. In one of his first acts, Senate Speaker Blan Maxwell appointed Burch as the chief sergeant-at-arms of the senate. Burch stayed in Nashville for much of the session. With Campbell in the state house and Hobart Carey in the state senate, and close relationships with Governor Cooper and Boss Crump, no one stood in the way of the Biggs machine in pushing through their legislation. "The Biggs Dynasty in Polk County will never lack for crown princes," The Knoxville Journal wrote. "Son Broughton Biggs is serving his second term as sheriff." The Journal referenced 21-year-old Burch Glen Biggs as "awaiting his turn." Referring to his son Tom, Broughton told the paper "And don't forget that I've got a boy 19 months old."

Burch was appointed chief sergeant-at-arms in the state senate for the 1939 legislative term. - Tennessee State Library and Archives

Campbell and Carey proposed three bills for Polk County. One created a county court appointed county attorney that paid a $1,200 annual salary, a position that was filled by Chattanoogan Harry Shafer. Another authorized the county court to issue $450,000 in bonds to help with their massive debt. A bill to create a county budget commission failed to pass.

Carey pushed through two bills benefiting the Democrats. The first created an office of business management for the Polk County Department of Education. Appointed to this position was none other than Hoyt Lillard. Already serving as school board chairman and as a director of the Benton Banking Company, this bill added to Lillard's immense power in the county. The bill stipulated that the county court would later appoint a different person and would be paid $2,400 annually, but that never happened. Carey's second bill gave county judge Vance Davis two salaries: $2,500 per year for judicial services and $1,100 per year for "services performed as county financial agent and accounting officer."[321]

In late January, Knoxville attorney Hal H. Clements, defeated candidate for state senate, received affidavits from several Polk County election officials alleging irregularities in the November 1938 election. Clements said he was still "pursuing my collection of these sworn statements to show the flagrant violations of the election laws in Polk County." Clements had reason to be skeptical of Carey's absurdly high margin of victory in Polk County.[322]

"The ballot box was taken from the polling place; no count or tally was ever made there; and no record of said election could be made by me under my official duty and oath," said P.H. Moore, election clerk at the Arthur's Shop precinct. JP Andrew Bates, a poll watcher at the Archville precinct, alleged that 50 more ballots than were actually cast were counted there. Archville precinct clerk Robert N. Woody, son of Dutch Woody, claimed 219 votes were counted despite only 177 registered voters. Two Old Fort precinct officials unsuccessfully protested several absentee ballots from non-residents. John Runion (brother of Scott and Elias Runion) and Thurston Taylor alleged the officer of election at Turtletown counted "50 or 60" more ballots than voters. "The election officer refused to lock or seal the box when the polls closed."[323]

No action was taken to investigate these election fraud allegations. The state election board reappointed Burch to the election commission. Despite prior complaints against him as a commissioner, Hoyt Lillard was also given a seat on the election commission. The Biggs machine was damn near unstoppable.

Burch lost a close friend when Congressman Sam McReynolds died of heart disease on July 11, 1939 at age 67. After the funeral, multiple newspapers reported that the Crump/McKellar faction considered asking Burch to run for the seat. Other candidates rumored to be entering the race were U.S. Attorney James B. Frazier Jr., Burch's cousin Estes Kefauver, and Judge L.D. Miller, endorsed by the Vance Davis faction in the 1938 primary. The Republicans hoped to win the seat if the Democrats failed to unite behind a candidate in the impending special election.

John Wrinkle, for many years a thorn in Burch's side, proposed a convention to nominate a candidate. The twelve counties comprising the Third

Congressional District would send a delegation, with only four counties having a larger delegation than Polk, giving Burch disproportionate influence. Burch was now becoming a kingmaker in Tennessee politics. He had "no intention" of entering the race himself, but served on a committee that ultimately decided to hold a primary to nominate a candidate. Judge L.D. Miller, State Sen. Lester Doak, and Estes Kefauver were set to face off in August. "I'm for Estes Kefauver," Burch announced, giving his cousin a major advantage in Polk County.[324] Kefauver selected Burch as his campaign manager for Polk County.

Estes Kefauver was elected to Congress in a special election in 1939, largely due to help from his cousin Burch. - Tennessee State Library and Archives

Two weeks before the primary, Miller and Doak withdrew from the race, claiming the primary was "set up against them." The *Chattanooga Times* published an editorial after Kefauver became the last candidate standing, calling it a "paradox" because of his reputation as an "enemy" of machine politics. "This does not mean that Mr. Kefauver has gone over to the machines. It means, rather, that the machine politicians, men like…former Sheriff Burch Biggs, of Polk, are hoping that by supporting a new political personality they can regain some of the prestige and influence they have lost." John Wrinkle announced he would run for Congress at the next regular election in 1940:

> "My reasons were perfectly obvious to all who were acquainted with the situation at the time. Statements now issued by Judge L.D. Miller and Senator Lester Doak confirm my reasons. It is now perfectly clear to all that Biggsism, under the leadership of former Sheriff Burch E. Biggs, is in complete control of this 'soap box' primary…My appeal will be direct to the people and I will not bow to a few bosses who wish to control the congressman. The Third Congressional District has never had a bossed or controlled Congressman."[325]

Kefauver went on to win the special election in a landslide over Republican nominee Casto Dodson. Of the twelve counties in the solidly blue Third Congressional District, only Bradley County voted for Dodson. Kefauver tallied 932 votes in Polk County to Dodson's 116 for 89 percent of the vote. Kefauver wrote to Burch in September: "I am gradually getting settled and have been to see Senator McKellar several times. He said he was 'awfully sorry' he did not get over to Benton during a recent trip to Chattanooga."[326]

For someone purportedly opposed to machine politics, Kefauver spent a lot of time with McKellar, Boss Crump's closest ally. He spent two days visiting with Burch in November. "Things look mighty good for us all over there," he wrote to Governor Cooper. The new congressman even recommended his elder cousin for U.S. Marshal after a potential new federal district court was discussed.[327] Burch's grandmother, Eliza Cooke Kimbrough, and Kefauver's great-grandfather, Robert Fielding Cooke, were siblings. Burch now had not just friends, but a cousin, in Washington.

Chapter 17

THE STRIKE

During Burch's third term as sheriff in 1916, the Copper Basin experienced its first labor strike. Since then, industries in the Basin had maintained cordial relations with unions in the region. The workers set up an American Federation of Labor (AFL) affiliate in 1936 and within two years had secured a contract that cut the work day down to eight hours, abolished the task system, and raised wages. Under the task system, workers sometimes had to work fifteen-hour days to get the job done. The area unions split in 1937 when the Ducktown and Isabella unions joined the Congress of Industrial Organizations (CIO).

On July 14, 1939, the TCC ceased operations for the first time in decades. The TCC was one of the county's largest taxpayers. "East Polk had all the money, but they had to give it to the county," Earl Oliver recalled.[328] The TCC praised Mitchell C. Anderson, a union organizer from Alabama, for his "fair-mindedness" during the pre-strike negotiations. But a deal could not be reached. After the International Union of Mine, Mill, and Smelter Workers (a CIO affiliate) voted to strike, company officials ordered a complete shutdown. The employees had taken a vote, and the CIO affiliate, dominant in Ducktown and Isabella, won out after being refused a closed shop and check-off. They had also demanded a 20-cent per day increase "as a restoration of a previous cut in wages," better safety conditions, and an arbitration clause that would turn over all labor disputes to the U.S. Department of Labor. AFL workers chose not to strike, and found themselves unable to go into work.[329] The families of 1,500 employees living in the Copper Basin would feel the effects of this labor dispute for several months.

Broughton went to Copperhill on the second day of the strike, describing the scene as "quiet and peaceful", with no signs of disorder along the picket lines. "My only interest in the strike is to see that peace and order is maintained."[330] CIO members picketed in front of the plants at the Isabella mine, the Ducktown flotation plant and mine, and the Copperhill smelting and acid plant. Local AFL members, dominant in Copperhill, were anxious to return to work.[331] Broughton set up temporary headquarters in the Copper Basin, and Burch Glen was appointed as a deputy.

"As yet, no negotiations between employer and employee have started toward reopening," the *Copper City Advance* reported a week later. Mining jobs provided the only means of livelihood for many Copper Basin residents, with several families "already destitute" after one week of striking.[332] Local merchants suffered without the thousands of dollars regularly circulating throughout the local economy, especially after pay day. Union representatives met on July 23 only to reject each other's proposals. Over 1,000 men requested unemployment compensation from the state. The unions worked to provide relief for their members during this trying time, providing commodities like flour, cornmeal, and grits, as well as medical supplies and fuel. Mitchell Anderson distributed union relief funds totaling $30,000.

On August 23, TCC employees opened their mail to find a letter informing them of the company's reopening on August 28. The CIO members were still striking, but all employees were welcome to return to work. The company made it clear they would replace striking employees. TCC paymaster Bob Barclay later wrote: "In all probability the strike would never have occurred had the rift not come about between the three unions. They turned to fighting each other and used their employer as the battleground."[333]

Burch was hated in the Copper Basin, especially in Copperhill. Earl Oliver and Rockford Patterson remembered how Burch's deputies frequently "harassed" people and "fee-grabbed" above the mountain because many of them had high-paying jobs in the mining industry. Several were outsiders who moved to the county for better pay, which spurred resentment among Burch's deputies.[334] These jobs in the Copper Basin helped rank Polk County in the state's top ten in per capita income in 1939.[335]

Despite all this, Burch maintained good relations with the TCC. Matt Witt later said the TCC "supported whichever side would win and keep tax assessment down."[336] With funds provided by the TCC, Broughton hired 200 additional deputies to "maintain peace and order" as some of the employees returned to work.[337] "I am prepared to give protection to all who wish to resume working when the plants reopen."[338] Many of them came from out of state, including some from "Bloody Harlan" County, Kentucky. Broughton later explained how the deputies were paid:

> "My budget didn't allow for the hiring of any extra deputies. Payroll was over a thousand dollars a day. I didn't want the company to pay the deputies so I paid them out of my personal account, and the company deposited the same amount to my name in the Hamilton National Bank in Knoxville."[339]

When asked about the character of the special deputies, deputy Frank Crawford later said they had "no character." Broughton said he "didn't have time to investigate their backgrounds" and claimed he wanted "men with hair on their chests who could handle the situation." An investigation later revealed that several convicted thieves, a confessed rapist, and a man who had murdered his father were among the special deputies.[340]

Copper mining was the most important industry in the county for over a century. - Ducktown Basin Museum

Reid Robinson, president of the International Union of Mine, Mill, and Smelter Workers, resented the hiring of additional deputies, claiming the money could be used to give the workers a wage increase. Broughton ordered a temporary ban on all beer and wine sales in the area, probably a good idea. "Businessmen in the Copper Basin are jubilant over the reopening of the plant, as business in this community has been practically at a standstill for more than a month," the *Copper City Advance* reported.

Ducktown, home to hundreds of people employed in the mining industry, lies in the heart of the Copper Basin. - Cleveland-Bradley County Public Library History Branch and Archives, Ridley Wills Collection

The day before the reopening, Broughton's special deputies paraded through the streets of Ducktown armed with Tommy guns, shotguns, .38 pistols, rifles, tear gas guns, clubs, and blackjacks.[341] Over a thousand employees, mostly AFL members, crossed picket lines to return to work on August 28. Fewer than 30 CIO workers returned to their jobs, and 200 men hoping to replace them filled out applications. Many non-union workers from North Carolina and Georgia were hired.

As the furnaces fired back on and miners put on their hardhats before descending back into the mines, hundreds of people paraded down Main Street in Ducktown protesting the reopening. As the strikers peacefully protested, the special deputies conducted warrantless searches of their vehicles. The deputies hurled threats and shouted profanities at them. Anderson informed the U.S. Department of Justice about the illegal searches. They referred him to the FBI, who then referred him to District Attorney Beecher Witt. No one intervened to stop the abuses.[342]

The second night after reopening, an unidentified gunman shot into two homes of TCC employees. Wes Helton, who lived in North Carolina, reported several shots, while Mineral Bluff, Georgia resident Fred Hyde reported 17 bullets shot into his house, with two entering the children's bedroom. A few days later, two men shot G.M. Queen, a miner, in Fannin County. Queen was on his way to work, and was not seriously wounded. Clyde Huffman and George Earley of Fannin County were arrested and charged with the shooting. As it turned out, both were CIO members. The strikers blamed the recently laid-off special deputies for the attacks on non-strikers. The special deputies allegedly wanted an excuse for Broughton to rehire them. Others placed the blame on angry strikers.

More employees gradually returned to work through September, with hundreds more applying for a job. The TCC tried to bring back the striking employees. The Kimsey Junior College Building had recently been converted to a county school. David Talley, a first-grader, remembered tension between kids during recess. "Your father is a scab!" he heard some students say to classmates. The teachers had to break up some fights.[343]

The county government in Benton distributed the lunches provided by the United States Surplus Commodities Program. The schools in Ducktown and Isabella, where most students had striking parents, received a bowl of soup, a piece

Miners on strike outside the Ducktown Hotel. - Library of Congress

Striking miners protest in front of a "scab" store in Ducktown. - Library of Congress

of bread, and spoiled milk. Several parents wrote to Governor Cooper asking for food for their children. The governor's office replied that their office in Benton "would be more than glad" to help, but it made no difference.[344] The rest of the county schools, including Copperhill, enjoyed a full, warm meal. Finally, Anderson contacted the Surplus Program's office in Washington, leading to an investigator visiting the Copper Basin, putting an end to the unequal lunch service.

The violent retaliation against new and returning workers was incessant. CIO member Luther Loudermilk dynamited Octavius Bingham's car in Stansbury Gap on the evening of September 9. The company had hired Bingham the day before. TCC employee Harve Ray, who lived near Blue Ridge, Georgia, was awoken by gunshots fired into his house.

While strikers continued terrorizing "scabs" and their families, local law enforcement, in cooperation with the TCC, continued terrorizing strikers and their families. Deputies from not only Polk County, but also Cherokee and Fannin Counties, conducted illegal searches of the strikers' vehicles and homes. The new deputies bullied peaceful picketers, "vilely" cursed them, and tried to stop them from distributing union literature.[345] TCC guard Pryor Crowe shoved strikers on the picket line. Deputy Frank Clayton, with his hand on his gun, threatened a group of strikers near the Ducktown Hotel:

> "Who in the hell are you hollering scab at? You God damn sons of bitches, I ought to kill every one of you. I ought to shoot your damn guts out!" …If you don't like what I said, God damn you, I will be here for a few days and I would love to blow you into hell!"[346]

Deputy Clyde Dale was with Clayton during the confrontation. Before searching everyone on the picket line, Clayton called the strikers "yellow sons of bitches" and said he was "getting damned tired of this foolishness." One striker alleged that he overheard Broughton say "If this hollering 'scab' doesn't stop, I'm aiming to leave every son of a bitch laying on the ground, doesn't matter who it is."[347]

On September 15, CIO member and striking TCC employee Jessie Boring forced fellow worker and AFL member Wade Anderson at gunpoint to get in his car. With the help of another man, Boring drove Anderson to Stansbury Mountain. They beat the hell out of Anderson before driving him to North Carolina. "Don't come back to Tennessee," Boring warned.[348]

The resilient Anderson walked all the way back to Copperhill and told Broughton what happened. He described Boring's sore nose, helping Deputies Frank Crawford and Clyde Dale find and arrest him in Turtletown. Boring confessed to the crimes of kidnaping and beating. Broughton arrested Clarence "Red" Sutton and Felton Woodward for assaulting TCC employee George Hunter on October 3.

On November 9, CIO attorneys filed a petition for an injunction to restrain the TCC and area law enforcement from interfering with union picketing activities, searching homes and cars, and hiring deputies and guards with criminal records. The CIO believed the AFL in Copperhill was in on the conspiracy. The petition alleged the defendants "conspired to and did carry out a series of threats and acts of intimidation, oppression, and coercion for the purpose of breaking the strike." The plaintiffs claimed their 1st, 4th, and 14th Amendment rights were being violated. Federal Judge Leslie Darr would hear the complaint soon, with John Wrinkle helping represent the CIO and Joe V. Williams representing the AFL.[349]

After four months, Jesse Deal of Greasy Creek could strike no longer. He had a family to support. They were almost out of food and his four kids needed clothes and shoes. He crossed the picket lines on November 13, returning to the mines. A third-shift employee, Deal never came home the next morning, but it did not take long to find him. His car was stuck in a ditch, with his dead body inside.

Broughton directly targeted the CIO by ordering the Ducktown courthouse closed on November 15. "I am custodian of the county building, and I want it closed." Having used the courthouse for years, the CIO had to find a new meeting place.[350]

Judge Darr heard the CIO's injunction request on November 22. The plaintiffs accused deputies and TCC guards of illegal searches, false arrests, excessive bonds, and detaining suspects for several days. Wrinkle went after the defendants like a bulldog, filing a motion for a subpoena demanding the Hamilton National Bank in Knoxville release the financial transactions of Broughton and the other defendants. Williams made several arguments to dismiss the petition, including a claim that federal courts had no jurisdiction and that the NLRB should settle the dispute.

Judge Darr gifted the Biggs machine and the TCC a big victory to begin the new decade. He dismissed the CIO's lawsuit against local law enforcement and the TCC and ruled that the plaintiffs "had no right to maintain the suit."[351] The CIO were denied a new trial.

Criminal Court Judge Sue K. Hicks had to dismiss four grand jurors at the January 1940 term of the Ducktown Law Court after they "no-billed" 15 felonious assault and drunkenness cases. Hicks granted the prosecution's motion to dismiss them for "connections either with the striking CIO union or the copper company" and insisted on "fair and disinterested investigations" from all jurors. Two of the jurors admitted they had picketed, while another juror turned out to be a union member.[352] The new jury returned with several indictments, including one against Clarence Sutton and Felton Woodward for assaulting George Hunter, and another against Jessie Boring for kidnapping and beating Wade Anderson. They also indicted James McMillan for shooting into the Ducktown home of Frank Ward.

The *Copper City Advance*, not usually as openly favorable to the Biggs machine as the *Polk County News*, complimented Broughton's "delicate" handling of the situation in the Copper Basin over the past several months. A few months later, the TCC reached a deal with the AFL to raise wages by 3.5 cents per hour. Employees now made $4.00 per shift and .50 cents an hour, reportedly "the highest common labor rate the basin has ever had."[353] It seemed peace had finally been restored in the Copper Basin.

The Tennessee Copper Company complex in Copperhill. - Ducktown Basin Museum

The Tennessee Copper Company office building in Copperhill. -Ducktown Basin Museum

Chapter 18
THE DYNAMITINGS

With the TVA's purchase of the Tennessee Power Company, Polk County would be losing $100,000 in annual property tax revenue, which was even more than the TCC paid. The sale of hundreds of thousands of acres in 1920 to help establish the Cherokee National Forest had also negatively impacted the county's ability to raise revenue. Burch traveled to Washington, D.C. with Hoyt Lillard and Leach Park to lobby the TVA to "make replacement for tax losses" to Polk County. Without reimbursement, the county court would have been forced to raise the tax rate from $2.11 to $3.51 per $100 valuation. The county only had 1,103 electricity users out of 15,685 people, ruling out a utility rate increase.

On February 25, 1940, a dynamite blast caused $3,000 in damages to the hoist house at the London mine near Ducktown. No one was injured. One of the guards had supposedly left early while the other went for a short walk just before the explosion. Broughton offered a $500 reward for information leading to the arrest and conviction of the perpetrators. "I was responsible for keeping peace in the Basin, and I made my own law," he later said.[354] This explosion ended the brief peace in the Copper Basin and proved to be the first of an increasingly brutal series of dynamite attacks. On March 29, an unidentified driver threw dynamite into the yards of Claude Chancey, Will Reed, and Reg Roach. No one was hurt in these blasts.

Around 1:00 AM on Monday April 1, three massive dynamite blasts "rocked the countryside," awakening several Copper Basin residents. Three TVA towers, carrying 66,000 volts of electricity from the Blue Ridge Dam and Parksville Dam, as well as an auxiliary line in Fannin County, were destroyed. Copperhill was left in "complete darkness" and vital industries were shut down for several hours.[355]

"This was the worst property loss since the outbreak of the strike," Broughton said, battling a flu. He blamed the dynamiting on the "labor troubles" and ordered the arrest of Marion Ellis, a striking CIO miner, pending further investigation. "I'm expecting anything to happen…I've got plenty of deputies all along the TVA power lines." TVA crews worked fast, setting new poles and stringing new wires in time to return power to the area before sunrise.[356]

The next morning, the CIO lost an appeal when the NLRB refused to file a complaint against the TCC for "unfair labor practices."[357] Two weeks after the first dynamiting, another series of blasts damaged a TVA tower near Hot House in Fannin County and destroyed a tower between the Ocoee River and Boyd's Gap, halting TCC operations for several hours. Copperhill police chief L.L. Cook said two striking CIO members had been arrested, but were later released. TVA officials called on the FBI to investigate.

According to a later testimony by Broughton, a former TCC employee named Freed Long approached him with information about the next dynamiting, implicating over twenty strikers. He mentioned alleged "secret conferences" to plan the attacks. Rather than find the men, Broughton contacted the FBI. He waited at the New York Hotel with Agents R.T. Manu and John Roach on the evening of April 23. Around 1:30 AM, another dynamiting left the area in darkness all night. Similar to the first series, these attacks targeted the lines running from the Blue Ridge and Parksville Dams. Long was right about the time and place of this dynamiting.[358]

Seventy percent of Copperhill residents used electricity to cook, leaving them no way to make breakfast before work. The blasts cost "huge losses" to the TCC. Broughton arrested four suspects, all CIO strikers, hoping to charge them right away. Knoxville FBI office chief H.E. Plaxico questioned the suspects.[359]

By the end of the month, the authorities believed they had found the main perpetrators. Eighteen other men were arrested in connection with the attacks. Felton Woodward, Ed Simonds, Earl Hubbard, Robert Rhodes, David Queen, Martin Simonds, Clint Huffman, Gordon Parr, L.B. Green, John McGee, Wayne Henry, R.S. (Oris) Postelle, and Marion Ellis pled not guilty. Robert Ballew, R.M. (Meigs) Collins, and Arthur Shillings were also arrested. Federal agents and the Polk County Sheriff's Department arrested Mitchell Anderson, the alleged ringleader, on April 29. Agent Plaxico charged him with "feloniously conspiring to and destroying federal property."[360]

Many of the suspects were not told the reason for their arrest, nor were they taken to a JP before being detained. Deputy Clyde Dale went to question Martin Simonds at his farm in North Carolina. "What's your authority?" Simonds asked. "This is my authority," Dale replied, brandishing his gun.[361]

Rather than charging and incarcerating the accused, local law enforcement and the FBI detained them at the Copperhill YMCA. They were held

The dynamiters targeted power lines along the Ocoee River Gorge. - Cleveland-Bradley County Public Library History Branch and Archives, Ridley Wills Collection

Parksville Lake, also known as Ocoee Lake, was created by the Tennessee Rural Electric Company in 1911 after the completion of Ocoee Dam #1, one of the state's first hydroelectric dams. - Tennessee State Library and Archives

for several days without their attorneys present or permission to notify their families. Some were thrown in a 6x8-foot cell in the Copperhill jail (presently the site of the Copper Grille). They were deprived of food, sleep, and subjected to third-degree questioning without an attorney present. Earl Hubbard, who was feeling ill after eating bologna sandwiches, was not permitted to wear his glasses and was forced to sit up. He was questioned for several hours without being given any water.[362]

The suspected dynamiters were held in the Copperhill YMCA building for "questioning." The building is presently Copperhill city hall. - Polk County Historical and Genealogical Society

Throughout the "questioning," the FBI agents remarked to the suspects "the union never helped you" and asked why they refused to return to work. But what they really wanted was anything linking Anderson to the dynamitings. "We're not really after you. We know you're alright. Anderson is the one we're after." When Ed Simonds (no relation to Martin) stood up to go to the bathroom, an agent grabbed his hair and slammed him back down in his chair.

The FBI obtained "confessions" from six suspects: Earl Hubbard, Ed Simonds, Felton Woodward, David Queen, Robert Rhodes, and Robert Lee Ballew. Worn down by several days of mistreatment, they were ready to do anything to get home to their families. They all signed papers with a typed confession under the signature line.[363]

Shortly after the suspects "confessed," the union voted to end the strike. Anderson made a reduced bond. The others all made $1,000 bond, and Ran Smith had also been arrested by the time of the grand jury hearing. Oris Postelle and Arthur Shillings were released due to insufficient evidence.

Van D. Jones was arrested and charged with conspiring with Mitchell Anderson. Broughton testified to the grand jury, showing records proving Anderson and Jones had stayed at the Key Hotel at the time of the dynamitings. An Alabama powder company employee claimed Woodward purchased dynamite on April 14 under the name "John Cash." E.B. Baker, defense attorney, said that the defendants confessed under duress and were denied proper food while in custody. Given the Biggs machine's success rate in court, the accused had little hope for an acquittal.

Chapter 19

THE REPUBLICANS GIVE UP

R.N. Price, chairman of what was left of the Polk County Republican Party, called a convention to nominate candidates for the 1940 election. Not one Republican ran for office. They elected Col. J.E. Adams, Copperhill attorney, as the new chairman, but made no nominations for county offices. "When we had a meeting, there wouldn't be two dozen there," Red Passmore remembered.[364]

At the Democratic convention, Broughton, Bob McClary and Abie Green were all renominated. Due to a falling out with Burch over liquor legislation, State Sen. Hobart Carey was replaced with Hugh Callaway of Loudon. Hardwick Stuart of Cleveland was nominated for state representative, succeeding Roxy Campbell. Hoyt Lillard was elected delegate to the Democratic National Convention in Chicago.

Burch was appointed to the Democratic State Executive Committee, his highest position to date. After her high school graduation, Burch took his daughter L'Ene to dine with Congressman Kefauver in Washington. "Wish Burch Biggs would swipe enough of the election money to fix the Wetmore bridge or sell one of those black steers or something anyway to get the bridge fixed," the *Polk County News* wrote.

In neighboring McMinn County, Burch's friend and ally Paul Cantrell was seeking a third term as sheriff. Violence at the polls in 1938 and accusations of voter fraud and intimidation prompted several voters to write Congressman John J. Jennings Jr. for help in ensuring fair elections. Jennings tried to convince Governor Cooper to send Maj. Tom Morris and "fifteen or twenty" highway patrolmen to "assist in preserving order" in the election.[365]

Hoping to upset Congressman Kefauver in the Democratic primary, John Wrinkle campaigned across the Third Congressional District. Kefauver barely campaigned, spending most of his time in Washington while Congress was still in session. Burch predicted Polk County would give his cousin "a nice majority."[366] A confident Wrinkle said, "I will carry Hamilton County by a substantial majority, and I will carry Polk and Bradley Counties also if I get a fair count. Burch Biggs will not give me a fair count in Polk if he has his way, and I understand he is trying to spread his influence into Bradley

County."[367] Wrinkle's first campaign for Congress was in 1934, years before he represented David McFadden, and his criticism of then-Congressman McReynolds did not endear him to Burch. Despite lack of opposition, Burch Glen, Roxy Campbell, Dr. W.A. Trevena, Frank Clayton, and Bill Rose were all assigned to work the polls.

The 1940 election did not go off as quietly as the 1938 election. Jim Lee got into a fight with seventeen-year-old Reuben Hamby near the Springtown precinct. The fight started on Deputy August Lewis' porch. Lee, who had been "drinking heavily," stabbed Hamby four times, including a fatal wound in the heart. According to the *Copper City Advance*, the murder had no connection to the election "so as could be learned."

Broughton, Bob McClary, and Abie Green received thousands of complimentary votes for sheriff, trustee, and tax assessor respectively. Charles Guinn won the Republican nomination for state senate and was set to face off against Hugh Callaway. State Sen. Hobart Carey, who won in Polk County in a landslide in 1938, lost the primary to Callaway by a vote of 3,305 to 14. Burch had made him, and Burch had broken him.

Crump's candidates, Governor Cooper and Senator McKellar, carried almost 99 percent of the vote in Polk County, shattering new records. The Republican challengers tallied five votes in Delano and zero votes in Turtletown. The *Chattanooga Times* reported that Biggs "showed as much power in Polk County as did Crump in Shelby." In the congressional primary, John Wrinkle tallied just 30 votes compared with 3,293 for Congressman Kefauver. The attorney who represented the McFadden family after his horrific death at the hands of a Polk County deputy sheriff supposedly won just thirty votes. Wrinkle lost Hamilton County and the district by a large margin, but his 0.9 percent vote share in Polk County screamed fraud. The county's absurdly lopsided margins were getting worse.

The *Knoxville Journal* ran an editorial on Polk County's astronomically-high vote total for the Crump-Biggs candidates. "The votes were so nearly unanimous for the Crump candidates that one could almost imagine that Benton, the county capital, bordered the bluffs of the Mississippi." Crump had only performed better in Shelby County once before. "Are the boys down there in Polk trying to leave the impression that the voters really cast them that way?"

The *Polk County News* mocked the "puzzled" *Knoxville Journal* editorial and defended the vote totals. "Senator McKellar is known to practically every Democrat in Polk County and has worked for and assisted Polk in every way possible." Explaining why Cooper received six less votes than McKellar, the *News* claimed the first-term governor "is not as well known." Callaway received fourteen less votes than Cooper because "he was practically unknown" until his candidacy. "We believe the votes were voted as counted," wrote the *News*. Callaway visited Burch's home a week after the election to thank him personally. With Carey out of the way, Burch had another state senator under his thumb in Nashville.

U.S. Senator Kenneth D. McKellar, a close ally of Boss Crump, went on to become Tennessee's longest-serving senator. - Tennessee State Library and Archives

McKellar had token opposition in the primary, but Burch would tolerate no opposition or criticism of Crump's number one ally. When the postmaster at Ocoee retired earlier that year, Burch rejected the names of three people recommended by the First Assistant Postmaster General for the position. "They were bitterly opposed to you and Senator McKellar in the primary," Burch wrote to Kefauver. One of them was Oliver W. Rice, a Republican. Another was Frank D. Lowery, son of former state legislator and Biggs critic Marvin Lowery. Burch recommended Dorothy Trevena Kimbrough, interim postmaster and daughter of JP Dr. W.A. Trevena.[368] She scored the lowest of all the applicants on the civil service exam, but only a top three scorer could be selected. Kefauver advised his cousin to "get the three people ahead of Mrs. Kimbrough to resign or withdraw."[369] McKellar wrote to Kefauver that it would be difficult to get them to resign, but said, "I should like to do anything that Mr. Biggs wants."[370] Kimbrough soon withdrew herself from consideration. Mabel Lowery, who had the third highest score, was eventually appointed. Nepotism and party loyalty won out over qualifications.

Devastated by the Biggs machine's dominance, only 150 Republicans met to reorganize in August. Col. Adams resigned as chairman and Cecil Lillard was elected to succeed him. A.C. Duncan of Copperhill was nominated to run against Hardwick Stuart for state representative.

Broughton took the oath of office for his third term on September 3, 1940, ensuring the Biggs family would hold the sheriff's office for at least twelve years. He reappointed Roxy Campbell as chief deputy, while Herman Wright, Ben Smith, Burch Maynor, W.B. Couch, and his brother Burch Glen were appointed as deputies. Deputy Louis Wright was assigned to Copperhill.

A few weeks later, Burch announced his candidacy for sheriff in 1942. With Broughton term-limited and Burch Glen preparing to enter the military, The Old Sheriff would be seeking a seventh term. "I plan to be sheriff of Polk County three more terms. I would rather be sheriff of Polk County than to have a seat in Congress."[371]

In October, Governor Cooper appointed Broughton chief of registration for the county draft board. Mostly veterans comprised the board: Hoyt Lillard, chairman; Bob Barclay, secretary; Charles E. Taylor, member, Dr. A.J. Guinn, examining physician; Parks Hyatt, government appeal agent; and Mrs. Joe H. Mabry, chief clerk. Hoyt Lillard, the sheriff's first cousin, now held the positions of president of the Benton Banking Company, school board chairman, election commission secretary, and draft board chairman. He also owned the grocery store in Benton. "He ran the show," Ralph Painter later said.[372] "What Burch didn't run, Hoyt did," Red Passmore recalled.[373] Bob Barclay resigned from the board after a couple of years, replaced by Gordon Daugherty.

Republican election commissioner Dutch Woody was powerless to stop fellow commissioners Burch and Hoyt Lillard from appointing friends, elected officials, and deputies to serve as officers of election or judges, including Leach Park, John Standridge, Constable Bill Hedden, JP Benson Hammons, Frank Clayton, Bill Rose, and Pryor Crowe.

In November, Democrats won by large margins in Polk County compared with surrounding counties and historical trends. Roosevelt was a popular president and beloved in the South, but Polk's results still raised eyebrows. Roosevelt garnered 3,611 votes to Wendell Willkie's 562 votes, nearly 87 percent of the vote. In 1932 and 1936 respectively, Roosevelt won 60 percent and 57 percent of the Polk vote. Polk's neighbors, aside from McMinn County, had no unusual deviations in their results. The Cantrell machine delivered McMinn County for Roosevelt by 14 points in the historically red county, but Wendell Willkie carried Bradley and Fannin Counties by double digits, keeping with their usual trends. Roosevelt won Monroe County by 14 points, not unusual for a purple county that had recently trended blue (due possibly to their new sheriff and aspiring boss W.O. Brakebill.) The president was popular in Meigs County because of the TVA, but he only won 60 percent of the vote there, and he lost a close contest in Loudon County. Cherokee County, normally a Republican county, voted 54 percent for Roosevelt. Republicans still dominated Fannin County where Roosevelt garnered nearly 45 percent of the vote, better than past Democratic candidates.

But the rest of the results screamed fraud this time. Hardwick Stuart tallied 3,347 votes to 494 for A.C. Duncan for state representative. Just a few elections prior, Republican candidates for state representative performed much better in Polk County, even in the height of the depression in the mid-1930s. Now, however, Burch's hand-picked election commissioners and precinct officials controlled the ballot boxes, and Bradley County's votes were diluted by Polk's absurdly high margins in the floterial house district. Several citizens made "well-supported" allegations that election officials carried off the ballot boxes to count the votes in the privacy of the county jail.[374] Governor Cooper tallied 89 percent of the Polk vote compared with 67 percent in Meigs County, 57 percent in Monroe County, and 59 percent in McMinn County, where even the Cantrell machine did not give him an unbelievably high margin. The governor only won 46 percent in Loudon County and lost a close race in Bradley County.

Congressman Kefauver tallied 90 percent of the vote in historically-purple Polk County. He only managed to win 80 percent in Grundy, Warren, and White Counties, longtime Democratic strongholds, and just 67 percent in solidly blue Meigs County. He lost Bradley County by 13 points but won the district with 69 percent of the vote. McMinn and Monroe Counties had close contests for Congress, with Republican John J. Jennings Jr. winning historically-red McMinn by just 80 votes (thanks to the Cantrell machine) and losing purple Monroe by 142 votes. But the congressman won 67 percent of the vote in unbossed red Loudon County. Congressman Jennings, first elected in 1939, would prove to be a thorn in the side of the Biggs and Cantrell machines.

Chapter 20
THE MACHINE CAN'T LOSE ANYWHERE

Shortly before the 1941 legislative session, Burch became a grandfather for the third time when Broughton and Louise welcomed a daughter, Mary Temple Biggs. Burch traveled to Nashville with George Woods, newly elected state representative from McMinn County, where he was once again appointed sergeant at arms of the state senate. His influence in the 1941 legislature would be felt in many ways. On January 21, Senate Speaker Blan Maxwell awarded Burch with a medal. The inscription read "All American Sheriff No. 1." All 33 senators were in attendance to witness Burch receive this honor.[375]

While campaigning for the State Senate, Hugh Callaway signed a pledge promising to vote for a state poll tax repeal. A majority of the Tennessee Democratic Executive Committee added support for the poll tax repeal to its platform at its 1940 convention, and even Governor Cooper and Boss Crump signaled support for repeal.

But Callaway quickly broke his pledge, announcing his opposition to the repeal. The *Nashville Tennessean* reported, because of Burch's power and influence, that Callaway was "privately unfriendly to the poll tax."

When asked about his flip-flop, Callaway said "Even a country boy legislator has a right to change his mind."[376] The *Knoxville-News Sentinel* called him out on his switch: "He heeded the wishes of the Biggs machine in Polk County instead of the rank-and-file voters of his district."[377] The repeal bills failed by a 2-1 margin in the state senate after the Crump faction voted them down. Representatives from the League of Women Voters were present for the vote, urging Callaway to keep his promise. "But…only a few feet to his rear stood Sergeant-At-Arms Burch Biggs, the man who holds the votes of Polk County in the hollow of his hand," the *Knoxville Journal* wrote. Recalling former State Sen. Hobart Carey's falling out with Burch, the *Journal* shared Polk County's 1940 primary results: Callaway 3,305; Carey, 14. "There was no hesitation in Callaway's voice when he voted to kill the poll tax repealer."[378]

State Rep. Hardwick Stuart authored a bill increasing the county attorney's salary to $1,800 per year. Stuart and Woods introduced "ripper bills" into the house of representatives in February. Stuart's bill would abolish the Republican-controlled Bradley County Court and replace it with a county commission, comprised of Democrats. Woods, a lieutenant in the Cantrell machine, introduced four bills handing over control of McMinn County's Republican controlled county court and school board to handpicked Democrats. Although still legal, ripper bills were beyond archaic by this time, and no one abused them quite like the Biggs and Cantrell machines.

The ripper bills easily passed the house and went to the senate, where Burch was there to "lobby" for them. The *Knoxville Journal* called Woods' maneuvering to get the bills passed "so frankly vicious that it is almost ingenious." Woods named his cousin superintendent in the school board bill, a move the *Journal* called a "blending of autocracy and nepotism." The *Journal* worried that the close friendship between Biggs and the Crump forces in the legislature would lead to the bills being "run over" Robert Lindsay, the Republican state senator representing the district including McMinn and Bradley Counties.

Paul Cantrell served three terms as sheriff of McMinn County before going onto the state senate in 1942. Burch helped secure legislation strengthening Cantrell's power in McMinn. - Tennessee State Library and Archives

Luckily for the Bradley County Court, a mix-up delayed Stuart's bill, effectively killing it. Senate Speaker Maxwell ruled all but one of the McMinn bills out of order on a technicality, but the bill to redistrict the McMinn County Court and place Democrats in office would be voted on. State Sen. Lindsay, powerless to stop them, appealed to his colleagues and requested "senatorial courtesy," wherein only bills introduced by senators from the district affected would be voted on:

> "Mr. Biggs, who has sponsored this thing, has been over here campaigning for this thing while he was serving this senate as the chief sergeant-at-arms, but I did not object to that…I thought you gentlemen would respect senatorial courtesy…I'd pull my shoes off and walk home barefooted before I'd vote against any of you senators on an issue like this."

On an almost party line vote, the bill passed 17-8.[379] Governor Cooper signed the McMinn County ripper bill into law on February 15. Disappointed in his Democratic colleagues, Lindsay called the bill "vicious."[380] Paul Cantrell now had total control of McMinn's government. Burch had a strong ally in his neighbor to the north, and the two were just getting started in their attempt to take control of southeastern Tennessee. Burch was now the undisputed boss in the region, and always hosted several politicians at his home when they visited the county, including Callaway and Kefauver.

While Burch and his allies in the legislature slowly amassed more power for themselves, the trials of the 21 strikers accused of dynamiting the TVA power lines began in federal court. A federal grand jury had recently indicted Mitchell Anderson and nineteen others. Defense counsel E.B. Baker argued that Broughton ordered the strikers arrested, held without a warrant, denied proper quarters and food, and subjected to lengthy questioning and "general mistreatment" by law enforcement, including FBI agents.[381]

The defense fought to get the suspects' confessions excluded, alleging they had been obtained "by coercion and duress." Judge Darr refused to exclude them, deciding that prosecutors showed the confessions "appeared as free and voluntary statements." But Darr did prohibit the confessions from being used to convict the defendants who never confessed.[382]

Prosecutors brought in two powder manufacturers from Alabama who testified that Felton and Theodore Woodward purchased three cases of dynamite under a different name. Several FBI agents testified, emphatically denying they mistreated or coerced confessions from the defendants. Broughton, Polk County deputies W.C. Rhodes and C.J. Cochran, Fannin County Sheriff H.C. Collins, Dr. H.P. Hyde, and YMCA cook J.J. Henslee all denied the allegations of mistreatment.

The defense finally caught a break when Judge Darr directed not guilty verdicts for Van D. Jones, James Gordon Parr, Leslie Bryant Green, Tate C. Green, Clyde L. Huffman, W. Clint Huffman, and Benjamin Cross, citing "inadequate proof" linking them to the conspiracy. The prosecution called Freed Long and three other witnesses who alleged they attended Anderson's planning meetings. Defense witnesses accused Long of accepting bribes for his testimony.[383] Earl Hubbard testified that the agents questioning him said they "knew what the truth was" and called him a "damned liar." Leon Howell testified to the good reputations of several of the defendants.[384]

Prosecuting attorneys objected to several of Baker's questions. "I will ask you if you didn't have a standing order on file that all your deputies were to search all these defendants' cars that were found out at night?" Baker asked Broughton. He rephrased the question, but Judge Darr again sustained the prosecution's objection. Broughton finally had to answer a question concerning how many special deputies he hired. "I put on a number of special deputies" he said, but was not forced to give a specific number.[385]

Baker questioned Agent N.H. McCabe about threatening Martin Simonds at his home and forcing him to come to the YMCA. McCabe claimed he had no idea he and Deputy Dale had crossed into North Carolina and had no adequate answer for why they could not question Simonds at home. Simonds testified about his long detention in the YMCA. But McCabe testified that Simonds was "turned loose" and chose to stay. "I have nothing to hide and would just as soon stay here," Simonds allegedly said.[386]

In his closing argument, defense counsel J.M.C. Townsend said the case was "the rottenest I have ever known." He accused the TCC of conspiring with the Biggs machine to break the strike. Townsend called the YMCA detentions "a damnable concentration camp, worse than any run by Hitler." He took a swipe at the FBI for their recent ambush killing of outlaw John Dillinger. U.S. Attorney James B. Frazier, Jr. made the prosecution's closing argument, saying he was "shocked and grieved" by the vilification of the FBI. He blamed the entire thing on Mitchell Anderson, "the brains behind the conspiracy."[387]

The jury began deliberations on January 28, 1941, telling Judge Darr they could not agree after a couple of hours. He recessed them until the next morning. They returned at noon with eight guilty verdicts and five acquittals. Mitchell Anderson, John Edward Simonds, Felton Woodward, Earl Hubbard, John David Queen, Robert Lee Rhodes, Robert Lee Ballew, and Marion Ellis were convicted. John McGee, Thomas Wayne Henry, Meigs Collins, William Ran Smith, and Martin Simonds were acquitted. Judge Darr sentenced them all to the maximum permitted by law. Anderson received two years and a $5,000 fine, while the rest received two-year sentences and $1,000 fines.[388] Coerced confessions and dubious testimony from Freed Long, who later admitted to accepting $10 from Deputy Bill Rose during the strike, led to the conviction of these men who had been denied due process rights. Their convictions would be appealed.

The striker's convictions seemed to have only emboldened the Polk County Sheriff's Department. In February 1941, a safe was stolen from the Clemmer Motor Company in Benton. Deputies found the safe on the side of the highway about a mile north of town. It had been busted open, with papers and checks scattered everywhere. Broughton inspected tire tracks in front of the motor company and dusted the safe for fingerprints. There were no eye witnesses, but a garage attendant said he saw Herbert Walker "looking about in a suspicion manner" shortly before the robbery. The sheriff decided who the guilty parties were.[389]

Broughton, along with Roxy Campbell, questioned Herbert Walker and William Pilgrim at the former's Cleveland home that morning. Walker admitted he had taken his car to the Clemmer Motor Company the day of the robbery. The sheriff got the keys to Walker's Buick Roadster and inspected the trunk where he found evidence that a heavy object had been hauled. He then claimed to have measured the dimensions of the stolen safe and that the imprint in the trunk was "exact."

Broughton and Campbell arrested Walker, Pilgrim, and another man named L.C. Miller. The sheriff allegedly cussed at them during the arrests. According to the suspects, Broughton denied offers of bond payments from six different people for Walker and threatened to prosecute the man who offered bond for Pilgrim. Walker had been previously indicted for multiple crimes, including assault and theft.

The defendants asked to be tried separately, but the court refused. Assistant DA Frank Bratton told the jury it was "up to you if you want to turn these defendants out to pasture to fleece everyone that happens along" and that they had a duty to "show these defendants that they can't come over here from Cleveland and rob in the very shadow of the courthouse." On March 18, they were convicted of grand larceny and sentenced to four years, after which they asked for a new trial. Miller alleged he was compelled to give evidence against himself and Walker called Bratton's arguments before the jury "illegal and improper" and "inspired by prejudice."

Charles Mayfield Sr., Pilgrim's attorney, worked with others to prove the accused trio's innocence. One week after their convictions, Mayfield learned that three men had been arrested in Kentucky after a series of robberies there as well as in Tennessee and Georgia. Checks from the safe at the Clemmer Motor Company were found in their possession. The FBI even investigated the three men, compiling strong evidence of their guilt. Mayfield tried unsuccessfully to obtain copies of the FBI files to convince Judge Pat Quinn to grant them a new trial. Their only recourse was to appeal to the state supreme court.

Broughton still refused to accept bond payments for Walker, Pilgrim, and Miller. They were held in the jail for over five months. Only being fed gravy, hoecake, and coffee for breakfast and potatoes, peas, and cornbread for lunch and dinner, they claimed they each lost over twenty pounds during their incarceration. They also said they had to sleep on the floor due to overcrowding.

On July 21, the state supreme court reversed their convictions and ordered a new trial. Broughton finally released them from jail that day. Cleveland's police chief testified about the measurements of the imprint in Walker's car, contradicting Broughton's findings. Walker's wife and another relative testified that they saw him and Pilgrim at home before midnight on the night of the robbery, which took place a few hours later according to multiple witnesses in Benton, including Dr. John Lillard. The state admitted it had insufficient evidence against Pilgrim and Miller, but still insisted on Walker's guilt. The jury found all three not guilty.[390]

It was a rare loss for Biggs machine in court, but it did not seem to teach them any lessons. A few weeks later, a fifteen-year-old boy from Copperhill named Ted Hallbrook was arrested for suspicion of arson in Cherokee County. He refused to go with the local authorities, so Deputy Bill Rose came to arrest him. Broughton held the boy in jail for over thirty days without charging him. Blanche Hallbrook, the boy's widowed mother, wrote to Governor Cooper asking for help. With four young children at home, she needed her eldest son there to help. "This is all done for spite anyway," she wrote. But the governor just advised her to talk to an attorney.[391]

The United States' entry into World War II was fast approaching, and several young Polk County men were drafted or enlisted in the armed forces. Burch Glen Biggs, Burch's 24-year-old son and new deputy under his brother, was stationed close by in Ft. Oglethorpe, Georgia. Nicknamed "Beefy" because of his size in his youth, the *Polk County News* wrote that Burch Glen would "make good in whatever department he will be placed in, even in the mess hall at mess time." Others drafted in summer 1941 included I.J. Wright, brother of deputies Herman and Louis Wright, George Painter (later a major player in McMinn County politics) and Frank D. Lowery.

By summer 1941, two anti-Biggs Democrats had left Polk County. Jim Park, brother of Leach Park, was no longer associated with the Benton Banking Company. Jim had previously served as election commissioner, promising a fair election. Winston Prince had tried to make peace with the Biggs machine for years, including supporting the 1938 harmony ticket. But he had had enough by 1941, and moved his family to Cleveland.

Charles Guinn also left Benton around this time, eventually settling in Etowah. "My dad didn't make any rash moves," his son Charlie Guinn said, recalling his father's frequent clashes with Burch. "He took things day by day." Charlie remembered growing up as a Republican in Polk County: "We had to watch everything we said. The walls had ears down there."[392] Mary Lethco Lewis recalled how the Biggs machine treated political opponents: "If you were a Republican, you were nothing."[393] The treatment was worse in the Copper Basin. "If you went into town and they didn't like your looks or if you was a Republican, they'd arrest you," Henry Watson said.[394] "Life was a lot easier if you were a Democrat" recalled one citizen whose father was a deputy.[395]

In October, Deputy Pryor Crowe was shot in Ducktown. Crowe was attempting to arrest Irving Crawford and John Brown for drunk driving, when Crawford pulled out a .405 caliber rifle and shot the deputy in the side of his face and neck. The car's side window shattered, showering Crowe with glass so badly it looked like he had been hit by a shotgun blast. The assailants sped toward the Hiwassee Dam, leaving Crowe without his left eye and in serious condition.

Drs. A.J. Guinn and H.H. Hyatt treated Crowe before he was transported to Erlanger Hospital in Chattanooga. He managed to survive the shooting. Local law enforcement found the perpetrators in Fannin County. They confessed to Broughton in Copperhill. It turned out that Crawford, a New York native living in North Carolina, had been using a fake name.

A few months later, Crawford was convicted and Judge Sue K. Hicks sentenced him to ten years in prison. Crowe returned to the force in January. According to the *Polk County News*, Crowe was "extremely popular" and Broughton regarded him as one of his most efficient officers. But others remembered Crowe as a "bully."[396] In Polk County, the punishment for a civilian shooting a deputy was a ten-year sentence, but deputies killing innocent civilians were acquitted.

Chapter 21

A Triple Murder in Greasy Creek

James "Jack" Hedden returned home from work on November 18, 1941 at 11:30 PM, expecting to find everyone asleep. What he found instead was his wife, Lecia, lying in the doorway with multiple gunshot wounds. She and their unborn child were dead. He rushed into the bedroom to check on their infant son, Ernest, who was sound asleep. Arlene Dillard Gowan, who had been staying with the Heddens, was laying lifeless on the bed, also with multiple gunshot wounds. Her 14-month-old son, Stephen, lay dead on the floor. In addition to gunshot wounds, Steven's head suffered major trauma. The *Copper City Advance* called it "probably the most brutal tragedy to ever happen in Polk County."

Jack Hedden frantically rushed to the home of his closest neighbor, Noah Bates, to call the police. Informed of the murders around midnight, Broughton got out of bed and went straight to work. Deputy Herman Wright accompanied him to the scene of the heinous crime. They arrived to find Noah Bates, Dave Rymer, and Rev. Melvin Ledford in the home with Jack. Deputies Frank Clayton, Ben Smith, and Bill Rose arrived shortly afterwards. They found shell casings of a .32 and .38 pistol inside the home and in the front yard. "I don't care who it is," Jack Hedden said to Broughton. "Get after him."

Constable Bill Hedden, Jack's brother, arrived with a friend, Julius Goforth. "Sheriff, we're going to catch the scoundrels that done this," Bill said. Broughton sent for bloodhounds from Brushy Mountain State Penitentiary. "It was the most horrible sight I ever looked on. I can't conceive of any human being shooting to death that baby boy," Broughton said.

Bill Hedden told Broughton that two cousins, Lawrence and Floyd Breeden, had been hanging around Jack and Lecia Hedden's home lately, trying to have their way with Arlene Gowan. She apparently had no interest in the two. Dr. Trevena, the county coroner, found .32 and .38 caliber bullets in the bodies of the victims. He was one man short of a coroner's jury. Deputy Herman Wright went outside to ask Julius Goforth to join them, but he was riding away in Bill's car. They were supposedly going to Elbert Campbell's store to call and inform family and friends of the murders.

When questioned, the Breedens seemed shocked when informed of the murders, but emphatically denied any involvement. They admitted to hanging around the Hedden home the day before and claimed that Bill Hedden had angrily run them off at gunpoint. A .38 pistol was sitting on their window sill. Broughton placed them under arrest for suspicion of murder.

Broughton questioned Noah Bates, who said he saw Julius Goforth sitting in a car and heard Bill Hedden's voice shortly before 6:00 PM. According to Bates, the car went in the direction of the Hedden home shortly before he heard gunshots and screams. Broughton asked Jack Hedden if Bill, who was married with several children, had also shown romantic interest in Arlene Gowan. Jack did not rule out the possibility, especially since Bill was so angry at the Breedens for hanging around her so much. He confirmed that he had seen Bill with his .32 and .38 pistols in his car the day before.

Deputy Bill Rose spoke with Elbert Campbell, who said Bill Hedden and Julius Goforth had not been to his store at all lately. Broughton was growing more suspicious of Bill. Rose mentioned that Bill had killed his own father, Riley Hedden, several years prior, successfully invoking self-defense. Burch had shot and killed Riley's brother, Garrett, in 1908.

Broughton had a cunning plan. He took a few deputies to Bill Hedden's house, where they also found Julius Goforth. The sheriff told them that they had the Breedens in jail and that he wanted them to come and help question the suspects. "Sure, I told you I would help in every way I could," Bill said.

According to a story passed down through the years, after Bill Hedden walked into a jail cell to help question the Breedens, Broughton slammed the door shut behind him, like he was trapping a wild animal.[397] Broughton questioned Bill about his gun, the bullets that were found at the crime scene, and his whereabouts during the murders. Bill claimed he was not feeling well and that he went to sleep around 5:00 PM, about an hour before the murders. But Broughton had heard enough, and placed Bill under arrest. "You know I wouldn't kill my own brother's wife!" Bill said in protest. He then claimed to have just remembered that he was briefly awoken around 9:00 PM by Julius Goforth placing his .38 pistol on top of his dresser. Bill said he did not want to imply that Goforth committed the murders, but that he had his gun while the crime took place. But Broughton was not buying Bill's excuse.

When informed that Bill Hedden tried to shift the blame to him, Julius Goforth broke into tears. "I hate to tell on Bill!" he said. The two were close friends, but Goforth told Broughton everything he allegedly witnessed. "He was crazy jealous about that woman that stayed there." Bill allegedly rode with Goforth to the house around 6:00 PM. Goforth said he had no idea what Bill was about to do. Goforth heard gunshots and screams just before Bill emerged from the house and returned to the car. "There's nobody left in there to tell the tale," Bill allegedly said to Goforth.[398]

Burch had allegedly used Bill Hedden as his "guard dog," but it now seemed he was not worth the trouble anymore. According to another account, in response to recent complaints about Bill's violent behavior, Burch told them, "He's your problem, not mine." Some said even Burch was scared of Bill.[399]

According to the *Chattanooga Times*, "investigating officers hinted that a pretrial confession had been obtained by one or both of the men in custody." Other newspapers printed similar reports. This erroneous report, confusing Goforth's confession that he knew Bill Hedden committed the murders, greatly damaged Bill's case. The *Polk County News* commended Broughton's "swift" work on the case. Within a few days, a grand jury indicted Bill on three counts of murder. No bond was allowed. Broughton said that Bill had possibly killed Gowan "in a fit of jealous passion" and killed his sister-in-law Lecia "to remove her as a witness."[400] The trial was set for December 3, a speedy trial indeed, as the next term of the circuit court was just around the corner.

Spectators crowded inside the courthouse in Benton for the county's most sensational murder trial since that of Emmett Gaddis in Ducktown. Beecher Witt led the prosecution, pressing hard for the death penalty. Etowah attorney Reuel Webb, along with Charles Guinn, represented Bill Hedden. Judge Pat Quinn denied Bill's request for a continuance after dismissing complaints of inadequate time to prepare and "prejudiced" newspaper reporting.[401] Clifford Lewis, Jim Rymer, Wilbur Rymer, Walter McDonald, Amos Bates, F.E. Bates, Charles Biggs, Sam Williams, Chester Linder, J.H. Hammons, Lester Donner, and Virgil Clark comprised the jury.

Jack Hedden was a prosecutor in the trial, sitting with Witt. Julius Goforth testified that he went with Bill Hedden to Jack and Lecia Hedden's home but stayed in the car. "I heard quarreling voices and a burst of gunfire shortly before Bill Hedden emerged with a pistol in his hand." Noah Bates also testified to what he heard and saw, albeit from a distance.[402]

Bill Hedden pled not guilty. "I first found out about the murder at 3:00 AM when a friend awoke me and told me about it," he said. When questioned about blood found in his car shortly after the murders, he claimed it was either from hauling some fresh meat or rescuing a bleeding hound dog.[403] Witt cross-examined Bill, who remained calm and emotionless his entire time on the stand. An FBI ballistics expert provided evidence that he claimed proved Bill's .38 pistol was used in the murders, but his .32 pistol was never recovered.

Millie Hedden swore her husband was innocent, blaming the murders on Goforth. Guinn called the evidence circumstantial and said others had "equal opportunity" to commit the crime. Witt called Bill Hedden "the most cowardly, most cruel, most dastardly killer who ever pulled the trigger on a pistol." Witt's closing arguments brought Jack Hedden, who had maintained his composure until this point, to tears.[404]

The trial lasted three days, and it only took the jury two hours of deliberation to find Bill Hedden "guilty of murder in the first degree, *without* mitigating circumstances." He received the verdict that his cousin James Allen had twice managed to evade. "I am not guilty," he told Judge Quinn, who sentenced him to death by electrocution on January 15.[405] For only the second time in its 102 years of existence, and after several controversial acquittals, a Polk County jury had sentenced a man to die.[406]

Broughton told Judge Quinn the Polk County Jail was not a safe place to keep Bill Hedden. Nearby jails would not suffice either, so he was transported to the state penitentiary in Nashville. Bill asked for a new trial, alleging the speed of his indictment and trial did not give his attorneys sufficient time to prepare a defense. He also claimed a guard was present while he spoke with his attorneys, violating their privacy. The motion for a new trial claimed the court erred during jury selection in several ways. Judge Quinn refused to dismiss a prospective juror who claimed to have formed an opinion after erroneous newspaper reports of Bill's confession. Three jurors, F.E. Bates, Jim Rymer, and Lester Donner, were too closely related to both Bill and Jack Hedden to qualify as competent jurors.[407]

Although the evidence looked really, really bad for Bill Hedden, it was argued that the state had violated his due process rights. Even worse, only one eyewitness allegedly saw him commit the nighttime killings, whereas numerous witnesses saw Emmett Gaddis and Manuel Price kill someone in broad daylight. Bill's case was better suited for a life sentence. But that was Polk County justice. Judge Quinn denied Bill a new trial at his January 15 hearing. His attorneys appealed the case to the state supreme court, delaying his execution.

Only days after Bill Hedden's conviction, Japan launched a surprise attack on the U.S. naval base at Pearl Harbor, killing thousands of people. The next day, President Franklin Roosevelt asked Congress for a declaration of war. The country was at war again, and hundreds of young Polk County men would be sent overseas to fight tyranny, leaving less resistance to tyranny at home.

Chapter 22

"The Biggs Machine Could Teach Crump Tricks"

Approaching his 68th birthday, Burch was near the peak of his power. "He was so powerful that a man could hardly go out to his own backhouse without asking Biggs first," a citizen later said.[408] Some of the big city newspapers had taken to calling Polk County "Biggs County." With Hoyt Lillard in charge of the county draft board, Burch held immense power during World War II.

It seemed to make no difference to the draft board that Henry Crox was 43 years of age and in poor health. He received a draft notice in spring 1942. Patsy Crox Underhill remembered her father's cousin, Dr. Boyd McClary, being "hoppin' mad" when Henry did not receive a deferment. Dr. McClary confronted Hoyt Lillard, demanding a deferment for his cousin. Lillard signed the papers. "Boyd said Daddy would not last through one march," Underhill later wrote. Crox was later diagnosed with histoplasmosis of the lungs.[409]

The draft board was accused of drafting Republicans first. A 1942 draft call included several married men, a majority of which were from the Copper Basin, home to several Republicans.[410] Buck Arp's son, "Little Buck," enlisted in the Navy before they had the chance to draft him early.[411] Red Passmore registered for the draft in Blount County, where he worked, but later received a referral after working for the TVA. But his brother, Paul, was one of the first ones drafted.

James O. "Red" Locke lived in Grassy Creek, a Republican stronghold. He was 34 years old, had six children, and another on the way, but it did not matter. He was among the first men drafted in Polk County, along with others with several children.[412] Marvin Lowery (not to be confused with the former state legislator) had a younger brother, Marshall, serving in the Army. His parents were disabled. They and their three youngest children depended on Marvin's income from his job at the TCC. But Marvin was drafted in early 1942, and was not even given time to sign up his family as dependents.[413] Mary Lethco Lewis remembered one way to avoid the draft, and that was to work Hoyt Lillard's farm.[414]

With Burch, McMinn Sheriff Paul Cantrell, and now Monroe County Sheriff W.O. Brakebill, Boss Crump had a strong alliance of bosses in East Tennessee as the 1942 election approached. Deputy Pat Mansfield was nominated to succeed Cantrell as McMinn County sheriff, while Cantrell was nominated for state senator. Burch attended the convention, urging McMinn Democrats to vote the remaining Republicans out of office. Following Burch, Cantrell was on the path to total control of his county.

For the ninth time in nearly forty years, Burch won his party's nomination for sheriff. Vance Davis was nominated for another term as county judge. Leach Park, Bob McClary, and John Harbison were all renominated for county court clerk, trustee, and register of deeds respectively. Deputy Bill Rose was nominated for JP for Copperhill. In an unexpected move, Broughton was nominated for state representative, succeeding Hardwick Stuart.

After five terms and two decades in office, George Gilliland, the only Democrat at the courthouse preceding the formation of Biggs machine, would not be on the ballot for circuit court clerk. His twenty years in office was the longest consecutive term for any county official in the same office. The year before, state auditors made an audit of the county offices. Of course, the only office found to have "shortages" was that of the circuit court clerk.[415]

A well-liked public servant, Gilliland was never really part of the machine, and Burch wanted him gone, hence the audit. In an attempt to remedy his casting aside of Roxy Campbell for Bob McClary in the trustee's office in 1938, Campbell was nominated to succeed Gilliland as circuit court clerk. Gilliland was so desperate for another job that he inquired about an opening at the Brushy Mountain State Penitentiary, a position well below his qualifications.[416]

The *Polk County News* reported the 1942 Democratic ticket was not expected to have any opposition. "Voting was pointless because Biggs would always win," Henry Watson recalled. He alleged the Biggs machine stuffed the ballot boxes and that people became afraid to talk about elections "because they did not want to be killed."[417] More than a few citizens told their kids about how Burch's men would dump ballots off a bridge on Highway 64 where one of the creeks emptied into the Ocoee River. Boxes full of marked ballots were always ready for transport to Benton.[418] George O. Rogers, who later served as a Democratic JP, told his family that the reported results would be "very different than what they really were."[419] Brad Kimbrough, a staunch Democrat, told his family all about how the Biggs machine stuffed the ballot boxes.[420]

Only seventeen people attended the Polk County Republican convention. Led by chairman Dutch Woody, they nominated a full ticket for the county offices: Frank Lillard for sheriff; Marion Payne for county judge; Dewey Carter for trustee; Amos Ballew for county court clerk; Cliff Panter for circuit court clerk; and M.C. Ledford for register of deeds. Buck Arp was nominated for state representative. None of the men nominated attended the meeting.

Burch's only viable rival in East Tennessee Democratic circles was Hamilton County judge candidate Wiley Couch. Cleveland attorney J. Lake McClary, Jr., claimed that Bradley County was "sick of Biggs" and wanted Couch to "dictate policies" in the Third Congressional District. Frustrated with Burch's nepotism, McClary spoke for Bradley's Democrats when he called for a "competitive examination" for Cleveland postmaster rather than someone handpicked by the Crump/McKellar faction at Burch's request.[421] Although still in Republican hands, Bradley County enjoyed a healthy two-party system. Bradley's Democrats also endorsed Broughton for state representative.

During the summer campaign season, *Chattanooga Times* reporter Fred Hixon wrote a complimentary article about Burch, praising his "loyalty and courage." Hixon lamented Tennessee's "rapidly vanishing rugged individualism," writing that Burch was one of the few remaining who almost "measured up" to the frontier leaders of the past. Those who charge that Burch is an "unscrupulous frontier bully" are mistaken, Hixon asserted. He admired Burch's "fighting fire with fire" style and insisted that if he did not rule Polk County with an "iron hand," then someone else would "rise to the occasion."

For Hixon, Burch's tears during the unveiling of the portrait of Congressman Sam McReynolds in the courthouse was a testament to how great a friend Burch was. He was correct that Burch lived for many years "astride a dynamite's nest." But he chose to overlook Burch's glaring character flaws through the years as he amassed more and more power for himself. "Above all, Burch Biggs is a man of high courage and his word is his bond."

Frank Lillard, son of John M. Lillard and nephew of former sheriff Abe Lillard III, initially accepted the Republican nomination for sheriff and planned to make the race, but he and most of the nominees later withdrew. Only M.C. Ledford stayed in, opposing John Harbison for register of deeds. Aluminum Company of America employee Mitchell Smith announced an independent bid for sheriff, but barely campaigned. He wrote to Governor

Cooper requesting that the National Guard or "disinterested federal employees" hold the election. "A great majority of the people in Polk County…are dissatisfied with the way elections have been held in the past," he claimed.[422] His plea for help was ignored.

"There are few places left these days where the old-time political barbecue, with all of its trimmings of pure hokum and rabble-rousing, would be attempted. Polk County is one," the *Knoxville News-Sentinel* wrote. Burch threw his biggest barbecue to date at Quinn Springs on July 18, entertaining over 2,000 people. If you give the people free food, they will come. At a time when many Polk Countians struggled to make ends meet, and the country was at war, Burch spent $1,000 on a party (the equivalent of $18,200 in 2023). Governor Cooper, Senators McKellar and Stewart, and Congressman Kefauver all attended. The *Copper City Advance* called it "the most distinguished political group ever to visit Polk County."

Burch, a candidate while also serving as election commissioner, led his fellow Democrats in their unopposed races, tallying 3,965 votes in August 1942. He had now been elected sheriff seven times. John Harbison won a second term as register of deeds, defeating M.C. Ledford by a vote of 3,778 to 164. Roxy Campbell was the new circuit court clerk. Vance Davis won another term as county judge. Arthur Dalton declined to run for reelection, leaving Bill Rose as the new JP from Copperhill, making the county court 7-1 Democratic. The other seven JPs were reelected. The same court that had, since 1938, raised the tax rate from $1.97 to $2.67, with nothing to show for it, would be in office until at least 1948. Burch also won a two-year term on the State Democratic Executive Committee. Buck Arp won the Republican nomination for state representative and campaigned on ending Tennessee's poll tax, saying he was 100 percent for repeal and that "nothing this side of hell" could change his position.[423] In the judicial cycle, District Attorney Beecher Witt and Judge Pat Quinn won unopposed races while Judge Sue K. Hicks defeated a Republican challenger.

In the statewide primaries, Crump's candidates dominated as usual. J. Ridley Mitchell, challenging Governor Cooper, lost Polk County by a vote of 3,870 to 50. U.S. Senator Tom Stewart tallied 3,899 votes to Edward W. Carmack Jr.'s 104 votes. These results starkly contrasted with the statewide numbers as Cooper and Stewart won their primaries with just under 60 percent of the vote. The *Nashville Tennessean* reported that challengers Mitchell and Carmack performed well in "un-bossed" counties. Cooper, a popular wartime governor, won an average of 82 percent of the vote in southeast Tennessee, but tallied 98.7 percent in Polk County. Republican election commissioner Henry Crox did not even sign the election certificates. Patsy Crox Underhill remembered the accusations of election fraud:

Edward H. "Boss" Crump of Memphis was the undisputed king of Tennessee politics during the 1930s and 1940s. - Tennessee State Library and Archives

"Daddy was the Republican county election commissioner. That position did not mean much because he was not allowed to see the ballots counted nor were the people he appointed as poll workers and watchers. He said he was never where he could see the actual ballots being counted. Men wearing guns, counting the votes had their backs to the others and a solid shield was between the ballots and the watchers with other men also armed lined up and guarding the doors. Boss Crump got what he needed from Polk is the story I have always heard."[424]

The *Chattanooga Times* was skeptical of Polk's election results, noting that over 4,000 votes were cast for governor despite the county's voting age population being just over 10,000. "If the rest of the state had voted as heavily, the vote in the gubernatorial race for the entire state would have been something like 732,264, whereas it was just a little over 300,000."[425] A *Knoxville News-Sentinel* editorial was even more critical. "And the worst of it is that this bloc of votes the Biggs family machine delivers is being used now by interests outside the county to control elections elsewhere. That even affects us in Knox County...We already have to accept Hugh Callaway for floterial senator without opposition, despite the fact that he flagrantly violated his pledge last session to vote and work for the repeal of the poll tax...The Biggs crowd is now tying up with the Couch organization in Chattanooga to wield sway in the Third District."

The *News-Sentinel* reminded voters that Congressman Kefauver attended Burch's July barbecue and how it surprised some of his supporters, especially given his reputation of "independence of machine domination." Unlike his colleague Congressman Jennings, Kefauver expressed no concern about fair elections in his district. In fact, after clerk and master John Standridge sent a copy of Polk County's election returns, Kefauver replied: "I appreciate the wonderful showing made in Polk County."[426] He was unopposed, but no doubt liked the almost 4,000 complementary votes. If he was skeptical of Cooper and Stewart's 98 percent vote tallies, he said nothing about it.

The *Knoxville Journal* reported that Burch's "row" with Congressman Jennings was brought out into the open after the 1942 elections. "Speechmaking Biggs avoids, maneuvering he excels in, and cultivating the individual is his specialty." On the floor of Congress, Jennings said he had been "trying in vain for 18 months to get the federal government through its district attorney to prosecute the violators of election laws in McMinn and Monroe Counties."[427] Beecher Witt, longtime Republican district attorney, never stood up to the bosses. If he ever had evidence that anyone in his district committed voter fraud, he took no action.

While serving as sergeant-at-arms in the state senate, Burch not only lobbied for the ripper bill that handed control of the McMinn County Court to the Democrats, but also another bill that reduced the voting precincts in the county from twenty-three to twelve, suppressing voter turnout. "To get these laws enacted," the *Journal* wrote, "Biggs kicked over a traditional barrier that had halted many a bit of spite legislation: the senatorial courtesy rule." The article reminded readers that a West Tennessee senator introduced the bills over protests of Sen. Robert Lindsay.

"The Polk County vote now decides, or almost decides, certain elections," the *Journal* wrote. Indeed, some close statewide elections had been decided by the lopsided returns in Polk County. Without his ridiculously high margins in Shelby, McMinn, and Polk Counties, Senator Stewart would have lost the primary. In the state senate, Burch was now handpicking the senator for Polk, Monroe, Loudon, and western Knox Counties. "The Polk County style of Democratic politics has been introduced into McMinn County," the *Journal* lamented.

Jennings had assisted with an ouster suit against Monroe County Sheriff W.O. Brakebill. "I'm making a fight on the political empire of Sheriff Burch

Biggs in Monroe, Polk, and McMinn Counties." Sweetwater attorney W.E. Michael, assisting Jennings, said, "I don't know if it is the Brakebill machine or the Biggs machine. It may be that Brakebill is just a little bug riding on the back of a bigger bug."[428] Jennings said he was "not against" Burch Biggs. "I'm just against his evil ways."[429]

Celebrating his return to the sheriff's office, Burch hosted a luncheon at the jail. Paul Cantrell, now a state senator, George Woods, Hugh Callaway, and Judge Sue K. Hicks attended. T.J. Addington, Joe Williams and E.A. Clark, the only surviving deputies from Burch's first term as sheriff in 1904, were his special guests. He reappointed Herman Wright as chief deputy and Ben Smith, Pryor Crowe, Frank Clayton, and Clyde Dale as deputies.

The county court elected Broughton as county coroner at their October meeting. He had done well for himself as sheriff. By the end of his six years in office, he owned a 312-acre river-bottom farm as well as another 267-acre spread near the river, the railroad, and Highway 411. All of this property was assessed at $18,500.[430]

In November 1942, Broughton tallied 3,586 votes in Polk County over Buck Arp on his way to winning the district. Arp won Bradley County by a small majority, but not near enough to overcome his deficit in Polk, where he only tallied 97 votes. Previously a successful candidate for county court clerk, receiving thousands of votes in several elections, Arp supposedly pulled in fewer than 100 votes in his home county. Charles Guinn, a former state representative, had reluctantly agreed to challenge Hugh Callaway for state senate. Just like Arp, he supposedly lost Polk County in a 3,529 to 101 vote blowout as Callaway won the district.

Governor Cooper's 97.6 percent total in Polk County was down 1.1 percent from his performance in the primary. According to the *Nashville Tennessean*, Cooper's haul in Polk "is thought to have set a new high percentage record." Cooper only managed to get 94.5 percent of the vote in Shelby County. The *Knoxville News-Sentinel* commented that the Biggs machine "could teach Crump tricks" after seeing the one-sided returns in Polk County. Edward B. Smith of the *Knoxville News-Sentinel* wrote:

"On election nights I always get a chuckle out of watching the returns come in from Polk County. They are always very late in being reported. And for some strange reason, in precinct after precinct the candidates opposing the Biggs ticket don't get a single vote."

Governor Cooper and Senator Stewart carried Polk County with their usual 3,000-plus votes over their opponent's fewer than 100 votes. The bosses in McMinn and Monroe Counties only delivered 70 and 60 percent respectively for Cooper. The governor won 82 percent in Hamilton County and 85 percent in Meigs County, but only managed 48 percent in Bradley County and 42 percent in Loudon County. Congressman Kefauver tallied 3,537 votes in Polk County, 98 percent of the vote. His Republican and Independent challengers combined for 80 votes. Kefauver won the district with 75 percent of the vote and did not tally more than 90 percent of the vote in any other county in the district, even in his adopted home of Hamilton County, where he won 87 percent of the vote. He lost Bradley County by eight votes. The Cantrell machine ensured Democrat John O'Connor tallied 67 percent of the vote against Congressman Jennings in McMinn County. O'Connor won 55 percent in Monroe County, but only won 30 percent in Loudon County. Jennings still won the district, dominating in the Knoxville metropolitan area. Burch's opponents were now screaming fraud at the top of their lungs. But no one in Nashville or Washington listened, except for that plucky congressman from Knoxville.

Republicans did well in Bradley County. The *Chattanooga Times* reported that Bradley's Democrats, and even some Republicans, "voiced their disapproval" of Polk County native Jess Rymer's appointment to the Tennessee Democratic Executive Committee for Bradley. Columbus Mee, an outspoken opponent of the Biggs machine in Bradley's Democratic circles, was passed over in favor of Rymer. If Bradley Countians thought they had seen the worst of Burch's meddling in their government, they had not seen anything yet.

Chapter 23

"A Small Payment for the Privilege of Voting"

After the November 1942 election, Burch came out firmly against repealing the state's poll tax. "There are five senators in East Tennessee who will oppose poll tax repeal, and you know those boys in Middle and West Tennessee don't want it." Two of those senators were Burch's allies Paul Cantrell and Hugh Callaway.[431] "We are going to do everything we can…I don't think it will ever pass," Burch said confidently. Governor Cooper and Boss Crump announced their support for repeal during the general election.[432] But multiple reporters, including Nat Caldwell of the *Nashville Tennessean*, wrote that Crump and Cooper may have always planned to break their promise on the poll tax repeal and that Burch had "tipped folks to the poll tax plans of the Memphis organization."

The *Nashville Tennessean* predicted that "little fuehrers" like Burch would "come out in their true colors again as soon as the votes could be dumped into a box." They noted that Burch defied his party by opposing the poll tax repeal after delivering 98.5 percent of Polk County's vote for the anti-poll tax Governor Cooper. "Should Tennessee's three million be without the heart to fight again for that right, then at least they should recognize their masters. Boss Biggs of Polk County (pop. 18,000) thinks he is one." The *Chattanooga Times* pointed out that six of the state's ten congressmen had voted to repeal the poll tax in federal elections. "The people of Tennessee want poll tax repeal." Burch denied reports that he had spoken for the Shelby County organization. "I was talking for Polk County."[433] Senator McKellar opposed the anti-poll tax bill in Congress, but predicted that Tennessee would repeal its own poll tax, citing the state party's platform.

Polk County clerk and master John Standridge defended Burch and his opposition to the poll tax repeal. "I know that Sheriff Biggs is respected by the citizens of Polk County…there are a great many people in the county named for him." He was certainly right about the second part. Burch Garfield Eaves, Burch Cheek, Burch L. Lewis, Burch E. Maynor, Burch Biggs White, Burch Ralph Brown, Burch Biggs Harbison, Burch E. Ellis, Burch Ray

Lee, Birch B. Bates, Burch Spencer Presswood, Burch Swafford, Burch Alvin Presswood, Burch G. Cronan, and Burch Lewis Perian were all born during Burch's terms as sheriff. In 1940, Burch E. Maynor named his twin boys Burch and Broughton. JP Benson Hammons named his son Oscar Burch Hammons after his close friend. Burch William Hutchins was the son of Deputy P.R. Hutchins. Standridge called the poll tax "a small payment for the privilege of voting."[434] Congressman Kefauver declined the opportunity to sponsor a new federal anti-poll tax bill in late December, a puzzling move for a politician supposedly opposed to the machines.

Broughton denied reports that he was in the running for house speaker.[435] Rep. Freddie Moses of Knoxville, a supporter of the poll tax repeal, wanted the position. Broughton went to Nashville to "line up support" for Rep. James Broome of Clarksville and "to get Moses out of the picture."[436] Just before Christmas, the *Nashville Tennessean* reported that there were already talks of legislation to change the Cleveland city and Bradley County governments, adding two more city commissioners "friendly" to Burch. "The Polk County sheriff is a master at this game of local legislation for purposes of extending the width of his political domain," Nat Caldwell of the *Tennessean* wrote.

Copperhill held its municipal election on December 5, having no idea that their duly elected city government would not be permitted to finish their term. The Copper Basin, and the city of Copperhill in particular, had given the Biggs machine a lot of trouble for years. Burch was prepared to lay the hammer down on them at the next session of the state legislature.

State Sen. W. French Grubb of Chattanooga introduced Senate Bill No.1 to "outright" repeal the state poll tax during the first week of the 1943 legislative session. Boss Crump supported it under the condition that a permanent voter registration system be passed concurrently. Burch, no longer sergeant-at-arms, went to Nashville to fight the repeal effort. This was more important to him than his job back home. That Broughton was there as a legislator did not matter. He said opposing repeal was the "principal purpose" of his visit. Rep. Broome was the new House Speaker, and several legislators were reportedly not "genuine" in their pledges to repeal. All this left Burch in a good position to get his way, as usual.[437]

State attorney general Roy Beeler helped prepare the repeal legislation. He worried a complete repeal would not survive in court because of the state constitutional requirement of a .50 cent levy to vote. The part of the poll tax required by a previous statute could be repealed without much trouble. In the event of the enactment of a full repeal bill, Beeler recommended an immediate legal challenge as a test of how the state supreme court would interpret it. On top of this impending legal challenge, the Shelby County delegation appeared to be making little effort toward repeal.

Prentice Cooper was governor of Tennessee during most of World War II. - Tennessee State Library and Archives

"It's a Republican scheme," Burch said, making no attempt to hide his motivation. "I'd be for it if I was a Republican. But it will hurt the Democrats, particularly in East Tennessee and in other counties where there are a lot of Negroes. If you let the Negroes vote the way they want to, most of them will just naturally vote for the Republican ticket." The *Knoxville Journal* reported that Burch could be seen "wherever there are two or more legislators talking things over in hotel lobbies on Capitol Hill."[438]

Burch was unconcerned about Governor Cooper's strong rhetoric in favor of repeal. "You know that if he intends to put pressure on any of the members, he would call me in." Broughton followed his father. "If there are ninety-eight members of this house who vote for poll tax repeal, there will be one vote against it and that vote will be mine."[439]

Burch traveled to Nashville every week to fight the poll tax repeal and lobby for more ripper bills, sometimes not even returning home for the weekend. On a rare weekend he did return home, he admitted "Somebody has got to be sheriff…When Burch (Glen) comes home from the Army, that day I'll resign and let the County Court elect him to fill my place. I'll never run for sheriff again."[440] The *Knoxville Journal* wrote of his reputation for doing favors for Republicans, so long as it is not a political one. "Politics has been a business with him."

The bills underwent several tweaks to please Boss Crump, and Beeler worked to ensure they were legal. As Cooper addressed the house of representatives urging repeal, Burch sat on the house floor with Broughton. Cooper was doing his best to fulfill a campaign promise from his first term, and the man who delivered huge majorities for him in Polk County was the leading opponent of repeal. "I'm here until the smoke of the battle clears," Burch said.[441]

The House Election Committee voted overwhelmingly to recommend passage of the poll tax repeal and permanent voter registration bills. After delivering an "impassioned plea" against the bills, Broughton cast one of a few nay votes. "Twenty years ago, the Republicans swept the eastern part of the state with a 70,000-vote majority. I predict that the same thing will happen within two years' time if this legislation becomes law," he said.[442]

Rural Middle Tennessee Democrats supported repeal, but opposed the permanent registration bill. Rural West Tennessee Democrats opposed the poll tax repeal. Boss Crump and the Shelby County delegation would only vote for the poll tax repeal after the permanent registration bill passed. Burch knew all he had to do was corral enough opposition to the permanent registration bill. Then, Boss Crump would drop support for the poll tax repeal, killing it altogether. The *Nashville Tennessean* had correctly predicted that Crump's refusal to support the poll tax repeal without first passing a permanent registration bill revealed his disingenuous support for the poll tax repeal.

On January 27, after three days of filibustering, the house passed the poll tax repeal and permanent registration bills by a wide margin. For a bill that was, according to Burch, a "Republican measure," it received significant Democratic support. A furious Broughton yelled at Speaker Broome demanding a motion to reconsider. Broome ruled Broughton "out of order."[443] Rep. George Woods blamed the editors of the *Nashville Banner* and the *Knoxville Journal*, both Republican papers, for the legislation's passage. "They can't dictate to this legislature," Woods said, with no sense of self-awareness.[444]

Burch took the loss better than the others. "I can take a licking as good as anybody else, and I'm still in good humor." He stood by his prediction of defeat in the senate, claiming only 12 or 14 senators would support it.[445] He knew he could count on Callaway and Cantrell to oppose it, and maybe more.

"I can't see why he wants to ruin things for someone else," Burch said of Governor Cooper. "I delivered more than 3,000 voters for him, to 46 for his opponent…I don't mind being called the boss of Polk County." Those who oppose him, he insisted, "just want to step into my shoes." Invoking the age-old "money for schools" argument, he defended buying poll taxes for people. "Is there anything wrong with that?"[446]

Burch attended a Democratic Party meeting in McMinn County in late January. "I have been accused of assisting McMinn County to become Democratic and also other counties of East Tennessee. I feel highly honored, and when we get through in Tennessee we will move down to Fannin County, Georgia, the only county in that state which went for Willkie in the presidential election." Monroe County Sheriff W.O. Brakebill also attended, boasting of major Democratic gains in his county.[447]

Burch sat at Callaway's desk as the senate voted on the poll tax repeal on February 1. Hamilton County Judge Wiley Couch attended in support of repeal, which passed by a vote of 22 to 10. The permanent registration bill also passed by a 19-13 vote. Callaway and Cantrell voted against both bills. "We will fight on in the courts," Burch said. Broughton told the press that those voting for repeal "will be sorry" for what they did. Governor Cooper was "delighted," calling it "the hardest legislative fight I have ever been through since I have been governor." Burch went to congratulate Cooper personally. Cooper and Beeler expected and even wanted a legal challenge to test the law's validity so the state would not waste time and money preparing a registration system only for it to later be ruled unconstitutional.[448] The *Chattanooga Times* celebrated the bills:

> "These new laws are two of the most far-reaching reforms in Tennessee election laws that have been made in many years. It comes nearer perhaps to ensuring universal suffrage to the people of Tennessee than any legislation that has been enacted by any general assembly in the history of the state."

Tennessee's poll tax appeared to be dead, but Burch would stop at nothing to revive it.

Chapter 24
"Skullduggery" in Bradley County and Copperhill

It was no secret that Burch and Cantrell were on a quest to take control of southeast Tennessee. Fearing a ripper bill, the Cleveland Chamber of Commerce and the Cleveland Lions Club passed resolutions asking their state legislators to oppose any legislation changing their city government "to the end that our town may continue to enjoy the blessings of good government administered with competence and integrity." Thanks to city commissioners "who have the general welfare of the city at heart and do not expect any personal gain," Cleveland was a model of fiscal responsibility and had exceptional schools and roads.[449]

In the first week of the 1943 legislative session, Broughton and Cantrell decided to go bigger than just Cleveland. They authored ripper bills handing control of Bradley County's government to the Democrats. One bill reduced the county's civil districts from four to two, giving the Democratic-leaning city of Cleveland more JPs than the much larger Republican-dominated rural areas. The five newly appointed JPs were all Democrats.[450] Another bill doubled the Democratic county judge Nat Eldridge's salary. They also introduced a bill to create a new county highway department and appoint Jess Rymer chairman of the highway commission. Rymer joined Burch to lobby for the bills.

Unlike with the ripper bills that were forced on McMinn County two years prior, there was no Robert Lindsay to oppose them this time. Cantrell enthusiastically sponsored the bills, while Broughton declined to comment. Bradley County had duly elected their ten-member county court, comprised of eight Republicans and two Democrats. The four county constables, all Republicans, were also getting kicked out of office. The bills moved quickly through the legislature, and Burch stood beside Cantrell as he finalized them.

The *Knoxville Journal* called the Bradley County ripper bills "outrageous," especially since neither Broughton nor Cantrell lived there. The *Journal* hoped the bills would "arouse" the electorate to demand constitutional reform and enact "home rule," removing the legislature's power over counties and municipalities. "Local governments will be returned to the people." The *Knoxville News-Sentinel* labeled the bills a "disgrace." The *Chattanooga Times* called the bills "offensive to Democrats and Republicans alike" and accused Burch of wanting to become a "sort of East Tennessee Crump" by branching out of Polk County. "It is a reprehensible piece of political skullduggery."

Governor Cooper delayed action on the bill that replaced the county court with Burch's hand-picked Democrats. Several prominent Cleveland residents, including attorney Charles Mayfield Sr., businessman George L. Hardwick, *Cleveland Daily Banner* editor Will Rodgers, H.L. Dethero, L.D. McDaris, and W.B. Parks, implored the governor to talk with them. Most of these men were Democrats. Mayfield claimed every Republican and three-fourths of Democrats in the county opposed the bills.[451] "I have got to have my program enacted by the legislature and in order to do that I must have the support of Cantrell and Biggs," the governor said. "I know it is vicious. I don't approve of it but I've got to sign it."[452]

Outraged Bradley Countians circulated flyers that read: "Bradley County government for Bradley County citizens by Bradley County voters."[453] Governor Cooper received nearly 150 telegrams from prominent Bradley County citizens, including ministers, doctors, businessmen, city commissioners C.L. Hardwick and Bethel Brown, Judge H.M. Fulbright, the American Legion Auxiliary, and the Business and Professional Women's Club.

Over 1,000 people attended a protest meeting on January 30, crowding inside the courthouse and out on the square. Most were rural citizens, and even some Democrats attended. *Cleveland Herald* editor Walter "Tino" Franklin led the meeting, urging his fellow citizens to "resist Biggs' dominance with everything you have, but in a peaceful way." The group formed a committee to challenge the bills in court, naming B.H. Fair, Jim Beaty, T.J. Marler, and Terrell Corn. They rousingly condemned Burch, Broughton, and Cantrell, and called the newly appointed JPs "quislings." One resolution called the new highway commission bill "a flagrant waste of public funds for no other purpose but to give a renegade Polk County politician a key to the treasury of Bradley County." Shouts of "Amen!" were frequent throughout the meeting, with many of the speakers comparing Burch to Hitler.[454] Another resolution called the bill increasing the county judge's salary "nothing short of legalized bribe."[455]

George L. Hardwick and Will Rodgers met with Governor Cooper and showed him several letters from prominent Bradley Countians, including Columbus Mee. Co-founder and president of the Cleveland Coca-Cola Bottling Company, Mee was the former chairman of the Bradley County Democratic Party. Under his leadership, the Democrats were historically competitive in Bradley, voting for Governor Cooper by remarkable margins.

Mee called the bills "the most vicious, unscrupulous legislation ever attempted in this county" and feared how it would hurt his party for decades to come. He also worried the bills "would end in possible violence." On the highway commission bill, he called Rymer "devoid of all honesty" and pleaded the governor not to give one man the power to handle all finances, make all purchases, do all the hiring and firing, and choose which roads would be included in the county's pike road system. "The taxpayers are revolting," Mee wrote, of the proposed road tax increases, especially during a time of war. Rymer's salary was set to be nearly double that of the current highway commissioner.[456]

Broughton represented Polk and Bradley Counties in the state legislature in the 1943 session, authoring legislation that weakened the machine's political opponents. - Tennessee State Library and Archives

Governor Cooper vetoed the highway commission bill. Broughton immediately called for an override vote, which passed by a 65-1 vote. Cantrell also led a successful override vote in the senate. The legislative session adjourned a few hours later. The *Knoxville Journal* wrote that the "vicious" ripper legislation demonstrated the long overdue need for "home rule," which could only happen with a constitutional convention, something that had not taken place in the state since 1870, before Burch was born.

George L. Hardwick led a group of Bradley County taxpayers, including W.T. Corn, W.E. Bacon, Perry Cecil, B.H. Fair, and T.J. Marler in obtaining an injunction from Chancellor J. Lon Foust in Chattanooga restraining Rymer and the new highway commissioners from taking office. It also claimed the new laws unconstitutionally increased the local road tax from .11 cents to .36 cents per $100 of assessed valuation. Nat Caldwell of the *Nashville Tennessean* cheered on the injunction, calling Rymer a "stooge" that Burch sent over to live in Bradley a few years earlier.

The group obtained the injunction the same week that state highway officials from all over the Southeast met in Chattanooga. The *Chattanooga Times* invited them to study "an experiment in the evil of political manipulation of highway departments which is close at hand." The *Times* hoped the fight over the Bradley County highway department would be a good lesson for the highway officials. "Political bosses very well know that control of highways means control of votes."[457]

On March 15, Chancellor Stewart ruled the Bradley County highway commission bill unconstitutional. The law violated a provision of the state constitution requiring all county officers to be elected by the people or the county court. Unfortunately for Bradley, the law changing the county court still stood, and they had the power to elect Rymer on their own. But before the new county court could meet, Cleveland attorneys Charles Mayfield Sr. and George Westerberg obtained an injunction from Chancellor Stewart enjoining the new court from "exercising the authority of their offices" and interfering with the court members elected by the people in August 1942.[458]

Chancellor Stewart later upheld the law changing the Bradley County Court. To the charge that the law aimed to replace duly-elected Republicans with appointed Democrats, Stewart wrote that "a court cannot inquire into the motives or conduct of the legislature in determining the validity of a statute." The state's archaic constitution did indeed give the legislature the power to, as Stewart wrote, "abolish civil districts in a county, and to create new districts, appoint justices of the peace to fill the same…" The defendants appealed the decision to the state supreme court.[459]

"Mr. Biggs apparently has the green light to continue his efforts to boss other counties in East Tennessee," the *Chattanooga Times* wrote. "Our state constitution is old fashioned and, in many ways, out of date." The argument for constitutional reform, particularly with respect to "home rule," was stronger than ever.

One month after the city's election, Broughton and Callaway authored a bill to change the government of Copperhill, a hotbed of anti-Biggs sentiment. The bill abolished the mayor and alderman form of government and replaced it with a mayor and three-man commission to be appointed for six-year terms. R.P. Taylor would remain as mayor, while only Granville Radcliffe and Leonard C. Goss would be retained as commissioners. Deputy Frank Clayton was appointed police commissioner. In true Biggs fashion, the new officials would receive generous salaries.[460] When asked what was wrong with the present Copperhill government, Callaway said, "Maybe they were not doing just right."[461]

"There is nothing for the taxpayers to be alarmed about in the bill," Mayor Taylor insisted. Cecil Kell, H.M. "Gid" Ware, and O.K. Lyle, later remembered by a Copperhill native as "upstanding citizens," would be removed from office under the proposed legislation. Its proponents justified it by emphasizing the consolidation of governmental departments.[462] The *Knoxville Journal*, while not encouraging violence, wrote that legislators who imposed such bills on constituents "richly deserves the ancient treatment of tar and feathers…This is the sort of legislation which makes a mockery of democratic government and an empty thing of the objectives for which we are sending millions of men across the high seas to fight."

These ripper bills met with immediate backlash. A group of women voters organized a mass meeting at the YMCA on the same day the bill passed in the house. Burch must be stopped, the *Chattanooga Times* warned, "before

Copperhill, on the northside of the river, was an anti-Biggs stronghold. A large majority of citizens protested the ripper bill that removed most of their duly-elected city government. - Cleveland-Bradley County Public Library History Branch and Archives, Ridley Wills Collection

he comes into Hamilton County and begins giving orders here." In response to the protests, Broughton and Callaway delayed action on the bill. They amended it to reduce the commissioners' salaries and removed the property tax increases. Governor Cooper signed the bill into law on January 27. The *Chattanooga Times* predicted Burch's ripper bills would lead to his political downfall.

> "In Tennessee many before Mr. Biggs have arisen to imagine that they could have become another Ed Crump in their own particular neck of the woods. They fail, utterly, to sense the real reason for Ed Crump's power…His strength lies chiefly in the fact that the people of Shelby County, en masse, think that he has done more for that county than any man of his time has done."

The new Copperhill city commissioners met in February and voted to audit the city's books. They alleged that the city's delinquent taxpayers owed the city $20,000. "We may be able to reduce the tax rate instead of increasing it," said one commissioner.[463] Copperhill citizens were now living under a municipal government they did not consent to govern them.

Chapter 25

A Landmark U.S. Supreme Court Decision

In January 1943, a group of McMinn County election workers, handpicked by the Cantrell machine, were convicted in federal court of acting "under color of law" of depriving certain citizens of the right to vote in 1940. They closed the Claxton precinct, not far from Polk County, at 10:00 AM after a fight broke out. They took the ballot box for "safekeeping." Judge Leslie Darr fined them one penny each.[464] The *Chattanooga Times* wrote that the slap on the wrist contributed to "the Napoleonic Complex developed by Sheriff Biggs of Polk County."

Congressman Jennings assailed Judge Darr's "miscarriage of justice" on the floor of Congress. He accused Burch of abolishing free elections in multiple southeast Tennessee counties "with his own particular brand of Hitlerism." Criticizing Congressman Kefauver for attending Burch's barbecue in 1942, Jennings asked, "On what beef did our friend feed at the Burch Biggs Barbecue that the bowels of compassion are so moved that he must rush into print in defense of the election frauds perpetrated by Biggs and his satellites?" Kefauver responded that he did not know the "particulars" of the McMinn election fraud case, but praised Darr's "integrity."[465]

More than two years had passed since Mitchell Anderson and seven other strikers were convicted for the dynamiting of federal power lines. Needing all the help they could get in the appeals process, they sent sworn statements to the National Committee for People's Rights in New York City. Local law enforcement and FBI agents, they alleged, used several "third-degree methods," including "drugging of witnesses, kidnaping of persons charged with a crime after long detention, holding of persons incommunicado, refusal to permit prisoners to see relatives or attorneys, and failure to notify families that men were held or where they were held."[466]

In a decision written by Associate Justice Felix Frankfurter on March 1, 1943, their convictions were overturned in the U.S. Supreme Court. "There was a working arrangement between federal officers and the sheriff of Polk County which made possible abuses revealed by this record." The landmark decision held that "incriminating statements obtained involuntarily cannot be made basis of convictions in federal courts." Frankfurter condemned the "unlawful detention" of the defendants in a "hostile atmosphere."[467]

Strong evidence pointed to the defendants' guilt. But thanks to the abuses of power by the Polk County Sheriff's Department and several FBI agents, they were free to go. The *Chattanooga Times* praised the decision for hitting at "one of the most prevalent abuses of civil liberties in the South" and criticized "petty political machines" that set themselves up as a "sort of inquisition" that violate legal rights.

The Tennessee Supreme Court upheld Bill Hedden's conviction, sending him to die in the electric chair. "Maintaining his innocence to the last," he was executed on March 30, 1943, aged 44. The evening before, he said that Julius Goforth's "lies" put him in prison. "I have no fear of death. I am ready to go if it is the Lord's will. I have nothing to say." The last letter he ever wrote was to his mother, Mary Hedden.[468]

Chapter 26
Bradley County Fights Back

Maude Brock answered the door on the evening of June 5, 1943 to find about 50 men standing outside. Her husband, Bradley County JP Lon Brock, was asleep. "We intend you no harm. Do not be alarmed." They handed her a typewritten, unsigned note for her husband.[469] Part of the note read:

> "The citizens have met in mass meeting and have protested the action of a few to have Bradley County redistricted and appoint new justices of the peace…Why should we citizens of this county that have brothers and sons fighting on the four corners of the world for freedom allow a dictator to come into our own county?...But as a final request, we are asking you to resign to the county judge and the local paper as justice of the peace or we will take it as acknowledged that you are openly a henchman or tool of Burch Biggs and will be dealt with as such…Remember that this request expires on June 8, 1943."[470]

Making no attempt to disguise themselves, the group also personally delivered letters to JPs John Million, who was not home, and Afton Mackey, who answered the door at his Walker Valley home. Brock steadfastly refused to resign. "I'm too old to be driven." Mackey claimed only a petition from a majority of the voters would make him resign. Million could not be reached for comment.[471]

By June 8, no action had been taken against them. A spokesperson for the JPs said a grand jury might investigate the threats, citing a state law classifying such "threats and intimidation" as a misdemeanor punishable by a fine up to $100 and a year imprisonment.[472] The ousted JPs appealed Chancellor Stewart's decision upholding the ripper bill. But the state supreme court could not hear the appeal until after the poll tax repeal case.

The new Bradley County Court was set to meet on July 5 to vote on the tax rate, school budget, and road commission. Over two dozen men confronted Mackey and Million in the courthouse. "You might as well leave, for we are not going to let you meet," one of them said. "If that is the way you feel about it, I'll leave," Mackey replied. "There goes your buddy now," one of them said before Mackey turned around to see Million walking toward the exit, followed by several men. With two more JPs absent due to illness, the court had no quorum and did not meet. A few nearby deputies did not arrive on the scene until after everyone left. Mackey and Million later said they did not feel threatened and refused to identify anyone in the group.[473]

The next day, Brock and Million announced their resignations. "On account of apparent opposition, we have decided to resign our offices as justices of the peace of Bradley County, to which we were appointed by the Tennessee state assembly."[474] Mackey, elected by the people, still refused to resign. The *Chattanooga Times* did not endorse the group's method of addressing the situation, but wrote that there was "nothing democratic in having the Tennessee state assembly appoint members of the Bradley County Court." The *Nashville Tennessean* wrote that "reports from Bradley indicate that the people are very serious about the matter of Biggs kicking out duly elected officials and putting in men of his choice." The citizens of Bradley had successfully fought back against Burch, who had no power to use the Bradley County Sheriff's Department to intimidate or retaliate against those who stood up to him. Bosses can only do so much without the gun.

Chapter 27
Shorty Richards Gets a "Raw Deal"

Recently discharged from the U.S. Navy to help his father on the farm, twenty-year-old Everett "Shorty" Richards liked to drink, probably a little too much. He had been arrested several times for drunkenness and once for breaking and entering and theft, but it was never proven. Everybody seemed to like him. "He's a pretty good boy. He works hard on the farm. He's good natured and not apt to start trouble with anybody," one citizen said.[475]

On May 22, 1943, he only drank three cans of beer. "I can drink nine or ten bottles of beer and not be drunk," he once said. "I'm going home," Shorty told the waitress as Deputies Flavis Bates and Ben Smith looked on. He walked down to Buck Arp's filling station. After circling the block, the deputies drove up behind him. "You 'aint running off on a pony like you did before," Bates said, grabbing Shorty's belt. "I don't guess I'll get away this time," Shorty replied. "Do you think I'm drunk?" Smith smiled and said nothing. They searched him before throwing him in the car, finding only a pocket knife. They drove him to the jail. "Bring the keys down," one of the deputies shouted. Bates exited the car, keeping one hand on the car door while opening the jail's screen door. Seeing an opportunity to make a run for it, the buzzed yet unarmed Shorty bolted towards the creek.[476]

"Halt!" Bates shouted. A few seconds later, a bullet whizzed by Shorty's head. He jumped into the creek, only to fall on a rock and break his leg. But that did not stop him from getting back on his feet and hobbling down the creek. Bates chased after Shorty, who crawled through a hole in a barbed wire fence. Another shot rang out.

Burch was sitting on his front porch visiting with Bertie Watson when he heard shots. Thinking a prisoner might be on the loose, he shouted, "Stop him at the bridge!" The Old Sheriff hopped in his car and drove to the south side of the bridge over Four Mile Creek on Highway 411. There were several witnesses near the bridge, including Frank Lillard, August Lewis, Mrs. Parnick McClary, Stella McClary, Mrs. Ethie Harrison, and Mrs. Joe Lewis.[477]

Shorty stumbled his way under the bridge. "Shorty, they are going to kill you if you don't stop!" a voice cried out. State Highway Patrolman Woodrow

Reece parked his car on the north side of the bridge. Mrs. Parnick McClary and her daughter-in-law, Stella, were in a car on the bridge. Reece exited his car and looked down in Shorty's direction. Burch was also on the bridge, and Bates and Smith came over soon after. Multiple shots were fired in Shorty's direction, about thirty feet east of the bridge. One of the bullets hit the creek, splashing water on Shorty. Another bullet struck him in the stomach. Still standing, he took a bullet to the arm, which knocked him off his feet.[478]

Shorty Richards ran from the jail, formerly located behind the fire hall on the right edge of this photo. Burch's house is in the center of the photo facing Main Street. - Author's photo

After he fled from custody, a deputy shot at Shorty, with the bullet whizzing past his head and causing him to jump off this bridge into Four Mile Creek. The old Haskins House, facing Town Creek Road, is visible on the right side of this photo. The jail was located to the left of where this photo was taken. - Author's photo

Having heard the commotion nearby, Broughton ran over to the bridge and saw a badly wounded Shorty laying on the bank. He ran down to help carry Shorty to Reece's patrol car. After discussing "what to do with him" for a few minutes, Reece and Bates drove him to the hospital in Cleveland. They took the scenic route along the back roads, and did little to help Shorty, telling him to press and hold his fingers on his wounds. "I thought each minute was the last," Shorty later said of his ride to the hospital. They rode past a doctor's office in Ocoee.[479]

The *Knoxville News-Sentinel* spoke with Shorty a couple of weeks later. He admitted he had been arrested for drunkenness before, but was not drunk this time. He told the reporter that Smith and Bates shot him. The reporter could not find Bates, and Patrolman Reece was allegedly on vacation.

"I don't know a thing about it," Smith insisted. "I was there, but I don't know who shot him." Smith claimed all of his information came from Burch. The reporter shared Shorty's version of the story. "None of it is right. He doesn't know who shot him," Smith said, smiling.[480]

The reporter visited Burch's house on Main Street, "probably the finest dwelling in Benton." Broughton answered the door. "My father is out of town. Gone over to Nashville to hear arguments in the poll tax case." He claimed there was no official report or statement about the shooting. "Do you know who did the shooting?" the reporter inquired. Broughton answered negatively, and said that Shorty would probably be prosecuted for drunkenness, a misdemeanor.[481]

Several witnesses saw what happened to Shorty, but were cautious when talking to the reporter. "Politics here is too thick to stir with a stick," one man said. Mrs. Joe Lewis, a relative of Deputy Bates, praised Burch before describing what she witnessed. "He's my friend and I voted for him. I've got nothing against Sheriff Biggs." She said she saw both deputies shoot at Shorty. "God holds me to the truth and this is the truth." She also saw Broughton help Shorty. "I couldn't sleep all night after it…It was a low-down, cowardly, dirty trick." Frank Lillard said that Shorty had been drinking but was not drunk. He said he saw Smith shoot at Shorty, followed shortly afterwards by Bates and Reece. "It would be hard to say just who hit him." Another bystander claimed that Shorty "wasn't drunk at all."[482] Burch would eventually hear from Shorty again.

Chapter 28

THE OCOEE SPEED TRAP

Knoxville resident E.M. Sims was driving the speed limit when he was pulled over by a Polk County deputy in Ocoee. The deputy accused him of driving 50 MPH in a 35 MPH zone. "You can plead guilty and pay a minimum fine or go to jail and make cash bond," a nearby JP told him. Sims had no choice but to plead guilty, and was fined $9. They refused to give him a receipt, telling him it would be available at the courthouse. Sims worried that the speed trap would hurt tourism in Tennessee. "A local condition of this kind fosters more ill will than anything I know of."[483]

Sims was the latest victim of what had become the notorious Ocoee speed trap. Having popped up in early 1943, several out-of-towners passing through on Highway 411 fell victim to this racket. Most drivers were not even speeding. Burch's deputies accused them of going "60 or 65 MPH." The *Knoxville Journal* received several letters reporting on the speed trap, including one from G.A. Sengebusch, a truck driver from Jefferson County. On a haul from Michigan to Florida, he and his driver Curley Spiker were pulled over and charged with speeding despite only going "about 30 MPH." Sengebusch protested the charges, resulting in the deputies upping the charges to reckless driving. The deputies were "reluctant" to tell him their names, but learned that one of them was Deputy Ben Smith.[484] A Maryville man claimed he was "enticed" into speeding by a slow car that sped up just above the speed limit as he was passing it. It turned out that the driver was a deputy.[485]

Burch downplayed the entire thing in his first statement on the controversy: "I have told my men to give drivers benefit of the doubt and not arrest anyone driving under 45 MPH, although the law sets the limit at 35 MPH."[486] JPs W.A. Kerr, J.J. Taylor, or M.B. Wimberly were always ready to hold a "roadside court" and fine those accused of speeding. "Why sometimes the squire will drive to the scene and save the drivers the extra fee," Burch said, trying to play it off as accommodating. But the JPs were always nearby ready to help the deputies shake down innocent travelers.[487]

On a business trip from Marietta, Georgia to Knoxville, M.L. McNeel Jr. was pulled over by deputies and fined $9 by JP W.A. Kerr. On his return trip the next day, McNeel was following a school bus. But that did not stop a deputy from pulling him over. "I was following a school bus," McNeel said. "We'll see about that," the deputy replied. Upon his arrival back home, he had two receipts totaling $18 in fines paid. He also had a card proving his perfect driving record from the Georgia Highway Patrol. In a letter to Governor Cooper, he signed it "a disappointed visitor."488

Governor Cooper received another letter, this time from three imprisoned salesmen, two from Chattanooga and one from Knoxville. They had pled not guilty to speeding while driving through Ocoee, so the JP upped the charge to reckless driving. Their refusal to pay a $15 fine (much higher than the customary $9) landed them behind bars.

Letters were pouring into Governor Cooper's office from all over the Southeast complaining about the Ocoee speed trap. The *Knoxville Journal* wrote that only a phone call from the governor could put a stop to the "banditry being practiced on our state highway." Complaints should have been sent to District Attorney Beecher Witt, but most everyone knew such efforts would have been futile.

An Etowah railroader passing through Ocoee was also refused a receipt after he paid a fine for doing absolutely nothing wrong. Unlike Sims, he at least received an explanation. "People show them [the receipts] around and get us unfavorable publicity," the JP said.489

Governor Cooper must have done something, because complaints were soon few and far between, until summer at least. On July 9, three drivers for the Hargis Lumber Company passed through Ocoee in their "heavily loaded" trucks on the way back from Georgia. A poultry truck with Polk County tags was riding between two of the lumber trucks, and none of the vehicles exceeded 30 MPH. A Polk County deputy and a state highway patrolman pulled the lumber trucks over for supposedly going 60 MPH. The drivers were fined $10.50, an increase from the usual excessive fine. Only one of the drivers could pay, so the deputy took the driver's license from the other two, who had to get a ride the next day to pay their fines. According to Hargis, this was not the first time one of his trucks had been stopped in Ocoee. Bradley County deputies said the same about several other Bradley Countians.490

"This Polk County speed trap is becoming notorious," wrote the *Chattanooga Times*. "The bootleggers and the deputies worked together to get people arrested," Patsy Crox Underhill remembered. "Out-of-towners would be arrested going through town for speeding and all. It was a mess."491

Chapter 29

A Summer in The Spotlight

Burch was all over the news in 1943. Between the ripper bills, the Ocoee speed trap, the shooting of Shorty Richards, and the poll tax repeal litigation, reporters were eager to sit down with the Old Sheriff. Louis Hofferbert of the *Knoxville News-Sentinel* and R.H. Fitzgerald Jr. of the *Chattanooga Times* conducted separate interviews with Burch in Benton.[492] Burch said he did not need to whitewash anything and that he wanted the "facts" to be known. "If Burch Biggs has committed any of the political misdemeanors charged by his critics, they weigh little on his conscience."

"The Biggs organization gets credit for everything — good or bad — that happens in Polk County, often being blamed as a machine for acts of individual members or acts of persons not directly linked to it," one reporter wrote. Burch admitted he had a machine and that his word was "law," but said he preferred to call it an organization, and referred to it as "our" rather than "my" organization. "I'm a machine man," Burch said. "Any kind of business needs a head. Here in Polk County, we have made a business of politics." He defended his lieutenants as "good, clean men" who do their duty. "I have always insisted on honesty." If a young man in the organization showed promise, Burch chose him for advancement and planned his career out for him "years ahead." One reporter noted that the Republicans have lost hope that they can beat the machine.

Now that Burch had admitted to having a machine, the conversation inevitably turned to Boss Crump. "I'm proud to be part of the Crump organization," Burch said. "I know they call Ed Crump a dictator, and maybe he is, but of my own knowledge I know that he has given Memphis and Shelby County good, clean government. That is what I am doing here." But the Old Sheriff made it clear that Crump "does not dictate to us." The two of them, he said, "see things alike."

Burch recalled first meeting Crump during the 1915 legislative session when he secured passage of his first ripper bill. One reporter pressed Burch a little on the recent ripper bills, writing that he "ran roughshod over democratic principles of government." But the reporter also believed that Burch spearheaded ripper bills in neighboring counties "not to increase his own power," but rather out of "friendship for certain of his lieutenants." Despite the fact that his son authored the Bradley County ripper bill and that he was sergeant-at-arms when the Senate passed the McMinn County ripper bill, Burch denied having any "direct designs" over any other county. He claimed to have known nothing about the Bradley County ripper bill. "I just wanted to see those counties Democratic, so I made them Democratic."

It was all just a game to Burch, and the object of the game was to accumulate more and more power for himself and his team. But the reporters, either naïve or dishonest, failed to see the contradictions in their apologia for Burch. "There is no evidence that Sheriff Biggs has attempted to dictate appointment of any local officials in either Bradley or McMinn." If this was true, and Burch had nothing to do with Paul Cantrell or Jess Rymer gaining power from the ripper bills, then how were the bills passed "out of friendship for certain of his lieutenants?"

When Burch returned to power in 1930, the election may or may not have been legitimate. Ripper bills undeniably helped him and his lieutenants increase their power. How he maintained his power, however, was a matter of dispute. "The Republicans charged him with fee-grabbing, stealing elections, voter intimidation, counting ballots behind closed doors, and running his opposition 'out of town,'" one reporter wrote. He called these accusations "sweeping generalities with few specific instances to support them." This reporter must not have read the well-documented and credible reports of election fraud in several previous elections, especially the 1936 election, for which extensive court transcripts were taken and reported on in all major state newspapers. He wrote that it was "plainly not true" that Burch had stolen elections. "Deputies work the polls to prevent disturbances," Burch said, laughing off the accusations. "Voter intimidation is not necessary."

Aside from its blatantly racist origins, the poll tax benefited bosses like Crump, Burch, and Cantrell. Burch said he "sees to it" that all Democrats are qualified to vote and unequivocally admitted to paying poll taxes for Democrats who could not pay their own. "I'm not interested in whether or not the poll tax is good or bad," he said. "Repeal would weaken the Democratic Party." "We don't steal elections. We don't have to," Burch insisted. He claimed that over 4,400 Democrats paid their poll tax in 1942 compared to just 63 Republicans. "These Polk County voters are not for sale. It does take organization work to get them out, especially in the mountains…It's the organization's job to get them to the polls. We get them there."

Burch asked why he and county judge Vance Davis were the only Democrats to win in the 1930 election. "It would have been as easy to steal all the offices as two of them." But he was not being truthful. Circuit court clerk George Gilliland and register of deeds Porter Campbell, both Democrats, also won in 1930. So did multiple JPs. He also omitted the fact that his organization did not control the election commission or the sheriff's department that year. Most importantly, the controversy in the 1930 election was over the Conasauga precinct, where every Democrat on the ticket won in an anomalous landslide.

In this instance, with great power came great wealth. The reporters could not avoid broaching the subject of Burch's increased wealth. Burch's opponents insisted he was "down and out" before the 1930 election, while his loyal defenders pointed to his family farm as the source of his financial success. Depending on who you asked, his net worth was estimated to be between $200,000 and $1,000,000.

Success on the farm, according to Burch's most ardent supporters, enabled him to feed several poor families during the darkest days of the depression. This generosity, they claim, explained his party's 98 percent vote share in recent elections. It is true that the Old Sheriff gave beef to many families in need from time to time. David Talley remembered the Biggs family as "benevolent people."[493] John B. Townsend publicly praised Burch for helping feed the needy.[494] But if Burch was feeding enough families to guarantee thousands of votes, how was his farm profitable, especially during an economic downturn and wartime rationing? Accusations of other illicit revenue streams were not unfounded.

The reporters each enjoyed a tour of Burch's beloved farm on Highway 411, where ten tenant farmers lived. Burch discussed his grandfather, pioneer settler William Biggs, who once lived on that very farm. Burch and Broughton's combined farmland, comprising more than 1,000 acres, was managed by Burch's nephew Charlie. "They've never been out of the family since we first owned them," he claimed. "We've always been here." But Burch was not being completely truthful. Only a small portion of the farmland he owned was inherited. Much of it was purchased from family members and others. In fact, one of these purchases was for 106 acres, and led to drawn out litigation with his cousin, Lillie Biggs.[495] His opponents were skeptical of how he managed to afford so much land on his income, especially with no mortgage.

On the subject of "fee-grabbing," one reporter wrote that "fee-grabbing" was more prevalent in neighboring counties, making no comment on Polk County and if it was wrong. It is unfortunate that he did not interview the many victims of fee-grabbing over the years. Ralph Painter remembered the "fee-grabbing" being much worse than reported. Painter was once arrested by a fee-grabbing deputy and fined by JP J.J. Taylor. He wrote "fee-grabbing" on the check. Taylor refused to accept it.[496]

According to Earl Oliver, if a sober person objected to being arrested, the deputy would say, "The judge won't know you weren't drunk in the morning." They were sometimes fined as much as $20. "Biggs would arrest you for just about anything," Oliver claimed. "They arrested you for no reason," Henry Watson alleged. "They harassed and arrested people all over the county." Wesley Lowery and his father-in-law were unjustly arrested by Constable Ernest McGee for drunkenness after parking their car at their auto body shop.[497]

In their interviews, the reporters gleaned more details of Burch's personal side and worldview. "A study of Burch Biggs would be incomplete without a reference to the simplicity and uprightness of his private life." The Old Sheriff's friends relayed stories of "kindness and generosity." His critics, however, who included John M. Lillard and his son, Frank, Henry Crox, Charlie Bates, and Buck Arp, were dubbed as "scattered, vocal, and impotent" opposition. "These men and many others bitterly assail the sheriff for his political activities, but none questions his courage or personal conduct," one reporter wrote. Burch claimed to hold "no malice" toward his political enemies.

Burch looked back on his comeback in the 1930 election with great pride: "They tried every way they knew to beat me out. They said I stole the election. They got out an injunction to keep the election commission from certifying me as the winner. I beat them on that. Then they got out an injunction to keep me from taking the oath of office, and I beat them on that." He shared perhaps his most candid quote of all: "I realized then that in politics your enemies will do anything to beat you. I knew the only way to win was to be so strong that there could never be any question. And this is what I have done."

With no "strong black cigar" in his mouth or "gold watch dangling across his heavy paunch," Burch did not meet the "standard look" of a political boss. One reporter described him as looking and acting like what he was: a successful farmer. "He has a shock of iron gray hair and blue-gray eyes that twinkle behind a pair of steel-rimmed spectacles…He has a ready smile and a deep bellow of a laugh." A "model of virtue," one reporter learned that Burch did not drink or swear and had quit smoking tobacco several decades ago.

Burch was happy to discuss family, even beyond the family business. "I'm just holding the office until young Burch gets back from the Army," he said. As Burch sat on his front porch with one reporter, his six-year-old grandson, Tom, rode up on his pony. The "apple of the sheriff's eye" had been deputized by his grandfather on the day he was born. "He's a Biggs," Burch said proudly.

Burch poses for a photo with one of his whiteface cattle on his Hiwassee River farm. - Chattanooga Times-Free Press

"He wants to be sheriff when he grows up." "Maybe you will see him sworn in one day," commented the reporter. "No," the Old Sheriff replied, "that would not be in the nature of things."

Around the time Burch was first elected sheriff, his mother Attie Kimbrough Biggs planted a pecan tree on the family farm. Burch loved showing the tree to visitors. He and Congressman Sam McReynolds used to sit under the tree. "We did a lot of planning here." Also on the farm were 225 head of whiteface cattle. "I don't raise show cattle...I breed for the market," Burch noted. He reluctantly agreed to pose for a photo beside a bull. "You can put that picture in the paper if you want to, but I know the first thing my political enemies will say. They'll want to know which one is the bull."

Before entering Burch's "spacious and handsomely furnished" living room, a reporter spotted a signed photo of the late Congressman McReynolds hanging "in a place of honor." Burch loved to tell the story of how McReynolds once visited London to dine with the king and queen at Buckingham Palace and then came to have lunch at the jail in Benton a week later. Also on the wall was a photo of Congressman Estes Kefauver. "He's sort of a nephew of mine," Burch said proudly.

The reporters praised Burch's "lack of aspiration for higher office," noting that he had once turned down the job of state prison warden. "He would rather kick off his shoes, lean back in his easy chair on his own front porch, and have his 'subjects' come to him for judgment." He reflected on the murder of his father and said the deadly raid on Garret Hedden's still was possibly the only time he had ever taken a man's life. "He looks back on his career without regret and faces the future with a serene mind."

Chapter 30

BIGGS VS. BEELER

"It will be a good, big lawsuit before it's over," Burch said referring to the poll tax repeal litigation. Judging by his previous track record in court, there was little reason to doubt him. State attorney general Roy Beeler said he would "vigorously" defend the repeal.[498] The *Nashville Tennessean* wrote that the poll tax would harm Burch's "ruthless little political machine" and that a "controlled vote" is his stock in trade.

Hoyt Lillard and Deputy Herman Wright joined Burch in filing suit. Due to their positions as election commissioners, Burch and Lillard were listed in the suit as plaintiffs and defendants. Burch argued that the repeal "attempts to deprive the public, the schools, and the school children of the state of many thousands of dollars," and that enforcement of the acts would require a burdensome tax increase. But the primary argument was that repeal violated Article 2, Section 28 of the state constitution requiring "all male citizens of this state over the age of 21 years…shall be liable to a poll tax of not less than .50 cents nor more than one dollar per anum."[499]

Chancellor Stewart granted Burch an injunction restraining Vance Davis and Bob McClary from spending any county funds to register voters under the new law. Burch's attorney contended that the permanent registration bill created a new county office to handle the records, something for which the state constitution did not provide. Republican election commissioner Henry Crox filed an answer to Burch's suit, claiming the provisions in the state constitution requiring the payment of a poll tax as a prerequisite to voting "are in direct conflict, in letter and in spirit, with the Constitution of the United States."[500]

Broughton was soon appointed to replace his father on the election commission, making Burch just a plaintiff in the suit. Hoyt Lillard and Henry Crox were reappointed. The state filed an answer to Burch's suit, declaring the repeal did not violate the state constitution because the provisions requiring a poll tax were not "self-executing." The legislature, according to their answer, had to pass legislation to activate the power to levy a poll tax.[501] Beeler emphasized a clause in the state constitution "as the legislature shall prescribe," while Burch's attorneys pointed to the clause "shall be liable to a poll tax..."[502]

Burch still made no attempt to conceal his motive. "The Democrats who supported this legislation are cutting their own throats. It will only serve to bring hordes of white Republican voters to the polls in East Tennessee and colored Republicans in Middle and West Tennessee."[503] Joe Hatcher of the *Nashville Tennessean* wrote of the "strange resemblance" between election returns in Polk and Shelby Counties, calling them "too one-sided to create the belief that a free-born, free-spoken, people agree so unanimously on any subject."

Chancellor Stewart presided over the demurrer hearing in Benton. Beeler's assistants, William F. Barry and Harry Phillips, made the principal arguments for the state. Charles Guinn represented Henry Crox. Judge R.A. Davis of Athens led Burch's team of attorneys, including Reuel Webb and county attorney Harry Schaffer. Cantrell, Woods, and Mansfield attended the hearing.

Barry cited a state supreme court decision, *Trammel vs. Griffin*, that ruled the legislature "may prescribe" qualifications to the right of suffrage, contending that the entire question of a poll tax was at the legislature's discretion. He surveyed the history of the state poll tax since 1870, including an 1873 law repealing the poll tax that stayed on the books until it was reinstated in the 1890s. Charles Guinn argued that the Fourteenth Amendment to the U.S. Constitution trumped the poll tax provision in the state constitution by "abridging" the right of suffrage granted to every citizen.[504]

"There is no higher law than the constitution," Davis said of Tennessee's governing document. He also cited previous state supreme court decisions, including *Tennessee vs. Old*. "It is not only, therefore, within the power of the legislature, but it was the duty of that body, to pass some such law as would define evidence...of the payment of a poll tax." Webb asserted that the registration law was discriminatory by proscribing a different means of registration for absentee voters and election day voters.[505] At the court's noon recess, Burch hosted a "feast of Tennessee delicacies" at the jail for Chancellor Stewart, the attorneys, and reporters.[506]

In a memorandum opinion, Chancellor Stewart ruled the poll tax repeal and permanent voter registration bills unconstitutional. Upon hearing the news, an elated Burch went to the clerk and master's office to read the decision. It turned out that Stewart "made his own investigation" rather than relying on the arguments in court. In a 20-page opinion, he found that the state constitution gave no authority to the legislature to "add to, change, or detract from liability for poll tax." Burch's attorneys successfully argued that the legislature had a "duty" to levy a poll tax. According to Stewart, the word "shall" in three sections of the state constitution imposed the duty. The argument for the common school fund, funded for years by the poll tax, also factored into Stewart's decision. Finally, Stewart agreed with the argument that the permanent voter registration bill granted a "special privilege" to absentee voters, including soldiers.[507]

Beeler appealed Stewart's decision to the state supreme court, filing a brief that contended payment of a poll tax is not mandatory "if there is no legislation requiring it."[508] The Tennessee Supreme Court heard the case of *Biggs vs. Beeler* on June 3, 1943. Barry argued that, since the poll tax was imposed by legislation in 1890, it could also be repealed by legislation. "No tax liability is placed upon citizens of Tennessee except when supported by appropriate legislation." Davis invoked the original intent argument: "The intention of the fathers of the (1870) constitution was to place an obligation on the voter to pay a poll tax." If the legislature was given the power to repeal the poll tax, Davis asserted, then they would have "the right to abolish all revenues."[509]

Referring to active-duty military outside the state, Davis claimed the permanent voter registration law exempted at least 40 percent of voters, creating a "special class of voters" that registered differently than civilians. Barry countered this argument, insisting that "those fighting should be permitted to vote for the democratic principles of democracy for which they are fighting."[510] Chattanooga attorney Carlyle Littleton joined the lawsuit to assist Guinn in representing Henry Crox. "I have made plans to take this case to the United States Supreme Court if it should be possible." He argued that the poll tax's purpose was "to disenfranchise the Negro" and that the state supreme court over the years avoided that issue by holding the poll tax as a "tax measure."[511]

On Saturday July 3, 1943, the weekend Tennesseans celebrated their country's independence from Great Britain, the state supreme court ruled the poll tax repeal bill unconstitutional. In a 3-2 decision, the court upheld Chancellor Stewart's ruling. Associate Justices Chambliss, Prewitt, and Gailor comprised the majority, while Associate Justice A.B. Neil and Chief Justice Grafton Green dissented.[512]

As to the question of the state constitution making the poll tax mandatory, all five justices agreed. But they disagreed on the legislature's obligation to pass laws enacting its power to repeal previous legislation enforcing a constitutional mandate. There was no precedent for such a case. The *Knoxville News-Sentinel* reported that Justices Prewitt and Gailor were "politicians" before being nominated to the court, and that Gailor was a "Crump henchman." He cast the deciding vote against repeal, indicating Boss Crump never wanted the poll tax repeal to stick. Green and Neil claimed the poll tax mandate was not "self-executing."[513] Green reasoned that one legislature cannot bind future legislatures. "If a constitutional provision requires the support of a statute in order to operate, it cannot function when that support is withdrawn — when the statute is repealed."[514]

The *Chattanooga Times* called it "one of the most significant victories of Biggs' career — it was a statewide fight and he emerges as a figure of statewide importance." Burch was "tickled to death" to get the news. "That is the way I thought it would be decided." He praised his attorney R.A. Davis as "the best constitutional lawyer in Tennessee."[515] Charles Guinn and Carlyle Littleton considered an appeal to the U.S. Supreme Court. But everyone knew the only way to permanently remove the state poll tax would be through a state constitutional amendment, something that had not happened in over 70 years. But until then, bosses like Burch continued using the poll tax to control and manipulate votes to maintain their power.

Chapter 31

Jennings Must Go

Governor Cooper was term-limited in 1944. George Woods wrote to state Democratic leaders suggesting that Paul Cantrell was "the proper man for the job." But most believed that Cantrell stood little chance against Chattanoogans James B. Frazier Jr. and Judge Wiley Couch. Knoxville Democrats showed no enthusiasm for Cantrell.

A federal grand jury indicted Etowah Police Chief Will Rucker, a close associate of the Cantrell machine, for violating election laws in the 1942 election. U.S. attorney James B. Frazier Jr. made it clear he was not involved in the indictments. Prosecuting election thieves would not earn endorsements from Burch and Boss Crump. A good friend of the late Gov. James B. Frazier Sr., Burch told Frazier he would support him if Boss Crump endorsed him.

In April, Boss Crump and Senator McKellar endorsed Congressman Jim McCord of the Fifth Congressional District. "I am standing by my guns — I'm for Jim McCord," Burch said. "He will be accorded the usual Democratic majority in Polk County."[516] He claimed that Democratic leaders in McMinn and Monroe Counties would also support him. Burch introduced McCord at the Democrats' Jefferson Day dinner at the Hermitage Hotel in Nashville.

After Broughton's one term in the state house, Burch was ready for his son to advance. His associates said it was his turn to be on the "receiving" end rather than the "giving" end in the sixth senatorial district.[517] Burch arranged for Republican State Rep. J.C.F. Herrell of Knox and Loudon Counties to step aside for Hugh Callaway. Broughton was to replace Callaway in the state senate. The *Knoxville Journal* even showed some sympathy for Callaway, who was being demoted after years of loyalty to Burch. The *Journal* feared the prospect of Broughton in the state senate making deals with local Republicans and the city administration to pass ripper bills in Knox County. Even Louis Hofferbert of the *Knoxville News-Sentinel* wrote that it was "well known" that Burch wished to "take a swing at Knox County."

Boss Crump was at the peak of his power in 1944. Charles Van Devander, Washington correspondent for the *New York Post*, was not a fan. In his new book, *The Big Bosses*, Van Devander chronicled political bosses from all over the country, including the Long dynasty in Louisiana and the Pendergast machine in St. Louis. Designating Tennessee as the nation's "most bossed state," he devoted extra attention to Boss Crump, Paul Cantrell, W.O. Brakebill, and Burch Biggs. He drew a distinction between the machines in Shelby and Polk Counties, giving Crump backhanded praise for his "highly efficient police force" and low taxes.[518] Burch's machine could claim neither. Van Devander saved his most scathing criticism for Burch:

> Sheriff Burch Biggs, the Democratic boss of a sizeable section of rural East Tennessee, is a bluff, hearty, loudmouthed, rough-and-tumble country man whose distinguishing accoutrements are a ten-gallon hat and free-swinging revolver…In what is normally a peaceful civilized community of farms and small towns, Sheriff Biggs rules principally by means of terrorism and intimidation, backed by the pistol and the blackjack.[519]

Van Devander did not mince words. He recounted how Burch's "army of strikebreakers created a reign of terror in Polk County."[520] The recent convictions of Cantrell's election workers in McMinn County and Brakebill's resignation in Monroe County convinced Van Devander that Burch's lopsided election returns were illegitimate. Unlike certain sycophantic reporters in Tennessee, Van Devander did his homework, utilizing court records of the election fraud trials, the striker's convictions, as well as interviews with reporters and politicians from East Tennessee.

Burch's defenders feigned indignation at the article's "exaggerations." B.L. Taylor, a veteran from Copperhill, reacted to the article by advocating for electing better candidates. "If there is the slightest trace of evidence," Taylor wrote, of machine politicians "bamboozling the poor taxpayers," then the voters had a "patriotic duty" to investigate and find the truth.[521]

The Polk County Republican Party hit an all-time low in 1944. With only 59 people in attendance, they elected R.N. Price as chairman and John Prince as secretary. The only nomination made was Dutch Woody for state representative. After the poll tax repeal was overturned, Burch had predicted they would not even put out a ticket. "They know they can't win," he said.[522] Walter Higgins of Chattanooga was the guest speaker, who said American soldiers overseas were "facing no more diabolical enemy than the Republicans are facing here in Polk County."[523]

Shortly after his 70th birthday, Burch won his party's nomination for the tenth time in forty years. Abie Green was nominated for a fifth term as tax assessor. George "Mutt" Gray was chosen to succeed the late John Harbison as register of deeds. Harbison passed away unexpectedly of a heart attack the previous November while visiting with friends on the mountain at Benton Springs. Bob McClary stepped aside after three terms as trustee for Charles Williams, who was nominated after twelve years as deputy trustee. Broughton was nominated for state senate and Deputy Bill Rose, also a JP in Copperhill, was nominated for state representative.

Burch and Cantrell needed Congressman John Jennings out of the way. His intervention had already caused Monroe County Sheriff Brakebill to resign, and although he had been critical of the Cantrell machine in McMinn County, he constantly assailed the Biggs machine on the floor of Congress. His enemies thought they finally had a way to get him out of the picture.

Cantrell and Woods met with Knoxville's Republican mayor, E.E. Patton, in April. Patton had previously run for Congress as an independent against Jennings' predecessor. Cantrell and Woods proposed that Patton challenge Jennings in the Republican primary, ensuring him plenty of cross-over Democratic votes. In return, they asked Patton to corral support amongst Knox County Republicans for Broughton in the state senate race. Broughton visited several Knoxville officials throughout the summer, including former Democratic mayor George Dempster.

Patton jumped in the race in May, bringing with him the support of many Democrats who knew Jennings was unbeatable in the general election. Jennings was never popular with the Republican establishment after winning a special election in 1939. Patton had significant support in Knox County Republican circles. The only question that remained was would enough Democrats cross over to vote for him.

Jennings made no apologies for his record in Congress, especially on the issue of election integrity. "I have abolished vote stealing in Monroe County," he said, reporting on an upcoming federal trial trying three of Brakebill's associates for election fraud. He called the Bradley County ripper bills an "outrage," maintaining his support for voters even outside of his district.[524] With Burch's cousin, Congressman Kefauver, Third Congressional District voters had no one else to turn to for help.

Congressman John J. Jennings Jr. of the Second Congressional District was a vocal opponent of the Biggs and Cantrell Machines. - Library of Congress

Nashville Tennessean columnist Joe Hatcher called Burch's pre-election barbecues at Quinn Springs "the forerunners of the Biggs vote-counting machine for the August primaries." Burch modeled his barbecues on the picnics and boat rides that Boss Crump used to host. Burch invited gubernatorial candidate Jim McCord. "The keynote will be 'It's one accord for Jim McCord!'"[525]

During a recent visit to Memphis, Burch and Broughton visited Boss Crump. "Do you know why Polk County and Shelby County are so close together politically?" Burch asked Crump. "It's because the sun rises on Polk County and sets on Shelby County," Burch said. "Why don't you come out to Polk County sometime?" Crump said he planned to visit soon as it was one of the few counties in the state he had never visited.[526] This was not surprising. Memphis is closer to Baton Rouge than it is to Benton, and Benton is closer to Cincinnati than it is to Memphis.

Over 2,000 people attended Burch's barbecue on July 8, including Congressman Kefauver and Chancellor Stewart, but most were there for the free food. Boss Crump was unable to attend, sending Shelby County District Attorney Will Gerber to represent him. "If we had more outstanding Democrats over the state like Sheriff Biggs there would never be any doubt about electing Democrats everywhere," Gerber told the crowd. Burch returned praise for praise: "Ed Crump is the greatest leader the sun ever shone upon. We have been accused here in Polk County of following his leadership and we plead guilty."[527]

Paul Cantrell addressed the crowd: "My mother taught Sheriff Biggs his ABCs…Sheriff Biggs started teaching me the ABCs in politics fourteen years ago and I am progressing fairly well." Congressman Kefauver defended Burch against accusations of election fraud. "How does he roll up such tremendous majorities for his ticket in Polk County? By rendering service and by hard work — by doing things for people he represents." Kefauver insisted there were no more Republicans in Polk County because "they all quit and joined Uncle Burch Biggs," as he referred to his much older cousin. "I have never known a greater leader than Uncle Burch Biggs." In a testament to Burch's influence in statewide elections, Governor Cooper visited Burch at his home to apologize personally for arriving late to the barbecue.[528]

Cleveland resident Robert John Standridge, a Polk County native, wrote a letter to the editor of the *Chattanooga Times* railing against Burch for his extravagant barbecue:

> "Scarcity of meat, tires, and gasoline cannot prevent this wild orgy. Let the planes be grounded around the world for the bosses must have gas. But the rations of meat for our fighting men throughout the world, for Biggs and his pompous henchmen must be fed well. Let the car of the farmer and working man stand idle for lack of tires, for these chosen men and women must ride in comfort. [529]

Standridge shared stories of soldiers coming home on leave to see family with only a few gallons of gas allotted for their use. Burch could ignore rationing orders, he explained, because of his "protection from men in state and federal offices who are the beneficiaries of his nefarious political machinations in Polk County."[530]

Broughton denied having plans for local legislation for Knox County if elected. He promised not to vote for any local legislation without giving the voters the opportunity to read the bills and express their opinions. When asked if he would serve as a "legislative mouthpiece" for his father, Broughton answered "No man has had a finer father than I" before adding that he would "stand on his own feet and vote his own convictions."[531]

In a speech in Etowah, Congressman Jennings called Judge Leslie Darr a "cheap, good-for-nothing judge" for giving Cantrell's convicted election workers a slap on the wrist. He seemed unconcerned about Patton's primary challenge. "I've been informed that the Democrats will import people in here from Polk County and as far away as Georgia and vote them by the truckloads. If they forced a 5,000 majority over me here, I'd still be nominated," Jennings promised. "I'm at eternal war with the Cantrells and the Biggs."[532]

An advertisement for one of Burch's legendary barbecues at Quinn Springs, where several citizens enjoyed free food and entertainment. - Polk County News

This pavilion at Quinn Springs, just off Highway 30 on the way to Reliance, still stands today. - Tennessee State Library and Archives

Cutting deals to help get Broughton elected to the state senate consumed much of Burch's time. But with the Democrats running unopposed for local offices, he had plenty of time for politics outside the county, as well as more lawsuits. Shortly before the primary, Shorty Richards filed a $25,000 damage suit against Burch and Deputies Flavis Bates and Ben Smith. Charging false arrest and excessive use of force, Shorty wanted compensation for the several injuries he suffered during his flight from alleged "false imprisonment" the year prior. Now residing in Dalton, Georgia, he had been unable to work for months.[533]

During the summer, Burch and Della's youngest child, L'Ene Biggs, married Everett Bryant in Cleveland. Burch and Della now had the house to themselves, and eagerly awaited more grandchildren. Burch almost had an opponent in 1944. The previous year, Mitchell Smith had announced another run for sheriff. He was inspired by the resignation of Monroe County Sheriff W.O. Brakebill in 1943. He wrote an open letter to his fellow Polk Countians, asking Burch to resign his post:

> "I estimate that Biggs and his son have made from a quarter-million to a half-million dollars off the taxpayers of Polk. The majority of people are opposed to him for he has crammed himself down their throats disregarding their wishes. His machine is as unscrupulous as Hitler's, the difference being size…I have a firm conviction that character, truth, sportsmanship, and decency will triumph over evil. If in the end right does not triumph over wrong, then everything I have learned is false…Good government should help to check the moral decadence of our country and give us strength to defeat our enemies. To have good government everyone must take an active interest and do his part. I request you to ask Biggs personally or by letter to resign, stating your reasons."[534]

The Old Sheriff refused to resign, claiming "my people elected me and I expect to be reelected…I am not a quitter."[535] Four decades after his first election to the job he loved, Burch was elected to an eighth term as sheriff, tallying 3,704 complementary votes. Mitchell Smith did not campaign or appear on the ballot, even as an independent. He received just two write-in votes, with one definitely from himself.[536] Several citizens thought it "foolish and reckless" for Smith to have been so outspoken against Burch, especially since he had no chance to win.[537]

Down the ballot, Abie Green won a fifth consecutive term as tax assessor and Charles Williams became the new trustee. Mutt Gray was elected register of deeds. In the primary, Jim McCord tallied 3,911 votes in Polk County against token opposition. Congressman Kefauver ran unopposed. Broughton, also unopposed, tallied 3,925 votes in his primary for state senate, more votes than his father and McCord. Bill Rose won the nomination for state representative.

James G. Crumbliss won the Republican nomination for state senate and would be facing off against Broughton in November. A former state legislator, U.S. Marshal, and Knoxville city commissioner, Crumbliss was a formidable candidate. Despite the best efforts of the Biggs-Cantrell forces, Patton lost the Republican primary to Congressman Jennings. Winning by a margin of four-to-one in the district, Jennings also defeated Patton easily in Knox County. Former Polk County resident Joseph Milburn Gregory of Oak Ridge threw "100 percent" of his support behind Jennings. "I know the Biggs clan...I'm in favor of anyone who can oust the Biggs machine."[538] Gregory's twin sister, Mildred, had recently married Vance Davis after his divorce from Claude Davis.

Even worse for Burch, the Republicans dominated in Bradley County, to the surprise of absolutely no one. Backlash over the ripper bill was so intense the Democrats did not even put out a ticket. The fact that Republicans controlled the sheriff's department in Bradley County, unlike in McMinn and Polk Counties, discouraged Democrats from even running for office since Republican voters would not be intimidated at the polls or have reason to be skeptical of the results.

Burch was receiving most of the blame for the situation in his neighboring county. Thanks to the ripper bill, Bradley County's government had barely functioned over the past year. The state supreme court upheld Chancellor Stewart's decision in favor of the ripper bill. The county court could not meet for several months.

On behalf of the ousted JPs, Charles Mayfield Sr. filed a writ of supersedeas to the state supreme court to allow the old county court to meet and function temporarily. They met with the new JPs only to set a tax rate and approve a school budget. The start of the 1943-1944 school year was chaotic, with Superintendent W.B. Cartwright saying the school system may not be able to operate due to a lack of finances. "I had hoped this change of laws in Bradley County would not interfere in any way with our schools...It is not fair to the youth of this county to have to suffer for the sins of a few foreign politicians."[539]

With the big election coming in November, Broughton was lucky Bradley County was not in the same senate district as Polk County, at least not yet.

Chapter 32

Taking a Swing at Knox County

A group of Bradley County Republicans, led by W.B. Parks, visited with Knox County Republican leaders to warn them of the prospect of Broughton's victory. "Don't accept any promises Biggs makes to you…Judas Iscariot is a credit to him. Hitler and Biggs are made of the same stuff." Parks told Crumbliss that 150 votes in Polk County would be a "compliment" from Burch Biggs and that "sometimes there are more votes than there are voters" in their elections. George Westerberg urged Knox Republicans to see that every voter is qualified and to "get out the vote" for Crumbliss. "The Biggs machine has bragged it's going to Knox County, and I warn you to be on the alert…See that your ballot boxes are not stuffed…They will try every kind of illegal practice."[540]

Congressman Jennings lambasted the Biggs-Cantrell machine for "substituting the rule of the pistol and the rule of the blackjack for the rule of the ballot."[541] Having received several affidavits from McMinn County voters accusing the Cantrell forces of election fraud and voter intimidation, Jennings shared the story of H.E. Williams. A resident of Etowah, the 69-year-old Williams had a near fatal encounter with Robert Biggs, Burch's nephew.

Williams, an election official in the 1944 Republican primary, refused to let Robert Biggs inside to watch the count. Robert, a Democratic election judge from a different precinct, had no right to enter. Two hundred twenty pounds and much younger than Williams, Robert angrily grabbed the senior citizen around the shoulders and tried to take his walking cane. Horace Reynolds, another elderly poll worker, tried to break up the scuffle.[542]

Williams struck Robert over the head with his cane, after which Robert pulled out his .45 pistol and struck Williams and Reynolds on the head. Aiming at Williams' chest, Robert said, "God damn you! I'll kill you!" Before Robert fired, Williams hit the pistol with his hand, causing the bullet to fire through the window over the heads of the other poll workers. Williams hit Robert again with his cane. Several people rushed over to restrain Robert before things turned deadly. Reynolds and another witness, John M. Guinn, corroborated Williams' story.[543]

Joseph Milburn Gregory campaigned for Crumbliss, serving as a spokesman for a group of Polk County refugees. "The people of Knox, Loudon, and Monroe Counties should know the peril and menace they face in the candidacy of Broughton Biggs," Gregory warned. "I have seen duly elected officials ripped out of office by his henchmen and voters intimidated and frightened away from the polls." He urged voters not to write his group's warning off as another "Biggs scare story." Nearly three dozen people signed Gregory's statement.[544]

In a speech in Tellico Plains, Crumbliss reached out to Polk County Democrats "who are anxious to regain a semblance of democracy at home in their county." He accused Broughton and "his crowd" of "permitting and encouraging evil." Jennings followed Crumbliss: "Now is the time, when our boys are so bravely fighting the battle of democracy overseas, to crush out the Biggs-Cantrell Storm Trooper rule here at home."[545]

Jennings eviscerated the Biggs-Cantrell machine in a speech at Karns High School in Knoxville: "In three places in the world today elections are a mockery — in Nazi Germany under the swastika, in Japan under the rule of the Rising Sun, and in Polk County under the heel of the Biggs-Cantrell machine." He reminded the crowd of Broughton's vote against the poll tax repeal. "They know that it is far easier for them to control a small vote than a large one …The Biggs are afraid of free elections, for they know that they cannot exist under a free, democratic, honest vote."[546]

The *Knoxville Journal*, a longtime Republican newspaper, gave Crumbliss a rousing endorsement. "We have a direct and personal interest in the depredations of this little machine that is trying to be Ed Crump in a little way. The Biggs-Cantrell crowd, drunk on the power they have seized in these neighboring counties, are stretching out their hands to include Knox in their control." The endorsement ended with a plea: "Beat Biggs for Senator, Beat Cantrell for Senator, Beat Woods for Representative." The *Chattanooga Times* predicted a "sweep" for Broughton in Polk and Monroe Counties, and the same for Crumbliss in Loudon County. "It appears Knox County may be a battleground in that race." Broughton ran ads solemnly promising to oppose any ripper bills for his district.

Shortly before the election, Crumbliss wrote a letter to the Polk County election commission, comprised of his opponent, his opponent's first cousin, and Henry Crox. Crumbliss wanted a certified copy of the absentee voters. He noted that at least 50 non-Polk residents appeared on the poll tax list. Jennings wrote the same letter to the McMinn County election commission and sent copies of each to U.S. Attorney General Francis Biddle. Jennings also noted that Broughton was "the sheriff of the county who figured in *Anderson et al* cited by the Supreme Court, March 1, 1943."[547]

Crumbliss received no response from election commission chairman Hoyt Lillard. Henry Crox, the long-suffering Republican election commissioner, also asked Lillard for the absentee voter list. John Prince joined him in a visit to Lillard's office. "It's a public record and I want to see it," Crox said. Lillard refused to let Crox and Prince see the list, claiming he had already posted it and that someone must have torn it down. The Cantrell forces had utilized this same trick where they would technically obey the law by post-

The Knoxville Journal published several cartoons that criticized machine politicians. - Knox County Public Library

ing it but then immediately take it down before anyone had a chance to read all of it.[548] Even the Democratic-leaning *Knoxville News-Sentinel*, who had given the Biggs machine mostly favorable coverage, called for reform when it reported on candidates Broughton and George Woods serving as election commissioners.

An outspoken opponent of Burch, Henry Crox received several threats over the years, but heroically carried on the fight. "Why don't you quit before Burch kills you?" an out-of-town attorney once asked him. He struggled to get Republicans to serve as poll watchers for the 1944 election. Many of those who turned him down said they had been "insulted and abused" while serving in elections for the past decade. "The Biggs Gang will just take the election just as they have in the past," one man claimed. Another man said that the Biggs machine always had "a gang of henchmen who were armed" that drove them away from the polls. "All those opposed to the Biggs Gang will not come to the election." Crox was turned down by a man who had been "getting on very well" with the Biggs Gang and did not want to "take the abuse" that he would have to take. One man who had once worked the Copperhill precinct was threatened by Deputy Frank Clayton. In an affidavit after the election, Crox did not mention the names of the men who turned him down out of fear for their safety.[549]

The usual members of the "Biggs Gang," as Crox had dubbed them, worked the precincts across the county. Leach Park was the officer of election in Benton. Other election workers included Dud White and Flavis Bates in Ocoee, Elias Runion in Turtletown, Louis Wright in Ducktown, and Frank Clayton in Copperhill. Crumbliss would need a lot of luck to do well in Polk County.

In an unusual move, Burch stayed away from the county's more "widely-known election hotspots" on election day. When the *Knoxville News-Sentinel* called him for a report, the jailer said "the sheriff has gone above the mountain."[550]

William M. Prince, Republican election judge at the Ocoee precinct, arrived five minutes before the polls opened. Voters were already casting ballots, and H.A. Adams had taken his place as Republican judge. Adams offered to let Prince take over, but Deputy Dud White, officer of election, would not allow it. "No, we have done started. He can't serve." Prince observed White marking ballots "for any and everybody who asked him to," even voters who were not disabled.[551]

Republican poll watcher W.C. Dalton reported to the Copperhill precinct, where he saw Democrat poll watcher Wayne Massengale hand three ballots, allegedly for his family, to Deputy Frank Clayton. Another Democratic poll watcher, Joe Coffee, warned Clayton to "be careful" with Dalton there. Clayton demanded to see Dalton's appointment papers. "You are not legally appointed," the armed deputy snarled. He tore up the papers and threw them into a stove. "If you want to vote, then vote and get out!" Dalton noticed that a Biggs man was already acting in his place as the "Republican" watcher.[552]

A half hour after the polls closed, officer of election Deputy Louis Wright ordered the counting at Ducktown stopped with some ballots uncounted. He put the counted ballots back into the box along with the scroll sheets and other records. "I'm taking them to Benton," the deputy said. "What are you going to do about the uncounted ballots?" asked election judge Theodore Shillings. Wright replied that the election commission would count them.[553]

Early returns showed Broughton trailing Crumbliss in the district by about 2,000 votes. Precincts reporting on late Tuesday night had Broughton trailing significantly in Knox and Loudon Counties, but Monroe County was a dead heat. When Burch returned to Benton, he said that results from Polk County were "entirely unavailable" at this time.[554]

By Wednesday evening, the Knox County returns were nearly complete. Crumbliss won 21,000 votes to Broughton's 15,000. Loudon County's complete returns showed an overwhelming victory for Crumbliss, while Monroe County's complete results showed that Crumbliss won by eight votes out of nearly 6,000 votes cast. To eke out a victory, Broughton would have to win Polk County by over 6,000 votes, where less than 4,000 votes were cast in 1942.

Congressman Jennings easily won reelection as the Republicans dominated Knox County. In the state representative race, Bradley County voters rejected Bill Rose, giving Will Bacon 2,498 votes to 879 for Rose. Bacon, Bradley's outgoing Republican tax assessor, ran as an independent. Republican Dutch Woody only tallied 79 votes in Bradley. But Rose could still win the district so long as Burch delivered his usual lopsided victories at home.

Polk County had yet to make one report. Broughton stayed at his campaign headquarters at the Hotel Farragut in Knoxville, claiming to know nothing of the results back home. Henry Crox tried to contact Hoyt Lillard for some answers, but he was also "out of town." For the past several years, the two Democratic election commissioners had frequently conducted business without Crox present.[555]

Crox said that the Democrats ran off a Republican election clerk in Benton and that election judge Frank Lillard reported that every non-military absentee ballot had Chattanooga return addresses. Crox added that election officials "wait until the official canvassing is held to bring in the ballot boxes," leaving them vulnerable for days in this instance.[556] "I have affidavits that at certain precincts, the count was stopped and officers said they were taking the ballot boxes to Benton…Some people in the county are afraid to talk."[557]

"It is perfectly apparent that Sheriff Biggs is waiting to see the total Crumbliss majority in the other three counties in the Sixth Senatorial District before turning in his county's vote," the *Knoxville Journal* wrote. Jennings asked the assistant attorney general in Washington for a federal investigation into "apparent fraudulent practices" in Polk and McMinn Counties. W.C. Dalton informed Jennings that Republican election officials had been refused admittance into several precincts.[558]

Copper City Advance editor Frank Middleton searched all over Benton to find an election official to get at least some results, but had no luck. Henry Crox said, "it is perfectly clear the Biggs people are trying to hold back Polk County returns to see what they need." He claimed to have the returns of only one precinct, Delano, insisting they held an honest election because the Republican election officials were present throughout. "It was 123 for Broughton Biggs and 70 for James G. Crumbliss," he reported, a much more believable tally compared to the typical 95 percent or higher for the Biggs candidates.[559] Crox reported that the county was "incapable" of legally casting more than 3,500 ballots."[560]

It was becoming more and more obvious that Broughton would not be going to the state senate. Before Polk County's election returns came in, the *Knoxville News-Sentinel* wrote that "for a long time the Biggs outfit has been too big for its pants — and trying to get bigger. It was time for a tailoring-down operation by the electorate."

By Friday morning, Polk County made national headlines again. They were now the only county in the United States that had not reported any election returns for the November 7, 1944 election. But Crumbliss was not worried. "That county doesn't have enough ballots to overcome my lead in

Knox, Monroe, and Loudon Counties…I figure he'll get about 3,000 votes and I'll get 300 in Polk County."[561]

Broughton returned to Benton later that morning. "There was no desire down here to do anything wrong or to outcount Mr. Crumbliss' lead in the other counties…We simply wanted to know what went on elsewhere before releasing our vote here."[562] Burch chimed in, accusing the newspapers of implicating election fraud. "I now want to concede defeat and offer congratulations to my friend Mr. Crumbliss. He is my senator," Broughton said.[563]

In his capacity as election commission secretary, Broughton announced Polk County's results. Crumbliss only tallied 232 votes to Broughton's 4,881 votes, an all-time record in Polk County history. This cut Crumbliss' lead in the district to 2,088. The final tally for the Sixth Senatorial District was 24,905 for Crumbliss and 22,817 for Broughton, the first loss for a Biggs candidate in over a decade.

Bill Rose comfortably won the state representative race against Will Bacon. Rose easily overcame his deficit in Bradley, tallying 4,829 votes to Bacon's 196 and Woody's 67 in Polk. In the state and federal races, Burch delivered his typical astronomically-high margins of victory for the Democrats, with President Roosevelt, Jim McCord, and Congressman Kefauver tallying over 4,800 votes each to their opponents 378, 261, and 118 respectively. Marion, Rhea, Warren, and White Counties, all similar in size, turned out far fewer voters than Polk County.

In 1940, Polk County had a population of 15,473, with 4,135 kids of school age. Subtracting all of the 0-5-year-olds, 18–20-year-olds, and the kids who did not go past the 8th grade (about 18 percent of students), the county only had about 10,000 people eligible to vote.[564] Assuming they all paid their poll tax (which was very unlikely), did the county really have voter turnout that high, and almost 5,000 people that eager to vote for Burch's preferred candidates?

Aside from the Cantrell-bossed McMinn County, Roosevelt's popularity had dwindled in Polk's neighboring counties, with Thomas Dewey carrying Monroe and Cherokee Counties for the Republicans for the first time since 1928. The historically Republican Bradley, Loudon, and Fannin Counties voted overwhelmingly for Dewey. In fact, this election was actually Roosevelt's worst showing nationwide in his four elections. But the president supposedly received a record 93 percent in Polk County. Not even the unbossed Democratic stronghold of Davidson County, which had voted overwhelmingly for the Democrat in all but one election since 1900, gave Roosevelt more than 72 percent of the vote. Meigs County, a rural and historically blue county that staunchly supported the TVA, only gave the president 58 percent of the vote. Solidly blue Murray County, Georgia voted overwhelmingly for the president in all four of his elections, but never gave him more than 83 percent, and only gave him 67 percent this time. On his way to reelection, Jennings easily won Loudon County and won a close race in Monroe County, but the Cantrell machine ensured he lost McMinn County by over 1,000 votes.

Cantrell was reelected in the Seventh Senatorial District by about 1,100 votes. Despite losing Bradley, Roane, and Anderson Counties, his machine delivered a Polk-like margin of victory in McMinn County, ensuring victory in the district. Burch no longer had the state senate seat for his county, but he still had Paul Cantrell and now Bill Rose in Nashville. Despite Burch's initial plans, Hugh Callaway was not even on the ballot for any office in this election. Cast aside only for Broughton to lose, he was reportedly expecting a lucrative job in state government, but received nothing.

The Knoxville News-Sentinel ran an editorial proposing a ban on candidates serving as election officials, criticizing Broughton for holding back the election returns for so long. The *Nashville Tennessean* relished in Broughton's defeat, writing that "the boss finds himself caught in the toils of the poll tax." Had the tax repeal been upheld, Burch could have reported far more than 4,000 votes in Polk County, possibly even enough to give Broughton a victory, since more people could have voted without paying the tax. The *Tennessean* took offense to Burch's claim that the election returns did not have to be legally announced until Monday:

> Seldom have the records of official abuse of authority showed examples of such wanton disregard of the personal rights of citizens as the Supreme Court found to have existed in Polk County under the domination of the Biggs machine. The story of how men were arrested without a warrant, taken to a building owned by the company with which they were in a labor dispute, where they were held and questioned intermittently over a period of six days during which they saw neither friends, relatives, or counsel, can be paralleled only where Gestapo methods are tolerated. But when it comes to letting the people know their election results, the henchmen of Sheriff Biggs are quite unwilling to do something "not required by law."

Congressman Jennings released two affidavits from W.C. Dalton and Theodore Shillings alleging election fraud in Polk County. The congressman claimed he had evidence that Polk County only cast 2,500 legal votes. "They brought them in from Georgia and North Carolina and drove them from precinct to precinct to vote." He also compared the number of absentee ballots cast in McMinn and Polk Counties to Knox County, which, despite being much larger, cast significantly fewer absentee ballots. "I have told the attorney general of the United States about these things and he says he intends to prosecute."[565] But in the end, no one was held accountable.

Horace Hughes was an alcoholic and no stranger to prison, but many believed Deputy Stephenson's lethal force was unnecessary in this instance. - Horace Hughes family

One young citizen, whose father was a deputy, once confronted Burch about his men stuffing the ballot boxes, telling him it was wrong and that he knew it was wrong. But the Old Sheriff just responded with a laugh.[566]

Burch's deputies may have grabbed and arrested many people who were not drunk at all, but that was not the case with Cherokee County native John Horace Hughes. The brother of a bootlegger, he was a raging alcoholic who often started fights. On December 16, 1944, Hughes broke into the jail. He was drunk, but he also had a knife. He had been released only a few days prior. The jailor, G.E. Stephenson, tried to arrest him. Hughes resisted, so Stepheson fatally shot him.

In this instance, there was an argument for Stephenson to defend himself with force, but the Hughes family believes such deadly force was unnecessary. The 36-year-old was survived by his young daughter, who had moved away with her mother after divorcing Hughes. Burch investigated the killing and said he would take no action against his jailer.[567] Polk County deputies had now unjustifiably killed five men on Burch's watch.

Chapter 33
CHOOSING THEIR VOTERS

State Rep. George Woods had been a loyal soldier for Cantrell, Burch, and Boss Crump. On the first day of the 1945 legislative session, he got his reward: the house speakership. Governor McCord supported Woods for speaker, upsetting the *Nashville Tennessean* who had supported the governor's candidacy despite his Crump ties. The *Knoxville Journal* called the selection of Woods "a gratuitous affront not only to East Tennessee Republicans but no less to a majority of East Tennessee Democrats who believe in a fair ballot and honest count." Speaker Woods denounced the *Tennessean* and the *Journal*, proclaiming he was "proud to be a member of the Biggs-Cantrell machine."[568] Following in his father's footsteps again, Broughton was appointed chief sergeant-at-arms, a consolation prize for losing the state senate race. Additionally, he received a higher per diem daily rate than the senators.

Burch and Cantrell would not waste any more time trying to get Congressman Jennings voted out. Rather, they would draw McMinn and Monroe Counties out of the Second Congressional District. Constitutionally-mandated redistricting always took place after the release of the U.S. Census results, not in the middle of the decade. But this particular thorn in their side had to go before he did any more damage to their machine.

Woods pushed through legislation to swap McMinn and Monroe Counties with Scott and Morgan Counties in the Second Congressional District. The Third Congressional District would gain McMinn and Monroe, to Congressman Kefauver's delight. Jennings had no issue with representing Scott and Morgan Counties, but hated to lose McMinn and Monroe, home to some of his strongest supporters. The two counties had happily been in the Knoxville-based district since 1932. "The handwriting is on the wall," wrote the *Chattanooga Times*, "Mr. Crump and Mr. Biggs are out to get full control of Tennessee."

The Hamilton County delegation opposed the legislation, wanting nothing to do with the Biggs-Cantrell territories of McMinn and Monroe Counties. Hamilton County Judge Wiley Couch, who had already broken with Burch over the poll tax repeal, feared his rival exerting more control in

Hamilton County. *The Chattanooga Times* worried Burch might handpick a challenger to primary Congressman Kefauver in 1946. Senator Crumbliss listened to his constituents and voted against the legislation.

In the capitol lobby, Burch, Broughton, Woods, Cantrell, and Judge Couch engaged in a heated argument. Couch called it "trick legislation." Burch denied it had been "slipped up" on anybody. "Monroe is the home county of Estes Kefauver, my cousin. I talked to him last night and he wants it." Burch pointed to Cantrell. "Here is the man who has made McMinn County Democratic. He wants to come back to the Third District where John Jennings won't aggravate him."[569]

Kefauver said he did not want the bill to pass "if there is to be a fight over it." Jennings said he would "rather go out of Congress than desert the decent people of Monroe and McMinn Counties…they want to get rid of me so they can steal elections." On the resignation of Monroe County Sheriff W.O. Brakebill, Jennings said "We have cleaned up Monroe. I am told that there was not a pistol or a blackjack at the polls in the county at the last election."[570]

The Crump-Biggs-Cantrell forces now had the power to kill local bills desired by lowly legislators if they refused to vote for the machine's legislation, so the redistricting bills passed overwhelmingly. *Chattanooga Times* editor Alfred Mynders lamented the prospect of a "Biggs stooge" in Congress and criticized the legislature for "permitting itself to become a Reichstag for Mr. Crump and Mr. Biggs."

In the state senate, Cantrell blocked legislation to weaken the poll tax. Governor McCord, unlike his predecessor, took no stand for or against the poll tax. Burch visited Nashville frequently, despite his job as sheriff of a county almost 200 miles away, keeping his allies in the anti-poll tax faction in line. State Rep. Bill Rose helped kill the anti-poll tax bills in committee. However, the bosses did support extending the poll tax exemption for military personnel.

Woods also co-sponsored a bill to "reform" absentee voting. The bill passed the senate, with Crumbliss casting one of only four votes against. The bill stipulated that absentee ballots "shall not be rejected by election officials because of technical irregularities or objections" and permitted absentee ballots to be cast up to two days before the election. Worst of all, the bill also forced election commissions to accept absentee ballots even if the absentee voter list is not posted. The bill easily passed in the house, but protests ensured it was moderated.[571]

The bosses would not stop at redistricting congressional seats. With Crump's blessing, Cantrell and Woods introduced a bill to redraw the Sixth and Seventh Senatorial Districts. For the longest time, Bradley, McMinn, Roane, and Anderson Counties comprised the Seventh District. These counties adjoin, but the district made little geographic sense. Still, the district had been a Republican stronghold since Reconstruction, with one Democrat representing it until Cantrell's election in 1942. The Sixth District, comprised of Polk, Monroe, Loudon, and western Knox Counties, had been a purple district, and made more sense geographically.

Under the proposed bill, Anderson and Roane Counties, both strongly Republican, would move into the Sixth District with Loudon and western Knox County, both solidly Republican. In exchange, the Seventh District would gain Monroe and Polk Counties, both purple counties, to join the Republican strongholds of Bradley and McMinn Counties. The new districts made more sense geographically. Woods even said it made the districts "more compact."[572]

But everyone knew the bill had nothing to do with geography. It was brazen gerrymandering. The *Knoxville News-Sentinel* wrote that the Biggs-Cantrell machine knew they had to "do something about the trouncing Broughton Biggs was given in Knox County" in the 1944 election. The *Nashville Tennessean* condemned the bill in an editorial called "Rigged for Biggs." The bill became law in record time, moving through both chambers without debate and signed by Governor McCord two days after being introduced.

Several members of the Sweetwater Lions Club protested the bill, only to be ignored. Forbidden by their constitution to take sides in political disputes, the club still voted to condemn the bill because Democrats and Republicans considered it a "civic" issue. "The Biggs-Cantrell-Brakebill Machine is at it again!" wrote the *Sweetwater Valley News* in a rare extra edition. They printed the names of sixteen Monroe Countians who "died for a clean democracy," and asked, "Have their lives been given in vain?"[573]

Chapter 34

SHERIFF BURCH GLEN BIGGS

On March 26, 1945, Burch did the unthinkable. He announced plans to resign the job he loved most. But the Biggs family would still control the sheriff's department, as Burch Glen, age 27, had just received his discharge from the Army. During a recent trip home, he was hospitalized with sciatic rheumatism. "I will resign as soon as my son is physically able to take over the duties of his office." The county court had the power to fill the vacancy.[574] "He has had his heart set on being sheriff," Burch said. "But he entered the army instead and I was elected."[575]

The *Chattanooga Times* was indignant about Burch's intention to hand over the sheriff's post to Burch Glen, accusing him of "violating the spirit" of the state constitution's limits on a sheriff's terms. "No family shall have a corner on the sheriff's job, the constitution seems to imply." The *Times* resented Burch's plan for Burch Glen to become sheriff in 1942 before the war intervened: "Apparently the people of Polk County would have nothing to say about it except to vote for junior." In reverence of Polk County's pioneer settlers, the *Times* listed Erby Boyd, Michael Hildebrand, Abraham Lillard, and other early settlers who would have never "belittled the constitutional rights of the citizens of Polk County."

Burch said his resignation would be effective July 2 and "recommended" the county court appoint Burch Glen as his replacement. "I have held the office of sheriff longer than any man in Tennessee, so I have been informed." According to the *Polk County News*, no one had served longer as sheriff of Polk County.[576]

Governor McCord's administration considered appointing Broughton to replace the resigning state prison warden, one of the highest paying jobs in the state. It was then reported that Burch might be offered the state prison warden job for a second time. But he had no interest in it. "I wouldn't take the job if it paid $20,000 a year." He said Broughton was not a candidate for the job either.[577]

There were also rumors Broughton would be running for Congress in 1946, but he debunked such talk. "We will be supporting Estes Kefauver for reelection next year. I have no intention of running for Congress. We just wanted to put Monroe and McMinn Counties back where they belong."[578] But many still speculated that Broughton would make a run for state senate in the new Seventh District, especially since Cantrell was planning another run for sheriff of McMinn County.

After a bitter fight with the state election board, Burch secured the appointment of two anti-Couch men to the Hamilton County election commission. He also succeeded in handpicking a commissioner for Bradley County. Broughton and Hoyt Lillard were reappointed as commissioners in Polk County. All of this, coupled with his close relationship with Congressman Kefauver, gave him virtual total control of the Third Congressional District. Alfred Mynders of the *Chattanooga Times* reported there might be a movement to rename the Chickamauga Dam to Burch Biggs Dam. "Chattanoogans would almost as soon see it given the name originally proposed – the General Sherman Dam. And it could only be named the Sherman Dam over the collective dead bodies of a whole lot of Chattanooga people."

The Polk County Court convened at 10:00 AM on July 2, 1945, when Burch's resignation became effective. He could finally "retire" to his farm. JP W.A. Kerr nominated Burch Glen to fill the vacancy. In a unanimous vote, the court elected Burch Glen, less than a week from his 28th birthday, to be the new sheriff.

Standing 6'3 and weighing in at 220 pounds, Burch Glen spent nearly four years in the service, working in army intelligence in Michigan and as a MP criminal investigator in Texas. Burch hosted a luncheon at the courthouse celebrating the new sheriff, ensuring the position would be in the family for at least sixteen consecutive years. In his first act in office, Burch Glen appointed his father chief deputy. "He had a great personality," the child of a deputy later remembered of the new sheriff.[579]

In its most scathing editorial yet, the *Knoxville News-Sentinel* wrote that Burch showed "contempt for the people by adding insult" to his attack on democracy by handing the sheriff's post over to Burch Glen. "Net effect of all this manipulation is to dig the Biggs family deeper into the public trough." The *Nashville Tennessean* called Polk County "a political circus."

In a column for the *Copper City Advance*, Bob Barclay discussed the history of Polk County's sheriffs, and made no criticism of Burch Glen's ascen-

The Biggs family held the office of sheriff for almost two decades. Burch Glen, standing left, became sheriff in 1945 after his father's resignation. L'Ene Biggs is standing between her brothers as their parents are seated. - Polk County News

sion to the office: "Young Burch, might, therefore, one day equal his daddy's record. He's young and husky, and has until 1986 in which to accomplish this rare feat." Barclay had maintained a cordial relationship with the Biggs machine. He recently served with John Standridge and others as officers in the Polk County Re-Elect Roosevelt Club, established by Burch himself.

~

Just like his father, Broughton continued doing well for himself after leaving office. He bought the R.W. Clemmer home and remodeled it into an apartment rental property.[580] While visiting a garage in Benton shortly after Christmas, he suffered a heart attack. The 41-year-old received treatment from a Chattanooga doctor and was expected to recover. His condition improved after a few weeks of rest.[581] But he would need to take it easy from now on.

Chapter 35

KEFAUVER'S SHIFT

A brilliant and calculating politician, Congressman Kefauver saw the writing on the wall. The war was over and the bosses were on their way out. As recently as spring 1944 he had written to Boss Crump about a visit while in Memphis.[582] His image was that of a reformer who opposed political machines, but he continued benefiting from their favors and took no meaningful action against them. He began a slow shift away from the bosses, planning his next big move.

Previously unenthusiastic about federal anti-poll tax legislation, Kefauver led efforts in summer 1945 to pass a bill removing the poll tax in elections involving federal officials. Burch was "disturbed" by his cousin's change of position. There was also speculation that Kefauver might challenge Senator McKellar in the 1946 primary. A longtime ally of Boss Crump, McKellar was going for a sixth term, and Burch supported him unwaveringly.[583] For the first time since helping Kefauver win a seat in Congress, Burch's relationship with his cousin started to cool. Kefauver later criticized the three state supreme court justices who voted to overturn the state poll tax repeal, including Alexander Chambliss, his former law partner.

Two of East Tennessee's most powerful political bosses reconciled in 1946. Burch and Judge Couch agreed to support Senator McKellar and Governor McCord for reelection. When asked about Kefauver, Burch said he would support him "if he behaves himself." He predicted a "mighty light vote" for McKellar's primary opponent, Edward W. Carmack, in Polk County.[584]

Kefauver's relationship with his cousin cooled even further when he declined to endorse McKellar for renomination. "I have no desire to be a hypocrite about it." Before endorsing Carmack, Kefauver informed Burch of his decision, saying it was the "fair thing to do." Burch did not lose his temper over his cousin's refusal to endorse Tennessee's senior senator for reelection, but he did say he "might not support the congressman in the primary…there are four or five fellows wanting to run."[585]

Monroe County Democrats endorsed Madisonville attorney Frank Bratton for Congress. "The Democratic Party tore his pants at the convention and slapped Rep. Estes Kefauver in his face right in his hometown at the order of Sheriff Burch Biggs of Polk County," the *Sweetwater Valley News* wrote. Bratton declined to make the race, complimenting both Burch and Kefauver. The *Sweetwater Valley News* wrote that Burch had "overreached himself" and predicted the citizens of Monroe "will tell him so at the polls on August 1."

Although "dissatisfied," the Cantrell machine still endorsed their congressman. Judge Couch indicated no desire to recruit a challenger to Kefauver. Burch spoke highly of the popular Hamilton County Judge Frank Darwin as a possible candidate. But he now seemed to be alone in his indecision over whether to endorse his cousin.[586]

Kefauver only had one formidable opponent in the primary: William F. McWhorter. The challenger claimed to have "no enmity" against Burch or Judge Couch. "I am not running against them. I am running against Estes Kefauver." McWhorter had little chance to pull an upset, but he made one comment that would prove to be prophetic: "If Wiley Couch and Burch Biggs throw their controlled votes to Kefauver in this election, they are going to be in a very embarrassing position two years from now when Estes Kefauver runs against Tom Stewart."[587]

Chapter 36

BOB BARCLAY SPEAKS OUT

Bob Barclay was born in Ringgold, Georgia and raised in Copperhill. He graduated from North Georgia Baptist College and played a year of professional baseball, pitching in the Georgia-Alabama League in 1914, the year after his father, Gus Barclay, was shot and killed in Copperhill. An infantryman in the American Expeditionary Force during World War I, he was awarded the Silver Star and French Croix de Guerre. He started at the TCC in 1916 as a water boy. After working as an office boy, rivet header, and electrician's helper, he had risen to the position of chief clerk and paymaster. Aside from an unsuccessful run for trustee in 1930, he had stayed out of politics. Like many at the TCC, he learned to coexist with the Biggs machine.

Some say the Copperhill ripper bill was the turning point for Barclay. But in April 1946, he wrote an open letter in the *Copper City Advance*, publicly condemning conditions in the county for the first time. A visit to the Copperhill grammar school building, where his youngest son was enrolled, moved him to write the scathing letter.

"The floors, seats, desks, and books were littered with water, dirt, plaster, and general debris as a result of rain that had broken through the flat roof at several places during the hard downpour." Barclay called the school's condition "the absolute depth of poverty in Polk County. I mean intellectual, civic, political, and not financial poverty." He said the building was "unfit for human occupancy" even before the rain. "It was dismal, dilapidated, and disgraceful." Anyone who had the opportunity to "take a stand," he insisted, but chose not to, was partly to blame. On the county's mineral wealth, he invoked Winston Churchill: "Never in the history of the world have so many done so little with so much."

Placing the blame on civic clubs, the PTA, local churches, and the *Polk County News*, Barclay saved his final finger-pointing for the Biggs machine. Although not mentioning Burch by name, Barclay remarked that, "If the rubble that is our school here represents anything, though, it is that of our Polk County political set up. The school is but one branch of the county political organization." He said the Biggs machine had "deadening effects" on the county and predicted they would "turn in virtual unanimous counts for its favorites" at the next election. "But behind this seeming solidarity lies a county prostrate in backwardness, decay, and indifference." Sally Hutchins Gregory, raised by staunch Democrats, described years of living under the Biggs machine as "pitiful."588

Burch claimed he had not read Barclay's article. Benton attorney John Prince commended Barclay for his courage to "speak against those who have assumed the leadership of the county and have so miserably failed at their stewardship."589

Bob Barclay, a lifelong Democrat and chief clerk at the TCC, had learned to co-exist with the Biggs Machine, but he finally spoke out about poor conditions in the county in spring 1946. - Polk County Historical and Genealogical Society

Barclay's concerns were not unfounded. Reuben M. Blair's 1941 graduate thesis on education in Polk County revealed that "many of the buildings are old and in need of repairs such as paint, roof mending, new floors, window sashes, replastering, and interior painting." Overcrowding was an increasing problem, especially at Polk County High School and Copperhill High School, where some classes were held in the study hall. "Laboratory equipment and supplies are inadequate, and lack of storage space and instructional space interferes with their best use," Blair wrote.590

Of the schools above the mountain, Copperhill saw the sharpest decline. Shortly before Christmas break in 1944, Copperhill students were sent home due to "inadequate heating facilities" in the buildings. According to one teacher, her classroom was 40 degrees that morning. "For a county as rich as Polk, our school buildings and equipment are in a pitiful condition," the *Copper City Advance* wrote. Attendance at Copperhill High School peaked at an average of 187 students in 1935. The numbers steadily decreased afterwards, and dipped under 100 for the first time in 1943.591 The schools in Ducktown fared better, especially with the Fourth Fractional Township Board wielding more influence than Hoyt Lillard.

Polk County Schools saw an increase in teacher resignations in the early 1940s, especially at the high schools. Although the teachers were paid well compared to surrounding rural districts, they had not received a raise in years, and some hated working under the Biggs machine. School board chairman Hoyt Lillard's new policy, implemented in 1942, required teachers to pay a $100 bond to insure they would not quit their job for the entire school year. The bond was increased to $250 in 1943 after the county lost thirteen high school teachers. An "uneasy atmosphere" prevailed among faculties, and several teachers left for better-paying jobs.[592] But not all teachers left on their own. Ruth Haskins taught for three years before becoming engaged to Red Passmore in 1938. She was told she would be fired if she married a Republican. Refusing to leave the man she loved, she lost her job at Benton Elementary.[593]

George Scarbrough spent years teaching at a "small, back-district" school. When he started, the school had poor attendance and was on the verge of closing. He worked with the students and parents to improve the school. But when Burch's men came around asking for "patronage" at election time, he refused, so they fired him. He later called the school officials "political puppets too spineless to protest" and accused the school board of passing on "legitimate teachers" in favor of those much less qualified, including some who barely attended college.[594] Under longtime school superintendent J.D. Clemmer, Polk County achieved educational excellence. But those days were long past.

Chapter 37

A Fatal Knock on the Door

Polk County saw an amplification of its culture of violence throughout 1946, especially in the Copper Basin. On April 4, Bill Rose got into a fight with former deputy Leroy Eller at the latter's Copperhill store. Both men were staying at a boarding house where they met later that night. Eller followed Rose into his room, moments before Rose shot him in the stomach. Eller was taken to a Chattanooga hospital, reportedly in serious condition. Deputy Frank Clayton arrested Rose, who was charged with felonious assault. He was released on a $5,000 bond. Rose never faced prosecution, most likely because Eller initiated the altercation.[595]

Copperhill police commissioner Frank Clayton, still on the force as a deputy, appointed Ottis "Shorty" Ensley as chief of police. On Sunday April 28, Richard Whitfield "Junior" Brown was accused of drunkenness at a restaurant in Copperhill. A veteran of World War II, Brown was awarded the Good Conduct Medal, among numerous other accolades. Chief Ensley arrived to arrest Brown, but Brown resisted. As the two men fought, a group of grammar school boys ran outside, leaving no witnesses. Brown allegedly grabbed Ensley's pistol from its holster and aimed it at the chief's head. Ensley then pulled his backup weapon from his pants pocket and shot Brown in the head. Brown was pronounced dead at a hospital only minutes later. He was survived by his new bride, infant daughter, parents, and several siblings, including his brother and fellow veteran Burton Brown.[596] "Bobby" Barclay Jr. a friend of Brown, felt "bitter" about Brown's death. "It's something you never forget," he later said.[597]

Burch Glen was the first officer on the scene. He swore out a warrant against Chief Ensley and wasted no time in arresting him. Ensley claimed self-defense and was held under $10,000 bond on a murder charge. He made bail and, despite the charges against him, was permitted to continue as chief of police. He was later indicted and would be tried at the January 1947 term of the criminal court.

Isabella native Jim Boggs re-enlisted in the Army after World War II, but disappeared after being granted leave in spring 1946. Most likely cited for being "drunk and disorderly," Deputy Clyde Dale had a warrant for Boggs' arrest. Boggs was believed to be at the home of Oscar Griffith in Chanceytown, a hamlet about a mile north of Ducktown. On May 2, 1946, Dale went to the Griffith home to learn that Boggs was not there. But he returned that evening with Deputy Frank Clayton and Copperhill Police Chief Shorty Ensley. They heard noises inside and knocked on the door, but no one answered. A group of friends, including Burton Brown, as well as a few small children, were in the home.[598]

Dale kicked the door open and saw Boggs sitting in a chair pointing a 12-gague shotgun at them. Before the deputies had time to react, Boggs fired a buckshot hitting Clayton in the chest, with a small part of the blast hitting Dale in the side. "Oh my God, he's shot me boys!" Clayton cried out. He died almost instantly, one day before his 32nd birthday.[599] He had been on the force for over decade, deputized by Burch in 1934. One of the men who killed Emmett Gaddis was dead.

Burch Glen led a county-wide manhunt for the 21-year-old Boggs. The sheriff went to see Boggs' parents at 2:00 AM. The next morning, Boggs' father convinced him to surrender. Under the condition that the sheriff return to the house alone, Boggs agreed to surrender. Burch Glen arrested Boggs, who was wearing his military uniform. Arraigned before JP Bill Rose, Boggs confessed to the killing.

Broughton served as a pallbearer at Clayton's memorial service, reportedly attended by over 3,000 people. The slain deputy was survived by his wife, four sisters, and a brother. Less than two months later, Boggs was tried in the Ducktown Law Court in June. He pled not guilty, claiming self-defense since he did not know the police had kicked open the door. But, Matt Witt later claimed Clayton and Dale intended to kill Boggs and that Boggs was tipped off.[600]

Cas Geer, an attorney from Sparta who had recently moved to Benton and befriended the Biggs machine, assisted Beecher Witt in the prosecution. The jury found Boggs guilty of second-degree murder, and Judge Sue K. Hicks sentenced him to ten years imprisonment. In Polk County, juries convicted cop-killers with ease, but refrained from convicting killer cops. A few months later, Judge Hicks gave a directed verdict of not-guilty for the now former Copperhill police chief Shortly Ensley in the death of Junior Brown, citing insufficient evidence.

Chapter 38

The Last of the Old Time Democratic Conventions

In what the *Chattanooga Times* called a "cut-and-dried" affair, Polk County Democrats nominated every incumbent for reelection in 1946: Burch Glen for sheriff, Charles Williams for trustee, Leach Park for county court clerk, Roxy Campbell for circuit court clerk, Ben Parks for tax assessor, and Mutt Gray for register of deeds. Hoyt Lillard was elected to succeed Charles Williams as party chairman. Pat Mansfield, in attendance with Speaker Woods, was nominated for state senate. JP Bill Rose was nominated for another term as state representative.

It is uncertain as to exactly why the Biggs-Cantrell machine endorsed McMinn County Sheriff Pat Mansfield for state senate in the new Seventh Senatorial District. Broughton's recent heart attack likely factored into his not making the race. But Mansfield had served two terms as sheriff and had been a loyal right-hand man to Paul Cantrell, who wanted to run for sheriff again. The two planned to swap jobs.

A little over two dozen Polk County Republicans gathered to reelect R.N. Price as chairman. They hoped to meet again to nominate several veterans and put out a full ticket for county offices. But no ticket was ever nominated. In fact, it would be a long time before the Republicans nominated a full ticket in the county.

Returning GIs were ready to enact change in local government, especially in the bossed counties. Bradley County Democrats, just as Monroe County Republicans had done, nominated an all-veteran ticket. Bradley County Republicans, led by W.B. Parks, denounced the Democratic ticket, claiming their all-GI ticket aimed to disguise their "impotence" as a party. "The ex-servicemen and people of the county will not be fooled by this trick… they did not name a single Republican soldier on their ticket." Parks accused Burch of "concocting" the idea in an attempt to "gain control of Bradley County."[601] Bill Lusk, Democratic nominee for sheriff, denied connections with "any person or group of persons outside Bradley County."[602]

McMinn County Republicans did not nominate a ticket for the 1946 election, instead endorsing a non-partisan ticket, comprised entirely of veterans. The Cantrell machine had been in power longer than any previous faction in McMinn's history, and a significant number of Democrats were ready to join with the Republicans to defeat the machine and clean up their county. Over 1,000 veterans met at the courthouse in Athens to nominate the GI Non-Partisan League ticket: Knox Henry (Republican) for sheriff; Frank Carmichael (Democrat) for trustee; George Painter (Democrat) for county court clerk; Bill Hamby (Democrat) for circuit court clerk; and Charlie Pickel (Republican) for register of deeds. Painter was raised in Conasauga. Pickel was a veteran of World War I, bringing wisdom and experience to the ticket.

After weeks of uncertainty over the position, they would take on Congressman Kefauver; the Polk County Democratic Party endorsed him for reelection. But, unlike with every other candidate for state and federal offices, they did not endorse their congressman's record. J. Creed Brock, former JP and deputy sheriff, unexpectedly called for everyone present "who likes Estes Kefauver" to stand. Two-thirds of those in attendance stood, and not one person in Burch's inner-circle stood. Brock complimented Kefauver's support for veterans and the TVA.[603] The *Nashville Tennessean* delighted in Burch endorsing Kefauver, no matter how begrudgingly it had been. "No other candidate wanted to run as Boss Biggs' choice…left out on his own limb, Boss Biggs had to crawl back or be sawed off."

Bob Barclay attended the convention to urge "road and school improvements." He even pledged to support a tax increase, despite their already high rates, if it was necessary. "The Biggs organization is something that we are all proud of," Barclay said, probably thinking something else. "It is up to the men elected to office to get the improvements we need."[604]

Barclay's profile had risen considerably in the past several years. He was an active member of the Copperhill Kiwanis Club and awaited publication of his first book, *Ducktown Back In Raht's Time*, a history of the early years of the Copper Basin. One citizen described Barclay as being "like a college professor."[605]

Burch addressed the convention, praising Boss Crump and reasserting what a "pleasure" it was to be a part of his organization. "The greatest Democrat Tennessee ever produced is Edward H. Crump," the 72-year-old former sheriff stated. This convention would prove to be the last time Burch Biggs and Bob Barclay ever met on friendly terms.[606]

County judge Vance Davis had begrudgingly accepted his subservient role in Polk County politics since the 1938 "harmony convention." Previous accusations of corruption on his part proved specious. He had "not paid much attention to politics" over the past few years and did not attend the county's Democratic convention. "I've been so busy looking after a business I opened a few years ago."[607] Davis was a successful fox dog breeder and owned a hotel in North Georgia. He had benefited little from politics since 1938, especially compared to the Biggs family and their close associates. Davis' financial success was not attributable to politics.

Part of the 1938 compromise stipulated that the Biggs and Davis factions could endorse different candidates for state and federal offices. The Carmack campaign, hoping to upset Senator McKellar, drafted Davis to manage his campaign in Polk County. Davis endorsed Congressman Kefauver rather enthusiastically. Davis also endorsed former governor Gordon Browning, who was challenging Governor McCord.

"The dictators in McMinn County will try to steal votes from me," Carmack said in a speech in Athens. Paul Cantrell and his associates sat at a window inside the courthouse as Carmack assailed them and praised the GI ticket. Despite a friend's request "not to make the speech about the dictator," he went ahead and did it anyway. "I'll make it again on the steps of the courthouse in a county where another dictator rules." Burch said Carmack was welcome in Polk County "to say anything he pleases." But he said confidently, "I don't think he would win or lose any votes by coming here."[608]

"I urge the voters of Polk County to follow the example of their neighbors in McMinn and fight for a clean election," Carmack said in Benton on July 23. While not referring to the Biggs machine by name, Carmack said he expected an attempt to take away votes from him and "any other candidate who opposes the rule of political machines." Burch watched the speech, as did several veterans, listening to Carmack's promise to support the GI Bill of Rights.[609]

The GIs in McMinn County campaigned extensively throughout the summer. They dubbed Paul Cantrell "The $100,000 sheriff" after Clyde Rogers, a former associate, fell out with the boss and revealed that Cantrell had been paid $109,104.58 under the fee system. Knox Henry, GI candidate for sheriff, promised if elected to only accept the $5,000 annual salary. One GI claimed Cantrell was "a nobody" until he tied in with Burch ten years ago and started imitating his neighbor's political tactics. "Biggs has got Polk County sewed up, and he spends his time helping Cantrell control McMinn County, including using Polk County voters at the polls," another GI supporter alleged.[610]

Three years after resigning from office after the threat of a federal lawsuit from Congressman Jennings, former Monroe County sheriff W.O. Brakebill attempted a comeback. The Democrats nominated him for county court clerk. GI supporters in Monroe said that Burch attended the Democratic convention to "put in a good word" for Brakebill. Fred Joins, frontrunner for county court clerk, had supposedly lost the nomination to Brakebill due to Biggs and Cantrell associates "stacking" the convention.[611]

"He wants to be a big political boss," a GI supporter said of Brakebill. "But Democrats here do not care for that type of machine rule." The GIs warned he was "seeking to extend the Biggs rule" to our county. "We don't want any election day monkey business which has characterized Polk and McMinn elections." The election commission appointed deputies as election officials, but the GIs had plenty of poll watchers ready.[612]

In late July, 150 McMinn County GIs sent a petition to U.S. Attorney General Tom Clark requesting federal officers to monitor elections in multiple Tennessee counties. Shelby, Polk, Monroe, and McMinn Counties, they claimed, would need FBI agents or Justice Department officials "to prevent violations of the federal statutes and to prevent frauds."[613] Their requests were ignored, causing them to resort to the only recourse they thought they had left.

Chapter 39

A Second Declaration of Independence in Athens

By 1946, McMinn Countians had lived under the Cantrell machine for a decade. Although not in power as long as Burch, Paul Cantrell's machine was nothing short of brutal, and had gained unprecedented power in the county. Multiple people were unjustifiably killed by deputies, including Carl Voiles and Hub Johnson. Most outrageous of all was the murder of Earl Ford, a Seabee from Meigs County. On leave in 1944, Ford was accused of "drunkeness" at a honkytonk outside of Athens. In an attempt to arrest Ford, Deputy Minus Wilburn deputized a thug named George Spurling on the spot. Spurling fatally shot Ford, who was resisting arrest, and planted a knife under his body. Witnesses testified that Ford, who wore a uniform without pockets, was unarmed, leading to Spurling's arrest for murder.

Voter intimidation and election fraud had become routine in McMinn County, with the perpetrators receiving little to no punishment. In 1938, a fight broke out at the Englewood precinct, resulting in a stabbing death. Tom Taylor, the son of Cantrell's opponent in 1940, was unjustifiably arrested and feared he would be killed. He made a daring escape by jerking the steering wheel to crash the police car into a creek. Thanks to ripper legislation, Cantrell had control of the county court and ordered the sale of their new voting machines. The fact that his opponents always won on the machines, but lost on paper ballots, might have had something to do with that.

The GI Ticket and their supporters tried every peaceful method imaginable to ensure a fair election. Throughout their campaign they promised voters that their vote would be "counted as cast." Observers knew if they kept that promise, violence would ensue.

In a move similar to the Biggs machine hiring extra deputies to break the miner's strike, the Cantrell machine hired dozens of outside deputies to "keep order" on election day. Massive crowds lined the streets of Athens as people went to vote on Thursday August 1, 1946. They had a front row seat, in broad daylight, to some of the worst instances of police brutality in the history of McMinn County. The machine would not relinquish its power without a war.

GI poll watcher Bob Harrill objected to a teenage girl voting at the Dixie Café precinct. Deputy Minus Wilburn blackjacked Harrill, who was hospitalized with a concussion. At the Waterworks precinct, Deputy Windy Wise shoved Tom Gillespie, an elderly black farmer, to the ground after using a racial slur. A highly respected citizen who was determined to exercise his right to vote, Gillespie got back on his feet. Wise shot him in the hip, but did not kill him.

Later that afternoon, two men barely evaded death at the Waterworks precinct. Deputy Wise refused to allow GI poll watchers Shy Scott and Ed Vestal to leave during the "counting," holding them at gun point. They were forced to stay in a corner where they could not see anything, but their presence inside the building as "witnesses" gave the election workers cover for their ballot stuffing. When a newspaper man walked in to get an update, the two GIs saw a brief opportunity to escape. They jumped through the window, shattering the glass all over the sidewalk on North Jackson Street. They had their hands up as they ran into the huge crowd. Deputy Wise almost snapped, shouting profanity and pointing his gun at the crowd.

Before the polls closed, Sheriff Pat Mansfield arrived at the Waterworks precinct and carried the ballot boxes back to his police car. He now had in his possession the ballot boxes from the county's largest precincts. He took them to the jail on White Street for "safekeeping." Feeling powerless, McMinn Countians watched as another election was being stolen from them.

But the GIs, especially ex-Marine Bill White, refused to surrender. He told his friends to go home and bring back as many guns as they could find. White led a group of GIs to the local armory, less than a mile from the jail, to acquire some heavy firepower. After sundown, they met on top of a hill across the street from the jail. Their requests for help from state and federal authorities had gone unanswered. They prepared to take their county back by force if necessary. After fighting the Japanese in the Pacific Theater, this would hardly be a challenge for Bill White.

Sheriff Mansfield, along with Paul Cantrell and dozens of deputies, were holed up in the jail. The GIs demanded they turn over the ballot boxes to ensure a fair count, but the sheriff refused. Shots were fired, kicking off a firefight that lasted several hours. Nearly two dozen GIs exchanged gunfire with the deputies. With the GIs having the high ground, and the deputies behind a thick brick wall, both sides avoided serious injuries. Pryor Crowe arrived to help the Cantrell forces but was run off.

At approximately 3:30 AM, the GIs obtained sticks of dynamite. They hurled them at the front of the jail three times, with the third one destroying the porch. The deputies finally surrendered, walking out the front door with their hands up. Sheriff Mansfield had escaped out the back earlier, but Cantrell blended in with the crowd and escaped into the darkness.

Filled with rage, a few GIs started beating the deputies in the street, and someone would probably be killed if they did not cool off. It was a blessing from above that no one died in the battle. GI supporter Ralph Duggan, an attorney and Navy veteran, stood on top of a car and screamed at the GIs to stop seeking retribution before someone was killed. He told them they had achieved their objective of securing the ballot boxes and that all of their credibility would be lost if they became vigilantes. They feared the National Guard was on their way and he wanted to show them that order had been restored in the county. The GIs calmed down, but not before one man slit the throat of Deputy Minus Wilburn. His wound was non-fatal.

The GIs found opened ballot boxes and piles of marked ballots strewn across the floor of the jail. They locked the deputies in the jail cells and collected the untampered ballot boxes. A three-man commission was formed to govern the county over the weekend to prevent anarchy, and the GIs patrolled the streets in place of the deputies.

Speaker Woods, also an election commissioner, agreed to return to Athens on Monday to canvass the election returns. Only certifying the ballots from boxes that had not been tampered with, the GI candidates won by an almost 2-1 margin. Woods certified the results, thus ending Cantrell's reign in McMinn County. Sheriff Mansfield withdrew from the state senate race.[614]

One can only imagine what went through Burch's head as he learned of the successful rebellion in Athens. With the fall of Cantrell, he had lost a powerful ally. But another man observed the aftermath of what became known as the "Battle of Athens" ever more intently: Bob Barclay. "This seems to mark the end of machine politics in McMinn County – and, I hope, everywhere else," Barclay wrote in his journal.[615] Burch Glen told reporters he had not seen any Cantrell associates in Polk County. "I'm saddened by the bloodshed." When asked if he was disappointed in Cantrell's defeat, he made no comment.[616]

Congressman Jennings blamed the U.S. Department of Justice for the bloodshed. "During the absence of some 6,000 voters in the armed services in 1942 and 1944 the Biggs-Cantrell machine used ex-convicts, murderers, armed deputy sheriffs, bootleggers, policemen, and other members of their official machine to win the elections," he said. "The days of the election thief are numbered. Polk County and the Biggs machine will be the next to be 'liberated.'"[617] The media also agreed: "Perhaps Polk is next on the revolt list," the *Knoxville News-Sentinel* wrote. Jim Buttram, GI campaign manager, also predicted the end of the Biggs machine:

> "This is the truth. Burch Biggs will never win another election. The Polk County machine is through now. I don't mean that we here in McMinn County are going to interfere. But people in Polk County and all over the state for that matter want clean, honest elections and good government. They know now it can be accomplished. This is just the start. The machine days are nearing their end."[618]

On Saturday August 3, the GIs heard rumors of an invasion from Polk County as Mansfield, along with several of his deputies and even some Polk deputies, would try to take back control of McMinn County. The GIs set up road blocks on US Highway 411 near the county line. They waited for several hours, but no one tried to invade.

Two GIs, George Painter and Bill Stansberry, visited Burch at his home. "We heard you were going to join Pat Mansfield and pay us a little visit in McMinn County," Painter said. "Do you think I'm crazy?" Burch answered.[619] He assured them he was "taking no part" in the McMinn County affair. Rev. Bernie Hampton, member of the three-man commission governing the county over the weekend, brushed off the rumors of a Mansfield-led invasion as "not serious." Although he did not expect any trouble, he said they wanted to "be ready."[620]

However, some Polk Countians did go to McMinn County that weekend when several young veterans visited the jail. According to the *Polk County News*, Herb Lillard and August Lewis were arrested in Athens on Saturday after they were found with guns in their car. They were released the next day. Lillard's family, including his father, John M. Lillard, and his brothers, Frank,

Cecil, and Cap, were staunch Republicans and longtime adversaries of the Biggs machine. Lewis had left the sheriff's department a few years prior.

The *Nashville Tennessean* contacted Burch about the uprising in Athens. "I know nothing about it," he told them. "I have no interest in what goes on in McMinn County. Goodbye!" But before hanging up, he told them he blamed the uprising on the newspapers.[621]

As the Cantrell machine did everything it could to hold onto power in McMinn County, the Biggs machine cruised to unopposed victory in Polk County. Elected in his own right for the first time, Burch Glen tallied 3,375 complementary votes to win a full term as sheriff. Leach Park won a fourth term as county court clerk while trustee Charles Williams, circuit court clerk Roxy Campbell, and register of deeds Mutt Gray all won a second term. Ben Parks was elected as the new tax assessor, succeeding the late Abie Green who had recently passed away.

In the state and federal primaries, Governor McCord and Senator McKellar won 96 percent of the Polk County vote. Former Governor Gordon Browning, fresh from service in the war, challenged McCord. The governor won the primary handily and won the contests in McMinn, Monroe, Bradley, Meigs, and Loudon Counties with an average of 78 percent, leaving Polk's unbelievable margin of victory as the massive outlier once again. Congressman Kefauver, despite recent tensions with his cousin, emerged victorious in Polk County against token opposition. Reporting on Pat Mansfield's total vote in an unopposed primary for state senate, the *Copper City Advance* wrote that Polk County gave him 3,719 complementary votes and McMinn County "gave him the boot." Bill Rose won the primary for state representative with no opposition. Burch won another term as state executive committeeman, as did Judge Wiley Couch. The Republican candidates tallied a combined 174 votes in the county. But, the one-party system in Polk County was about to be blown up.

Chapter 40

THE ORIGINS OF THE GOOD GOVERNMENT LEAGUE

In the August 8, 1946 edition of the *Copper City Advance*, Bob Barclay wrote a column titled "A Second Declaration of Independence."

"A Second Declaration of Independence was written at Athens on election day of last week…The Athens Declaration will be repeated many times and in many communities over the next few years. All the people needed was fearless leadership in their efforts to rid the country of political domination by the few. This is the leadership they now have, and they will follow it. It is the same brand of leadership that led our boys to victory from the North Atlantic to Tokyo. And the home victory will be just as complete and decisive as were the foreign victories."

Barclay discouraged any immediate action on the part of frustrated veterans in other bossed counties: "The time for action in county elections in Tennessee for 1946 is past…The McMinn County GIs did not go off half-cocked. They were ready beforehand with both an organization and objective. Without these, they would have been both defeated and put in jail."

Gone was Barclay's friendly attitude towards the Biggs machine. It was as if the McMinn GIs fueled him with unlimited courage. "Political bossism in Tennessee is out of date." He urged an "orderly" preparation for the 1948 elections. A commander of the American Legion Post No. 96 in Copperhill and a veteran of World War I, Barclay was ready to lead the reform movement. "The time was ripe in Polk…People were sick of Biggs and his relatives and henchmen and high-handed manipulations and they looked around for a leader here. That's when Bob Barclay stepped in," one citizen later remembered.[622]

On August 19, U.S. Navy veteran Chuck Talley announced the organization of a veterans committee in Polk County. "Our goal is the complete destruction of the Biggs-Couch machine in Polk County." A former Copperhill police officer and deputy sheriff, Talley led over one hundred Copper Basin veterans of both world wars in signing the statement. The group planned to recruit veterans from below the mountain as well. They congratulated the McMinn GIs on their victory.⁶²³

"We have been governed too much by legislative fiat from Nashville," read their statement as they planned to take back the Copperhill city government. Another objective was to hold a convention of veterans from every county in the Third Congressional District to select GI candidates for the state legislature. They hoped to "destroy machine rule in this part of Tennessee and to strengthen the election laws so as to make it a felony to steal an election or conspire with others to steal an election."⁶²⁴

The new veterans organization decided not to oppose Congressman Kefauver. "We know he has been the beneficiary of election thefts in Polk County," Talley said. But they were confident he would "sever his connection" with the machine, or else they would fight to defeat him, too.⁶²⁵ Talley enlisted the help of longtime Biggs foe John Wrinkle when preparing the group's statement.

"They have a right to organize," Burch said when informed of the veterans organization. "We have six veterans holding office in the courthouse, including my son, who served three years in World War II." Another was John Standridge, the clerk and master, who served in the Coast Guard.⁶²⁶

Missing in action since the Battle of Athens, Paul Cantrell made his first public appearance in nearly a month when he spoke to reporters at the Hermitage Hotel in Nashville. He declined to comment on the revolt that ousted him from power, and discussed his business ventures and life after politics. Burch walked right by Cantrell and stopped to talk with some friends. When asked to pose for a photo with his former ally, he refused. Commenting on Burch's snub, the *Knoxville Journal* wrote that it "should be a great lesson in human nature" since Burch treated Cantrell like he was "of little political value" to him. The *Nashville Tennessean* commented that Burch may have written a caption for the photo in his head: "One Down, One to Go."

A group of veterans met in Benton on August 23 to elect temporary officers to lead the "Good Government League," or GGL for short. Chairman

James R. "Newt" Shoemaker and Secretary Alfred R. "Little Buck" Arp Jr. initiated a membership drive and called a mass meeting to be held at Ducktown High School on August 31. Bob Sartin and Wade McGee also served as officers. Citizens "interested in good government" were invited.[627]

"The veterans seemed disturbed about recently published stories which they said were 'prematurely released.' These stories announced an all-out war against the 'Burch Biggs-Wiley Couch political machine' and indicated that the veterans group intended waging an active campaign for reforms in county, state, and national offices," the *Chattanooga Times* wrote. GGL officials claimed to be interested "primarily in better government in our own county and our own district." Chuck Talley said he had no plans to form a separate group from the GGL and wanted to work with Shoemaker and Arp. There was speculation that John Wrinkle leaked the plans for the veterans group led by Talley.[628]

Back at the courthouse, some of Burch's men called the GGL a "Republican movement," but most of them ignored it. Burch, of course, had more to say about it: "I'm all for the boys. If the GI is qualified for the post, I'm for him." With the nepotism flying right over his head, he bragged about "turning over his job to a veteran" the year before. "I can't understand how anyone could get the impression that I'm against the GIs."[629]

Burch Glen denied rumors that he would be replacing all of his deputies with GIs. "If I find it possible, I will have three GI deputies and three non-GIs." The young sheriff insisted he had "pretty high requirements" for a deputy. "I won't hire a deputy who drinks – not even a beer." You had to be at least 6 feet tall and weigh 200 pounds. "Little men make good officers elsewhere, but not in Polk County." Burch Glen added that "You must also be cool and level-headed" to serve on the force.[630] His deputies included Herman and Louis Wright, "Big Jim" Ellis, Clyde Dale, Ernest Hunt, Jim Spurling, and J.L. McClure. Herman Wright had been on the force since Burch first appointed him in 1930, and Spurling had replaced the slain Frank Clayton.

With the support of the McMinn GIs, James P. "Jobo" Cartwright emerged as the frontrunner for state senate. "I pledge to do everything in my power to break the Burch Biggs political machine in Polk County," he said.[631] Although not a veteran, Cartwright had served on the three-man commission that briefly governed McMinn County after the Battle of Athens.

Cleveland attorney Hardwick Stuart, a former Marine and state representative, mulled a run for the state senate. "I'm not going to be bound to any one party or faction."[632] But his previous ties with the Biggs machine made him unacceptable to the GGL. "We don't want any candidates who have had anything to do with the Biggs organization," Wade McGee said.[633]

With McMinn, Monroe, and Bradley Counties now all unbossed, the state senate race would be an easy win for the veterans. But the contest for state representative for Polk and Bradley Counties was the contest to watch. Bill Rose, well-liked and popular, hoped to win a second term. Burch's support made Rose, a veteran of World War I, a formidable opponent for the eventual GGL nominee. "The man will be well qualified," a GGL spokesman said.[634]

The *Chattanooga Times* wrote that "Veterans leaders, themselves, are anxious to prevent some of the old-line anti-Biggs factional leaders from identifying themselves too closely with the GI cause since they fear such connections would give the idea that the veterans are being used to grind the political axes for this group."[635] David Talley recalled some veterans in the GGL as "downright mean."[636] Sally Hutchins Gregory remembered some "vicious" men among GGL membership, but praised Barclay as a "gentleman."[637] Most GGL supporters simply advocated for positive change.

Chapter 41
CHAIRMAN BARCLAY

On August 31, 1946, 400 Polk Countians, including several veterans, gathered inside Ducktown High School (originally the Kimsey Junior College Building) to elect permanent officers for the GGL and endorse candidates for the state legislature. Newt Shoemaker called for the nomination of a permanent chairman. "Bob Barclay!" H.M. Love shouted as he jumped to his feet. Wade McGee competed with Warren Crye for Shoemaker's attention. A few people shouted "No!" Shoemaker recognized McGee, who made a motion to end nominations and elect Barclay by acclamation. The motion carried. Bob Barclay was now the leader of the Good Government League of Polk County.[638]

Now presiding, Barclay called for the nomination of a permanent secretary. "Little Vance" Davis nominated "Little Buck" Arp. Barclay ignored all other nominations, including a name put forth by A.J. Trotter. A noisy group of Biggs men crowded outside the building, hoping to get inside and influence the nominations. Unphased by their disruptive tactics, Barclay addressed the crowd:

> "Too many people in this county have been thinking of too many things other than good government. The tide is now turning…While you boys were away fighting the enemies of democracy abroad, those same evils were developing here at home. We are not here to persecute or ask for persecution or defeat of any man in office. We are here to defend a principle – freedom to do as you please as long as you don't become a nuisance or a menace to your community, and the right to run for any public office for which you can qualify with the assurance that if you get the most votes you will win…You boys came back home to see the results of political machines in Polk County. You see our county buildings – particularly the schools – in dilapidation. The Copperhill and Benton school buildings are a disgrace to a civilized county…With your help and with the help of all the good people of this county who will rally around us we will have some changes in Polk County."[639]

The *Chattanooga Times* reported that disinterested observers called the selection of Barclay for chairman "a masterstroke" that "lent an additional flavor of nonpartisanship to the organization." Although the *Times* wrote that Barclay had not been identified with "any political party or faction," he was a known Democrat.[640] "A fiery, gray-topped spellbinder," Barclay was not popular with everyone. "Some said that Barclay was just a natural-born rabble rouser with a lust for power."[641] Matt Witt later said it was "strictly a power and ego trip" for Barclay, but noted that he was not in it for the money.[642] "He whipped those guys up into believing what they were going to do was an extension of their war service," David Talley later recalled.[643] "They became restless and longed for the action they had seen overseas." A talented orator, Barclay gave speeches "in the style of a preacher at a camp meeting revival."[644]

The GGL passed the following resolutions: commending the McMinn GIs for their successful fight against the Cantrell machine; condemning election thieves; abolishing the poll tax; opening a county health department; strict enforcement of the salary system for sheriffs set up by the 1921 law that regulated the fee system; and starting a school and road building program.

The convention endorsed Frank Lowery for state representative. A son and grandson of former state legislators Marvin Lowery and William Frank Lowery, he enlisted in the Army and became an artillery captain. He fought in North Africa, Italy, and Germany. His superiors asked him to remain in the armed forces, but he returned home to work for his father's cotton gin business. After Marvin Lowery fell out with Burch, deputies frequently harassed Lowery's drivers as they hauled cotton to market. Burch's "fee-grabbing" only further motivated the Lowerys to support the GGL. A veteran, college graduate, and member of a longtime Democratic family, Frank Lowery proved to be a fine choice to take on the Biggs machine in Nashville.[645]

Jobo Cartwright of Athens easily won the GGL's endorsement for state senate over Hardwick Stuart. Cartwright vowed to "serve all the people and no factions" if elected.[646] Barclay formed several committees and appointed chairmen for each, including Lake McGee, Newt Shoemaker, Chucky Talley, and Hubert C. "Buck" Sartin.

McMinn GI leader Ralph Duggan addressed the convention, urging the organization to remain non-partisan. "Decent citizens must work together for a common aim regardless of political party." Barclay would later exchange letters with Duggan, seeking advice on how to successfully lead a nonpartisan reform group.[647] Burch Glen was in Ducktown the night of the meeting. "I'm just visiting over here," he said.[648] The *Copper City Advance* wrote that the GGL candidates "were steamrolled through with watch-like precision." The *Advance* commended the GIs for their "show of interest in county affairs" and urged them to keep the organization "non-partisan."

Dr. John Lillard, a veteran desirous of reform, quickly distanced himself from the GGL. Disturbed by the selection of Barclay as chairman, the Benton physician alleged the group only formed to "wrest political authority from the Biggs group."[649] Chuck Talley eventually left the GGL as well. Skepticism about some GGL members was not totally unfounded. Frank Lowery later attended a secret meeting of political dissidents. He had to walk "off the beaten path" while holding a lantern in the mountains near Reliance. "Let's kill 'em all," one of the men said. Lowery shut down that attitude promptly. "No, let's organize and vote them out."[650]

Bob Barclay, a decorated World War I veteran, was elected as the first chairman of the GGL. - Polk County Historical and Genealogical Society

The GGL held their first meeting in the auditorium of the Ducktown School on August 31, 1946. The privately-owned building, now known as Kimsey Ridge, still stands today. - Author's photo

Chapter 42

"THE FEE BUSINESS WAS GOOD FOR THE SHERIFF"

In addition to campaigning against the GGL, Burch and Broughton had dates in Judge Darr's court in September 1946. Seeking $50,000 in damages for "conspiracy to arrest and imprison, wrongful imprisonment, and malicious prosecution," Herbert Walker and William Pilgrim sued Broughton and Roxy Campbell in federal court.[651] M.E. Clemmer, owner of the garage that was robbed in 1941, was a co-defendant. The state supreme court had recently overturned Walker and Pilgrim's convictions, after which they served in the war. "Justice is a farce in Polk County," Walker said. He claimed he had to leave the state "to live down the blotch on my name."[652]

Burch's old friend Joe V. Williams defended Broughton. The defendants, represented by who else but John Wrinkle, testified to their long and miserable stay in the jail. "The jail was always packed...The fee business was good for the sheriff."[653] Wrinkle explained in a brief:

> "We think the great weight of the evidence is that Biggs was keeping the jail full of prisoners because of the amount of money that he could get and the profit made out of the poor ration that he fed the prisoners. The proof showed that the jail was stacked with prisoners, some of them having to sleep on a steel floor unless they slept three in a cot. Sheriff Biggs did not deny this, did not give any statement of the number of prisoners that he had, or the total income for the period that Walker was in jail."[654]

Wrinkle said the fingerprints found on the safe did not match those of the suspects. Walker accused Broughton of "procuring" the grand jury to indict him without probable cause. In his testimony, Broughton said he held "no malice" towards Walker and Pilgrim, and admitted the evidence was circumstantial. "I still think they did it."[655] Explaining why he denied their bond, he claimed he investigated those offering bond payments, concluding they were insolvent. But Wrinkle claimed that Broughton refused several reputable bond offers. "These bonds were certified by the Clerk of the Circuit Court of Bradley County, and it was the duty of Sheriff Biggs to recognize an official in an adjoining county that said the bond was good. We say that this refusal alone showed he was malicious in his prosecution…and that the imprisonment was false and unwarranted."[656]

The jury decided in favor of Pilgrim, but Broughton only had to pay him $1,500 in damages. Campbell and Clemmer were held not liable and Walker walked away empty-handed. Prior to the trial, a juror made prejudicial remarks against Walker, claiming he had a "bad reputation." Wrinkle wanted an appeal.[657] The *Chattanooga Times* suggested a new law to force sheriffs to "make a complete and official accounting" of fees accumulated, funds spent on food, and their net profits. A few months later, L.C. Miller, the third man imprisoned for stealing the safe, filed a $25,000 suit against Broughton.

Two years after initially filing suit, Shorty Richards' damages suit against Burch was finally tried in late September. He claimed his injuries left him partially paralyzed and rendered him unable to do most work, especially heavy lifting. Now living in North Georgia, he struggled to find gainful employment. Chattanooga attorney Carlyle Littleton, who helped defend the poll tax repeal before the state supreme court, represented Shorty. The only difference in his testimony and the story he told reporters was who shot him. He was now claiming Burch shot him from the bridge.

Littleton charged a "conspiracy to harm" Richards and said the defendants were guilty of attempted manslaughter since they had no right to shoot a suspect fleeing from a misdemeanor charge. "My client could reasonably have been apprehended without bloodshed." Judge Darr quoted a state law that said "the power of arrest for a misdemeanor in such manner as to be perilous to human life is not authorized by law." He also said the deputies had "no right to sacrifice human life or shed blood to prevent the escape of petty offenders."

Russell Kramer, Burch's defense counsel, objected to several of Littleton's questions. Littleton asked Shorty: "Did you consider Polk County, with Burch Biggs there, a healthy place…" before a livid Kramer objected. Littleton also asked Shorty how many times he had been arrested in Polk County and if they "made a practice" of arresting people like him on Saturday nights after having "a beer or two." The objective, according to Littleton, was to show malice and prove that they wanted to "get rid of Shorty in the county." Shorty testified that Deputies Ben Smith, Flavis Bates, Herman Wright, or Pryor Crowe would arrest him before he was fined between $11 and $15. Judge Darr sustained most of Kramer's objections, forcing Littleton to reword or withdraw his questions.

Burch, Smith, and Bates all denied shooting or even shooting at Shorty. They all pinned the blame on highway patrolman Woodrow Reece. Burch testified that he left his house unarmed and that the McClary car was not on the bridge. Littleton irritated Kramer again when he asked Burch if he "ever admitted to killing anybody." Kramer objected to another question about "if there has been some killing up there by the deputies." Darr sustained all of them. Littleton emphasized that Burch did not arrest Reece despite testifying he saw Reece shoot Shorty.

Judge Leslie R. Darr, appointed to the federal bench by President Franklin D. Roosevelt, frequently gave preferential treatment to the political bosses in East Tennessee. - Chattanooga Public Library

Bates testified that he did not shoot at Shorty when he first ran off and that Shorty later said he did not know who shot him. "Do you know what would have happened to this boy if he said Burch Biggs shot him?" Littleton said. This led to a rare Kramer objection that Darr overruled. But Littleton then said "they shoot to kill" in Polk County, leading to Darr sustaining Kramer's objection and telling Littleton he would have to prove a pattern in this case, not previous events. Smith claimed that the only shots he fired were warning shots up in the air as he chased Shorty. Even Broughton blamed Reece for shooting Shorty in his testimony and said his father was unarmed.

The plaintiff accused State Patrolman Reece of participating in the conspiracy to harm, but the defense claimed he acted on his own. In his testimony, Reece admitted he fired shots in Shorty's direction down in the creek but did not specify if any of the shots hit Shorty. Kramer asked him if he wished to end his testimony to prevent possible self-incrimination. Reece agreed and left the witness stand.

Several people who witnessed the incident testified. Stella McClary and her mother-in-law, Mrs. Parnick McClary, swore they saw Burch shoot Shorty from the bridge while in their car. But Mrs. Parnick McClary said she also saw Reece shoot at Shorty. Kramer accused the McClarys of "some rather bad feeling" between her and the Biggs family over a recent financial transaction, but they denied it, saying they liked the Biggs family.

Former deputy August Lewis, who now owned and operated a hardware store at the corner of Main Street and Highway 411, testified that he saw Reece shoot down at Shorty and saw "one or two cars" on the bridge. It is puzzling that Littleton did not ask Lewis about his days as a deputy sheriff. But he did ask if Burch bought a school bus for him when he was a driver. "You know he controls politics over there," Littleton said. Kramer objected, but Littleton said he wanted to show that Lewis held a "lucrative position" because of the sheriff. Darr still sustained the objection. Littleton asked "Could anybody get any sort of political job over there without Mr. Biggs' support?" Darr again sustained Kramer's objection. When asked if he was a "good friend" of Burch Biggs, Lewis answered "I hope I am."

Frank Lillard played dumb during most of his testimony, denying that he ever spoke to reporters after the incident. He lived on the west side of Highway 411 and said he was blind in one eye. He testified that he saw Reece shoot down at Shorty but did not see Burch shoot. Neil Howard testified he saw Burch on the bridge and heard several shots.

The jury only deliberated for an hour and ruled in favor of Shorty, handing the Biggs machine its second defeat in Judge Darr's court in the same month. Burch was ordered to pay Shorty $5,000, while Bates and Smith would have to pay $500 each. The defense asked for a new trial, but the case was later declared a mistrial and would have to be retried.[658] With the trials concluded for now, Burch and Broughton could get back to campaigning against the GGL.

Chapter 43

"We Haven't Enjoyed a Clean Election in the Past 16 Years"

A month out from the election, the Biggs machine circulated campaign pamphlets. "For the first time in the history of the present political monarchs in Polk County, they have found it necessary to resort to printed pamphlets to attract voters," Barclay said with amusement. He called the effort "a hodgepodge of truth distortions." In the spirit of the McMinn GIs, he guaranteed the November election would be fair and that Polk Countians could vote "with the assurance that as they mark their ballots, so they will be counted."[659] The GGL ran ads urging the election of Lowery and Cartwright:

> "McMinn County threw off the Biggs-Cantrell Yoke on Aug. 1st. Bradley County was threatened with the Biggs Shackles, but refused to wear them. Polk Count CAN and WILL free itself on Nov. 5 with the help and support of the good people of the county!"[660]

Barclay spoke at a rally in Ducktown on October 1, telling voters that electing Lowery and Cartwright would be the first step towards "liquidation" of the Biggs machine. "There are four things, principally, wrong with Polk County: poor schools, poor highways, little knowledge of the county's finances, and the method of holding elections." He blamed the people's lack of cooperation for the present situation. On the subject of election fraud, Barclay claimed he had no "first-hand evidence," but said that "where there is so much smoke there is bound to be a fire." He lamented the lack of school improvements, but made it clear that he meant no criticism of the teachers.[661]

Others shared Barclay's desire for improved roads. Copper Basin resident Henry Watson remembered the roads being in "terrible shape."[662] But the same was true below the mountain. Linsdale native Mary Lethco Lewis remembered the roads being so bad that sometimes people had to fix them themselves.[663] Billy Rice lived in Ocoee and often struggled to get to school when the bus got stuck in the mud.[664] Roy G. Lillard, son of former sheriff Abe Lillard III, later wrote that the roads had been "sadly neglected."[665]

Several of the roads needed to be hard-surfaced. A few years prior, the Men's Community Club of Ducktown passed a resolution asking the governor and the road commissioner to pave the unfinished section of U.S. Highway 64. They complained of hazards due to "dust, loose gravel, mud, holes, and rocks."[666] Given that a road contractor had been extorted and killed by a Polk County deputy, it was unsurprising that such little progress had been made on the federal highway through the county.

Very few Copperhill businessmen attended the rallies, much to Barclay's disappointment. "Copperhill has been a pawn in the hands of the county machine for years," he said. Frank Lowery also spoke, insisting that the framers of the state constitution did not intend for any political subdivision to "be under the control of any one family."[667] Lowery and Rose both campaigned on a promise to repeal the Copperhill ripper bill.

Most GGL sympathizers remained anonymous, with very few openly aiding the new reform organization. Pearl Haskins, a Democrat from a family vocally opposed to the Biggs machine, permitted the GGL to meet in her Corner Lunch restaurant in Benton. "People were threatened with violence if they went to her lunchroom to eat." Haskins was forced out of business.[668]

The Biggs machine hatched an idea to peel away some veteran support from the GGL. A group of 400 pro-Biggs veterans formed the Veterans League of Polk County. Ben Witt was elected chairman. Warren Crye and A.J. Trotter, unsuccessful in their attempt to influence the election of officers at the first GGL meeting, helped organize the new group. Three Republicans were elected officers: Warren Crye, Raymond McMahan, and Hal Dalton. I.J. Wright, brother of Deputies Herman and Louis Wright, joined the group.

Their platform was almost a carbon copy of the GGL's platform. But one resolution stood out, directed at the McMinn County GIs: "We condemn mob violence and are opposed to outside influence in the affairs of Polk County." Witt denied the new group had any ties to the Biggs machine. "This organization has no affiliation with any political faction or political leader."[669] The county court later unanimously endorsed the Veterans League platform.

Ralph Duggan shared helpful election information with Barclay. "We found that the machine had misinformed people for so long and so badly that they did not know what their rights were," Duggan wrote.[670] Barclay wrote to state attorney general Roy Beeler requesting legal information about state elections. "I am also doing this as a precautionary measure against uncalled for squabbles at the polls which could very well happen as much from ignorance of our election laws as from outright attempts to take the election by malicious disregard of these same election laws."[671]

Barclay had two questions: Where are the ballots to be counted, and who is and is not permitted by law to see the ballots read off to be sure they are being called as the voters marked them? "Citizens here have been frightened into believing that when they have cast their ballots that their rights and privileges end there, and that the safest thing for them to do is to 'scat' and not be seen at the polls any more that day."[672] Beeler's office responded by sharing Tennessee Code Section 2087:

> "When the election is finished the returning officer and judges shall in the presence of such the electors as may choose to attend open the box and read aloud the names of the persons which shall appear on each ballot…"[673]

Citing the case of *United States vs. Badinelli 37, Fed. 138*, Beeler's office wrote that "taking a ballot box from the polls to a private room to count the votes was unlawful." They also wrote that electors who have the right to vote in the precinct have the right to be present at the counting of the ballots in the polling place appointed for that purpose. Barclay said it seemed as if "our laws are okay if they are properly and fairly executed."[674] Barclay also sent telegrams to Governor McCord and Senator McKellar. An excerpt from the message read:

> "Machine rule has brought decay and stagnation to progress in Polk County, and citizens have at last rebelled by endorsing the foregoing nominees. These nominees can win in Polk through a fair election on November 5. Do you favor a fair election here on that date, or will you by remaining silent tacitly endorse a continuation of scandalous conditions at the polls here which would well bring revolt of the citizens of Polk on November 5 similar to that which occurred in McMinn County on August 1? Please answer."[675]

Governor McCord replied with one-sentence: "Re your telegram of October 14, I favor clean elections in every ward and precinct in Tennessee."

He told the Associated Press that he had no plans to send officers into Polk County "to watch for trouble" on election day. "We will not have a streamlined carpet-bagging government in Tennessee!"[676] He cited a federal injunction that restrained former governor Gordon Browning from sending troops to patrol Shelby County's election in 1938, where Browning was crushed by Boss Crump's candidate Prentice Cooper. The state courts, the governor insisted, can investigate the "disturbances."[677] W.O. "Chink" Lowe, the Republican nominee for governor, promised if elected to send in the state guard "to enable all qualified persons to vote and assure count of the votes as cast."[678]

Five hundred people attended a GGL rally at the courthouse on October 12. Discussing the Veterans League, Barclay commended the members as "good boys, just like the veterans in the GGL." By November 5, he predicted, "many of them will be in the GGL."[679] He responded to the charge that he had a personal vendetta against the Biggs machine:

> "I did not start this purging movement in Polk County, and I won't stop it. I could not do so if I tried. The citizens are beginning to awaken to their sense of responsibility, and are determined to regain control of the county. It's no pleasure for me to be fighting my old political buddies."[680]

"November 5 should be made a public holiday," Barclay declared. He called on all merchants to close their business and all farmers, workers, and housewives to come out to the polls "to see how the election is won." This, he insisted, would ensure they could defeat the Biggs machine "without mob violence." Barclay asserted the GGL would not permit outside armed deputies near any precinct and that every vote "would be counted as cast." Other speakers included Frank Lowery, Jobo Cartwright, Ralph Duggan, and Willis Park, who had fled Polk County for Cleveland. Cartwright named increased salaries for teachers as a "major plank" of his platform.[681]

At a rally of 200 people in Copperhill, Barclay demanded a more-detailed report of the county's finances. "Copperhill is under the domination of the Biggs organization...I am campaigning to return this city to the people, as well as the whole of Polk County." He lamented the flight of "several good families" from the county in recent years. "They left because they can no longer stand local political conditions." The GGL chairman blamed Polk County Republican leaders for "selling out" the party. "We have no true Republican or Democratic parties in this county. The only difference in Polk now is between those who favor progress and decency in the county and those who do not." He claimed the Biggs machine only cared about its own welfare and the majorities it can "roll up" at elections. "We can win the election without violence, and none of us want violence."[682]

Courage is contagious, and Barclay proved an inspiration to many young veterans longing for change. Henry Watson recalled why he decided to join the GGL: "At the time everybody was afraid to even say anything about the elections, afraid of being killed, or their stuff being burnt up or their kids being bothered or something. Anybody that got in their way they either killed or had killed…That's the reason that I was interested in trying to stop some of it."[683]

Campaign poster for Frank Lowery, the GGL candidate for state representative, in November 1946. - Lamon Lowery Rose

Speaking at a Democratic Party barbecue in Cleveland, Hardwick Stuart struggled to shake off his past ties with the Biggs machine. "I would like to have everybody's vote, but damn the influence…Anybody who supports me should expect nothing in return."[684] Burch and several associates attended the barbecue, as did Governor McCord, who referred to Stuart as "Senator Stuart."

Henry Crox and Red Passmore met with Bradley County Republicans to ensure their support for Lowery. After initially declining to endorse, the Tennessee Republican Party endorsed Cartwright on October 19, saying "We are supporting generally all anti-Biggs movements in the state."[685]

In response to several newspapers predicting violence and "outside interference" on election day, Burch Glen asked Governor McCord if he could send in the National Guard to help "preserve law and order."[686] The governor consulted Attorney General Beeler who cited a 1941 Public Act prohibiting the Guard from "supervising, guarding, holding, or investigating" any election. The Guard could only be dispatched in the event of an "invasion, rebellion, insurrection, or riot." Due to their limited police powers in the state, Beeler also said the State Highway Patrol could only be dispatched to help preserve order if they were made special deputies by the sheriff.[687]

School board chairman Hoyt Lillard sent a letter to every county teacher and school employee urging them to vote for Bill Rose. He listed Rose's promises for increased salaries, improved facilities, and new school buses. "Help keep a board of education that will keep you secure in your positions and see that you get your money every month." He falsely claimed that the "opposing faction" had been in control before 1930 and warned they would again "lower the standard of our school system."[688] According to Ralph Painter, his mother, Doris, was paid $45 per month as a teacher, but Lillard always kept $5 for himself out of each paycheck. Painter taught at Conasauga for many years, but did not teach long after Lillard took over the school system.[689]

A week before the election, Ralph Duggan alleged the Biggs machine was "stating openly" that they intended to count the ballots in the jail. In response to Duggan's warning that there "may be trouble" on November 5, Burch said "There'll be no fight unless Duggan starts it."[690] On November 1, election commission chairman Hoyt Lillard released a statement:

> "Orders and instructions have been given to all precinct election officers appointed to hold the Nov. 5 general election in Polk County to carry out the election as prescribed by law and they have been specifically instructed to hold a fair and impartial election, that the votes must be counted where cast in the respective precincts and that any legal voter of the respective precincts shall have the right to see the ballots counted as prescribed by law."[691]

Lillard's statement almost read like an admission of prior guilt. Broughton, the election commission secretary, ensured that "any person qualified to vote in any precinct in the county will be free to watch the count in that precinct." Another Biggs supporter insisted the election would be fair "unless we are invaded by outsiders."[692]

Governor McCord said he was "greatly relieved" to read Lillard's statement. Barclay commended the statement, and discussed past election abuses, including ballot stuffing and altering election scrolls after leaving the precincts. "If they can beat us in a fair election, we will go along with them," the GGL chairman promised.[693] Burch seemed confident he would survive the challenge: "My people will take care of me in this county."[694] The *Nashville*

Tennessean was still skeptical: "We can't help wondering if instructions in past elections have been that specific. There's a slight air of too meticulous virtue about the whole thing."

Fewer deputies than usual were assigned to work the precincts. Leach Park and John Standridge were in Benton, Deputy Clyde Dale in Ducktown, I. J. Wright in Conasauga, and Joe Coffee in Copperhill. W.C. Higgins was a Democrat election worker at Conasauga. His cousin, Wayne Higgins, was a GGL poll watcher. "I'll take care of my cousin, if necessary," Wayne said.[695]

William B. Ladd, Senator McKellar's opponent in the primary, listed six demands for the Polk County election commission. He wanted a record of absentee voters who requested ballots, for their envelopes to be preserved, and for a posted list of everyone who voted absentee. He also wanted Burch Glen to forbid his deputies from serving as election officers and to refrain from stationing them at any precinct "for the purpose of intimidating, terrorizing, assaulting, and aiding in stealing the election."[696]

Election commissioner Henry Crox said the Biggs machine "has run the county long enough" and predicted victory for Lowery and Cartwright only if a clean election is held. He feared a repeat of the Battle of Athens. "We haven't enjoyed a clean election in the past 16 years."[697] In reply to Burch's comment that "little Republican opposition" had challenged the Democrats for the past decade, Crox said it was useless to run for office "when they knew the election would be taken from them." Crox shared stories of the Biggs machine bringing in "thugs" and voters from North Carolina and Georgia to ensure victory at the polls. "Biggs officials have for years hustled the ballot boxes off to some secluded spot immediately after closing of the polls to count them, threatening the Republican officials with bodily harm if they interfered."[698]

GGL Secretary Little Buck Arp warned that, "We'll fight if the election is conducted like previous elections." Attorney John Prince said he would be watching Biggs closely on election day and that "our boys will not be tricked." Little Vance Davis chimed in: "If the Biggs crowd resorts to unfair methods to win the election, we'll be ready with guns." Burch Glen said the county would have "law and order" and a "fair count of the votes." But the young sheriff reminded everyone that "we can put up a pretty good scrap if trouble starts." Sitting on the courthouse steps, an old farmer came to Burch's defense: "Burch Biggs always has conducted fair elections and if there's any trouble, it'll be stirred up by Republicans."[699]

The election commission failed to post the list of absentee voters in the courthouse ten days before the election as required by law. "We still haven't

Bill Rose, left, was a deputy sheriff, justice of the peace, and state legislator under the Biggs Machine. - Lori Rosenbloom

found out what happened to the mail ballots," Little Buck Arp said. As usual, Hoyt Lillard claimed it had been posted and that someone must have taken it down. "No one knows just how ready we are for tomorrow," Arp said. "There will be trouble."[700]

The GGL had opened their election headquarters in an abandoned cotton gin, and Buck Arp's filling station across from the courthouse served as secondary headquarters. A 24-hour guard had to be stationed there after someone was seen snooping around it two nights before the election.

An anonymous Polk County citizen wrote an indignant letter to the editor of the *Chattanooga Times* in defense of Burch. He accused the paper of being a "severe critic" of Burch for several years and insisted the editor, Alfred Mynders, would change his opinion of him if he ever met him. He praised Burch as a "God-fearing man" who helped many people "in distress and trouble." Accusing the *Times* of portraying all Polk Countians as "ruffians," the nameless scribe asked the press to "let them alone" so they could get along better. "Burch Biggs is a loyal friend, a devoted husband, loving father, a leader in all religious and charitable activities in this section.[701]

The day before the election, two dozen GGL men stood outside the Arp filling station as Broughton, Hoyt Lillard, and several other Biggs men walked into the courthouse. "Even an outsider could feel the tension thickening as the leaguers glared out across the street at the little group tramping toward the courthouse, the *Nashville Tennessean* reported. "Another Athens is the only alternative if the Biggs machine starts using the same methods it has for the past 16 years," Barclay said.[702]

Worried for his family's safety, Burch had a "cordon" of guards stationed around his Main Street home that night. "We'll have no disorder unless outsiders come in and stir it up," he said. "I count many men in the GGL as my friends and I don't think they will instigate trouble." Ignoring the group's bipartisan composition, he insisted the GGL was nothing but a front for the Republicans. "They can't win any other way." GGL leaders easily refuted this by reminding voters that well over half their membership was Democratic and that one of the two candidates they endorsed for the state legislature was from a longtime Democratic family.[703]

In a last-minute campaign flyer, a desperate Bill Rose attempted to tie Lowery to Banjo Presswood, claiming it was "general knowledge" that the bootlegger was supporting Lowery and that he had contacted Copperhill city officials to "guarantee" that the ripper bill would not be repealed if Lowery won. Most voters knew Burch protected Banjo's racket, and Barclay later said that very few voters believed Rose's accusations.[704]

The *Copper City Advance* urged every eligible voter to get out and vote:

> "Throughout the world today, there are millions who would gladly exchange whatever small possessions they may have left to them for our greatest American privilege – the right to vote."

The *Advance* hoped a repeat of the "McMinn County affair" could be avoided and reminded the election commissioners, elected officials, and the people that they all had a role to play to ensure a fair and non-violent election. The GGL ran a full-page ad asking voters to support Lowery and Cartwright and "celebrate the return of freedom in Polk County!"[705]

Chapter 44

THE GGL'S FIRST TEST

Anticipating another shootout between veterans and sheriff's deputies, newspaper reporters from Nashville, Knoxville, Chattanooga, and even Atlanta descended upon Benton on election day. The Associated Press even installed equipment to transmit wire photos. The GGL stationed spotters at every precinct who "will not be shoved about when the counting begins."[706] Several McMinn County GIs were also in town ready to help if necessary. The GGL denied a report that some GIs were found in possession of machine guns and dynamite.

Burch Glen heard rumors that GGL supporters planned to kidnap his father in an attempt to draw the deputies into the mountains and away from the polls. He escorted Burch as he cast his vote in Springtown. No one tried to kidnap the Old Sheriff.

According to the old-timers, Polk County had its "quietest and most orderly" election they had ever seen. GGL leaders admitted it was the fairest election in the county since 1930. Turnout was high as voters countywide cast their ballots without any trouble. Beer sales were banned in Copperhill the day before the election. Tension was reportedly "a little higher" in the Copper Basin, but Barclay reported that "everything went along smoothly there."[707]

No one reported seeing any guns at the polls except for one incident in Benton that was quicky defused. A man who had too much to drink, according to Burch Glen, "came in and tried to raise a racket." The drunk, allegedly a Biggs supporter, pulled a gun on another man, but was quickly arrested and imprisoned. "I don't care what side they're on, we're going to see that nobody raises a disturbance in Benton today," Burch Glen insisted.[708]

"From the time the polls opened, Benton assumed the peaceful air of a country town conducting a routine election," the *Chattanooga Times* reported. At the Benton precinct, officer of election Leach Park laughed with GGL election judge H.M. Love as he called off the ballots. Ol Harrison, Burch's opponent in 1930, watched the count. "Here in Copperhill, the *Copper City Advance* reported, "the returns were counted in the presence of all who desired to stay, and was completed by eight o'clock."

Without incident, the ballot boxes were transported to the courthouse that evening. Broughton stood outside and welcomed reporters and photographers to come in and watch. "Everything will be peaceful," he assured them. More than 200 people from both sides watched as Hoyt Lillard tabulated the results.[709]

"POLK WAR VETERANS SMASH BIGGS MACHINE," reported the *Nashville Tennessean*. The *Chattanooga Times* ran the headline "BURCH BIGGS GIVEN BEATING." The election results proved what everyone who was not a Biggs devotee knew: in a fair election, the Biggs machine would lose. Frank Lowery and Jobo Cartwright won by comfortable margins in Polk County on their way to resounding victory in their districts. Lowery won 1,636 votes to Rose's 1,376 votes (54 percent of the vote). Lowery and Rose virtually split the county's nine precincts, with Lowery winning big in Ocoee, Conasauga, and Ducktown and Rose easily taking the mountain precincts and winning close contests in Benton and Copperhill. Cartwright won 1,751 votes to Stuart's 1,152 votes (60 percent of the vote). These results reminded Polk voters of the election days of old when the county was consistently purple. The winners took Bradley County by larger margins, with Lowery winning 4,079 votes to Rose's 2,287. Cartwright blew out Stuart in Bradley and McMinn Counties and won Monroe County by about 300 votes, winning 8,893 votes to 5,175 for Stuart.

The most damning indicator of just how clean the election was showed in the gubernatorial contest. In what the *Copper City Advance* called a "stunning surprise," Republican nominee Chink Lowe, although losing the race statewide, won 1,307 votes to Governor McCord's 1,188 votes (52 percent of

Anticipating another violent election, newspaper reporters from all over the region descended upon Benton for the November 5, 1946 election, only to find the streets of Benton calm and peaceful. - Polk County News

the vote). Just two years prior, Burch delivered 4,802 votes for McCord and 251 for his opponent. It was Polk's closest election for governor since 1930 and the first since 1936 where the winner received under 75 percent of the vote. As expected, Lowe won comfortably in Bradley and McMinn Counties and narrowly carried Monroe and Loudon Counties. The governor barely won Meigs County.

In the federal races, Kefauver and McKellar won Polk County as expected, but they did not receive the customary 95 percent-plus vote share. Kefauver won 1,410 votes to 825 for his opponent, independent candidate George Bagwell, while McKellar won 1,291 votes to 826 for Ladd. Both were reelected, but did not break 65 percent of the vote in Polk County. In 1944, Kefauver had tallied 4,818 votes in Polk. In fact, more than half of Bagwell's votes in the district came from McMinn and Polk Counties, whose voters knew of Kefauver's close ties to Burch.

Certainly, 1946 was a good year for Republicans nationwide. But the Democrats still won everywhere they had historically been strong, including in the Third Congressional District. Nevertheless, Polk County had just proven how purple they really were with such mixed election results and the absence of any landslide victories. For the first time in nearly two decades, their results matched with their historical trends and those of their neighboring counties. Only one question remained: could it continue?

Bob Barclay was more satisfied than anybody. "All we have asked for is a fair and honest election...We seem to be getting it." Ralph Duggan called it "the most peaceful election ever conducted." John Prince, who had accused the Biggs machine of buying votes, said it was the "most orderly election" he had seen in his 53 years.[710]

Burch sat beside his radio listening to results from around the nation. "Nobody can take defeat any better than I can," he told reporters. "I'll see 'em again." Bill Rose, who had recently said he was quitting politics "win, lose, or draw" after the 1947 legislative term, graciously accepted defeat. "Politics takes too much time from my business." Hoyt Lillard just made excuses: "The newspapers so terrorized the voters by predictions of violence that our supporters were afraid to come to the polls."[711]

John Wrinkle celebrated the GGL victory: "Everybody knows that his (Biggs) 4,000 vote majorities were in the counting, not in the voting." He credited the *Chattanooga Times* for playing an important part in its "impartial" coverage of the Biggs machine.[712] Barclay also thanked the *Times* for "helping build up sentiment against the political machine in this county."

He insisted the GGL would "crush" the last signs of machine rule in Polk in August 1948.[713] Thanking Copper Basin voters, Barclay wrote of the "dawn of a new day in Polk County's search for better things."[714] The *Copper City Advance* celebrated the "honest" election that had been "much too rare" in the county.

Veterans in both parties emerged victorious at the polls all over East Tennessee, with six GIs winning seats in the state legislature. John Peck, a Democrat who was elected as McMinn County's state representative, ran as an independent. Monroe County also elected an ex-GI Democrat. Good Government Leagues popped up all over the region. Alfred Mynders observed the bipartisan rejection of bossism: "The issues in this campaign were not Republican versus Democrat…The issue…was good government against machine politics." In neighboring Cherokee County, North Carolina, former Polk County deputy Frank Crawford was elected sheriff.

The *Chattanooga Times* speculated on the chances that Governor McCord would sign any potential anti-Biggs bills at the next legislative session. "The fact that Polk County voted against McCord and for Lowe doesn't offer much encouragement to Biggs supporters."

In his weekly column, Barclay compared the results of the 1944 county election to the results from 1946, claiming "not over 2,000" of the 1944 votes were legal. "I wonder whose face is red now?" he said of McCord's loss in Polk County. He hoped the GGL victory would inspire other counties across the state "to clear the state of political thievery and vandalism from the capitol building down to the smallest county office." The GGL chairman praised the "boys" in the organization for bearing the "brunt of the fight" in ensuring a fair election. "The name of Polk has once more been added to the list of civilized counties in Tennessee. We intend to keep it there by putting the finishing touches to the political machine in this county in 1948."[715]

The GGL held a victory rally on November 16 in Benton where they unveiled their new slogan: "A Clean Slate in '48!" Barclay wanted the entire county court replaced with GIs from both parties. "The League is still active and growing…Just wait until 1948. It will be pitiful.[716] Barclay had done a commendable job of forming a broad coalition of Republicans, Democrats, and independent voters, many of whom had many disagreements on national issues, and getting them to the polls to defeat the Biggs machine's candidates and advocate for long overdue reforms.

The November election was free of violence, but the month was not. On November 19, a dynamite explosion went off at the Copperhill home of Deputy Ernest Hunt. No one was harmed in the attack, as Hunt was sleeping at the house he had just bought next door. "I was asleep when the explosion woke me up and I heard an automobile drive away."[717] The perpetrators were probably men ready to see the Biggs machine overthrown, by any means necessary.

Frank Lowery's victory in the contest for state legislature in November 1946 was a crucial early victory for the GGL. - Polk County Historical and Genealogical Society

The *Chattanooga Times* reported that Cartwright was planning legislation to "curtail" the power of the Biggs machine and that he wanted to return McMinn and Monroe Counties to the Second Congressional District. Cartwright vehemently denied reports that he would curtail Biggs in the legislature and he said he would not be sponsoring any "spite legislation" and claimed had given "no consideration" to redistricting. "I have no personal legislative plans whatever, but I will do the very best I can for the counties I represent." Discussing potential GGL legislation, he said he would cooperate with them as long as their bills are "reasonable and fair."[718]

Almost one hundred Copperhill citizens met on November 18 with one goal in mind: repealing the Copperhill ripper bill. W. Q. Higdon and E. A. Middleton were elected chairman and secretary for the group. Proving that he was not just making an empty campaign promise, Bill Rose took to the floor first, stating his desire to see the city government "go back as before." W.G. Tallant, W.O. Tallant, and Pat Terry also spoke.[719]

The GGL executive committee met in December to draft a resolution to increase salaries for the county's teachers. They had not received a pay increase since 1941, and there was no automatic annual increment.[720] The resolution called for the pay increase to be retroactive to the start of the 1946-1947 school year and for the county court to "institute an economy drive in the county's affairs whereby any useless or extravagant expenditures may be terminated."[721]

A few weeks before Christmas, young veterans John Standridge and Ben Witt purchased the *Polk County News* from longtime publisher John Shamblin. Standridge was still clerk and master for the Chancery Court. The duo would lead the paper to a more pronounced bias towards the Biggs machine. During the Fall 1946 campaign, Barclay had asked Shamblin to run one of his columns from the *Copper City Advance*. A reluctant Shamblin replied, "There seems to be a political scrap between two factions in Polk, and I don't want to get mixed up in it." Barclay wrote that Shamblin was only concerned with "self-preservation" and that he was a "typical editor" who had "been cowed into submission by political machines."[722] The new owners listed a program they "would like to see" on the paper's masthead. Much of it was a blatant rip-off of the GGL's platform, including modern schools and improved roads.

The state comptroller's office released the results of their audit of the county's revenue collecting offices. Anticipating a GGL-initiated audit, Burch arranged for an audit of several county offices. Unsurprisingly, they all received glowing praise. The state auditor commended their "neat and accurate recordkeeping" and assured voters that all state and county funds "are accounted for and have been paid into the proper channels." Standridge ran the story on the front page of his newspaper the same week Lowery and Cartwright introduced legislation to take on the Biggs machine.[723]

Chapter 45

REPEALING THE RIPPERS

Former state legislator Marvin Lowery had a talk with his son, Frank, before the 1947 legislative session. "Only stay over there long enough to do what you need to do and then get out," he warned him. Elected as an independent, Frank Lowery caucused with the Democrats. Not long after he settled in the capitol, a Biggs associate stopped in for a visit. He dropped an envelope full of money on a table in front of the freshman legislator. "If you don't do anything to hurt us, consider this a down payment." Lowery refused to take the bribe. "I'm going to do what I came here to do."[724] Burch had every reason to fear private acts stripping him of his power, especially since it was partly how he accumulated so much of it to begin with.

When Burch visited Nashville during this session, at least he was not neglecting his duties as sheriff. His first stop was Governor McCord's office. *Nashville Tennessean* photographers spotted him, wearing his trademark ten-gallon hat, engaged in conversation with Will Gerber, Boss Crump's right-hand man. When approached by reporters, Gerber walked away. Burch said he was "just looking around" and refused to comment further. "He wasn't the same jovial 'boss politician,'" the *Tennessean* wrote.[725]

"The plan is to completely destroy the Biggs machine and establish more efficient government in Polk County," Lowery said of his legislation. He planned repeals of several previous bills, including some authored by his father. The budget commissioner and county school manager positions, which had proven to be very lucrative for Hoyt Lillard, would be abolished, as would the chief deputy's salary. Cartwright, who observed that Burch was spending much of his time conferring with senators, planned to introduce the same bills in the senate.[726]

Burch and Broughton looked on as Lowery introduced his bills in the house chamber. The bills also abolished the $1,800 annual salary for a county attorney, currently held by Cas Geer, and the $2,100 annual salary paid to the sheriff for "assisting in holding court at Ducktown." For years, the sheriff drew an additional salary just for doing his job by opening court on both sides of the county as all previous sheriffs had done for no extra compensation.[727]

"This is not spite legislation," Lowery insisted. "We are primarily interested in saving money for Polk County." Burch barely spoke a word to Lowery, and told the press he had no comment. He was trying to garner enough support to block the bills, telling other legislators they would "cripple the Democratic Party in East Tennessee and turn Polk County over to the Republicans."728 The next day, Lowery and Cartwright introduced another bill, this time to abolish the $2,100 annual salary paid to the circuit court clerk for attending court at Benton and Ducktown. Roxy Campbell, and formerly George Gilliland, drew this extra salary for many years.

"Mr. Biggs has the right to lobby for or against any bill he chooses," Bob Barclay told the *Chattanooga Times*. He discussed the $6,000 annual savings ensured by the bills by gutting "salaries poured down the drain, insofar as benefit to the county is concerned."729 "It is almost unheard of for members of the legislature to fight any local bill," the *Knoxville News-Sentinel* reported. Burch was in Nashville all week and said he did not know if his friends would fight the Lowery and Cartwright legislation. The next week, Broughton, Burch Glen, and Roxy Campbell issued a joint statement alleging the proposed bills "are not applicable to the officeholders." They claimed the chief deputy salary law had already been ruled unconstitutional and that Campbell had never drawn a salary under the circuit court clerk salary law.730

Burch's lobbying efforts failed, and local courtesy prevailed. The bills passed the senate on January 13. Governor McCord's office made no efforts to block or stall their passage. Burch and Broughton were not present when the house easily passed the bills on January 15. McCord signed two of the bills the next day, eliminating the county school business manager position and the chief deputy's salary. On January 21, he signed the remaining three bills. Lowery and Cartwright had accomplished much of their agenda in just a few weeks.

Lowery's work was far from over. He introduced a bill to restore the Bradley County Court districts to their pre-1943 boundaries.731 The bill would not affect the tenure of any current JP and would become effective in September 1948. After passing the senate, McCord signed it into law on January 31.

On January 24, Lowery kept his most important campaign promise when he introduced legislation to repeal the Copperhill ripper bill. Barclay wrote that a repeal would have "a tremendously favorable effect on the morale of the people here in the Basin." It could not have come at a better time, as city clerk Louise Styles had recently been charged with embezzlement.[732]

The bill restored the city's aldermanic government, and the present mayor and commissioners, R.P. Taylor, Granville Radcliffe, and Leonard C. Goss, would be removed from office. Taylor had now been put in and taken out of office by state legislation. The bill named a new mayor and board of aldermen handpicked by the GGL: Pat Terry, Buck McCay, William G. Tallant, Emil A. Greene, Carl E. Panter, and former commissioner Gid Ware. Unlike the Bradley County bill, this would go into effect immediately and the city would not hold another election until December 1948.[733]

Pat Terry, a WWI veteran and longtime TCC employee, was appointed mayor of Copperhill under legislation sponsored by the GGL. - Ducktown Basin Museum

On February 14, the Copperhill bill became law after the governor made no attempt to sign or veto it. He gave no explanation for his decision. Bill Rose swore in the new city aldermen, comprised of Democrats and Republicans. New mayor Pat Terry was a longtime resident, TCC employee, World War I veteran, and father of two World War II veterans. Three of the new aldermen were veterans.

Lowery and Cartwright voted against a proposed increase in funding for the State Highway Patrol. Cartwright alleged that Sgt. C.W. Strader assisted the Cantrell forces during the Battle of Athens. "They ought to cut the highway patrol appropriation in half. All the patrolmen do is hang around back alleys and wait a chance to raid bootleggers." Lowery resented the highway patrol for refusing to "help preserve order" during the 1946 county election.[734] Lowery's distrust of the highway patrol would soon be vindicated further.

Chapter 46

THE POLK COUNTY COMMISSION ACT

In addition to controlling the sheriff's department since 1930 and every county office since 1934, Burch had the Polk County Court completely under his thumb. Only one or two Republicans, usually from Copperhill, ever won a seat on the eight-person legislative body and the court was powerless to stop anything Burch wanted. Bob Barclay and the GGL knew they had to find a way to cut off the machine's purse strings if they were to liberate their county in 1948. "We must take control of the county away from our 'enemies' as soon as possible," Barclay wrote to Lowery.[735]

On February 4, 1947, Frank Lowery introduced one of the most important private acts in the county's history: the Polk County Commission Act. Under the bill, a three-person commission would control all county business and finances except those powers given to the county court by the state constitution. Lowery claimed the bill would "increase efficiency" in the county government. The bill appointed three people to serve as county commissioners until the 1948 election: Bob Barclay, Little Buck Arp, and W.P. McGee.[736]

The county court could not be abolished through legislation, but it could be weakened. It would still have the power to elect the school board and superintendent, but would require budget approval from the new county commission. "This bill will place almost complete control of the county in the hands of three competent men. They will control all purchases and all public funds and be responsible to the people," Lowery said. The commissioners would be paid $200 per month.[737]

The appointment of W.P. McGee caused enough controversy to force Lowery and Cartwright to replace him. They chose Abraham Watson Gregory, son of former sheriff Joseph N. Gregory and brother of outspoken Biggs critic Joseph Milburn Gregory, as the third commissioner. Newt Shoemaker soon replaced Little Buck Arp. Governor McCord signed the bill on February 28. The Polk County Commission Act took effect the next day.

At Frank Lowery's office in Ocoee, county judge Vance Davis administered the oath of office to Barclay, Shoemaker and Gregory (Davis' brother-in-law). Barclay was elected chairman and would serve as finance commissioner and purchasing agent. Gregory became highway commissioner, and Shoemaker would oversee the county's institutions as welfare commissioner. They reported a "friendly and gracious reception" from the Biggs men at the courthouse.[738]

Lowery and Cartwright soon found a way to wrest control of the school board from the county court. They introduced bills to abolish the current school board and appoint a new board. Appointed to serve on the new board were Paul P. McClary, Frank Rymer, H.M. Love Jr., Jessie W. Chastain, Sam Sharp, Walter Higdon, and Wendell Kilpatrick. Unlike the previous board, the new board would be elected by the people starting in 1948.

Watson Gregory, son of former sheriff Joseph N. Gregory, was appointed to the newly-created Polk County Commission, serving with Bob Barclay and James "Newt" Shoemaker. - Doug Gregory

Vance Davis came out in support of the GGL's reforms. At their February meeting, he persuaded the county court to pass a resolution, introduced by Bill Rose, requesting Lowery and Cartwright authorize the county to borrow money for school and other building construction. The legislative duo happily introduced bills to authorize over half a million dollars in bonds to build new high school buildings in Copperhill and Benton as well as repair many existing schools. The bills also included funds to rebuild the Ducktown Law Court. Condemned after years of neglect, the court building was later destroyed by fire. In April, the new county school board voted for a "complete rejuvenation" of Polk County High School and a rewiring of all the schools in Benton.[739]

Alfred Mynders praised Lowery and Cartwright's "exemplary" work in the legislature. But the editor was mistaken in his claim that the GGL had "cleaned out the last remnants of the Biggs machine." Certainly, the county's schools, roads, and finances were all under GGL control, but Burch still had all the courthouse offices, including and especially trustee Charles Williams and county court clerk Leach Park. But most important of all, through his younger son, Burch still had the gun. The *Copper City Advance* commended Lowery and Cartwright for keeping their campaign promises and believed their legislation would "pull the county out of the deplorable and even pitiful condition into which is has fallen."

In a test case, GGL supporters John W. Crewse, Buck Arp, Bob McClary, August Lewis, and Henry Crox filed a bill in chancery court declaring the Polk County Commission Act unconstitutional. The bill named the three commissioners and state attorney general Roy Beeler as defendants. The bill said the act "seeks to suspend the general law relative to the powers and duties of the quarterly county court provided in the Tennessee Code." It also charged that the act placed an "additional burden" on Polk County taxpayers due to the bonds issued by the new commission.[740] The county court hired attorneys Cas Geer and R.A. Davis, who requested the act be declared "null and void."[741]

On June 26, Judge Alan Kelley ruled the Polk County Commission Act valid, although an appeal was inevitable. Unlike their *Polk County News* articles reporting on the initiation of the lawsuit, Standridge and Witt placed their article reporting on the act being upheld in a small blurb near the bottom of the page. "We are over the hump in so far as the legality of our positions is concerned," Barclay said. "Beginning on July 1, we will be operating the county on our own budget, and from then on payments will be made only for services to the county and not for services to self."[742] Now in control of the county's new legislative body, the GGL had never appeared stronger.

Chapter 47

THE KEYS TO THE BALLOT BOXES AND THE TREASURY

In a letter to Tennessee Secretary of State Joe C. Carr, Bob Barclay requested that the GGL be permitted to select an election commissioner for the county:

> "...Let me remind you that Polk is a small county. The influence it has exerted in elections over the past several years has been not only ridiculous, but preposterous. Given fair, honest elections, and divided on strictly party lines, neither side can gain more than a nominal majority. The county is almost equally divided between Democrats and Republicans... Honest elections should remove this county from the ranks of election titans, in which rank it has been foolishly placed by some...All conception of the right of equal franchise had been driven out of the minds of Polk citizens. But we know of numerous cases where the Biggs machine have voted one citizen as many as from five to ten times at a single election. And just recently a Democrat of Fannin County, Georgia, told me that at one election he voted 13 times in Polk County...All we want is the assurance of a fair election next year... We want no second Athens here, for the Lord knows Polk County's reputation is already a thing to blush over."[743]

Burch also appealed to the state election board. Due to Broughton's poor health, he asked the board to appoint Cas Geer and reappoint Hoyt Lillard. Unintimidated, Frank Lowery insisted "with equal vigor" that W.H. Ritchie, a chemist from Copperhill, be appointed. In fact, he only wanted one Democrat appointed. "Nine-tenths of Polk County Democrats are backing the GGL," Lowery said as he eviscerated the Biggs machine's 16-year record.[744]

"I am Burch Biggs – the man Republicans have talked about more in East Tennessee than they have Mr. Crump," Burch said. "This man Lowery is not a Democrat. He didn't attend our county Democratic convention and he voted against Senator McKellar and Governor McCord in the primary." He warned that Ritchie, if appointed, would work with Henry Crox. "Give us these two Democrats and this will be Lowery's last trip down here as a member of the legislature."⁷⁴⁵

"How do you know I voted against – or think I voted against Governor McCord?" Lowery asked Burch. Laughter broke out at the young legislator's apparent slip of the tongue. "Because you worked for and voted for the Republican nominee for governor, because any person votes for the man he works for in an election," Burch replied. "I might have voted for my opponent," Lowery suggested. He claimed the 1946 election results in Polk was not reflective of the reality, alleging that Governor McCord lost the county because of his association with the Biggs machine, not because the county was turning Republican. "I won't be responsible for what happens to the Democratic Party in Polk County," Lowery said, warning against the appointment of Geer and Lillard. "We are not dead, we are coming back," Burch insisted.⁷⁴⁶

The state election board waited weeks to make their appointments, during which time Broughton stayed in Nashville to lobby. Lowery put forth another recommendation: Bob Barclay. That the GGL chairman was now serving on the county commission, Lowery's recommendation appeared to violate a GGL plank opposing county officials serving as election commissioners. But Lillard and Geer seemed a lock, and Burch's confidence was telling. Lowery showed no signs of discouragement if the GGL did not get their men on the commission, predicting a GGL victory in 1948.

"The Crump political machine has put out a rescue hand to the battered Burch Biggs organization in Polk County" wrote the *Nashville Tennessean* as the state election board appointed Burch's men. Henry Crox was also reappointed. Broughton "beamed with confidence" after the appointments were announced. "I believe the organization could stage a comeback next year."⁷⁴⁷

Buck Sartin and Matt Witt remembered Burch using county road crews to fix and improve his properties, including his rental properties.⁷⁴⁸ But now the road department was in the hands of the GGL, and the Biggs machine suddenly became vigilant watchdogs for alleged misuse of public works.

Chattanooga Times reporter Fred Hixon wrote a series of articles in July 1947 detailing allegations that the county commission used funds from the gas tax for the benefit of private property owners. Barclay and Shoemaker reportedly approved construction of a baseball diamond, excavating a basement for a church, excavating a six-foot embankment, and delivering crushed stone to improve private roads and driveways. "These projects, no doubt, have considerable vote-getting qualities..." Hixon wrote.[749]

Benton Station Baptist Church had its basement excavated. Fred Casada, brother of road grader Roy Casada, received a new private road to his house. The baseball field was constructed on C.C. Rice's property. George Lillard and James Crumley, openly friendly with GGL leaders, had their property improved by county road crews, including leveling the embankment on U.S. 411. Shoemaker had crushed stone delivered to his driveway that only connected to one neighbor's driveway, but he claimed it was a long-neglected public road. A new filling station in Benton also received crushed stone.[750]

Barclay and Shoemaker said they had "nothing to hide" and that similar projects were planned, including for several churches. Shoemaker called the baseball diamond a recreation project for the good of the community and claimed the Biggs machine had built one at Stillwell Station. Barclay expressed no interest in the county buying or leasing the baseball field.[751]

"A detailed audit is now in progress in Polk County," Barclay told the *Times*, hinting at "glaring irregularities" in the sheriff's office. Barclay said the county commission had not paid the last two claims, totaling $3,300, submitted by Burch Glen for boarding prisoners. "No payment will be tendered the sheriff until we ascertain the correct amounts we are due him," Lowery said. Lowery became clerk of the county commission, drawing a $200 per month salary.[752]

A longtime advocate of cemetery preservation, Barclay was passionate about maintaining the resting places of Polk Countians. "The voters of Polk County will have an opportunity to register their approval or disapproval in the county elections next year."[753] He brushed off accusations of using county funds and equipment for private property improvements, calling such work "isolated acts of good faith in the part of an accommodating bulldozer driver and not the policy of the county commission." He vowed to keep improving roads to cemeteries and school playgrounds "even if it means cutting down on the mileage allowed officers for transporting doubtful drunks to jail."[754]

Barclay criticized the *Times* for taking his and Shoemaker's comments out of context, since they had been interviewed separately and on different days. "We did not, do not, and will not approve of our highway department using county resources and equipment in improving private property," the GGL chairman said. He justified improving private roads to churches and cemeteries, alleging that some of them had become "impassable" due to years of neglect. "We know full well that the policy we have inaugurated of giving the average citizen of our county some benefits of the county's revenue in such ways as I have explained above is a radical departure for Polk County," Barclay said with pride.[755] He organized a local cemetery project with Rev. Frank Trotter, Virginia Middleton, and Joe Harbison.

In July, the county court asked J. Creed Brock to resign from his $200 per month highway department supervisor job after his arrest for drunk driving. Roxy Campbell pulled court records from 1936 documenting Brock's conviction for grand larceny. Campbell also pulled files on W.P. McGee, another highway department supervisor, who pled guilty to possession of liquor in 1943. Three of McGee's sons, Lake, Wade, and Jack, also worked for the highway department.

A new pro-Biggs organization appeared around this time: The Good County League. Led by T.J. Kincaid, they demanded that Brock and McGee be fired. Barclay called the group "idiots" and refused to meet their demands. The GGL chairman saw nothing wrong with having the two men working for the highway department, especially since they did not make policy. Lowery claimed he was unaware of McGee's arrest and called it an "isolated case." The Biggs machine did not seem to mind working with Brock when he was a Democratic JP, but now that he worked for the GGL-controlled road department, his criminal record suddenly became relevant. Standridge alleged in the *Polk County News* that recent road work had contaminated the water supply running to the courthouse and the jail.[756]

The county commission worked on the budget for several months. They claimed the approval of the county court for the budget or any changes in the tax rate was not required. The new budget would increase education spending by almost $150,000, with nearly half coming from the county treasury. The elementary and high school taxes would both increase, resulting in significant changes in the allocation of tax revenue.

Determined to put an end to years of graft, Lowery reported that four deputy sheriffs had been drawing money out of the county's general fund. The money came from a .4 cents tax intended for a building fund that the commission scrapped and put toward the schools.[757] In a more serious charge, Lowery alleged that Roxy Campbell, Leach Park, John Standridge, and Mutt Gray had spent years illegally drawing a $1,800 annual salary from the county treasury. John Prince, legal counsel for the GGL, made the investigation and urged them to file suit to recover the money.[758]

As discussed previously, a 1921 public act capped earnings for county officials in a county the size of Polk at $5,000 per year. Any fees collected in excess of that amount were to be paid into the county treasury. Campbell, Park, Standridge, and Gray had even obtained decrees from "various courts in Polk County" authorizing the payment of the extra salaries. Judge Pat Quinn awarded a decree to former circuit court clerk George Gilliland for an extra $1,800 salary, but it was authorized by a 1937 law that was quickly overruled by the state supreme court. Judge Quinn had also awarded a decree to Roxy Campbell based on no law at all, while Chancellor Stewart awarded a decree to John Standridge because he, in the chancellor's view, "was not being paid enough." No decree at all was found for Gray's extra salary.[759]

Another graft Lowery brought to light included the costs charged by JPs and deputy sheriffs. They charged prisoners who were unable to pay the fine an $8 transportation fee if tried in the Copper Basin. Since the county had no workhouse, prisoners sentenced to "the workhouse" were sent to the jail to "lay it out." Prisoners were allowed $1 daily on their fine and cost bill. "While the prisoner is laying out," Lowery said, "the county is paying the sheriff .90 cents per day to board the prisoner." Transporting officers received a mileage fee as well as a $2 guarding fee. If an officer transported five prisoners from the Copper Basin, they charged $40. "If unable to settle the fine and costs in their case, prisoners have been required to spend additional time in jail to pay the transportation and guard costs," Lowery explained. He claimed that JP W.G. Davis had accumulated $444 in fine and costs, but had kept no records. The county commission initiated an audit of the sheriff's department.[760]

At their July meeting, the county court voted to move the authority to spend the county's portion of the state gas tax to the state highway department. Desperate to take back the purse strings from the county commission, the county court criticized the commission's expenditures improving private property. Trustee Charles Williams was enjoined from honoring any more warrants issued by the commission on the gas tax fund. Barclay claimed the county court had no legal right to do this, citing the Polk County Commission Act.[761] He called the move "one of the most vicious and high-handed actions ever perpetrated" upon the citizens of the county.[762]

The *Chattanooga Times* resented the action of the Polk County Court: "The Biggs machine seems to have kept a record of every spadeful of gravel a highway worker in Polk County, under the new regime, may have put in a mudhole in his neighbor's lane. This was interpreted as "using state gasoline tax funds on private property." The *Times* called the evidence "inconsequential," and commended the county commission for improving roads leading to churches and cemeteries that the Biggs machine had long neglected. "The people of Polk County appreciate it…they are now getting a taste of good government for the first time in many years."

State law required that the county department, commission, or agency controlling the road funds had to concur with the county court before the state highway department could take control of the county's gas tax fund. But the law never stopped the Biggs machine before. Because of the injunction, road work was at a standstill. Of the 95 counties in the state, only one county had its gas tax fund administered by the state highway department. The state highway commissioner refused to get involved in the dispute between the county's two legislative bodies. Several Polk Countians sent the state highway commissioner telegrams asking him to side with the county commission. "They've given us the first decent roads and services we have had in this county in many years."[763]

Less than a week before school started, Lowery said opening might be delayed due to the county court's "tampering" with the school budget. Rather than adopting the tax rate recommended by the county commission, the court cut property taxes by .3 cents and shifted $23,000 allotted for education to the general fund. From there, $12,000 was allotted to the county jail for boarding prisoners. This reduced the school fund to a level below the minimum required to receive matching state funds provided by the sales tax. The state education commissioner said it was "inconceivable that a county court would do anything like that to a school budget."[764] Burch was not going to give up control of the county's money willingly.

"Look for anything to happen in Polk," Alfred Mynders warned. "The people are sick of the machinations of the defeated and discredited machine." Barclay compared the actions of the county court to pre-war Germany and accused them of "starving the youth" of the county. "They did it because their lord and master told them to do it, and they knew nothing else to do." The school board was in a "quandary," the GGL chairman wrote, asking if they should open the schools or follow the court's lead and let the education of Polk's school children "go to hell." Barclay made his preference known: "Open the schools and let the county court go to hell." He expected a fight and knew Burch would not back down. "And if the county is goaded to the point where the march breaks into a storm, then I'll second Mr. Shakespeare when he said '…and damned be he who first cries, 'Hold Enough.'"[765]

Barclay summarized the GGL's accomplishments so far. "County affairs had ceased to drift and had reached a static condition. Responsibility for aggressive action did not exist under the old system."[766] He discussed the changes in the Fourth Fractional Township and committed to supporting the new commissioners, Leon Howell, Pat Terry, and S.E. Sharp. Over $300,000 was paid to the commission through new legislation. He lamented the decades of reduced spending on the township's schools, long before the Biggs machine came to power.[767]

According to Barclay, the Biggs machine might have been able to "prolong" their control if they had never passed the Copperhill ripper bill. The new city commissioners named in the repeal bill found the city in a "deplorable" condition.[768] Some citizens still resented the former city commissioners that had been put in office by the ripper bill. Someone rode by Granville Radcliffe's home one evening and threw a stick of dynamite in his yard. The perpetrators were never caught.

Barclay discussed the new school board and its upcoming popular election. "Of all the tasks facing the GGL in its efforts to lift Polk County out of the doldrums, none is more formidable than that of improving the county's educational system and facilities." Schools in Benton, Copperhill, and Isabella needed extensive repairs. Barclay estimated that at least a million dollars would be required to put the county's schools in "first-class" condition. "The scars they leave on a community are visible for years after their overthrow."[769]

The GGL chairman lamented the loss of some of the county's best teachers during the war years. He reminded the citizens that progress would be slow. "…Not to further the interests of a few who have long since grown admittedly opulent and overbearingly insolent from the public funds that should have gone for educational purposes in this county."[770] Lowell Posey's family eagerly supported the GGL. "The GGL had to win so we could get better schools." Posey recalled improvements in the Copper Basin's schools before he started high school in the early 1950s.[771]

Copper Basin native Henry Watson remembered that one school "was like an outhouse" before the GGL made improvements.[772] Over the summer, the school board made significant repairs to several school buildings below the mountain, including roofing, rewiring, and painting. Polk County High School received several new desks, lockers, and typewriters. Students in the First and Second Civil Districts set a record for attendance. Much work had yet to be done, as most classrooms were overcrowded. A new school building for Old Fort prepared to break ground.

Copperhill High School principal J.M. Reedy thanked the new government officials for repairing the Copper Basin's school buildings. "You will now be able to drive your children to school without fear of sliding into a ditch or over the hill."[773] Thanks to Barclay encouraging increased attendance, the Tennessee Department of Education soon upgraded Copperhill High School from a "B" to "A," a grade the school had not received since 1943.

Barclay was confident the Polk County Commission would endure, and advocated for state constitutional reform to "bring it up to date."[774] In a thinly-veiled shot at Hoyt Lillard, Barclay claimed the county had a "one man school board" before the GGL's first victory in 1946. "The Good Government League is nothing more than a league of Polk County citizens determined to regain their rightful place around the council tables where their county's business is carried on," Barclay said before accusing the Biggs machine of making the county a "laughing stock."[775]

Chapter 48
THE CROWN PRINCE PASSES

During the 1947 legislative session, Broughton suffered a second heart attack, forcing him to further withdraw from politics. Dubbed the "crown prince" of the Biggs machine, it was anticipated that he would lead the machine once Burch finally "retired." But Burch was in better health than his son, and was not about to let go of his power without giving the GGL a hell of a fight.

On August 8, 1947, Broughton met with Governor McCord at the Read House in Chattanooga. Fearing he was having another heart attack, Broughton left the hotel and took a cab to the office of Dr. James L. Bibb at the Providence Building. A patrolman saw him exit the cab, looking gravely ill. He helped Broughton inside the doctor's office. As Dr. Bibb was away, other doctors treated him for about an hour. They called for an ambulance to take him to Erlanger Hospital. Shortly before the ambulance arrived, Broughton had a convulsion and passed away. He was only 42 years old.[776]

Burch and Della had, for the second time, suffered the worst loss any person can ever imagine. They would be burying their second child. Broughton's wife of fourteen years, Louise Higgins Biggs, and his three children, Joann, Tom, and Mary Temple, ages thirteen, ten, and six, survived him, as did his brother Burch Glen Biggs and sister L'Ene Biggs Bryant. He was reunited with his sister, Etholeen.

The family rushed to Chattanooga upon the news of Broughton's tragic passing, and Governor McCord visited the funeral home to give his condolences. Several newspapers, even ones critical of him and his father, penned thoughtful articles in his memory. An "extremely large crowd" of family and friends attended the memorial service at the Ocoee Baptist Church prior to laying the former sheriff to rest in the Benton Cemetery. Pallbearers included former deputy Pryor Crowe, former state legislator Col. James F. Corn, and Drs. H. Guinn and H.H. Hyatt.[777] "Broughton Biggs undoubtably had a notable career lying before him which might have landed him some day in the halls of Congress and he had within him the ability to make Tennessee proud of him," wrote the *Hamilton County Herald*.[778]

Chapter 49

The Draewell Audit

Filling in for Chancellor T.L. Stewart, Circuit Court Judge Alan Kelly dissolved the county court's injunction that removed the county commission's authority to dispense with the county's share of the state gas tax. The county commission went "running full blast in our highway work."[779] Barclay advocated for a new road into Grassy Creek. The narrow, dangerous road to Roger's Ferry bridge, as well as the bridge itself, had been the site of several accidents. He suggested building a new road on a more direct route from Copperhill.

Barclay attended a Benton Lions Club meeting featuring local civic groups that launched a campaign to improve the river road that connected the two sides of the county via U.S. Highway 64. Barclay suggested the road be renamed. He put forward the name "The Old Copper Road," which was the name he used in his book *Ducktown Back In Raht's Time*.

Acting on a hot tip, deputies arrested J. Creed Brock for allegedly driving drunk while transporting liquor. Barclay said the "crime-detecting deputies" made the arrest for purely political reasons. "Here indeed was a knockout blow for the GGL," Barclay wrote. "Here was – some thought – a startling crime for whose detection the sane and honest citizens would cry out with heartfelt convulsions and vow that the Biggs political machine should be kept in power to save the county from repetition of such baseless criminality." Brock was acquitted of the charges, and Barclay credited an "unusually large number" of good citizens presenting themselves for jury duty for the first time in many years.[780]

In their incessant litigation, the county commission was represented by three fine attorneys: John Prince, Lewis Pope, and Charles S. Mayfield Jr. A Republican, Prince was a longtime Biggs foe. Pope had his law practice in Nashville. Mayfield was the son of the late Cleveland attorney Charles S. Mayfield, Sr., who had represented the Vance Davis faction in litigation against the Biggs machine. Nicknamed "Stax," the younger Mayfield was a graduate of Harvard Law School, a veteran of the navy, and had worked for the FBI.

The GGL had even more at stake in late October when Chancellor Glenn Woodlee ruled on three crucial issues. Burch Glen filed suit to secure a $12,500 judgement for boarding and guarding prisoners that the county commission refused to pay. The county court and commission both claimed the power to set the county's tax rate and budget. Although the injunction had been dissolved, the gas tax question was unresolved.

Woodlee dismissed the gas tax case in a big win for the county commission. He made no ruling on the other two cases. The county had been unable to collect property taxes for several months. To ensure the schools could operate, the county commission was forced to move money from the general fund and take out a loan just to qualify for matching funds from the state sales tax.

In November, Judge Pat Quinn ordered a thorough inspection of the county's public facilities. Their findings spelled bad news for the Biggs machine. The well pump at Polk County High School needed repairs to prevent polluted water, and falling ceiling plaster plagued many classrooms. The sick had not been quarantined at the Poor Farm, which needed sanitary improvements. At the jail, prisoners had been sleeping on torn mattresses and dirty blankets. The building also needed new windows. Burch Glen said he would make the necessary improvements.[781]

Two intersections in particular had become so dangerous that multiple automobile fatalities had occurred. The grand jury urged the highway department to appeal to the state for help making the curve and bridge near Ledford Hill on Highway 411 and the intersection of Highways 68 and 64 safer. Perhaps worst of all, the inspection revealed that multiple school bus drivers had been working under the influence of alcohol.[782]

On November 8, 1947, Barclay authorized the release of an extensive audit into years of the county's finances under the Biggs machine. He permitted the *Chattanooga Times* and the *Copper City Advance* to print it. The county commission hired O.T. Draewell, a Chattanooga CPA, to conduct the audit. His findings appeared to confirm the suspicions of many Polk Countians: The Biggs machine had been grafting the county. David Talley said Burch stole from the county: "They wanted to accumulate wealth." The child of a deputy had similar recollections, commenting that Burch never aspired to higher office because "he could steal more as the sheriff."[783] Henry Watson accused Burch, Hoyt Lillard, and Vance Davis of taking money straight out of the treasury. "They all come out millionaires," Watson later claimed.[784]

The audit thoroughly examined each and every county office. "No centralized bookkeeping was maintained by the county," Draewell reported.[785] The amount of money spent on "excessive, unauthorized, or property not accounted for" items totaled at least $47,000. Draewell examined the county's finances from June 1944 to February 1947, during which time Burch and Burch Glen were paid nearly $16,000 from prisoner's board bills alone (state law capped boarding charges at .90 cents per day). Draewell said the turnkey fees "seemed excessive." During a 10-month period, Burch Glen charged prison board bills or turnkey fees for 265 people who were never committed to jail by a JP and charged board for 240 people who had already been released. He collected $4,414.60 during this time. Mae West and Roy Rogers, among numerous other fake names, appeared on the jail board list for public drunkenness in December 1946. The usual fee for transporting prisoners from Ducktown to Benton was .10 per mile plus a $2 guard fee. But a typical entry showed that they charged the county $48 for transporting two prisoners.[786] David Talley remembered Burch's deputies arresting people and keeping them in a holding cell in Copperhill. "He charged the county for transports that were never made."[787]

It was revealed that Leach Park, Roxy Campbell, and Mutt Gray had, for a 32-month period, collected a combined $14,550 in salaries from the general fund "for which no authorities exist." Per state law, their offices were to be paid by fees. John and Gena Standridge collected $4,800 in salary, per state law, for their work as clerk and master, but they also collected fees. Charles Williams and Leach Park were found to have kept much better records than Roxy Campbell and John Standridge, and the income and expense statements of their offices came out clean.[788]

John Standridge denied receiving any unauthorized income and claimed neither he nor Charles Williams were permitted to see the audit. Neither did Roxy Campbell, who said the auditors had no right to come into his office when they did.[789]

Draewell found that several JPs failed to keep records "in a manner required by state law" by recording cases out of order and not using cash or receipt books. Two JPs had not remitted $800 in fees to the county as of July

1947. M.B. Wimberly and J.J. Taylor made the best attempts at record keeping, while W.G. Davis had scribbled his on unorganized sheets of paper, and W.A. Kerr was always behind by at least a month.[790]

The audit of the sheriff's jail account and board bills revealed the following: Several prisoners who served time in the jail could not be traced to the trial dockets of the JPs; the sheriff charged the county for taking care of 58 prisoners per day while the jail's capacity was only 40; and the sheriff overcharged the county for each prisoner by making it appear the prisoner was incarcerated longer than they really were. Draewell was unable to establish a basis for the excessive turnkey fees.[791]

"The sheriff is required to make an accounting for the fees and earnings of his office, including profit for boarding prisoners." Neither Burch nor his younger son had maintained such a record. Deputy sheriffs depended upon their salaries from income collected by the sheriff. But the audit revealed that Burch paid them with money from county funds. Broughton, Pryor Crowe, Flavis Bates, Herman Wright, Louis Wright, Ben Smith, E.M. Rymer, Jim Ellis, and Tate Kimbrough were all paid extra salaries ranging from $150 to $1,300.[792]

"I never drew a dollar illegally in my life," Burch said. "They got a little old auditor from Chattanooga and took him over there. There's nothing to it." Insisting the jail's capacity was well over 40, he claimed that he once held 91 prisoners during the Hoover administration "when they didn't have any money and couldn't get out."[793] In fact, a look at the list of prisoners in 1936 and 1941 reveal the names of several men who are not buried in Polk County or any surrounding counties. Most of them, if they even existed, were jailed for "public drunkenness."[794] Burch told the *Chattanooga Times* that state auditors "examined my books at least four times while I was sheriff, and usually they found small balances due me from the county."[795] In an ideal situation, state auditors can serve as an impartial check on local officials, but given Burch's close relationship with the state administration for the previous two decades, there was a strong distrust of the state auditor's reports.

Burch claimed he always submitted his jail account to county judge Vance Davis every month. "He approved them and gave me a warrant. They claim that Judge Davis belongs to them. So, there must not be anything wrong with them or Judge Davis, who, they say, is not on my side, would not have approved them."[796]

Burch Glen also made a statement: "I emphatically deny that my office has received any excess fees. In fact, I have sued the county commission for back

The old Polk County jail, which stood for the first half of the 20th century, was located at the corner of Main Street and Town Creek Road. Part of the former site is now a fire hall. - Polk County News

salary and fees amounting to $12,500. My salary hasn't been paid in nine months." He alleged the audit was politically motivated and said the charges against him were "malicious, vicious, and corrupt in all respects." He worried the release of the audit would affect his lawsuit against the commission and claimed he paid out of pocket to maintain the sheriff department's operations. "My records are available to anyone who wants to see them."[797]

Vance Davis played a key role in the entire grafting controversy. Still serving as county judge, he had to sign warrants for all claims made by the sheriff's department. Burch pointed to Davis' signatures as proof he was not in on the grafting, especially since Davis was known to be sympathetic to the GGL. But the reality was that Burch and Burch Glen were misrepresenting Davis' role.

In his lawsuit against the county commission, Burch Glen said he was owed almost $16,194.90. The county commission refused to issue warrants to pay him because they believed he was grossly overcharging the county for expenses in operating the sheriff's department and pocketing the profits. According to Burch Glen, Davis' signature on the claims was proof that they had been audited and were, therefore, accurate. But when the matter was brought to his attention in the lawsuit, Davis said it was his understanding that he was signing the warrants "subject to an audit to be made later" and that he wrote "not audited" on the documents. Burch Glen denied any knowledge of this, and claimed the auditor for the 4th Judicial District had already looked them over.[798]

Much to the sheriff's frustration, the Polk County Commission Act required the county commission to audit all claims submitted by the sheriff.[799] Burch's attorneys disputed this by invoking one of their go-to arguments, claiming that particular clause of the act "would require more" of the sheriff of Polk County than that of other sheriffs in the state and should be ruled unconstitutional. Barclay's duties as finance commissioner in this matter, they argued, were ministerial and not discretionary.

To the charge that he had never paid excess fees into the county treasury, Burch Glen admitted as much, alleging he never received a salary in excess of $5,000 annually. But from the day he took office in July 1945 to the day the Polk County Commission Act became law, Burch Glen's sheriff's department was paid $60,168.75 out of the treasury. "The very mentioning of these staggering figures that have been paid to this sheriff of this small county should be enough to convince the Court that there is bound to be something wrong somewhere," attorneys for the county commission said. Barclay and the commission wanted to make sure the sheriff was paid what he was owed and nothing more.

Also troubling was the fact that Burch Glen refused to turn over the sufficient records required to complete an audit. Tennessee Code Sections 10729 and 10730 required all sheriffs to account for all fees received, all salaries paid, and all expenses in itemized detail.

"The facts exposed by the audit are likely to put the finishing touches on the Biggs organization," the *Chattanooga Times* wrote. No matter the accuracy of the Draewell audit, it was undeniable that Burch was wealthier than most rural sheriffs could ever dream of being. He still had his Main Street home in Benton, his 421-acre river bottom farm, and ten other properties across the first civil district totaling nearly 500 acres.[800]

Chapter 50
"A Clean Slate in '48"

At their November meeting, the GGL agreed to nominate a full ticket of veterans for all county offices, equally divided among Democrats and Republicans. "We must take into consideration that none of us is in this for any personal gain," Barclay said. Gid Ware was elected treasurer, replacing Charles Taylor, president of the Ducktown Banking Company.[801]

It was rumored that Vance Davis' son, "Little Vance," would be the candidate for sheriff, but the Davis family quickly debunked the rumor, claiming his father sent him to live in Mississippi "to get him out of the current political speculation."[802] Vance Davis did not publicly state his support for the GGL, but several Biggs men accused him of favoring the reform group.[803] Barclay denied any involvement with Davis, but the two did meet in private several times.

Despite the death of his oldest son, Burch remained as politically active as ever. He attended a dinner in Nashville in early 1948 where he predicted a "big comeback" in the August election. "My opponents know I'm going to win," he said confidently.[804] The Old Sheriff had a loyal base of die-hard Democrats and voters who depended on him for jobs and favors, but Lowery and Cartwright's victories proved that a strong majority opposed him, and had for some time.

With Kefauver now challenging U.S. Senator Tom Stewart, Boss Crump looked to endorse another candidate. Burch believed Stewart had no chance and pledged to support whoever Crump endorsed. If the race came down to Stewart and Kefauver in the primary, Burch said he would pick his cousin. Crump spoke highly of Circuit Judge John Mitchell of Cookeville. Although Crump had dropped Stewart, the senator still had significant support in East Tennessee. But Burch appeared to be backing Mitchell.

Barclay frequently drove above and below the mountain, along the poorly-surfaced Highway 64 through the Ocoee River Gorge, to attend political meetings. Former Deputy August Lewis hosted GGL executive committee meetings at his hardware store in Benton. Rev. G.W. Passmore, former trustee, opened the meetings with a prayer.

The GGL held their first meeting of the new year on February 13, 1948 in Ducktown. "Our first objective is honest elections. Good schools and good roads will follow as a natural result." Barclay summarized the party's continuing accomplishments and announced that they would soon nominate 28 candidates, ranging from county officers to JPs and school board.[805] Copperhill mayor Pat Terry discussed recent improvements and Sam Sharp reported on progress in the schools. "Ducktown School now has the finest cafeteria in Tennessee."[806] Barclay released the county commission's first semi-annual financial statement on February 17. Ever the recruiter, the GGL chairman encouraged the county's business and professional citizens to serve on the GGL's advisory committee.

In March, Chancellor Woodlee finally put an end to the county's financial crisis when he ordered the county commission to adopt the county court's budget. "The county's finances are fast becoming in a state of chaos," he said, compelling him to dissolve the commission's injunction.[807] But he did write in his ruling that the county commission would have the authority to prepare all subsequent budgets. Now that the county could collect property and poll taxes again, Barclay urged voters to pay their poll taxes as soon as possible.

An indignant John Standridge blamed the county commission for the financial crisis and criticized them for failing to mention they funded the schools with sales tax revenue and borrowed money. He accused the *Chattanooga Times* of "prejudice."[808] The *Times* also drew the ire of Jake Higgins, who challenged Alfred Mynders to "let one of your men come here and get the facts" instead of "getting all your information from Bob Barclay."[809] Having worked as IRS division chief for East Tennessee, the state's deputy poll tax collector, and running an auditing business, Higgins decided to take it easy. He started a weekly column in the *Polk County News* called "Jake Higgins Says." He could now opine freely on the political scene. "I am to have a few things to say this year about politics."

Still authorized to spend some money, the county court had recently voted to pay Burch Glen $750 for ex-officio services. "The sheriff is required to render a tremendous amount of service under the duties of his office…for which he does not receive any compensation."[810] Even with the county commission refusing to pay the fees allegedly owed the young sheriff, Burch used his stranglehold over the county court to continue lining his family's pockets. At their April meeting, the county court recommended that the school board give all the county's teachers a $120 salary bonus for the current school year. Bill Rose made a motion to adopt the resolution, which passed unanimously.

On April 13, just days before the GGL met to nominate their county ticket, Thomas R. Hickey resigned as an officer in the party. Unhappy with the results of the recent nominating committee meeting, Hickey wrote an open letter of resignation expressing his fear that the GGL was becoming partisan and "falling into the hands of men who have knowingly been desirous of political authority for years."[811]

There was already bad blood between Hickey and other GGL supporters. The previous summer, Everett Henson and Wade McGee passed Hickey on Highway 68 just north of Ducktown and fired shotgun rounds into Hickey's car. With two pellets in his neck, Hickey drove himself to the TCC hospital. Burch Glen and Deputy Ernest Hunt arrested Henson and McGee, who later made bond.

The GGL met at the courthouse on April 16 to nominate their slate of candidates for county offices. The courtroom could not hold the nearly 500 people in attendance, forcing several people to stand in the hallway. Two bands, a hillbilly quartet, and a brass band that "blared out fighting music," entertained.[812] Since he was to be nominated for public office, Bob Barclay did not preside over this meeting, handing over the gavel to vice-chairman Isham Lyle.

At the top of the ticket would be 51-year-old John Edwards, a steely-eyed, no-nonsense World War I veteran living in Ocoee. Nominated for sheriff, Edwards was candid about his past, confessing he once made a living manufacturing illegal whisky. He swore he was forced to pay $100 in protection money to longtime Biggs associate George Williams.[813]

Buck Sartin, a Delano businessman who fought with the Third Army under General Patton in the Battle of the Bulge, was nominated for trustee. Edwards and Sartin were both Democrats. Luther Taylor, a farmer and Turtletown businessman, won the nomination for tax assessor. Most of these men had shown little to no interest in politics before the war. The incumbent county commissioners, Bob Barclay, Watson Gregory, and Newt Shoemaker, were renominated.

For the first justices of the peace election since 1942, the GGL nominated Joe Ben Mayfield, August Lewis, Grant White, Andrew Bates, James Rucker, Arthur Dalton, John V. "Chili" Newman, and Lester Kimsey. Starting out as a bus driver and later deputy sheriff for Burch, Lewis had undergone an

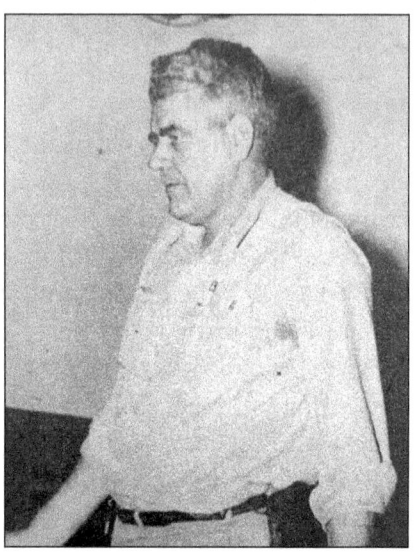

John Edwards, a lifelong Democrat, became the GGL nominee for sheriff in 1948. - Lura Edwards Ward

After working as a county school bus driver and deputy sheriff for the Biggs Machine, August Lewis opened a hardware store in Benton. He later joined the GGL and was nominated for First District JP in 1948. - Polk County Historical and Genealogical Society

interesting transformation to the GGL side. Paul McClary, H.M. Love, Frank Rymer, Clifford Tilson, Dr. J.B. Boggess, Sam Sharp, and George Sosebee were all nominated for school board. The nominees for constables were W.I. Bates, Ben Woody, Toy Lee, and Copperhill police officer Bud Payne.

The ticket was adopted by the convention unanimously, followed by one of Barclay's rousing speeches. "Honest elections are our foremost objective!" he said to thundering applause. He also emphasized the continued need for road and school improvements. The party adhered to its founding principles of nonpartisanship with its nomination of several known Republicans and refrained from endorsing candidates for state or federal offices.[814]

Burch was in the courthouse during the convention, but never entered the courtroom. "I'm not afraid of Bob Barclay," he told reporters. "He doesn't worry me the least bit." He said that Burch Glen would be the Democratic nominee for sheriff.[815]

Wilma Edwards Jones, daughter of John Edwards, remembered that his family had no idea he was running for political office until he was nominated. Edwards was a "talker" and knew just about everybody in the county. Some were skeptical of his nomination, concerned over his questionable qualifications. He grew up in Sylco, and had worked as a farmer, carpenter, CCC foreman, and bootlegger. He was remembered as a decent man, and one citizen said he was "as straight as an arrow."[816]

Former deputy sheriff and Copperhill police chief Clyde Dale was now police chief in McCaysville. He announced an independent bid for sheriff, but quickly dropped out after taking a security job with the TVA. He denied anyone influenced him to withdraw. It now seemed the sheriff's contest would be between John Edwards and Burch Glen Biggs. But one week later, James F. Kerr, a 26-year-old veteran from Benton, announced he was seeking the Democratic nomination for sheriff, and Carl Hammons, another veteran, jumped in the race for tax assessor. The duo announced their campaigns in Chattanooga and demanded a secret ballot. "Many have told me they would vote for us if there is a secret ballot," Kerr claimed. They said they could not afford to vote against the Biggs crowd openly.[817]

The GGL received another boost on May 3 when the state supreme court upheld Judge Kelly's decision on the constitutionality of the Polk County Commission Act. Preparation of the budget and determination of the tax rate would be an exclusive power of the commission from this point forward, so long as the commission existed.

At the Republican state convention, Congressman Jennings accused trustee Charles Williams of refusing to issue poll tax receipts to Republicans. He said Burch controlled Williams "lock, stock, and barrel." He scheduled a meeting with several Polk Countians, who were not even his constituents, to "look into a legal procedure" to protect their right to vote.[818] Burch blamed the county commission for anyone struggling to pay their poll tax. "They enjoined the county court clerk from preparing the tax books."[819] But state law did not prohibit the trustee from issuing poll tax receipts if the county tax books were not in order.[820]

Jennings met with Henry Crox, H.M. Love, Newt Shoemaker, John Edwards, Isham Lyle, and attorney John Prince on May 3. The group prepared an ouster suit against Charles Williams and Leach Park for alleged refusal to issue poll tax receipts to citizens "opposed to the Burch Biggs organization." Williams claimed he was powerless to issue receipts until Park sent him the certified list. Park blamed the county commission for delaying his ability to finish the tax lists on time. But neither Williams or Park mentioned that the county court's refusal to adopt the county commission's budget led to the injunction in the first place. To prove his assertion that no one, not even a Democrat, had been issued a poll tax receipt, Williams offered a "substantial reward" for anyone who brought him a signed receipt.[821] The *Chattanooga Times* did not accept their excuses. "This blockade of the poll tax certificates is too highhanded to be tolerated."

On May 4, Burch stood in the courthouse with a smile on his face as almost 400 people marched inside demanding that Charles Williams accept their poll tax payments. Williams was not in his office, leaving his deputy trustee Harvey Hammons to deal with the fiery crowd, led by H.M. Love, John Edwards, and Joe Ben Mayfield. Hammons stood his ground, refusing to accept a penny from anyone. "No poll tax receipts today…Not until the tax books come from the county court clerk's office."[822]

The crowd piled into the county court clerk's office. "Aren't the tax books a matter of public record?" school board chairman Paul McClary asked Leach Park. "They're public information when I'm done with them," Park responded. Refusing to have his picture taken, Park said something Burch would have never said: "It doesn't ever do a politician any good to have his picture in the papers." He told the crowd he might have the tax books finished at the end of the month, close to the state's poll tax deadline.[823]

County commissioner Shoemaker welcomed everyone to his office, where he recorded the name and address of everyone who attempted to pay their poll tax. "This is a conspiracy against the voters!" H.M. Love said. Especially upset was Grady Stewart, an Army veteran who offered Hammons $10 for the $4 poll tax. "While I was in the Army, I fought from Omaha Beach through Belgium into Germany, and I say that if we're going to have a Fuhrer or Kaiser here that we've got to bow down to — and it sure looks as if we have, not only the veteran, but every man, wife, and child is getting a dirty deal!"[824] McClary warned that if trouble ever came, it would "make the Battle of Athens look like a dress rehearsal by comparison."[825] An overconfident Park said, "I'll be up for reelection in two years, and by that time this whole thing will have blown over."[826] Love vowed the GGL would not quit "until we have unseated the Biggs bunch."

Before the GGL met on May 5, Burch said the poll tax books would be ready by May 15, sooner than Park had claimed. Over 300 GGL supporters, dressed mostly in work clothes, argued that evening over whether or not to "do something" about the poll tax receipts before May 15. Bob Barclay implored everyone to take no action until then. "I don't want you boys to do anything." At least fifteen men shouted, "Too late! To hell with 'em!"[827]

Their chairman told them to "swallow their pride" and see what happens on May 15. "I have talked with you against violence. I have told you not to pack guns or carry dynamite, but the pressure is tremendous…I don't want any widows or orphans made in Polk County. I'm not going to give the word." A majority voted to heed Barclay's advice. But his patience was wearing thin. "It's the last time I'm going to ask you to meet about the poll tax question. I'm not going to ask them another damn time when they are going to get out the poll tax receipts. If they do drive the people of Polk County to a point of desperation, then the guilt will be on their hands, if there are any hands left."[828]

Charles Williams, son of former trustee George Williams, served as deputy trustee and later trustee for many years. - Polk County Historical and Genealogical Society

John Edwards joined Barclay in urging restraint. "It's in our interest not to start anything too early." GGL treasurer Gid Ware said his family intended to vote on August 5, "poll tax receipts or no poll tax receipts." Everett "Eb" Bates told the crowd they would be voting "even if we have to take up our guns and march to the polls."[829]

From his Nashville law office, Lewis Pope worked vigorously to ensure Polk Countians would have a chance to pay their poll tax before the state deadline

This poll tax receipt, issued to a Third District voter in 1948, was signed by deputy trustee Harvey Hammons. - Author's collection

in June. Roy Beeler refused to intervene, but a distressed Beecher Witt discussed the matter with Burch, Leach Park, and Charles Williams. "I was scared someone would get killed unless the matter was cleared up." The longtime DA worked quietly to "smooth" it all out. "All of them promised the tax books would be ready by May 15 and receipts would be available at that time," Witt said.[830]

Minus Wilburn had a long scar on his throat from the aftermath of the Battle of Athens. He barely survived the attack from the man who slit his throat. Authorities failed to charge him in the beating of GI poll watcher Bob Harrill. Almost two years later, Wilburn was accused of assaulting another veteran supporting a reform party, this time in Polk County.

On the evening of May 8, a friend dropped off H.M. Love at his home on Highway 411 north of Benton. Another car pulled into his driveway. "Are we on the right road to Knoxville?" the driver asked. Love answered affirmatively. The driver then jumped out of the car, joined by two others, and blackjacked Love. Love had just enough strength remaining to pull out his pistol and fired in their direction, unsure if he hit any of them. They piled back into the car and sped off towards Etowah.[831]

Love suffered numerous bruises and lacerations, requiring seventeen stitches. He did not recognize the men, but described the vehicle. He suspected Wilburn was one of them, having seen the former McMinn County deputy following him in a similar vehicle earlier that day. "It was bound to be a put-up job of some kind." In addition to two "John Doe" warrants, Love swore out a warrant charging Wilburn with felonious assault and intent to commit murder.[832] Bob Barclay wrote in his journal after a committee meeting the next day:

> "…Everyone was too concerned about the treatment received by H.M. Love last night. The opinion was general that this marked the opening of a reign of terror by the Biggs' forces to frighten and intimidate the GGL. But Biggs and his followers are crazy if they think such tactics will be of help to them in the coming election."[833]

McMinn County deputies arrested Wilburn and took him to Benton. Wilburn posted a $5,000 bond and returned home. Upon hearing rumors that a group of Polk County boys were "out to get him," Chief Deputy Sheriff Otto Kennedy took Wilburn into custody as he was entering McMinn County High School to attend the Democratic county convention. They held him in the jail in Athens for protection. "Apparently he won't be satisfied until he loses his head entirely," Barclay wrote in reference to Wilburn's brush with death in the aftermath of the Battle of Athens. Burch Glen said he was investigating the assault on Love in connection with the political rivalry "from another angle." He refused to elaborate.[834]

JP W.A. Kerr later dismissed the charges against Wilburn citing a "lack of sufficient evidence." Love and two witnesses testified, but could not convince Kerr of the identities of his assailants. Wilburn and Love shook hands after the hearing. Wilburn's attorney denied reports he was in danger.[835]

The *Chattanooga Times* called the beating of Love an "outrage that cries out for a grand jury hearing" and alleged the Biggs machine was attempting to frighten the citizens from paying their poll taxes. "There have been some bloody and murderous crimes committed on Polk County highways in the past, with political angles involved. Too many of those crimes remain unsolved." The *Times* worried that Burch was "inviting disaster," but they were careful not to blame Burch for the attack on Love.

Thanks to a mandatory injunction by Chancellor Woodlee, Charles Williams began issuing poll tax receipts on May 10. Forty-eight people paid their poll tax that day. It was later revealed that several citizens, including Bill Moats, Grady Stewart, F.W. Higgins, J.C. Higgins, Rex Cronan, Jack Stewart, Spence Stone, Virgil Calhoun, Lake McGee and W.M. Lowery Jr. signed the injunction petition. Williams permitted voters to buy receipts, costing $2.04 each, for family members and neighbors, a great benefit for voters above the mountain.

James Kerr and Carl Hammons, hoping to win the Democratic nominations for sheriff and tax assessor respectively, met with Burch about ensuring a secret ballot at the Democratic convention. "I have nothing to do with the convention," the most powerful Democrat in East Tennessee told them. They kept pestering him, asking him who was in charge of the convention and the nomination process. "I don't know" was the only answer they could get out of the Old Sheriff, until he finally told them to talk to Hoyt Lillard, who told them the same thing. When they found out Burch had paid $200 for a brass band to play at the convention, Kerr and Hammons said, "I think the Democrats of Polk County would rather have the chance of picking the candidate to represent them than to hear Burch Biggs' band play 'Long Live the King.'"[836]

Chapter 51
"Mark Your Ballot, Mark it Well, Mark it Straight for the GGL!"

The evening before the Democratic convention, the Old Sheriff made a shocking announcement: Burch Glen would not be a candidate for renomination. For the first time in two decades, someone with the Biggs surname would not appear on the Democratic ticket for sheriff, or any other office. Burch tapped trustee Charles Williams to run at the top of the ticket. A longtime associate, and with Leach Park and Roxy Campbell halfway through their terms in office, Williams was the natural choice to run for sheriff.

So satisfied was James Kerr that he withdrew from the sheriff's race. Carl Hammons also dropped his bid for tax assessor, leaving Ben Parks unopposed for renomination. But Frank Lowery refused to believe the Biggs family would ever relinquish the sheriff's office voluntarily. "If Charlie Williams were to get elected, he would resign and the county court would elect "Beefy" (Burch Glen). But Lowery thought Williams was a strong candidate.[837] He was one of the more well-liked associates in the Biggs machine. "I don't know how he got mixed up with that bunch," Ralph Painter later said.[838]

Over 500 people attended the Democratic convention on May 15, 1948. Burch Glen made the motion to nominate Charles Williams for sheriff, predicting that he would win by an "overwhelming" majority.[839] "I am stepping down so that there may be harmony in the Democratic Party."[840] Williams said he had "no idea" he would ever be nominated for sheriff until the day before. To replace Williams, Roxy Campbell nominated deputy trustee Harvey Hammons.[841]

Burch sat quietly during the convention, only arising to nominate Bill Rose for county commission. Robert "Little Bob" Rymer Jr. and Ben Witt were also nominated for county commission. With the exception of Benson Hammons, who had been a JP since 1906, a new slate of JP candidates was nominated, including George O. Rogers and Elmo Lyle. Hoyt Lillard was among the school board nominees, hoping to regain control of the county schools since his removal from office. Lillard requested that the nominees conduct a clean campaign and "tell nothing but the truth about your enemies." The Democrats nominated several veterans in an attempt to peel away votes from the GGL.[842]

"There is going to be peace after the August election," county attorney and election commissioner Cas Geer said.[843] The *Copper City Advance* called Williams "undoubtedly the strongest man in the Biggs organization," but still endorsed the GGL ticket. Barclay said that the nomination of Williams for sheriff "suites me just fine" and predicted Edwards could beat him.[844] For Barclay, Witt's nomination for county commission proved the short-lived Polk County Veterans League had been nothing but a Biggs group in disguise. The GGL chairman insisted that Rose was ineligible to run for county commission since he had yet to resign as a JP.

Most observers agreed that Burch decided to withdraw his son from the race because the Democrats stood a better chance against the GGL if the Biggs name was not on the ticket. Others said Burch knew 1948 was a loss for the Democrats and did not want his son to go on record having lost an election. But the *Nashville Tennessean* suspected that he worried his son would be killed if he was a candidate. "August might produce fireworks that could outshine the doings in McMinn County two years ago."[845]

Burch made sure to generate as much good publicity as possible during the summer campaign. In a ceremony officiated by Rev. M.W. Little at the Ocoee Baptist Church on May 18, Burch and Della celebrated their 50th wedding anniversary by renewing their vows. Over 80 guests enjoyed the music of Margaret Evelyn Smith, who sang "Love's Old Sweet Song." Smith would later become Burch Glen's bride. Joann Biggs, Burch and Della's oldest grandchild, joined a quartet to perform "When Your Hair Has Turned to Silver." The social event of the season, the ceremony made the front page of the *Polk County News*. "Burch looked as happy as a 16-year-old," Jake Higgins wrote in his column.

The *Polk County News* endorsed the "men of character and ability" on the Democratic ticket. The paper began a weekly column "Who Should Operate Our County Government," supposedly informing readers about "the truth" about the candidates and vowing not to mudsling or agitate violence. The second column praised Charles Williams who, according to state auditors, "has the best kept records in the state." Williams had been accused of forging signatures on poll tax receipts, but the *News* insisted he "has never in his life been associated with lawlessness." The *News* condemned third parties as having a history of "shame, disgrace, and mismanagement" and said their membership is always comprised of people who had been rejected by both major parties.

If the Democrats were good at anything, it was projection. They ran ads accusing the GGL of hiring drunk school bus drivers and politicizing the school system. They also included "a much-needed school building program" on their platform, a blatant imitation of a core GGL objective.[846] Barclay asked for campaign contributions. "It costs more than 'pore' boys have, and the GGL has no rich members running for office." The Biggs machine was rumored to be spending ten dollars for every dollar spent by the GGL. Barclay predicted the GGL would receive five votes for every three votes cast for the Democrats.

Burch and Della celebrated their fiftieth wedding anniversary in May 1948. - Polk County News

Polk County's bootleggers and honky-tonk operators were near the top of Barclay's list of factions opposing the GGL. For years, Banjo Presswood had enjoyed protection from the Biggs machine, driving his "big, expensive" sedan equipped with an official police siren. His customers frequented his taxi-dispatching shed in Ducktown. They got their whiskey by tapping on the window "in a friendly fashion." But one deputy went after every lawbreaker, even those that were off-limits. Louis Wright arrested Banjo Presswood multiple times, but the bootlegger was always turned loose right away. Frustrated to no end, Wright had had enough and resigned from the force. Although, his days as a lawman were far from over.[847]

The GGL held their first major rally in Copperhill on June 18. "Every nominee on the GGL ticket pledged himself to a fair, honest election with the votes honestly cast and honestly counted, and we hereby call on our opponents as a group to so pledge themselves," Barclay said. "More work has been done on the roads during the past 15 months than has been done in the past 15 years."[848]

"We have cut out unauthorized salaries! "We have wrecked the machine beyond repair!" Without even raising taxes, the GGL chairman promised to work for increased teacher salaries, improved school buildings, hard-surfaced main county roads, a modern home for aged and needy citizens, a more efficient accounting system, and fair and impartial law enforcement.[849] Throughout June, the GGL held rallies in Greasy Creek, Conasauga, and Isabella. Proving their commitment to the schools, the county commission proposed the largest increase in the school budget in many years. State funding would help with the large increase in education spending.

The Democrats rode in a 70-vehicle motorcade, some of which were county vehicles, from Benton to the Copper Basin on June 26. Signs that read "Get on the bandwagon — vote Democratic" were plastered on several of the vehicles. The motorcade stopped for a rally at Ducktown High School, drawing nearly 2,000 people.[850] "They have had enough of mismanagement in the local government," the *Polk County News* wrote. "No threats of arms, or stores of dynamite, or any threats of violence were made." Former state senator Wayne Parkey was a guest speaker, urging the preservation of the two party-system. "A man should always vote for the party nominees" he said in a direct shot at the non-partisan GGL, whom he branded as "selfish politicians." In contrast to one of Burch's legendary Quinn Springs barbecues, attendees had to settle for sandwiches and soft drinks in the school cafeteria.[851]

Hoping to regain control of the education system in the county, Hoyt Lillard was nominated for school board in the First District in 1948. - Author's photo

After two terms as deputy trustee, Harvey Hammons was nominated for trustee in 1948. - Author's photo

On June 30, Burch Glen had a massive heart attack and was taken to Epperson Hospital in Athens. A few weeks shy of his 31st birthday, the young sheriff was reportedly in serious condition and put under an oxygen tent.[852] The decision to remove him from the Democratic ticket had proven to be a wise one, as Burch and Della were on the verge of burying a third child. His condition improved after a few days. "He will have to take it easy for a long time to come," Burch said of his only surviving son.[853]

If Burch ever entertained the idea of giving up politics for his family's sake, he never acted on it. His drive to hold onto power consumed him. Burch Glen returned home from the hospital on July 12, but his doctors ordered him to bed rest with no visitors. Burch, who was the county coroner, served as acting sheriff during his son's recovery period.

The Polk County election was crucial to the statewide races. When Judge John Mitchell made a campaign stop in Benton on July 10, Burch attended, but changed his tune, claiming he was "neutral" in the Senate race. Mitchell, a veteran, was well-received in Polk County, but Kefauver was still the favorite, especially amongst labor groups in the Copper Basin.[854] Cas Geer was appointed Mitchell's campaign manager for Polk County. A longtime friend of Mitchell, Geer faced no backlash from Burch. Overlooking his machine ties, the *Copper City Advance* endorsed Kefauver, praising his character and thanking him for his support for TVA.

On July 1, Burch came out in support of his cousin, claiming, "I've always been for Estes," predicting he would win Polk County.[855] Change was coming in the statewide elections. He knew Kefauver was likely to win the three-man Senate primary and that Governor McCord would likely lose to Browning. It was time to change horses again, and Burch had no reason to fall out with his soon-to-be even more powerful cousin.

The *Knoxville Journal* saw right through Kefauver's strategy of presenting himself as the "anti-machine" candidate in the Senate race, writing that his opposition to the Crump machine "was based upon the fact that the machine is not for Kefauver." The *Journal* reminded readers how Burch helped get Kefauver a seat in Congress and how he "got along in perfect harmony" with Judge Wiley Couch. "If there was ever a word of criticism by him of the disenfranchisement of thousands of citizens in his own home district by the use of machine methods there exists no record of it." The *Journal* asked why

Kefauver never "came to the rescue" of his constituents by involving federal authorities.

Facing little press scrutiny for his connections to the Biggs machine, Kefauver increased his support across the state by eviscerating Boss Crump. But he could not always avoid the subject of Polk County entirely. At a speech in Knoxville, he called the Biggs machine "small compared to Crump" and denied ever taking orders from Burch. "They have and they haven't," a red-faced Kefauver said when asked if they were backing him. "I have never been dictated to by any political boss or clique."[856]

At a speech in Greeneville, Kefauver said it "makes no difference whether Biggs supports me…This political organization is no factor at all in my complete independence as a candidate for the U.S. Senate."[857] After Kefauver called for an FBI investigation into voting in Memphis, the *Knoxville Journal* wrote that there was no danger of his votes being counted in Polk County because they would be using "multiplication instead of division." Kefauver even drew praise from the *London Observer* for his "battle" against Boss Crump in Memphis. "Our British friends ought to be told about Estes' friends in Polk County," the *Journal* wrote.

Over a thousand people attended Burch's pre-election barbecue at Quinn Springs on July 24. A motorcade of 250 vehicles departed the Copper Basin, passed through Parksville, Ocoee, Conasauga, and Benton before arriving at the barbecue. Even Senator McKellar and Boss Crump made the trip over from Memphis. Jake Higgins had a big time, and told all about it in his column. He likely exaggerated the number of attendees, claiming 2,500 were there.

"Mark Your Ballot, Mark It Well, Mark It Straight for the GGL!" and "Freedom from tyranny in Polk County!" were among the GGL's most effective slogans.[858] Two hundred people attended a GGL rally in Ducktown on July 17. Throughout July, rallies were also held in Springtown, Ocoee and Linsdale. The final GGL rally was held at the courthouse on July 31 with over 1,500 people in attendance. The GGL rode to the rally in a motorcade nearly twice the size of the Democrats' motorcade.

But they ran into some trouble while traveling below the mountain to Benton. Hundreds of roofing nails had been sprinkled all over the road near Boyd's Gap, resulting in about twenty cars with flat tires. Burch took a seat on his favorite bench outside a filling station across the street to watch as nearly 600 people

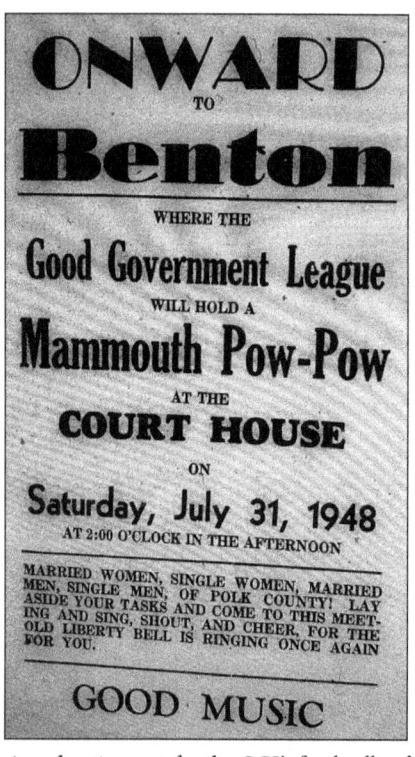

An advertisement for the GGL's final rally of the 1948 election campaign. - Tennessee State Library and Archives

poured into the courthouse, leaving almost a thousand on the lawn. "This looks like the return of freedom to Polk County," said one GGL supporter.[859] Ruth Haskins Passmore, whose father had criticized the Biggs machine, shook her fist and said, "This is the United States of America, and Polk County is our home! We have the right to vote just like every other American citizen does!"[860]

"The fifth day of August will be the most eventful day in the history of Polk County!" Barclay said kicking off the rally. "We have met today to decide if Russian Communism, German Nazism, or Italian Fascism is any worse than Polk County Bossism." He eviscerated the editors of the *Polk County News*, calling them "liars since birth." "Their mothers taught them to lie!"[861]

Buck Arp's Esso Station, across the street from the courthouse on Highway 411, served as one of the GGL's campaign headquarters. - Polk County News

The chairman then channeled a more positive tune: "We stand for good roads, good schools, and honest law enforcement…But the Biggs machine has stolen our platform — all except the plank that calls for law enforcement." Laughing off accusations of misuse of county road equipment in North Carolina, Barclay remarked "maybe we should repair the North Carolina roads so the people who have been supporting Biggs for the past 16 years can get to Benton to vote."[862]

"The County Court has no right to alter the budget, but they are holding up its passage 'for discussion' making it impossible for the Commission to pay the county's debts including the salaries of the school teachers," Barclay alleged. He accused Hoyt Lillard and Leach Park of threatening the TCC with an increase in taxes if it paid its 1947 taxes before the election. "Biggs and his followers know if the Copper Company's taxes are paid, the County Commission can pay off its debts." Park called Barclay's claims an "absolute falsehood." To the Biggs machine's complaint of the county commission moving certain teachers from Benton to various rural schools, Barclay defended the policy: "His faction during its reign has moved all of the good teachers into Benton and we are merely decentralizing the education system for the benefit of the rest of the county."[863]

Barclay told the crowd he expected no trouble at the polls on election day. "But I have heard reports that Biggs has asked Governor Jim McCord to send National Guardsmen to Benton."[864] Barclay said the GGL did not want violence, but warned that "we don't expect to have the election taken away from us by illegal means."[865] He wrote in his journal that evening: "It was an enthusiastic meeting, and the people were not lured there by the promise of refreshments, as our opponents had to do at their two mass meetings."[866]

Shortly before the election, Frank Lowery alleged the Polk County election commission "emphatically refused" to let him or anyone see the absentee voter list. Hoyt Lillard claimed he posted the list before three witnesses. Chancellor Woodlee issued an injunction against "secreting and hiding the list of absentee voters."[867] To Lowery's charge that the list had over 1,800 names, Lillard said "There's not a word of truth in it," claiming it had less than 200. Lowery also alleged many of the absentee voters had not resided in the county for many years.[868] The list turned out to have 288 names. Lowery remained unsatisfied, noting the pages were not numbered. "I do not know if the list Lillard released is a complete one."[869] Red Passmore recalled that very few GGL supporters voted absentee out of fear their ballots would be discarded before election day.[870] Barclay noted that Davidson County, the state's second largest county, only had 356 absentee voters.[871]

Amused at Lowery's allegations, Burch said he was in no position to pass on voter eligibility. "He didn't tell the newspapers that his twin brother, Sam and his wife, who live in Chatsworth, Georgia, had paid poll tax in Polk County with the intention of supporting their candidates." If Burch was worried about the election, he did not show it. He predicted the Democrats would win back all offices.[872]

Above the mountain in Copperhill, Bob Barclay posted a list of 400 certified voters in the window of a vacant store. "These voters have all been illegally certified," he alleged, and claimed every person on the list was dead, underage, or no longer a legal resident. "The Good Government League does not believe these persons should be eligible to vote in the August 5 election." Burch laughed off Barclay's accusations. "Those fellas are just scared because they know the Democrats will win on election day."[873] He predicted a "quiet election."[874]

At least 5,000 votes were expected to be cast on election day, and the possibility of breaking the county's previous record of 5,400 was not out of the question. Although many suspected that not all of those 5,400 votes were legitimate. The election commission, just as they had done for over a decade, assigned Biggs men as officers of election at most precincts. Leach Park served as officer of election in Benton, assisted by Pryor Crowe, Roxy Campbell, Traynor Witt, and Burch E. Maynor. Former sheriff Ol Harrison served as a Republican election judge and Eb Bates was a clerk.

Other officers of election included Elias L. Runion in Turtletown, Hoyt Taylor in Ducktown, and R.P. Taylor in Copperhill. John Runion was a Republican judge at Turtletown. Lake Ledford, a qualified voter in Turtletown, signed an affidavit alleging that Elias Runion offered him $25 if he would take his family of five to "vote right."[875] R.P. Taylor was the former Copperhill mayor who supported the ripper bill that threw some of his colleagues out of office. Granville Radcliffe, former Copperhill city commissioner, served as a Democratic judge there, while W.C. Dalton was the Republican judge and Amos Ballew was a clerk. Flavis Bates, the deputy with the itchy trigger finger, was an election judge in Ocoee.

The election workers and sheriff's deputies had permitted an honest and peaceful election in November 1946, resulting in a GGL victory. Would they permit the same result this time?

Chapter 52

"The Most Eventful Day in the History of Polk County"

Burch's prediction of a quiet election proved accurate for the early part of the day as thousands of people cast their ballots at the county's nine precincts. Reporters and photographers from Knoxville, Chattanooga, and Atlanta returned to cover the highly-anticipated election.

August Lewis, GGL candidate for JP, and his friend Long Cross were released from prison at 9:00 AM, right as the polls opened. Cross used to keep half pints in his inner coat pockets. The night before, they had been unexpectedly arrested on Lewis' property for carrying weapons. Lewis called the arrests "an outrage."[876]

Continuing his election day tradition, Burch cast his ballot in Springtown. A photographer snapped a picture of him talking with Harvey Hammons. "This is the first time in 20 years of Polk County political history that a member of the Biggs family is not seeking the sheriff's post," he said. Of his close ally in Memphis, he remarked that Crump "would be through" if Kefauver and Browning were elected.[877] Burch hoped to survive the revolt against the bosses in Tennessee, and had already hitched his wagon to Kefauver, the obvious favorite. An alliance with Crump was no longer beneficial to him.

The courthouse was packed with voters. The Democrats had Sally Hutchins Gregory, aged 15, working the election. She remembered distributing a pint of whiskey to everyone who exited the courthouse after voting the Democratic ticket.[878]

AP reporter James Callaway entered the courthouse to get an update on the balloting. Leach Park grabbed Callaway and "escorted" him outside. "I'm only trying to get some information, Callaway said. They did not argue for long as Deputy Willie Green placed Callaway under arrest. "If any of the reporters try to come back in, put them in jail!" Park ordered Green, a special "election day" deputy. Other reporters looked on as Green "manhandled" Callaway and hauled him to the jail.[879]

"He was very crude and unmannerly," *Knoxville News-Sentinel* reporter Frank Larkin said of Park. Callaway was later charged with "disturbing the peace and violating election statutes."⁸⁸⁰ Other reporters attempted to secure Callaway's release, prompting a few deputies to follow them around, "apparently seeking any excuse to take others into custody." When asked, Cas Geer and John Standridge made no effort to help. Put off by their "attitude," the two said Callaway "can stay in jail till he rots for all we care."⁸⁸¹

Jailer Bill Epperson refused to let Callaway make a phone call. After a few hours, two men arrived to pay his $500 bond: Deputy Bill Barnes and *Chattanooga News-Free Press* correspondent Roy G. Lillard. That a deputy helped secure Callaway's release seemed to indicate that some of Burch's men realized they may have overstepped their bounds.⁸⁸²

"The general tenseness seemed to increase as the day wore on," reported the *Chattanooga Times*. A shell exploded inside one of Pryor Crowe's cars at his lot in Benton. Crowe was working the election in the courthouse, but Deputy James Kerr was in the car at the time. Kerr was unharmed, but a small fire had to be extinguished. Just after the shell exploded, several witnesses saw men with rifles appear on the roof of Harvey Hammons' radio shop. Newt Green, his son George, and Farrell Gilliland identified them as "Biggs men."⁸⁸³

Crowds formed around the key precincts as the polls were closing. GGL supporters surrounded the county building in Copperhill, considerably increasing tensions. "There were so many guns in Benton that day it looked like an army," Red Passmore recalled, although he noted most of them were

The election at the courthouse in Benton grew increasingly tense as the day wore on. - courthousephotos.com

concealed. But Passmore never carried a gun. He said it would give "the law" an excuse to kill him. During the counting, the Democratic election judges permitted several challenges of mail-in ballots. Newspaper reporters encountered no opposition from any officers of election in the Copper Basin. The same was true in Ocoee and Springtown.

At approximately 6:00 PM, Turtletown election workers Donald Land and Edwin Shearer allegedly heard a noise across the street from the precinct. Located near the present site of the Turtletown Post Office, the precinct sat on stilts in front of a creek on the east side of Highway 68. Land and Shearer were allegedly informed of a group of armed men hiding in the woods up on the hill near the Old Farner Road. It was said that Shearer always carried a gun. He and Land left the precinct to investigate, walking up a woodland trail. Another account claimed they were just going outside to relieve themselves.[884]

As the two Democrat poll watchers emerged from the woods, an unidentified assassin with a high-powered weapon shot Land right between the eyes, killing him instantly. Shearer was also shot in the head, and fell to the ground with a critical wound.[885] "They were going to take away the ballot boxes," Henry Watson later alleged. "And that's when the killing started."[886] Shortly after hearing the shots, William Melton, a nearby resident, saw three veterans turn off the Old Farner Road and speed toward Ducktown.[887]

The election was quiet no more. According to Jim Shearer, Democratic candidate for JP and Edwin's father, "25 or 30 shots" were fired over the precinct. "The shots were of different caliber, I heard them sing as they passed over the building." Deputy Ernest Hunt found a pile of cigarette butts beside a tree where the shots likely came from. He also found shattered bark and bullets stuck in a few trees that had to be dug out with an axe.[888] The election workers, including Edwin's brother, Morris, stopped the counting and quickly secured the ballot box. Election judge Carl Payne "straddled" the ballot box with a shotgun all day.[889]

Worried about more trouble should they pass through Ducktown, Jim Shearer had the ambulance drive his son to a hospital in Andrews, North Carolina, forty miles away. Earl Oliver and Sonny Ledford helped paramedics retrieve the bodies.[890] A half-hour after the shooting, a coroner's jury led by JP W.G. Davis determined Land had been "murdered by bushwhacking."

Jim Shearer, a former Republican who lost to Vance Davis in the race for county judge in 1930, blamed the GGL. Deputy Hunt agreed.

Land was a 29-year-old World War II veteran who drove for the TCC. He was survived by his wife and five-year-old son.[891] Shearer had a wife and three sons. "They were promised a new car apiece if they would steal the ballot boxes," Henry Watson claimed.[892] Earl Oliver also heard they had tried to steal the boxes.[893] But another citizen complimented them as "good Democrats."[894] Jim Shearer said they had been transporting voters to the precinct throughout the day.[895]

The Turtletown precinct was located near the present site of the post office, pictured here on the right. - Author's photo

Donald Land was killed instantly by an unknown assailant outside the Turtletown precinct. - Donald Land family

Edwin Shearer was mortally wounded by an unknown assailant outside the Turtletown precinct. - Danny Shearer

Below the mountain in Benton, GGL poll watchers Red Passmore and Watson Gregory stood by helpless as Leach Park moved the ballot box against a wall out of their view. *Chattanooga News-Free Press* photographer John Goforth tried to get a picture of the counting through an open courthouse window. Park rushed over and snatched the lens off Goforth's camera. Park also took *Knoxville News-Sentinel* photographer Homer Anderson by the arm and shoved him out of the room. "Get out!" Park barked at *News-Sentinel* reporter Frank Larkin after ejecting Anderson.[896] Two unidentified men confronted Associated Press photographer Rudy Faircloth at the filling station across the street. "Get out fast," one of them said after pulling a knife. The man tried to slash Faircloth, but missed.[897]

As the sun was setting, the crowd around the courthouse grew larger. Well over a thousand people had gathered on the lawn by 10:00 PM, anxiously awaiting the election results. "On the night of the election, no one went to bed," one citizen recalled. "People stood outside looking in the open windows of the courthouse…" Park only allowed election workers and select candidates inside.[898] In a "courageous act," Bull Kennedy, Etowah police chief and brother of McMinn's Chief Deputy Otto Kennedy, came to Benton and spoke with some Biggs men at a filling station across from the courthouse.[899]

Around 3:00 AM, the lights went out at the Ducktown precinct during the counting. Moments later, an unidentified shooter drove by and fired a fusillade into the precinct, wounding four men inside: Wayne Kimsey, Richard Jacks, Chester Goode, and Ernest Loudermilk. Kimsey worked for Banjo Presswood, and Jacks and Goode were GGL supporters. Loudermilk, a 40-year-old truck driver, suffered fatal wounds. He lay in the street about two hundred yards from the precinct, located on the present site of the Ducktown Law Court at the corner of Main and Hiwassee Streets.[900]

According to Loudermilk's family, he was wearing the coat of his brother-in-law, Banjo Presswood. Loudermilk was not even living in the county anymore, but had agreed to come and work the election. The assassins mistook him for his brother-in-law, their intended target.[901]

Bill McGee later claimed he was sitting in his car just before the lights went out. "A car came down from the direction of the mines with guns blaz-

Ernest Loudermilk was killed by an unknown assailant at the Ducktown precinct. - Cheryl Loudermilk Kear

ing," McGee recalled. "I instinctively fell to the floor of my car." According to McGee and other witnesses, the shooting lasted half an hour.[902]

Accompanied by Chuck Talley and Shorty Ensley, Banjo Presswood hid out at one of his buildings. A young veteran, who they all recognized, drove by and threw five sticks of dynamite at the front of the building. Talley convinced Banjo and Ensley not to shoot the assailant, and defused the dynamite just in time.[903]

After the gunfire in Ducktown ceased, GGL supporters took the Ducktown ballot box to Copperhill, allegedly for "safekeeping." Biggs supporters Hardy "Cobby" Loudermilk and his wife followed them. What the Loudermilks did not know was that the GGL had men, including Jim Boggs and Burton Brown, stationed on rooftops in Copperhill "prepared for battle." Boggs and Brown had not been back in town for long. Boggs had just received an early release from prison after killing Frank Clayton. Now living in Los Angeles, Burton Brown was visiting family, still upset over the death of his brother, Junior, at the hands of Shorty Ensley.

Cobby Loudermilk reportedly fired into the county building on Ocoee Street. Bullets flew into Loudermilk's car, allegedly fired by Boggs and Brown. The cou-

The lights were cut off outside the new Ducktown Law Court as the votes were being counted. The ensuing gunfire killed Ernest Loudermilk and wounded four others. - Author's photo

ple collided with another car and hit a telephone poll in front of the Georgia Corner Grocery. Cobby was badly hurt, but his wife only suffered "superficial" wounds. Several people nearby, including Granville Radcliffe, heard the gunshots. Barclay arrived to help carry Cobby to Dr. Thomas J. Hicks' clinic.[904]

Earl Oliver and Henry Watson later said Burch sent Cobby Loudermilk to steal the ballot box and brought his wife to "dispel suspicion." Watson also said the GGL thought the Loudermilks' presence near the Copperhill precinct late at night was "too significant to ignore."[905] Barclay thought the Loudermilks wanted to see "where the ballot boxes were taken."[906]

Under heavy guard, the Turtletown ballot box arrived at the courthouse before dawn. A "rumble" went through the huge crowd after it was learned that people had been killed above the mountain. Onlookers said it was a "miracle" the news did not trigger a violent reaction in the crowd.[907] Barclay feared an attempt to steal the Copperhill ballot box before sunrise, but nothing happened. "Our strength was too great," he wrote in his journal. Around 7:00 AM, he led GGL supporters in returning the Ducktown ballot box to the precinct to finish the counting.[908]

Burton Brown disarmed Floyd "Bad Eye" Dalton, L.C. Ganues, Ed Westmoreland, and Lee Johnson and locked them in the Copperhill jail. Bad Eye Dalton had long been muscle for the Biggs machine and Ganues was a "special deputy." With those men out of their way, at least a half dozen cars left the Copper Basin around 11:00 AM to deliver the last two ballot boxes to Benton. Raymond Radford, a cab driver from McCaysville, drove with Burton Brown and James Freeman with the Ducktown box. Barclay rode in W.C. Dalton's car with two Democratic poll workers, Leroy Eller and Wayne Massengale, in possession of the Copperhill box. They stopped in Parksville to call Frank Lowery. "Don't try to come into Benton," Lowery said. "You will probably be fired upon. Wait for the highway patrol." They waited for a time, but then proceeded "without incident."[909]

The men delivering the Ducktown ballot box were not so fortunate. Perched upon a mountaintop, an unidentified gunman fired on Radford, Brown, and Freeman as their car passed through Parksville. Radford suffered wounds in his neck and shoulder from the shattered glass. The other passengers were unharmed.[910] Cas Geer later said that GGL supporters, rather than election officers, delivered the boxes from Ducktown and Copperhill.[911] This was true about Ducktown, but not Copperhill.

Still recovering from his recent heart attack, Burch Glen was resting at the Cleveland home of his sister, L'Ene Biggs Bryant. As the county coroner, Burch was in charge during his son's absence. After being informed of the deadly shootings in the Copper Basin and Deputy Ernest Hunt's warning of an "armed mob" preparing to invade Benton, Burch Glen called Governor McCord to request National Guard support.[912] He made the call at approximately 7:30 AM.[913]

According to multiple witnesses, including Red Passmore, Frank Lowery had asked Governor McCord to send in the National Guard before the election as a precaution. Despite his lack of authority to do so, Lowery allegedly called the governor early Friday morning before Burch Glen, begging him to help prevent a "massacre."[914]

Governor McCord also sent the State Highway Patrol into the county. He ordered both the guard and the patrol "to see that the trouble stops immediately." But one citizen insisted Burch made the request: "The governor would do anything Burch asked him to do." Chief Deputy Jim Ellis claimed Burch Glen asked the governor for additional support from the highway patrol. State Safety Commissioner Lynn Bomar led thirty highway patrolmen down to Benton early Friday morning.[915]

Burch had returned home late Thursday night after a visit to Benton Springs. In a phone call with the *Nashville Tennessean* early Friday morning, he said he did not know if the killings in the Copper Basin were connected with the election. "All I know is that they were shot from ambush."[916]

The election returns were incomplete on Friday morning. With four out of nine precincts reporting, John Edwards led Charles Williams in the sheriff's race 654 to 509, with the other GGL candidates holding similar leads. The ballots had yet to be counted in the three key precincts: Benton, Ducktown, and Copperhill. Outraged at Callaway's imprisonment, the *Chattanooga Times* condemned the "Biggs tyranny" of jailing Callaway for "wanting to get the information which is the right of every American." "They may not have been doing anything wrong," wrote the *Nashville Tennessean* of the Benton precinct officials, "but the implication seems to be that they were."

Earl Oliver and Sonny Ledford found Ernest Loudermilk's body on the street Friday morning. They also found dynamite under a pickup truck near the Ducktown precinct.[917] Guns were reportedly being issued outside the courthouse.[918] Polk County was out of control.

Chapter 53

Occupied Polk

Newspapers from coast to coast printed front-page headlines on Polk County's deadly election in their Friday August 6, 1948 editions. "SLAYING MARS PRIMARY VOTE IN TENNESSEE," reported the *Richmond Times Dispatch*. "BLOODSHED IN CONGRESS BALLOTING" was the headline in the *Atlanta Constitution*. "GUNS BLAZE IN PRIMARY," the *Denver Post* wrote. *The Olympian* in Olympia, Washington accurately reported the number of casualties. The violence even caught the attention of the *New York Times*: "2 DIE IN TENNESSEE PRIMARY AMBUSH."

Under the command of Lt. Col. Glenn R. Aytes, more than 150 guardsmen from the 278th Infantry Regiment, comprised of Company A from Etowah and Company D from Athens, were ordered to move into Benton. Many were World War II veterans, but some were just out of high school.[919] Seventeen-year-old Billy Stewart and four of his fellow guardsmen were sitting in an Etowah drug store when their officers came in and ordered them to suit up and report to the armory. They were issued M-1 30 cal. rifles before going through Athens and then Cleveland. Stewart later remembered:

> "We then mounted our vehicles and proceeded toward Benton. We traveled the old Benton Highway instead of using the new Highway 64. About halfway to Benton we was stopped by four men who told us there was a road block ahead and that the men there said we was not going to Benton. Capt. Earl Carmichael told the men he would give them ten minutes to go back and tell the men to make a hole because we was coming through. He also told 2nd Lt. Charles Ballew to load the machine gun and told us to lock and load our weapons. At this point we considered this operation serious and someone could get killed."[920]

Additional guardsmen from Cleveland, equipped with gas masks, arrived shortly afterward under the command of Col. Dwight L. McReynolds.[921] Bob Barclay was there to welcome the guardsmen.[922] Tensions were high as a crowd of over 500 Polk Countians, comprised of Biggs supporters and GGL sympathizers, stood silently outside the courthouse "watching each other wearily."

McReynolds addressed the crowd: "We have been sent in by Governor McCord at the request of Sheriff Biggs to restore order." After the guardsmen took firm positions, the crowd dispersed within minutes. "Move on! Move on!" a guardsman said as he entered the crowd carrying his fixed bayonet. A few guardsmen drove jeeps equipped with loudspeakers ordering everyone to keep off the streets unless they had business abroad. Guard groups departed for the Copper Basin to restore order in Ducktown and Copperhill. "From that point on we was the law," Stewart later said.[923]

The guard set up headquarters in the courthouse where they found the ballot boxes in the trustee's office. Most of the boxes sat inside the trustee's vault, but the boxes from the Copper Basin precincts sat just inside the office door. Pfc. Frank Haren was ordered to guard the boxes inside the vault. Election commissioners Hoyt Lillard and Henry Crox were absent, but Cas Geer said there would be no results until Monday. "Old Biggs is out now, and he knows it," one citizen told a reporter.[924] August Lewis and his uncle, George O. Rogers, both JP candidates on opposing sides, discussed the election. "I'm the GGL man they arrested and put under bond on charges of carrying a pistol on my own property," Lewis said."[925]

The State Highway Patrol arrived shortly after the National Guard, establishing its headquarters in the jail with Bill Epperson. Given Burch's relationship with the state administration, many citizens resented the presence of the highway patrol, validating Frank Lowery's previous concerns. The *Nashville Tennessean* observed an "undercurrent of enmity between the two law preserving forces." The guard was reportedly enthusiastic to assist the veteran-dominated GGL.[926] Barclay wrote in his journal that the highway patrol arrived "to try, or so it appears, to help Mr. Biggs to win the election."[927]

Road blocks were set up on the main highways to check vehicles entering and leaving town. One family sent their daughter on a bus to her aunt's house in Zion Valley, hoping she would be safer there. "Members of the National Guard checked all the luggage for concealed weapons but passed me by. I asked if they wanted to search me, an eight-year-old child, which seemed to embarrass them."[928]

Edwin Shearer's sister-in law and her husband, Shirley and Cecil Hamby, were in town visiting with their infant son, David. They decided to return home to Maryville, only to be stopped by a group of guardsmen conducting searches. One of the guardsmen dumped Cecil's dirty work clothes out of his

The first National Guard troops arrived in Benton the morning after the election. - Cleveland Daily Banner

Bob Barclay, third from left wearing a hat with his left foot slightly off the ground, converses with other GGL supporters as the guardsmen arrive in Benton. - Cleveland Daily Banner

trunk onto the road and rummaged through them with his bayonet. After a guardsman searched their glove compartment, Shirley asked if he wanted to search David's diaper, too.[929]

Col. McReynolds ordered a temporary confiscation of all weapons in the county. Hardware stores had to lock up their supply of guns and ammunition. The day before, T. Blair Lillard, aged 13, was surprised to find a loaded rifle in the family's hardware store. "Put that down!" his father Herb Lillard told him. Herb feared there would be trouble on election day, and was prepared for a fight. But he now had to lock up his entire supply of firearms.[930]

Guardsmen and patrolmen made simultaneous raids in the three cities, finding multiple arsenals, including pistols, rifles, shotguns, and homemade dynamite bombs "powerful enough to wreck a good-sized building."[931] One of the biggest raids of the day was at the "Dog House," a mile east of Benton, where Maj. Zeb Sherrill's guard detail found handmade grenades, dynamite sticks, and cached ammunition. Austin Lewis was found at the one-story building at the edge of the woods, claiming the owner, Charles Webb, was not home.[932]

Everyone in the county had to give up their weapons, even the sheriff's department. "You can't do this to me!" Chief Deputy Ellis protested. "I'm the law around here." Lt. Col. Aytes replied: "No, brother, I'm the law now."[933] But Aytes later denied that Ellis refused to surrender his weapon, contradicting a report by the International News Service.[934] Perhaps for the first time ever, only state authorities had a monopoly on the use of deadly force in Polk County. Every weapon confiscated was stored in either the courthouse or the jail.

One citizen, almost seven-years-old, remembered sleeping over at his aunt's house. He and a cousin shared a bed, with the family's guns hidden under their mattress. The parents figured the guardsmen, if they even conducted a search, would not check under a child's mattress.[935] The guard did not search every home. In response to death threats, Henry and Ruth Crox spent Thursday night in their bedroom with a shotgun and pistol near at hand. But starting on Friday night, guardsmen stood watch outside their home.[936]

The *Nashville Tennessean* snapped a photo of Pfc. Wesley Barker and Sgt. Wayne Carpenter storing weapons in the courthouse. Commissioner Bomar reported on two busloads of weapons that escaped into the mountains before the highway patrol arrived. "We know that there are some machine guns that got away from here," Lt. Col. Aytes said.[937] A group of citizens said the "presence of these bombs indicate that someone has foreseen the possibility that the Biggs forces might attempt to barricade themselves in the jail and count the ballots there."⁹³⁸ Aytes thumbed through a military manual discussing riot control. "This is one thing we won't have to use," he said. "This is a revolt that never came off."⁹³⁹ Observing the number of guns and ammunition confiscated, the *Etowah Enterprise* wrote that "the citizens of Polk County were planning on an election war to surpass that of Athens in 1946."⁹⁴⁰

The guardsmen knew they were in for a long weekend on duty. They got rest whenever and wherever they could, with many sleeping in the courthouse or on the lawn in front of the jail. Billy Stewart was awakened and dispatched to the Copper Basin at 2:00 AM on Saturday morning. His group would be patrolling the streets of Ducktown at sunrise, so they had to get some sleep in the precinct there. "When we turned the lights on, we could see the bullet holes and all the blood on the floor," Stewart recalled. "How did they think we could get any rest?"⁹⁴¹

Late Friday night, Banjo Presswood was driving to Chattanooga. Chuck and Florene Talley were with him. Equipped with a machine gun at Boyd's Gap on Highway 64, Burton Brown and Jim Boggs waited on him for hours. Just after they packed up and started to leave, Banjo's car safely passed by.⁹⁴²

Guardsmen patrolling above the mountain had to make radio contact with Benton every four hours, day and night. David Talley remembered walking around Ducktown before the National Guard arrived. "There were over one hundred people on the street, far more than usual, armed to the teeth." Talley watched from his front porch as guardsmen made hourly patrols up Highway 68 to Turtletown and Farner.⁹⁴³

Equipped with submachine guns, the highway patrol had made nine arrests by early Saturday morning. Burton Brown, Raymond Radford, and James Freeman were charged with reckless driving and carrying concealed weapons. Albert Owens, Walter Campbell and Alvin Goforth, all of Archville, were charged with drunk driving and carrying pistols. Carl Derryberry and J.E. Loudermilk of Pearltown were charged with carrying pistols.⁹⁴⁴ Bomar later said Brown, Radford, and Freeman, the trio that were fired upon while delivering the Ducktown ballot box, were being held under "suspicion of murder." Bill McGee, who later claimed to witness the shooting at the Ducktown precinct, was arrested and charged with attempted murder.⁹⁴⁵

The arrests infuriated Bob Barclay, who accused Bomar and the highway patrol of "taking sides." The GGL leader called Brown, Radford, and Freeman "his boys" and said it was not possible that they were involved in the killings.[946] Bomar said they were being held for questioning about "election day gunplay" but were not held in connection "with any particular slaying."[947] Matt Witt later alleged that Brown was "imported" by Bob Barclay to "intimidate the opposition."[948] David Talley remembered Burton Brown and Jim Boggs as "nice guys" who later became "terrors", and suspected that Barclay secured Boggs' early release from prison.[949] Talley believed Brown and Boggs only helped fight the Biggs machine so they could "take over the rackets and graft" after running Banjo Presswood out of town.[950] According to Bomar, Brown, Radford, and Freeman admitted that they were "seeking revenge" for the death of Burton's brother, Junior, and that they were "out to get" Shorty Ensley. It was alleged that Copperhill mayor Pat Terry had sworn Brown in as a "special policeman" two days before the election.[951]

"The situation at Benton was grimly tense," wrote the *Copper City Advance*, "and it is almost certain that more violence would have occurred" if the National Guard had not moved in." The *Polk County News* reported that "by Saturday morning, peace was restored to Polk County." The *Chattanooga Times* gave Governor McCord lukewarm praise for sending in the guard and patrol, but had not forgiven him for his inaction during the Battle of Athens. "Everything is under control," Maj. Sherrill told the *Cleveland Daily Banner*. Nearly one hundred weapons had been confiscated.[952] Bomar said the patrol and the guard would not leave the county until after the election results were officially tabulated.[953]

Edwin Shearer, aged thirty-five, passed away at an Andrews, North Carolina hospital on Saturday morning, raising the election day death toll to three. Bob Barclay and other GGL members, including Brown's father, posted the $32,000 bond for Brown, Radford, and Freeman, who had officially been charged with suspicion of murder. "We think the high bonds are harassing tactics," Barclay said. He wrote in his journal: "No doubt that the cases will ever come to trial."[954]

With the results still unofficial, the GGL claimed victory. Frank Lowery released figures indicating a near clean sweep for the GGL. Tax assessor Ben Parks conceded no contests to the GGL with the exception of the sheriff's race.[955] H.M. Love called Browning and Kefauver's victories over the Crump-backed candidates "the best thing that has happened in Tennessee in twenty years." But he was even more excited that Burch's reign, 18 "long" years, was over: "Of course, the victory in Polk County brings the real cheer…Words can't express the feeling."[956]

Reporters caught up with the Old Sheriff on Saturday for the first time since state authorities took control of the county. He declined to make a statement, saying, "the newspapers won't give a truthful account if I make a statement." Hugh Stoval, *Atlanta Constitution* photographer, prepared to take Burch's picture. Looking away from the camera with his chin up high and suspenders holding up his pants around his belly, Burch snarled at Stoval after he took a picture: "How'd you feel if I bounced a rock between your eyes?" He told the reporters to "get on down the road."[957]

Everything remained calm over the weekend with a few minor exceptions. The first was when guardsmen shot out the tires of a vehicle driving down Highway 411 into Benton after it failed to yield to the guard's signals to halt. It turned out to be a group of men from Knoxville that had been drinking, and only one passenger suffered a minor injury. The same thing happened with another car that failed to stop at a barricade. The drivers of both cars claimed they had no idea they were required to stop. One citizen, seated on a porch swing, remembered a car that tried to get around a road block: "An A Model Ford tried to drive around the blockade. The guardsmen shot holes in the tires, and the car went through a fence and into the pasture in front of the house. Everyone was scared, but no one was hurt."[958]

Although still very strict, Lt. Col. Aytes allowed citizens to walk the streets and get around. "The people feel free to come out on the streets, but we keep them moving and don't allow them to congregate." He said things were "very peaceful."[959] The roadblocks were removed on Sunday morning, and several people drove through Benton to see the guardsmen on duty. Etowah Police Chief Bull Kennedy drove down to "look over the situation," only to have his pistol and shotgun confiscated.[960]

Burch met with Maj. Gen. Hilton Butler, Brig. Gen. Paul Jordan, and Col. Dwight McReynolds at a conference in Chattanooga on Sunday. The election commission was set to meet on Monday to canvass the votes and release the official results. Butler threatened to send Jordan in with more guardsmen if necessary. "If more trouble breaks out, we are going to put Polk County under martial law." He proposed a deal where both the Democrats and the GGL could send in five representatives to witness the count. "No one is going in there with guns on."[961]

Cleveland attorney Charles Mayfield Jr. hosted a GGL committee meeting at his Parksville Lake cabin on Sunday afternoon. Watson Gregory, August

Guardsmen stored all confiscated weapons in the courthouse and jail. - Paul Bates

Guardsmen stand guard outside the courthouse as peace and order is restored in the county over the weekend of August 6-8, 1948. - Polk County Historical and Genealogical Society

Lewis, Lake McGee, Emil Greene, Dr. Boggess, Bob Barclay, and 23-year-old World War II veteran "Bobby" Barclay Jr. attended. They discussed rumors that the election commission would try to throw out the ballots from Ducktown and Copperhill, ensuring a victory for the Biggs machine. After he returned home, Barclay received a visit from Lt. Col. Giles and Capt. Carl Anderson of the National Guard, informing him of the plans for Monday's vote count.[962]

To the surprise of absolutely no one, election commission chairman Hoyt Lillard whined about the ballot boxes from Ducktown and Copperhill, asking for them to be discarded. Burch Glen made the same complaint. It was true that GGL supporters, not the officers of election, transported one of the boxes to Benton. But Lillard never complained when Burch's deputies served as officers of election and transported ballot boxes, always counting the votes out of public view. The GGL, knowing they would almost certainly lose without the Ducktown and Copperhill ballots, refused to allow them to be discarded. The margins of victory at each precinct would prove which boxes, if any, had been tampered with.

Over the weekend, the families of Ernest Loudermilk and Donald Land buried their loves ones in the Zion Hill Baptist Church Cemetery. Burch Glen returned to Benton on Monday, but the National Guard was still in charge, with the State Highway Patrol assisting.[963] An Athens man tried to sneak into the county with a gun, but was arrested at a road block early on Monday. The same thing happened to two deputy sheriffs from Copperhill.[964]

Bomar sent for 15 additional patrolmen, for a total of 65, to help keep the peace during the counting. The guard used loudspeakers to order everyone outside to clear the courthouse square. To prevent any potential attack on the building, the guard placed M2 Browning .50 caliber machine guns, known as the "Ma Deuce," at each corner of the courthouse lawn. Under the protection and supervision of guardsmen, the election commissioners carried the ballot boxes from the vault to an upstairs courtroom. The count was about to begin.[965]

Chapter 54

COUNTING THE VOTES

Edwin Shearer was laid to rest in the Liberty Community Cemetery in Cherokee County, North Carolina at 1:00 PM on Monday. Around the same time, the final vote canvass began in Benton. 32 men entered the upstairs chancery court room: five GGL representatives, five Democrat representatives, the three election commissioners, three reporters, and a guardsmen assigned to escort each. All sixteen civilians were searched for weapons. "We were armed with a nightstick and we was told if they made any sign to the outside like they were indicating how the count was going we was to drop them with our nightstick," Billy Stewart remembered. A Chattanooga reporter arrived late, but was searched and allowed to enter with a guard escort.[966]

Bob Barclay, Frank Lowery, John Edwards, John Prince, and Charles Mayfield Jr. represented the GGL. Charles Williams, Harvey Hammons, Ben Parks, Traynor Witt, and Jake Higgins were the Democratic representatives. Among the reporters was C.C.L. Ray of the *Cleveland Daily Banner*. Capt. Jim McKenzie stood next to the table to react immediately in case anyone initiated an altercation.

The commissioners began the count, with Henry Crox calling off the count from each scroll sheet. A little over an hour passed before three of the reporters left, leaving Ray as the only newsman.[967] Highway patrolmen escorted the reporters to the county line "to prevent the spread of any unauthorized rumors" about the results.[968]

Hoyt Lillard opened the Turtletown ballot box at 5:00 PM. Henry Crox discovered that two tally sheets reported different numbers. Cas Geer signed the sheet that had thirty fewer votes cast. The Ducktown box only had one tally sheet. Everything in the Copperhill box appeared to be in order.[969]

At the end of the count, the result was a victory for the GGL. The Democrats demanded the commissioners throw out the "illegal" boxes from Ducktown and Copperhill. The two warring factions struggled to control their tempers and discussed the matter for a half hour. The GGL argued that the commission had no authority to throw out any boxes, and that the losing candidates could challenge the results in court.[970]

"Are you going to certify these election returns, Mr. Lillard, or aren't you?" Barclay said, raising his voice for the first time all day. "I don't know," replied Lillard. "I want to do what is right and what is legal." Barclay snapped back at Burch's nephew and right-hand man: "All you want to do is what they have ordered you to do!" Henry Crox asked Ben Parks: "Are you in on this, too?" Parks replied that the Democrats would have won "if you hadn't stole it from us." This infuriated Barclay. "What do you mean we stole it from you? All we did was keep a bunch of your thugs from running off with the ballot box when the lights were cut off at Ducktown." Barclay described his election night experience, recounting how his GGL men took the Ducktown box to Copperhill for safekeeping until Friday morning. Upon returning the box, the Biggs-appointed election officials in Ducktown refused to complete the count, leading Barclay and his associates to finish the counting and transport the box to Benton.[971]

Cas Geer's decision might have averted another bitter fight when he shared his thoughts: "My advice is to go ahead and certify the election on the basis of the returns we have. Then, if any candidate desires to contest their election, the courts can decide whether or not the election is valid." Ralph Painter remembered Geer as a "good guy" and remarked that, "He wasn't crooked enough to stay in Benton too long."[972]

With that, the election commission certified the results. At the request of Col. McReynolds, Lillard and Barclay agreed to "help keep down further trouble" on both sides so the guard could finally leave the county. "I'm not mad any anybody," Parks said. "I thought I had won, but I guess not." He shook hands with Barclay, ending the nearly ten-hour vote count.[973] After eighteen long years, the Biggs machine was finally out of power.

The GGL won almost every contest. Edwards defeated Williams in the sheriff's race 2,653 to 2,266 (54 percent of the vote), while independent candidate Claude Harrison tallied 59 votes. Buck Sartin was now trustee, defeating Harvey Hammons by almost 400 votes. Incumbent tax assessor Ben Parks lost to Luther Taylor by about 300 votes. Bob Barclay and Watson Gregory both tallied over 2,300 votes to remain on the county commission while Democrat Bill Rose won a seat by placing third, with incumbent commissioner Newt Shoemaker coming in fifth place.

August Lewis and Joe B. Mayfield, GGL, and George O. Rogers, Democrat, became JPs in the First District. Burch's longtime ally Benson Hammons won yet another term as JP from the second district, as did Democrat Broughton Campbell. The GGL swept the third district JP races with L.L.

Kimsey and John V. "Chili" Newman emerging victorious over Jim Shearer. Republican stalwart Arthur Dalton won the JP contest in Copperhill. The GGL made a clean sweep in the constable races and all but one seat on the school board. H.M. Love won a school board seat in the First District. Bud Payne was the new constable for the Third District. Former deputy Manuel Price, the man who was acquitted for killing George Ledford, lost the Second District constable race to Toy Lee by 17 votes.

The GGL's margins of victory proved they did not stuff the ballot boxes in the precincts above the

Henry Crox, the long-suffering Republican election commissioner, carries a ballot box to the chancery courtroom to begin the most important vote count in the history of the county. - Etowah Enterprise

M2 Browning .50 caliber machine guns, known as the "Ma Deuce," were mounted on all four corners of the courthouse lawn to discourage any attacks on the building during the vote count. - Etowah Enterprise

mountain. Edwards won the Copperhill and Ducktown precincts by just over 60 percent, a believable margin for the GGL strongholds and much lower than the Biggs machine's typical 98 percent margins at their peak of power. Williams won 61 percent of the votes in Turtletown, where the Democrat election workers jealously guarded the ballot box after Land and Shearer were shot. Aside from the Second District and Benton, the GGL performed well below the mountain. If the Biggs machine stuffed the ballot boxes anywhere, it was in Benton, where every Democrat on the ticket won. Judging by how Leach Park ran that precinct, the Democrats were fortunate that Barclay did not demand the results be thrown out there.

The election commissioners, watchers, and guardsmen left the courthouse around 11:00 PM to find the town square virtually deserted. The highway patrol left the next day, but the guard was ordered to stick around a little while longer. They left at noon on Wednesday after returning all confiscated weapons, including those belonging to the sheriff's department. Benton was reportedly quiet after the guard departed.[974] The *Copper City Advance* praised the guard on "a job well done" and complimented their impartiality. The Copper Basin found itself without its two sheriff's deputies as Ernest Hunt and his family left "hurriedly" and L.C. Ganues "vanished."[975] Billy Stewart would never forget his experience: "I spent my entire military career stateside, but the closest I ever got to actual combat was down the road in Polk County."[976]

Although the complete results from the Democratic State Executive Committee race were not yet available, it appeared Burch would be losing in that contest. Jim Park, brother of Leach Park who had left Benton for Cleveland nearly a decade prior, had a chance to win a seat on the committee. But he tallied 500 fewer votes in Polk County than Burch. When the results finally came out a couple of weeks later, neither Burch nor Park won a seat, with Burch only tallying 11,132 votes to his opponents' 18,667 and 17,296. The Third Congressional District was done with Burch Biggs.

Burch's unpopularity in Polk County had no effect on his cousin's U.S. Senate primary, as Congressman Kefauver won nearly 1,500 votes in Polk, crushing his opponents. After Kefauver's rather unimpressive performance against an independent candidate for Congress in 1946, Polk Countians had warmed to him again. In some of the slickest maneuvering and wily politicking in Tennessee history, Kefauver managed to gain the support of the anti-Crump/McKellar faction and win the statewide primary. A congressman who was openly and closely aligned with Burch for nearly a decade went

The votes were counted under National Guard supervision on August 9, 1948. Seated behind the table are L-R: John Prince, Charles S. Mayfield Jr., Frank Lowery, Bob Barclay, and John Edwards. Henry Crox is at the head of the table on the left, Hoyt Lillard is facing the camera, and Cas Geer has his back to the camera. - Etowah Enterprise

Hoyt Lillard examines scroll sheets as others look on during the nine-hour vote canvassing. - Paul Bates

on to become the next Senator from Tennessee. His victory would not have been possible without Burch's support in winning the special congressional election in 1939. However inadvertently and unenthusiastically towards the end, Burch had made his cousin a U.S. Senator, and it happened the same day his machine was toppled.

In another upset for the Crump machine, former Governor Gordon Browning defeated Governor Jim McCord in the primary. But McCord edged out Browning in Polk by just over 150 votes. In the congressional primary, Republican John Hammer defeated James B. Frazier Jr. in Polk, but Frazier won the primary and would be the new Third District Congressman. Winston Prince won the Democratic primary for state senate and would be facing off against the Republican nominee, Harry T. Burn of Niota, who defeated incumbent Jobo Cartwright in the primary.

Bob Barclay made a statement after the final election results:

> "I wish to express my gratitude and undying admiration for our Good Government League men and young men who at the risk of their lives upheld in the Third District the principles of fair, honest elections upon which the Good Government League pledged itself over the past two years. Polk County will, I feel sure, witness the dawn of a new day in the months and years ahead through the efforts of these men on August 5. I also want to express my appreciation for the National Guard because I am confident that their presence in Polk County averted further violence…In conclusion, let me request that all dissension and strife cease. Henceforth let us look forward to peace and cooperation between all parties in Polk County."[977]

McMinn GI leader Ralph Duggan released a statement on yet another violent election:

> Another tragic chapter in the sordid history of bossism in Tennessee affairs was written in Polk County…The McMinn County story of the August election of 1946 was partially reenacted…We sincerely regret that Burch Biggs, because of his greed and lust for power, brought about the situation that resulted in the deaths of three men and the wounding of others…The story is as old as history itself. The people of counties, states, and nations, after enduring tyranny and oppression until they can stand no more, always arise and regain the power so ruthlessly tak-

en from them…It was our pleasure to assist the Good Government League in Polk County in their efforts to elect their ticket in the legislative race in 1946… All right-thinking people deplore violence at elections, but it is not the violence in itself which is deplorable; it is rather the existing conditions which make violence necessary. We do not deplore the fact that decent, right-thinking citizens carried their muskets to the polls with them and enforced their rights as citizens. We do condemn Burch Biggs for making it necessary that honest men had to resort to these methods.[978]

Frank Lillard, left, and Bob Barclay celebrate the GGL victory outside the Lillard Hardware store on Main Street in Benton. - Laura Lillard

The *Nashville Tennessean* echoed Duggan's sentiment: "As much as the gun play and bloodshed are to be regretted, perhaps it was inevitable that a ruthless dictatorship like the Burch Biggs machine, which had long lived by force, should pass away in a whirlwind of violence. Certainly, it is in harmony with the Biblical principle by living and dying by the sword. There has perhaps been no counterpart in all America to the unrefined political arts which flourished in hapless Polk County. Brute force made open mockery of democratic principles. Suppression was the order of the day." The *Knoxville News-Sentinel* called for the state authorities to prevent future "election mobbery" in Polk County. The *Knoxville Journal* wrote that years of Biggs rule "invited exactly the kind of violence" that resulted. But the *Journal* also wrote that the "medicine used was almost as dangerous as the disease." Only time would tell if the *Journal* was right.

Epilogue

"A Man on the Sunset of Life"

Burch did not withdraw from politics entirely after the 1948 election, remaining a popular and respected figure in the eyes of many Polk County Democrats. Making no attempt to lead the party, he stayed in the background. Burch Glen won his lawsuit against the county commission, receiving the back pay he was allegedly "owed." He would have nothing further to do with politics after that. The Old Sheriff ran his mouth on occasion. When Congressman Jennings lost the 1950 primary to Howard Baker Sr., Burch reveled in his longtime adversary's defeat. He sent a telegram:

> "I want to congratulate you on your defeat. The people of the Second District have at last realized you failed them completely."[979]

Even in retirement, Burch was not free of litigation. He waited five years to get another trial in Shorty Richards' damages suit in federal court. A second trial was held in early 1951 in Judge Robert Taylor's court in Knoxville, with Flavis Bates and Ben Smith as co-defendants.

Charles Guinn assisted Carlyle Littleton to represent Shorty, who wanted $25,000 in damages and claimed his injuries prevented him from performing farm work. Russell Kramer, still Burch's go-to defense attorney, objected to a question about Burch's financial status. The judge overruled the objection, forcing Burch to discuss all the property he owned, including farmland, buildings, tools, machinery, and stock.[980] Without Judge Darr presiding, the plaintiffs could finally get a fair shake.

Burch's beloved river-bottom farm had grown to encompass 741 acres and was assessed at $21,700 (almost $250,000 in 2023). Richard Jones, a young boy from Ducktown, later remembered his parents taking him to see the Biggs farm in the early 1950s. "My mother had us count the cows. Then she said that every one of us owned at least one of those cows."[981] She knew that such wealth, on a sheriff's salary, and during the depression, was not legitimate. Burch's nieces, nephews, and cousins also had property nearby, but nowhere near as much as him. The farm was located on the present site of the Chilhowee Gliderport and Super Sod on Highway 411 a few miles north of Benton.[982]

The defense called Frank Lillard and August Lewis, neither of whom were friendly with Burch, to the stand. Both testified they saw Burch on the bridge, unarmed. Burch actually claimed he never carried a firearm during his eight terms as sheriff. Lewis said he saw Woodrow Reece shoot in Shorty's direction from the bridge. When asked if Burch had controlled the county politically and could secure political jobs for people, Lewis answered negatively. The jury deliberated for two hours and could not agree, resulting in a mistrial.[983]

The continued political turmoil after the GGL took control of the county in September 1948 will be discussed extensively in a second volume. In 1950, Frank Lowery appeared to have won the election for state representative, but his opponent, Thomas Lynn Johnston, charged fraud. Burch traveled to Nashville as the state legislature investigated, relishing in Lowery's impending expulsion. Lowery was eventually expelled, and Johnston, a Bradley County Democrat with no machine ties, was seated in his place. Along with State Sen. Harry T. Burn, Johnston blamed the GGL for the fraud and authored legislation abolishing the Polk County Commission.

When JP August Lewis switched back to the Democrats in early 1951, the GGL lost control of the county court by one seat. The GGL blockaded the courthouse before the county court was to meet in March. Burch was in the courthouse with several other people, who were demanding mass resignations of county officials. "Nothing like this would have happened when I was sheriff," Burch told a reporter. "I'm taking no part in the controversy."[984]

What seemed like endless political killings is one of the greatest tragedies in this era of Polk County history. On the evening of May 11, 1951, August Lewis and his family had just returned home in Benton. After he parked the car in the garage, an unidentified, shotgun-wielding assassin bushwhacked him, blasting three shots into his chest. Lewis stumbled inside where his family saw him fall to the floor. Before he passed away, he said he did not know who shot him.

Of all the murders in the county's history, Lewis' murder may have been the most terrorizing one of all. Just when everybody thought the killings were over, especially with the Biggs machine out of power, Lewis' murder proved a major setback in the county's trajectory. Everyone walked on eggshells afterward, terrified to discuss the murder at all. What few political discussions that took place were discreet.

With Lewis gone, the county court was deadlocked between the GGL and the Democrats, plunging the county into a state of borderline anarchy. The county court had not met for several months. Teachers did not receive their paychecks and road maintenance was paused. Several citizens contemplated selling their property and leaving the county. Governor Browning seriously considered abolishing the county and dividing it between Bradley, McMinn, and Monroe Counties. Burch's response to the crisis was not at all surprising. "I don't care what they do with the county."[985] Alfred Mynders was disappointed in Burch's reaction, hoping that he would "snap out of it in a hurry and go to bat for the county his ancestor helped establish."

Polk County's troubles attracted national attention, with major publications criticizing the Biggs machine and the GGL. Burch and Bob Barclay both received unflattering portrayals in a *Collier's* article. "They will have to pay for untrue remarks about me and my family," Burch said. "They'll find they can't tell a lie on me and get by with it."[986] Barclay said the articles took his comments out of context.

In 1952, Shorty Richards got a third trial in federal court, this time with Judge George Taylor in Knoxville. Still asking for $25,000 in damages, Shorty now had John Wrinkle and Charles Guinn on his legal team in place of the late Carlyle Littleton. He alleged Burch shot "straight down at him" from a bridge and that Flavis Bates held a gun on him during the ride to the hospital.[987]

During jury selection, Wrinkle and Guinn inquired about Polk County's "turbulent" political past. Two jurors admitted to casting votes in the 1946 McMinn County election (one for Paul Cantrell and one for Knox Henry) and were dismissed, as was the wife of former Hamilton County Sheriff Frank Burns and a Bradley County constable who had "cooperated" with Burch in the past.[988]

A new witness, Mrs. Bertie Watson, testified for the plaintiffs. She claimed she was visiting with Burch on his front porch when they heard a gunshot. "A criminal might be trying to get away," Burch allegedly said. "Stop him at the bridge! I'll be along as soon as I get my gun." But Watson also said she did not see Burch with a gun. Mrs. Parnick McClary Dobbs and Mrs. Stella McClary alleged that Shorty was shot from the bridge by someone who appeared to be Burch.[989] Kramer asked why Mrs. Watson waited nine years to "tell her story."[990] Likely fearing retaliation, perhaps the fact that Burch was no longer in power had something to do with her hesitation.

Russell Kramer described Burch as a "78-year-old man on the sunset of life."[991] He insisted that only one deputy fired at Shorty but did not hit him, and claimed someone else must have shot him from across the creek. Woodrow Reece was unavailable for the second trial. But the defense paid his travel expenses for this trial, where he testified that he shot at Shorty.[992] Kramer alleged discrepancies in the plaintiff's witnesses. "In the excitement and confusion, they were mistaken. He also accused Shorty of exaggerating his injuries, but Shorty still occasionally bled from the mouth.[993]

Since the initial trial in 1946, three defense witnesses had died. In addition to Broughton Biggs and August Lewis, Frank Lillard had passed away. He took his own life less than a month before the trial in September 1952. He was only 55 years old. Kramer relied heavily on their testimonies. Wrinkle claimed that Lillard had committed suicide "in order not to testify in the case." But Lillard had recently suffered a family tragedy.

In his testimony, Burch admitted he went to the bridge after hearing the shots but denied that Mrs. Watson was visiting with him at the time. Attempting to establish a pattern, Wrinkle grilled Burch during his cross-examination. "He was virtually in charge of Polk County." He asked the elderly farmer, "How many men have you shot and killed?" Judge Taylor asked why such questioning was necessary. "There's probably been more people shot in Polk County than in Hamilton County, although Hamilton is much the larger county," Wrinkle said. Judge Taylor excused the jury during Wrinkle's questioning of Burch. "How many men have you shot?" "How many have been shot in Polk County while you were in office?" "How many when you were in Etowah as chief of police?" Burch answered that one man was shot in Etowah while transporting whiskey. "There were no others."

Garrett Hedden. James Spurling. David McFadden. Scott Runion. Jack Haddock. Mattie Haddock. George Ledford. Emmett Gaddis. Horace Hughes. Burch neglected to mention any of these men (and one woman) that were shot by him or his deputies. Runion and the Haddocks did not die, and shooting Hedden was possibly justified. But Burch failed to answer the question honestly. Wrinkle questioned him about some of the men he omitted, but since some of the shootings occurred during Broughton's administration, the court deemed them irrelevant.[994]

The jury only deliberated for a few hours before returning with a verdict in favor of Shorty, awarding him $2,000 in compensatory damages from each of the three defendants, but no punitive damages.⁹⁹⁵ After nine years and life-altering injuries, Shorty Richards only received $6,000 for his suffering. Burch, Flavis Bates, and Ben Smith received little more than a slap on the wrist. Although this was a federal jury, it certainly felt like Polk County justice.

Burch followed state politics until the end. In summer 1952, gubernatorial candidate Frank Clement delivered a fiery speech in front of the courthouse in Benton, eviscerating Governor Browning and his supposed failure to bring August Lewis' killer to justice. Burch delighted in hearing Clement assail the GGL. After the speech, Burch rushed over to the young candidate. "You're the next governor of Tennessee, so help me God!" Clement had the support of Boss Crump, who was not really a boss anymore, at least outside of Memphis.⁹⁹⁶ Senator McKellar lost his bid for a seventh term to Congressman Albert Gore Sr. The days of Crump and McKellar dominating Tennessee politics were over.

Crump had little to do with it, but Clement did go on to become governor. Burch and several Polk County Democrats attended his inauguration. Alfred Mynders wrote that "amiable, good-natured, likable Sheriff Biggs belongs to a political era which has vanished forever from the Tennessee scene, we hope, we hope."

Burch spent his final years enjoying time with family. He loved to relax in his rocking chair. On March 17, 1954, shortly after suffering a heart attack, he celebrated his 80th birthday. Birthday cards poured in, including one from a janitor at the state capitol who owed his job to Burch, and another from a woman of modest means who appreciated how Burch once helped her troubled son.

Burch especially enjoyed time spent with his grandchildren. L'Ene had three daughters, Becky, Carol, and Nancy, all born after her husband, Everett Bryant, returned home from the war. Burch went to Cleveland to visit them often. Broughton's son, Tom, was a football star at Polk County High School, and his youngest daughter, Mary Temple, was a standout basketball player. Burch lived to see his eldest grandchild, Joann, get married.

The family remained close by. Burch Glen went on to work for the post office and L'Ene taught at Bradley Central High School. Burch made his final appearance at a political meeting in April 1954 when he was named to a committee to count the votes for nominees at the county's Democratic convention. Leach Park and Herman Wright also attended.

Suffering from a kidney ailment and other health complications, a critically-ill Burch was hospitalized in late summer. With his family at his side, Burch Euclid Biggs passed away at Bradley County Memorial Hospital in Cleveland on the afternoon of September 12, 1954. He was 80 years old. In addition to his wife Della, children Burch Glen and L'Ene, and six grandchildren, he was survived by his two younger brothers, Duke Biggs of Kirkland, Texas and Gus Biggs of Benton.

Newspapers all over the country ran his obituary. Held at the First Baptist Church of Benton (formerly Ocoee Baptist Church), his funeral was one of the largest in the county's history, with several visitors from all over the state in attendance. Herman Wright, Pryor Crowe, Tom Kelly, Leach Park, George Crawford, and his nephew Charles Biggs were pallbearers.

Burch was laid to rest in the Benton Cemetery next to his slain father, Tom, and his oldest child, Della Etholeen. A small stone inscribed "The Old

Burch E. Biggs is buried in the Biggs family plot in the Benton Town Cemetery. - Author's photo

Sheriff" was placed in front of his headstone. He lies at rest with a beautiful view of the Chilhowee Mountains. One month after his passing, Boss Crump, also aged 80, died.

The *Chattanooga Times* remembered Burch in a column titled "End of An Era." Although still mildly critical, the *Times* complimented his "warmth that was hard to resist" and the way he carried himself with dignity. In a swipe at the GGL and their troubles in Burch's final years, the *Times* commented that "One by one, political bosses have been dethroned in recent years, their machines broken up, their power assumed in some cases by hands no better suited to serve democracy." Sheriff John Edwards commented that Burch was "the only true politician Polk County has ever produced."[997]

Jake Higgins was perhaps Burch's oldest and closest friend. He penned a heartfelt tribute in his *Polk County News* column, sharing a story that perfectly encapsulated how Burch was simultaneously a ruthless political boss and a warm, affable, person who made friends easy:

> "I know of one newspaper publisher friend of mine that had indulged in a lot of criticism of Burch. He was talking to me one time and I asked him if he had ever met him and he said he hadn't. I asked him to come to Benton and have a talk with him. This newspaper man came to a barbecue at Quinn Springs given by Burch and I introduced them, and after a long talk, this man left Polk County and was a warm friend of his ever afterwards. You had to know him to love him."[998]

About the Author

Tyler L. Boyd's first book, *Tennessee Statesman Harry T. Burn: Woman Suffrage, Free Elections and a Life of Service*, published in 2019. It was selected for the Tennessee State Museum's 2020 Book Club, won the Award of Distinction from the East Tennessee Historical Society, and the Award for Historic Preservation from the National Society Daughters of the American Revolution. His second book, *Nellie Kenyon: Trailblazing Tennessee Journalist*, published in 2022.

Boyd studies history, civics, economics, geography, and philosophy. He enjoys genealogy, running, traveling, and the cinema. He has a B.A. in history and a M.S. in teacher education, both from the University of Tennessee. He has taught high school in Loudon, Bradley, and McMinn Counties. He currently serves as a Programs committee member at the McMinn County Living Heritage Museum, as vice president of the McMinn County Historical Society, and on the McMinn County Library Board. Born and raised in Athens, he resides in East Tennessee.

Bibliography

Primary Sources

Bill Davidson and Harold Twitty. "Terror in Tennessee." *Collier's*, September 8, 1951.

Billy Benton Stewart. "278th Regimental Combat Team Sent to Polk County," n.d.

Charles Van Devander. "Mailed Fist in Tennessee." *American Mercury*, May 1944.

David L. Talley. *The Polk County Tennessee Election War of 1948*. 2000.

David L. Talley. *The Streets of Ducktown*. 2015.

Estes Kefauver Papers, MPA.0144. University of Tennessee Libraries, Knoxville, Special Collections.

Hugh Sparrow. "In Kefauver's Backyard." *Inside Detective*, June 1952.

Governor Hill McAlister (1875-1959) Papers 1933-1937, GP 42, TSLA

Governor Jim Nance McCord (1879-1968) Papers 1945-1949, GP 45, TSLA

Governor Prentice Cooper (1895-1969) Papers 1939-1945, GP 44, TSLA

John Jennings Papers, MPA.113. University of Tennessee Libraries, Knoxville, Special Collections.

L.D. Miller. "Murder at Twilight." *Master Detective*, March 1944.

Patsy Crox Underhill. *Polk County Politics*. n.d.

Polk County, Tennessee Election of 1948 Collection. University of West Georgia Center for Public History.

Robert Edward Barclay Papers, 1854-1977. Tennessee State Library and Archives

Sue K. Hicks Papers, MPA.0136. University of Tennessee Libraries, Knoxville, Special Collections.

The National Committee For People's Rights. *Report on the Ducktown (Tennessee) Dynamiting Convictions*. December 1941.

Government Records

Etowah City Commission Minutes

Polk County Quarterly Court Minutes

Polk County Tax Books
Public Acts of the State of Tennessee
Private Acts of the State of Tennessee

Tennessee Chancery Court Cases
Lillie Biggs, et al vs. B.E. Biggs, et al, No. 1434, Polk County Chancery Court at Benton (1938)

Tennessee Circuit Court Cases
R.G. Hood vs. A.B. Green, No. 1070, Polk County Circuit Court at Benton (1936)

G.S. Runion vs. B.E. Biggs and August Lewis, Polk County Circuit Court at Benton (1938)

Tennessee Criminal Court Cases
State vs. Burch Biggs, No. 5415, McMinn County Criminal Court (1926)

State vs. Burch Biggs, No. 5557, McMinn County Criminal Court (1927)

State vs. Emmett Gaddis, Clarence Brooks, Lloyd Parton, No. 50, Polk County Criminal Court at Ducktown (1937)

State vs. James Boggs, No. 675, Polk County Criminal Court at Ducktown (1946)

State vs. L.C. Miller, Herbert Walker, and William Pilgrim, No. 2526-7-8, Polk County Criminal Court at Benton (1941)

State vs. M.D. Price, No. 2337, Polk County Criminal Court at Benton (1937)

State vs. T.W. Dalton, M.D. Price, and Jack Hedden, No. 2581-82-83, Polk County Criminal Court at Benton (1941)

State vs. William Hedden, No. 2587, Polk County Criminal Court at Benton (1941)

Tennessee Supreme Court Cases
Biggs vs. Beeler, 180 Tenn. 198 (1943)

Bill Grooms, Johnnie Grooms, and Ralph Grooms vs. B.E. Biggs, Jr., Sheriff, Polk Law (1938)

George H. Ledford, et al., Appellees, vs. Hoyt L. Lillard, et al., Appellants, No. 4 Polk County Equity (1936)

State of Tennessee, ex. rel. vs. B.E. Biggs, Law Cause No. 3 from Polk County (1931)

State of Tennessee Ex Rel Burch G. Biggs, Sheriff of Polk County, Tennessee vs. R.E. Barclay, Commissioner of Finance and Chairman of the Board of County Commissioners of Polk County, Tennessee, et als, Polk Equity (1948)

United States District Court Cases

Everett Richards vs. Burch E. Biggs, et al, No. 606, Eastern District of Tennessee, Southern Division (1944)

Herbert Walker vs. B.E. Biggs, Jr., M.E. Clemmer, and C.L. Campbell, Civil No. 459, Eastern District of Tennessee, Southern Division (1946)

Rozelle McFadden, Administratrix, etc., vs. B.E. Biggs, et al, No. 2200 Law, Eastern District of Tennessee, Southern Division (1938)

U.S. vs. George Crawford et al, No. 20620, Northern District of Georgia, Atlanta Division (1936)

U.S. vs. Mitchell Clifton Anderson, et al, No. 8100 Criminal, Eastern District of Tennessee, Southern Division (1941)

Interviews

Billy Rice, phone interview with the author
Buck Arp family, phone interview with the author
Charles Clifford Guinn, Jr., interview with the author
Charles Matt Witt, interview with Loel Oldham
Cheryl Loudermilk Kear, phone interview with the author
George O. Rogers family, phone interview with the author
David Talley, phone interview with the author
Earl Oliver, interview with Kristin N. Patterson
Hubert C. Sartin family, interview with the author
James Lucius Passmore, interview with Kristin N. Patterson
Lowell Posey, phone interview with the author
Manuel Price family, phone interview with the author
Mary Lethco Lewis, interview with the author
Ralph Painter, interview with the author
Robert E. Barclay Jr., interview with Kristin N. Patterson
Rusty Arp, phone interview with the author
Sally Hutchins Gregory, interview with Margaret Gregory
Sandy Osborne, phone interview with the author
Shirley Watkins Hamby, phone interview with Katherine Goodman Smith
Stephen Byrd, phone interview with the author

T. Blair Lillard II, phone interview with the author
Wesley J. Lowery, interview with Kristin N. Patterson
William Frank Lowery, interview with the author
William Henry Watson, interview with Kristin N. Patterson
Wilma Edwards Jones, phone interview with the author

Secondary Sources

Barclay, R.E. *The Copper Basin: 1890 to 1963*. Knoxville: White Wing Publishing House and Press, 1975.

Blair, Reuben Moore. "The Development of Education in Polk County, Tennessee." M.A. thesis, University of Tennessee, 1941.

DeRose, Chris. *The Fighting Bunch: The Battle of Athens and How World War II Veterans Won the Only Successful Armed Rebellion Since the Revolution*. New York: St. Martin's Press, 2020.

Guy, Joe. *Hidden History of East Tennessee*. Charleston, SC: The History Press, 2008.

Lemond, Thomas Addison, Jr. "The Good Government League and Polk County (Tennessee) Politics, 1946-1965." M.A. thesis, Vanderbilt University, 1970.

Lillard, Roy G. "Some Aspects of Polk County Politics." Term paper, University of Tennessee, 1958.

Lillard, Roy G. *The History of Polk County Tennessee*. Maryville, TN: Stinnett Printing Company, 1999.

Parish, Thurman. *Mountain Memories: History, People, Legends & Tales of the Polk County Mountains in Southeast Tennessee*. Privately published, 2010.

Patterson, Kristin Nicole. "Stealing Democracy: Sheriff Biggs, The Good Government League, and Politics in Polk County, Tennessee 1930-1948." M.A. thesis, University of West Georgia, 2005.

Smith, Robert N. *An Evil Day in Georgia: The Killing of Coleman Osborn and the Death Penalty in the Progressive-Era South*. Knoxville, TN: University of Tennessee Press, 2015.

Newspapers

Asheville Citizen-Times
Atlanta Constitution
Bristol Herald-Courier
Chattanooga Times

Chattanooga News
Chattanooga News-Free Press
Charlotte News
Cleveland Daily Banner
Cleveland Herald
Cleveland Journal and Banner
Columbus Ledger
Copper City Advance
Daily Post-Athenian
Denver Post
Etowah Enterprise
Kingsport News
Knoxville Journal
Knoxville Journal and Tribune
Knoxville News-Sentinel
Nashville Banner
Nashville Tennessean
New York Times
The Olympian
Polk County News
Polk County Republican
Richmond Times Dispatch
Sweetwater Valley News

ENDNOTES

1. Brock, Carol Bryant; Williams, Nancy Bryant. "Biggs Family History." Biggs Family file. Polk County Historical and Genealogical Society; "Times Reporter Spends Day With Sheriff Burch E. Biggs," *Chattanooga Times*, June 30, 1943
2. Lillard, *The History of Polk County Tennessee*, p. 274
3. "Times Reporter Spends Day With Sheriff Burch E. Biggs"
4. "Burch Biggs, 80, Is Dead; Power in Politics of Polk," *Chattanooga Times*, September 13, 1954
5. Lillard, *The History of Polk County Tennessee*, p. 68
6. Barclay, *The Copper Basin: 1890-1963*
7. "Two Young Men Are Expelled From School," Clemmer Scrapbook, 1893
8. Bryant, L'Ene Biggs, "Cherished Memories," Biggs family file
9. "Mr. Cody Is a Very Bad Man," *Chattanooga Times*, September 26, 1905
10. Polk County Tax Books (1906)
11. "That Murder At M'Cays," *Chattanooga Times*, January 21, 1907
12. "Clemency Is Disapproved," *Chattanooga Times*, January 15, 1908
13. "Times Reporter Spends Day With Sheriff Burch E. Biggs;" "Burch Biggs, 80, Is Dead; Power in Politics of Polk"
14. Ibid
15. Lillard, *The History of Polk County Tennessee*, p. 261
16. Fratricide Meets Doom," *Chattanooga Times*, February 5, 1908
17. "Fratricide Meets Doom;" "Noted Moonshiner and Outlaw Killed," *Knoxville Journal and Tribune*, January 5, 1908; "Long Defiance of Laws of Land," *Nashville American*, January 5, 1908
18. Etowah City Commission Minutes, July 6, 1910
19. "Ex-Polk Politico, Burch Biggs, Dies," *Knoxville News-Sentinel*, September 13, 1954
20. Letter, W.H. Williamson to Newton Rogers, February 12, 1913
21. Barclay, *The Copper Basin: 1890-1963*, p. 150
22. "Deputy Sheriff Shoots and Kills Chief of Police," *Chattanooga News*, December 24, 1913
23. "Circuit Court," *Polk County Republican*, March 27, 1914; "Officers Fight Fatal Duel At Copperhill," *Nashville Tennessean*, December 25, 1913; "Tragedy At Copperhill," *Knoxville Journal and Tribune*, December 26, 1913
24. "Hood Acquitted," *Cleveland Journal and Banner*, March 31, 1914
25. Letter, W.F. Russell to Gov. Prentice Cooper, August 8, 1938, Governor Prentice Cooper (1895-1969) Papers 1939-1945, GP 44, TSLA
26. W.H. Williamson to Newton Rogers, May 12, 1912
27. "Son Killed By Deputy Sheriff Basis Of Suit," *Chattanooga News*, January 13, 1916
28. "Etholeen Biggs (1915)," clipping from Amanda Higdon Scrapbook, Polk County Historical and Genealogical Society

29 Polk County Tax Books (1923)
30 State vs. Burch Biggs, No. 5415, McMinn County Criminal Court (1927); "Blair Leaves Athens For Other Sessions," *Chattanooga Times*, May 15, 1927; State vs. Burch Biggs, No. 5557, McMinn County Criminal Court (1927)
31 Smith, *An Evil Day In Georgia*, p. 41-42
32 "Election Officers Under Indictment," *Chattanooga Times*, August 11, 1926
34 Anonymous source #1
35 "Burch Biggs, Dictator of Polk County, Says He Provides 'Clean Government,'" *Knoxville News-Sentinel*, June 21, 1943
36 Davidson, Bill; Twitty, Harold. "Terror in Tennessee." *Collier's*, September 8, 1951.
37 "Guns Used in Polk To Control Count," *Chattanooga Times*, August 13, 1930
38 "Polk Squire's Election Contested By Opponent," *Chattanooga Times*, January 16, 1930; "J.P. Contest Is Filed In Court," *Polk County News*, January 22, 1931
39 State of Tennessee, ex. rel. vs. B.E. Biggs, Law Cause No. 3 from Polk County (1931)
40 Tennessee Private Acts (1931), p. 2004-2005
41 "Bill Reduces Polk District And Court 2," *Polk County News*, July 9, 1931; Tennessee Private Acts (1931) p. 1846-1848
42 James Lucius Passmore, interview with Kristin N. Patterson
43 Ibid
44 Underhill, Patsy. "Polk County Politics," n.d.
45 Earl Oliver, interview with Kristin N. Patterson
46 Lowell Posey, phone interview with the author
47 David Talley, phone interview with the author
48 Tennessee Private Acts (1933), p. 1377-1379
49 Ibid, p. 1826-1828
50 Anonymous source #2
51 Tennessee Public Acts (1921), p. 188-200
52 "Court Writ Curbs Officials In Polk," *Chattanooga Times*, February 10, 1933
53 "High Cost of County Government," *Polk County News*, March 16, 1933
54 Polk County Quarterly Court Minutes (August 1935)
55 Buck Arp family, phone interview with the author
56 "Clerk Asserts Shortage Slur Political Bunk," *Chattanooga Times*, January 5, 1934
57 Polk County Tax Books (1934); "Terror In Tennessee"
58 Hubert C. Sartin family, interview with the author
59 "Polk County Politics"
60 Letter, James F. Corn to Gov. Prentice Cooper, September 23, 1943, Cooper Papers
61 "Polk County Politics"
62 "Republicans of Polk Are For The Fusion Ticket," *Polk County News*, September 13, 1934
63 "Polk County Politics"

64 Parish, *Mountain Memories*, p. 121
65 Sally Hutchins Gregory, interview with Margaret Gregory
66 "Ouster Ignored by Polk Judge," *Polk County News*, April 4, 1935
67 "Relief Job Scene Of Riot, Shooting," *Chattanooga Times*, November 28, 1935
68 "Eight Hurt in Labor Outbreak At Copperhill," *Chattanooga News*, November 27, 1935
69 "Relief Job Scene Of Riot, Shooting"
70 "Road Crew Asks For Protection," *Knoxville-News Sentinel*, November 28, 1935
71 Letter, John S. Wrinkle to Gov. Hill McAlister, May 17, 1936, Governor Hill McAlister (1875-1959) Papers 1933-1937, GP 42, TSLA
72 Rozelle McFadden, Administratrix, etc., vs. B.E. Biggs, et al, No. 2200 Law, Eastern District of Tennessee, Southern Division (1938)
73 Ibid; "Polk Deputy Shot On Porch Of Home," *Chattanooga Times*, December 25, 1935
74 "M'Fadden Warrant Still Not Served," *Chattanooga Times*, January 10, 1936
75 "McFadden To Attempt Alibi In Polk Shooting," *Chattanooga Times*, December 25, 1935
76 "Sheriff At Cleveland Asked To Help Search," *Chattanooga Times*, December 25, 1935
77 "Denies He Shot Deputy Sheriff," *Knoxville Journal*, January 1, 1936
78 "Denies Shooting Deputy In Polk," *Knoxville Journal*, January 30, 1936
79 "M'Fadden Hearing Slated Thursday," *Chattanooga Times*, February 11, 1936
80 "D.W. M'Fadden Charges Biggs Seeks His Life," *Chattanooga Times*, February 15, 1936
81 Ibid
82 "McFadden Held In Shooting of Deputy in Polk," *Chattanooga News*, February 15, 1936
83 Ibid
84 "M'Fadden Guarded As He Makes Bond," *Chattanooga Times*, February 18, 1936
85 "Locals," *Polk County News*, April 23, 1935
86 "Foust Enjoins Polk Salaries; Fees Assailed," *Polk County News*, February 13, 1936
87 Ibid; "Biggs Fights Back Against Salary Attack," *Chattanooga Times*, June 5, 1936
88 "Foust Enjoins Polk Salaries; Fees Assailed," *Chattanooga Times*, February 11, 1936
89 George H. Ledford, et al., Appellees, vs. Hoyt L. Lillard, et al., Appellants, No. 4 Polk County Equity (1936)
90 Ibid
91 Gregory interview
92 "Says Officers Beat His Head At Copperhill," *Chattanooga Times*, April 6, 1935
93 "Story Quinn Told Branded As False," *Chattanooga Times*, April 13, 1935

94	"Deputy Fired On CCC Truck; G-Men Report," *Chattanooga Times*, July 17, 1936
95	"Three Sentenced in CCC Shooting," *Chattanooga Times,* October 9, 1936; U.S. vs. George Crawford et al., No. 20620, Northern District of Georgia, Atlanta Division (1936)
96	Anonymous source #3
97	"Political Announcements: For Sheriff," *Polk County News*, March 19, 1936
98	"Guinn New Leader of Polk Republicans," *Polk County News*, April 2, 1936
99	"Polk Leaders State Revolt Against Biggs," *Chattanooga News*, May 5, 1936
100	Anonymous source #1
101	"Polk's Democrats Swing Into Fight," *Chattanooga Times*, May 17, 1936
102	Ibid
103	Ibid
104	"McFadden Met Death Avoiding Longer Trip," *Chattanooga Times*, May 19, 1936
105	"Gaddis, Two Pals On Trial Tuesday," *Chattanooga Times*, January 17, 1937
106	"Agents of U.S. Investigating Polk Shooting," *Chattanooga Times*, May 21, 1936
107	"Theory of the State," Sue K. Hicks Papers, MPA.0136. University of Tennessee Libraries, Knoxville, Special Collections; "McFadden Slain As Bullets Fly In Polk County," *Chattanooga Times*, May 18, 1936
108	"M'Fadden Slain In Gun Mystery In Polk," *Polk County News*, May 21, 1936
109	"McFadden Death Will Be Probed By Grand Jury," *Chattanooga Times*, May 19, 1936; McFadden vs. Biggs (1938)
110	"McFadden Slain As Bullets Fly In Polk County"
111	"McFadden Death Will Be Probed By Grand Jury" ; "Declares First Shot Was Fired By McFadden," *Chattanooga News*, May 18, 1936
112	"M'Fadden Slain In Gun Mystery In Polk"
113	"McFadden Death Will Be Probed By Grand Jury"
114	"Jury To Probe Road Slaying," *Knoxville Journal*, May 19, 1936
115	"Biggs Told Governor He Would Shield Man," *Chattanooga Times*, May 18, 1936; "McFadden Petitioned McAlister for Troops," *Chattanooga Times*, May 19, 1936
116	"McFadden Met Death Avoiding Longer Trip"
117	"Blair Puts Off M'Fadden Case Pending Probe," *Chattanooga Times*, May 20, 1936
118	"Brooks, Parton With Gaddis At Killing – Biggs," *Chattanooga News*, May 22, 1936
119	"Blair Puts Off M'Fadden Case Pending Probe"
120	Ibid
121	"Brooks, Parton With Gaddis At Killing – Biggs"
122	"Blair Puts Off M'Fadden Case Pending Probe"
123	"Brooks, Parton With Gaddis At Killing – Biggs"
124	"Tension Grows At Copperhill," *Chattanooga Times*, May 22, 1936
125	"Biggs Ready to Serve Any McFadden Papers," *Chattanooga Times*, May 23, 1936

126 "Probe In Polk To Start Soon," *Chattanooga Times*, May 23, 1936
127 "Clear Case of First Degree Murder – Witt," *Chattanooga News*, May 23, 1936
128 "Gaddis Is Held To Grand Jury," *Chattanooga Times*, May 31, 1936; "Ex-Deputy Sheriff Held For Murder," *Nashville Tennessean*, May 31, 1936
129 "Gaddis Is Held To Grand Jury"
130 "Wrinkle Asks Help Of G-Men In Gaddis Case," *Chattanooga Times*, June 2, 1936
131 "M'Fadden Slaying Studied By G-Men," *Chattanooga Times*, June 4, 1936
132 "Help Of Leaders Offered In Probe," *Chattanooga Times*, June 13, 1936
133 "Polk Riot Matter For State Courts," *Chattanooga Times*, June 14, 1936
134 "Automobile Club Travels New Road," *Chattanooga Times*, July 24, 1936
135 "Road Man's Son Asks U.S. Aid," *Knoxville News-Sentinel*, July 5, 1936
136 "Biggs Fights Back Against Salary Attack"
137 "Fusion May Seek To Unhorse Biggs," *Chattanooga Times*, May 23, 1936
138 "F.D.R. Indorsed; Dossett Forces Run Convention," *Chattanooga Times*, May 22, 1936
139 "Both Legs of Man Broken By Bullet," *Chattanooga Times*, June 2, 1936
140 "Miners Will Visit Benton Tomorrow," *Chattanooga Times*, June 3, 1936; "Fusion Completed By Action In Polk," *Chattanooga Times*, May 29, 1936
141 "Fusionists Report Tacks Put In Road," *Chattanooga Times*, June 4, 1936
142 "Polk Trustee Denies Charges Foes Issued," *Chattanooga Times*, June 4, 1936
143 "Miners At Benton Buy 300 Receipts," *Chattanooga Times*, June 5, 1936
144 Parish, *Mountain Memories*, p. 121
145 "Sheriff Biggs Is Main Issue As Son Seeks Father's Office," *Chattanooga News*, July 23, 1936
146 "Young Biggs Says He Is Unfettered," *Chattanooga Times*, July 17, 1936
147 Ibid
148 "Harbison Sees Victory By Majority of 1,500," *Chattanooga Times*, August 6, 1936
149 "'Bogus' Poll Taxes in Polk Vote Charged," *Chattanooga News*, March 30, 1937
150 "Howell To Stand For Polk Honesty," *Chattanooga Times*, August 2, 1936
151 "Polk's WPA Set-Up Target Of Attack," *Chattanooga Times*, August 1, 1936
152 Ibid
153 "Probe Charges Politics Cost Job Of Worker," *Knoxville Journal*, August 6, 1936
154 "Polk Deputy Runs As Shots Hit Two," *Chattanooga Times*, August 4, 1936; "Polk's First Election Shot Fired Sunday," *Cleveland Daily Banner*, August 4, 1936
155 Ibid
156 Ibid
157 "Polk's First Election Shot Fired Sunday"
158 "Polk Deputy Runs As Shots Hit Two"
159 "Youth and Woman Shot at Conasauga," *Chattanooga News*, August 4, 1936

160 "Judge Davis Urges Polk Voters To Defeat Biggs-Trevena Court," *Chattanooga Times*, August 4, 1936

161 Henry Watson, interview with Kristin N. Patterson

162 "Georgian Swears Three Were Paid $5 Each to Support Biggs Ticket," *Chattanooga Times*, August 11, 1936

163 "Writ By Eldridge Bans Intimidation," *Chattanooga Times*, August 6, 1936

164 Ibid

165 "Interest Centers On Battle In Polk," *Chattanooga Times*, August 6, 1936

166 "Conasauga Vote Stopped," *Chattanooga Times*, August 7, 1936; "Crowd Blocks Opening Polls At Conasauga," *Chattanooga News*, August 6, 1936; "Armed Crowd Goes To Poll," *Knoxville News-Sentinel*, August 6, 1946; "Witnesses Tell of Vote Battle At Conasauga," *Chattanooga News*, April 2, 1937

167 "Witnesses Tell Of Vote Battle At Conasauga;" "Display Of Guns Described In Polk Vote Hearing," *Chattanooga Times*, April 2, 1937

168 Ibid

169 "Polk Man Charges Illegal Balloting," *Chattanooga Times*, April 1, 1937

170 "Biggs Elected Behind Rifles," *Chattanooga Times*, August 7, 1936

171 "Georgian Swears Three Were Paid $5 Each to Support Biggs Ticket"

172 "Writ Granted Against Green in Polk Voting," *Chattanooga Times*, August 28, 1936

173 "Polk Vote Fraud Charged In Court," *Chattanooga Times*, March 30, 1937; "'Bogus' Poll Taxes in Polk Vote Charged," *Chattanooga News*, March 30, 1937

174 "Writ Granted Against Green in Polk Voting"

175 "Terror In Tennessee"

176 "Polk Vote Fraud Charged In Court,"; "'Bogus' Poll Taxes in Polk Vote Charged"

177 Ibid; "Polk County Election Judge Is Slugged, Reportedly By Constable," *Knoxville Journal*, August 7, 1936; "Polk Man Named As Vote Marker," *Chattanooga Times*, March 31, 1937

178 "Polk Man Charges Illegal Balloting"; "Non-Residents Cast Ballots, Witnesses Say," *Chattanooga Times*, April 3, 1937

179 "Prosecution In Polk Vote Trial Completes Case," *Chattanooga News*, April 1, 1937

180 "Biggs Elected Behind Rifles"

181 Ibid

182 Ibid

183 "Biggs Elected Behind Rifles"

184 "False Bottoms Found In Polk County Ballot Boxes," *Chattanooga News*, August 7, 1936

185 "Polk Fraud Uncovered," *Chattanooga Times*, August 8, 1936

186 "Standridge Slaps At Park Charges," *Chattanooga Times*, October 24, 1936

187 "Terror In Tennessee"

188 "Polk Election Returns May Be Contested," *Chattanooga News*, August 8, 1936

189 "Biggs Elected Behind Rifles"
190 "Chief Quits In Polk County," *Chattanooga Times*, August 9, 1936
191 "Who Keeps Biggs In Power?" *Chattanooga News*, August 12, 1936
192 Ibid
193 "Georgian Swears Three Were Paid $5 Each to Support Biggs Ticket"
194 "Polk County Politics," *Chattanooga Times*, August 17, 1936
195 Ibid
196 Charles Matt Witt, interview with Loel Oldham
197 Anonymous source #4
198 Witt interview
199 "Burch Biggs Looks Like a Farmer, Not the Powerful Politician He Is," *Knoxville News-Sentinel*, June 25, 1943
200 Gregory interview
201 Anonymous source #5
202 Charles Clifford Guinn, Jr., interview with the author
203 Billy Rice, phone interview with the author
204 "Attempt Made To Assassinate McFadden, Jr." *Chattanooga News*, August 13, 1936; "M'Fadden Machine Struck By Shots," *Chattanooga Times*, August 15, 1936
205 Ibid
206 "M'Fadden Links Shooting With Tennessee Row," *Asheville Citizen-Times*, August 14, 1936
207 "Writ Granted Against Green In Polk Voting," *Chattanooga Times*, August 28, 1936
208 "New Biggs Rules As Polk Sheriff," *Chattanooga Times*, September 2, 1936
209 "Sheriff Biggs Serving Notice On Slot Machine Operators," *Polk County News*, September 24, 1936
210 Anonymous source #4, Anonymous source #6, Anonymous source #7
211 "Polk County Politics"
212 Witt interview
213 "Sheriff Biggs Serving Notice On Slot Machine Operators"
214 "Terror in Tennessee;" David L. Talley. "The Streets of Ducktown." 2015
215 "The Streets of Ducktown"
216 Ibid
217 State vs. Emmett Gaddis, Clarence Brooks, Lloyd Parton, No. 50, Polk County Criminal Court at Ducktown (1937)
218 "Gaddis Trial Jury Sought," *Knoxville-News Sentinel*, January 19, 1937
219 "Only Two Jurors Selected For Gaddis Trial," *Chattanooga News*, January 19, 1937
220 "Surprise Seen In Gaddis Case," *Chattanooga Times*, January 20, 1937
221 "Atlanta Matron One of Surprise State Witnesses," *Chattanooga News*, January 20, 1937
222 "Hear Witnesses In Feud Death," *Knoxville News-Sentinel*, January 20, 1937
223 "Gaddis Wounded by Parton, Woman Eyewitness States," *Chattanooga Times*, January 21, 1937

224 "Atlanta Matron One of Surprise State Witnesses;" "Gaddis Wounded by Parton, Woman Eyewitness States"
225 "Atlanta Matron One of Surprise State Witnesses"
226 Ibid
227 "Youth 'Saw Father' Kill Contractor," *Knoxville News-Sentinel*, January 21, 1937
228 Ibid
229 Ibid
230 "'Pappy' Killed McFadden, Said Son of Gaddis," *Chattanooga News*, January 21, 1937
231 "M'Fadden Shot First Bullets, Gaddis Swears," *Chattanooga Times*, January 22, 1937
232 Ibid
233 Ibid
234 Ibid
235 Ibid
236 Ibid
237 "Judge Halts Gaddis Trial To Quiz Jury," *Knoxville News-Sentinel*, January 22, 1937
238 "Theory of the Defendants," Hicks Papers; "McFadden Shot First Bullets, Gaddis Swears"
239 "McFadden Shot First Bullets, Gaddis Swears"
240 "Jury-Fixing Report Heard In Gaddis Case," *Chattanooga News*, January 22, 1937
241 "Judge Halts Gaddis Trial To Quiz Jury"
242 "Judge Probes 'Fixing' Rumor," *Chattanooga Times,* January 23, 1937
243 Ibid
244 Ibid
245 "Gaddis Jurors Quickly Acquit Three In Trial," *Chattanooga Times*, January 24, 1937
246 Ibid
247 Ibid
248 Ibid
249 "Gaddis Jurors Quickly Acquit Three In Trial"
250 "Polk Deputy Is Given Bail," *Polk County News*, March 25, 1937
251 Ibid; "Deputy Facing Murder Charge In Polk County," *Cleveland Herald*, March 19, 1937; Sandy Osborne, phone interview with the author
252 "Polk Deputy Held On Murder Count," *Chattanooga Times*, March 18, 1937
253 Ibid; George Ledford Killed By Deputy Sheriff E.D. Price," *Polk County News*, March 18, 1937
254 "Polk Deputy Held On Murder Count"
255 State vs. M.D. Price, No. 2337, Polk County Criminal Court at Benton (1937)
256 "Trial For Deputy Started At Benton," *Copper City Advance*, March 25, 1938
257 Ibid

258 "M.D. Price Acquitted In Polk County Death," *Chattanooga Times*, March 25, 1938
259 Gregory interview
260 State vs. T.W. Dalton, M.D. Price, and Jack Hedden, No. 2581-82-83, Polk County Criminal Court at Benton (1941)
261 Osborne family interview; Manuel Price family, phone interview with the author
262 R.G. Hood vs. A.B. Green, No. 1070, Polk County Circuit Court at Benton (1936)
263 "Polk Man Charges Illegal Balloting"
264 "Display Of Guns Described In Polk Vote Hearing," *Chattanooga Times*, April 2, 1937
265 Ibid
266 "Polk Election Suits Dropped," *Chattanooga Times*, June 20, 1937
267 "Woody Withdraws Polk County Bill," *Chattanooga Times*, February 20, 1937
268 Rozelle McFadden, Administratrix, etc., vs. B.E. Biggs, et al, No. 2200 Law, Eastern District of Tennessee, Southern Division (1938); "Gaddis, Biggs Sued By Widow In U.S. Court," *Copper City Advance*, May 13, 1937
269 "Gaddis, Biggs Sued By Widow In U.S. Court," *Chattanooga Times*, May 11, 1937
270 McFadden vs. Biggs (1938)
271 Ibid
272 "Crippen Tells of 'Road Mob,'" *Knoxville News-Sentinel*, January 31, 1938; "Claims Gaddis Asked A Bribe," *Chattanooga Times*, February 1, 1938
273 "Claims Gaddis Asked A Bribe;" "Gaddis Asked 'Protection,' Witness Says," *Chattanooga News*, January 31, 1938
274 "Claims Gaddis Asked A Bribe"
275 "Plea Filed To Dismiss Suit Against Biggs," *Chattanooga News*, February 2, 1938
276 Ibid
277 McFadden vs. Biggs (1938); "Gaddis Asked 'Protection,' Witness Says"
278 McFadden vs. Biggs (1938)
279 Ibid
280 "Polk Commission Still Not Named," *Chattanooga Times*, September 3, 1937
281 "Polk Democrats In Harmony Move," *Chattanooga Times*, May 25, 1938
282 "Groups To Divide Offices In Polk," *Chattanooga Times*, May 27, 1938
283 "Harmony Ticket Put Out By Polk County Democrats Saturday," *Polk County News*, June 2, 1938
284 Ralph Painter, interview with the author
285 "'Harmony Ticket' Selected By Polk County Democrats"
286 G.S. Runion vs. B.E. Biggs and August Lewis, Polk County Circuit Court at Benton (1938); "Judge Quinn Holding Court," *Polk County News*, June 2, 1938
287 Bill Grooms, Johnnie Grooms, and Ralph Grooms vs. B.E. Biggs, Jr., Sheriff, Polk Law (1938)
288 Painter interview

289 Grooms vs. Biggs (1938)
290 "New Polk Candidate," *Polk County News*, June 23, 1938
291 "Democrats Meet In Rally At Ducktown," *Copper City Advance*, July 15, 1938
292 "Polk County Politics"
293 Lillard, *The History of Polk County Tennessee*, p. 215-216
294 Sartin family interview
295 "3 Buyers Acquire Big Tract in Polk," *Chattanooga Times*, August 13, 1945
296 Anonymous source #3
297 ""Socials," *Polk County News*, September 2, 1937; "Locals," *Polk County News*, November 11, 1938
298 "Terror In Tennessee"
299 Gregory interview
300 Polk County Tax Books (1938)
301 Lemond, "The Good Government League and Polk County (Tennessee) Politics, 1946-1965", p. 4
302 Witt interview; "Terror In Tennessee"
303 Posey interview; Painter interview; "Terror In Tennessee"
304 Witt interview
305 Anonymous source #8
306 Anonymous source #4
307 Sartin family interview
308 Witt interview; Anonymous source #9
309 Gregory interview
310 "The Streets of Ducktown"
311 "Clayton, Polk Deputy, Is Slain; Biggs Leasing Search for Killer," *Chattanooga Times*, May 3, 1946
312 "So Far No Charges Filed Against Polk Deputies," *Polk County News*, September 15, 1938
313 "The Streets of Ducktown"
314 Ibid
315 "Gaddis Is Slain In Gun Battle; Deputies Held," *Chattanooga Times*, September 15, 1938
316 "Gaddis Is Slain In Gun Battle; Deputies Held"
317 Talley interview
318 Oliver interview
319 Watson interview
320 Talley interview
321 "Legislation Proposed To Put Polk Leaders, Lillard and Davis, Into Jobs," *Polk County News*, February 2, 1939
322 "Polk County Poll Officials Charge Many Irregularities," *Knoxville Journal*, January 19, 1939
323 Ibid
324 "All Candidates Agree On Plan To Pick Nominee," *Chattanooga Times*, July 22, 1939; "Organization in Polk to Support Kefauver," *Chattanooga Times*, August 6, 1939

325 "Wrinkle To Make House Race In '40," *Chattanooga Times*, August 22, 1939
326 Letter, Estes Kefauver to Burch Biggs, September 30, 1939, Estes Kefauver Papers, MPA.0144. University of Tennessee Libraries, Knoxville, Special Collections.
327 Letter, Estes Kefauver to Gov. Prentice Cooper, December 6, 1939, Cooper Papers
328 "Tenn. Copper Co. Ceases Operations," *Copper City Advance*, July 21, 1939; Oliver interview
329 "Copper Workers Are Adamant On Checkoff," *Polk County News*, July 20, 1939; "Special Deputies Guard Reopening," *Chattanooga Times*, August 28, 1939; National Committee for People's Rights. "Report on the Ducktown (Tennessee) Dynamiting Convictions." December 1941
330 "Copper Plans Set For Siege," *Chattanooga Times*, July 16, 1939
331 "Tenn. Copper Co. Ceases Operations"; "Copper Workers Are Adamant On Checkoff"
332 Ibid
333 Barclay, *The Copper Basin*, p. 71
334 Oliver interview
335 Lemond, "The Good Government League and Polk County (Tennessee) Politics, 1946-1965," p. 4
336 Witt interview
337 Ibid; "Report on the Ducktown (Tennessee) Dynamiting Convictions"
338 "Final Talk Fails At Copper Plants,'" *Chattanooga Times*, August 27, 1939
339 "Report on the Ducktown (Tennessee) Dynamiting Convictions"
340 Ibid
341 "Report on the Ducktown (Tennessee) Dynamiting Convictions"
342 Ibid
343 "The Streets of Ducktown"
344 Letter, Paul Savage to Mrs. Maude Ineen, September 29, 1939, Cooper Papers
345 "Judge Will Hear Union Complaint," *Chattanooga Times*, November 11, 1939; "The Streets of Ducktown;" "Report on the Ducktown (Tennessee) Dynamiting Convictions"
346 "Report on the Ducktown (Tennessee) Dynamiting Convictions"
347 Ibid
348 "Miner Forced To Enter Car, Is Beaten," *Copper City Advance*, September 22, 1939
349 "Judge Will Hear Union Complaint;" "Union Complains To Be Aired Today," *Chattanooga Times*, November 22, 1939
350 "Polk Courthouse Barred To Union," *Chattanooga Times*, November 16, 1939
351 "Judge Dismisses Suit Filed By CIO Against Tenn. Copper Co.," *Copper City Advance*, January 26, 1940
352 "Hicks 'Fires' 4 Polk Jurors," *Polk County News*, January 18, 1940
353 "Tennessee Copper Company Increases Wages," *Copper City Advance*, October 4, 1940
354 "Report on the Ducktown (Tennessee) Dynamiting Convictions"

355 "Three TVA Towers Dynamited In Copper Basin; Striker Held," *Chattanooga Times*, April 2, 1940; "Three TVA Towers Dynamited In Basin," *Copper City Advance*, April 5, 1940
356 Ibid
357 "Three TVA Towers Dynamited In Basin"
358 "Report on the Ducktown (Tennessee) Dynamiting Convictions"
359 "Blasts Demolish TVA Line Tower," *Chattanooga Times*, April 25, 1940; "F.B.I. Chief Plaxico Here In Investigation: Questions Men Arrested in Dynamiting of Towers Wednesday," *Copper City Advance*, April 16, 1940
360 "Nineteen Arrested In Dynamiting Of Towers," *Copper City Advance*, May 3, 1940; U.S. vs. Mitchell Clifton Anderson, et al, No. 8100 Criminal, Eastern District of Tennessee, Southern Division (1941)
361 "Report on the Ducktown (Tennessee) Dynamiting Convictions"
362 Ibid; U.S. vs. Anderson, et al (1941)
363 "Report on the Ducktown (Tennessee) Dynamiting Convictions"
364 Passmore interview
365 "State Polices M'Minn Voting," *Chattanooga Times*, August 1, 1940
366 "Cooper Forces Expecting Big Victory," *Nashville Banner*, August 1, 1940
367 "Wrinkle Claims Victory," *Chattanooga Times*, August 1, 1940
368 Letter, Burch E. Biggs to Estes Kefauver, August 8, 1940, Kefauver Papers
369 Letter, Estes Kefauver to Burch E. Biggs, August 20, 1940, Kefauver Papers
370 Letter, Kenneth McKellar to Estes Kefauver, August 16, 1940, Kefauver Papers
371 "Burch Biggs Will Run Again In Polk County," *Chattanooga Times*, September 28, 1940
372 Painter interview
373 Passmore interview
374 "Terror In Tennessee"
375 "Senate Medal Given "Ex-Sheriff Biggs," *Polk County News*, January 23, 1941
376 "Knox Group For Poll Tax Repeal 'In Campaign,'" *Nashville Tennessean*, January 15, 1941
377 "Poll Repeal Issue Not Dead," *Knoxville-News Sentinel*, January 16, 1941
378 "Knox Senator Voids Pledge," *Knoxville Journal*, January 16, 1941
379 "Cooper Given Bill Changing M'Minn Court," *Chattanooga Times*, February 16, 1941
380 "Ripper Bill For McMinn Is Enacted," *Knoxville Journal*, February 16, 1941
381 "Three Confessions Admitted By Darr," *Chattanooga Times*, January 18, 1941
382 "Confessions Of Three Are Held Evidence," *Copper City Advance*, January 17, 1941
383 "7 Defendants Are Acquitted Of Dynamiting," *Chattanooga Times*, January 22, 1941
384 Ibid, "Report on the Ducktown (Tennessee) Dynamiting Convictions"
385 "Report on the Ducktown (Tennessee) Dynamiting Convictions"
386 Ibid
387 "TVA Case Jury Cannot Agree, Given Recess," *Chattanooga Times*, January 29, 1941

388 "Eight Defendants In Dynamiting Sentenced," *Copper City Advance*, February 7, 1941
389 "Darr Adjourns Biggs Hearing Until Monday," *Chattanooga Times*, September 7, 1946
390 State of Tennessee vs. L.C. Miller, Herbert Walker, and William Pilgrim, Nos. 2526-7-8, Polk County Criminal Court at Benton (1941); Herbert Walker vs. B.E. Biggs, Jr., M.E. Clemmer, and C.L. Campbell, Civil No. 459, Eastern District of Tennessee, Southern Division (1946)
391 Letter, Blanche Hallbrook to Gov. Prentice Cooper, September 6, 1941, Cooper Papers
392 Guinn interview
393 Mary Lethco Lewis, interview with the author
394 Watson interview
395 Anonymous source #5
396 Talley, David, "The Polk County Tennessee Election War of 1948," 2000
397 Anonymous source #10
398 "Two Young Mothers, Baby Murdered; 4 Men Arrested, *Polk County News*, November 20, 1941; "Four Men Charged With Murder In Shooting of Baby, Two Women," *Chattanooga Times*, November 20, 1941; Miller, L.D. "Murder at Twilight." *Master Detective Magazine*, March 1944
399 Anonymous source #4, Anonymous source #10
400 "Hedden Indicted In Triple Killing: Trial Set For Dec. 3; Goforth Held As Witness For State," Copper City Advance, November 28, 1941
401 State vs. William Hedden, No, 2587, Polk County Criminal Court at Benton (1941); "Polk Officer Goes On Trial For Murder," *Polk County News*, December 4, 1941
402 "Defendant Denies Slayings In Polk," *Chattanooga Times*, December 5, 1941
403 Ibid
404 "Hedden Gets Death In Polk Murders," *Knoxville Journal*, December 6, 1941
405 Ibid
406 "Bill Hedden Sentenced To Die In Electric Chair," *Polk County News*, December 11, 1941; "Death Sentence and 99 Years," *Nashville Banner*, April 2, 1921
407 State vs. Hedden (1941)
408 Hugh Sparrow. "In Kefauver's Backyard." *Inside Detective*. June 1952.
409 "Polk County Politics"
410 "Many Married Men in Polk Draft List," *Chattanooga Times*, December 7, 1942
411 Rusty Arp, phone interview with the author
412 Passmore interview
413 Letter, Martha Lowery to Gov. Prentice Cooper, June 10, 1942, Cooper Papers
414 Lewis interview
415 Letter, B.E. Biggs to Gov. Prentice Cooper, June 6, 1941, Cooper Papers
416 Letter, James Hardin to Herbert Russell, October 13, 1942, Cooper Papers
417 Watson interview

418 Stephen Byrd, phone interview with the author; Anonymous source #4
419 George O. Rogers family, phone interview with the author
420 T. Blair Lillard II, phone interview with the author
421 "M'Clary Favors Couch Over Biggs,'" *Chattanooga Times*, April 15, 1942
422 Letter, Mitchell Smith to Gov. Prentice Cooper, May 18, 1942, Cooper Papers
423 "Says Guinn Will Run From Polk Against Hugh Callaway," *Knoxville News-Sentinel*," August 14, 1942
424 "Polk County Politics"
425 "Prodigious Polk," *Chattanooga Times*, September 22, 1942
426 Letter, Estes Kefauver to John Standridge, August 14, 1942, Kefauver Papers
427 "Jennings Election Violation Charges Brings Row With Biggs Out," *Knoxville Journal*, August 23, 1942
428 "Seek To Oust Monroe Sheriff," *Knoxville News-Sentinel*," September 14, 1942
429 "Congressmen Flooded With Hubbies' Pleas For U.S. Commissions," *Nashville Tennessean*, September 20, 1942
430 Polk County Tax Books (1943)
431 "Biggs Opposes State Repeal Of Poll Tax," *Chattanooga Times*, November 9, 1942
432 Ibid
433 "He Talks For Polk, Says Sheriff Biggs," *Chattanooga Times*, November 11, 1942
434 "Biggs' Tax Stand Defended In Polk," *Chattanooga Times*, November 20, 1942
435 "Speculation Rife On Assembly Jobs: State Treasurer, Comptroller to Be Elected in January," *Chattanooga Times*, December 3, 1942
436 "Speakership Fight Looms," *Knoxville News-Sentinel*, December 22, 1942
437 "Grubb Offers Poll Tax Bill Asking Repeal," *Chattanooga Times*, January 5, 1943
438 "Head Tax To Help Schools Is Broached," *Knoxville Journal*, January 6, 1943
439 "Beeler Doubts If All Of Tax Can Be Lifted," *Chattanooga Times*, January 6, 1943
440 "Legislature Close In Two Weeks Seen," *Knoxville Journal*, January 24, 1943
441 "Cooper Seeks Vote Pledges On Tax Repeal," *Chattanooga Times*, January 26, 1943
442 "Poll Tax Bill Wins Approval Of Committee," *Chattanooga Times*, January 22, 1943
443 "Poll Tax, Registration Bills Pass in House by Big Margin," *Chattanooga Times*, January 28, 1943
444 "Rep. Woods of McMinn Attacks Journal Editor," *Knoxville Journal*, January 28, 1943
445 "Repeal of State Poll Tax, Permanent Registration, Voted Easily By House," *Nashville Tennessean*, January 28, 1943
446 "Poll Tax Ban Sticks In Craw Of Burch Biggs," *Knoxville News-Sentinel*, January 29, 1943

447 "M'Minn Group Battles State Poll Repealer," *Knoxville News-Sentinel*, January 31, 1943
448 "Skirmish Over Poll Tax Ends As Senate Passes Repeal Measure, 22-10," *Chattanooga Times*, February 2, 1943; "'My Hardest Fight,' Says Cooper; Sees Session End Feb. 11," *Knoxville Journal*, February 2, 1943
449 Resolution, Cleveland Lions Club, January 6, 1943, Cooper Papers; Letter, Harry L. Dethero to Gov. Prentice Cooper, January 5, 1943, Cooper Papers
450 Tennessee Private Acts (1943), p. 49-51
451 Letter, Charles S. Mayfield to Gov. Prentice Cooper, February 6, 1943, Cooper Papers
452 "Biggs Political Machine Is Gunning For Knox GOP Scalp, Parks Charges," *Knoxville Journal*, August 27, 1944
453 "Cleveland Plans Protest Meeting," *Chattanooga Times*, January 30, 1943
454 Ibid
455 Letter, Walter L. Franklin to Gov. Prentice Cooper, February 1, 1943, Cooper Papers
456 Letter, Columbus A. Mee to Gov. Prentice Cooper, February 6, 1943, Cooper Papers
457 "An Object Lesson," *Chattanooga Times*, February 17, 1943
458 "Chancellor Signs Restraining Fiat," *Chattanooga Times*, April 3, 1943
459 "Bradley Court Ouster Upheld," *Chattanooga Times*, May 20, 1943
460 Tennessee Private Acts (1943), p. 517-526
461 "Biggs Hopes To Change Copperhill Officials," *Knoxville Journal*, January 20, 1943
462 "New Bill Changes Copperhill Board," *Copper City Advance*, January 22, 1943
463 "New City Commissioners Take Over In Copperhill," *Copper City Advance*, February 5, 1943
464 "3 Found Guilty In Vote Fraud," *Chattanooga Times*, January 29, 1943
465 "Biggs Barbecue Potent, Jennings Tells Kefauver," *Knoxville Journal*, March 4, 1943
466 "Report on the Ducktown (Tennessee) Dynamiting Convictions"
467 US vs. Anderson et al. (1943); "Court Lays Polk 'Abuses' To Biggs-Federal Deal," *Knoxville Journal*, March 3, 1943
468 "Hedden Dies In Electric Chair," *Copper City Advance*, April 2, 1943
469 "New Bradley Squires Told to Quit Or Be Treated as Biggs Henchmen," *Chattanooga Times*, June 6, 1943
470 Ibid
471 Ibid
472 "Jurors May Probe Bradley Warning," *Chattanooga Times*, June 11, 1943
473 "Squires Fail to Meet in Bradley, 2 Are Escorted From Courthouse," *Chattanooga Times*, July 6, 1943
474 "Two New Bradley County Squires Announce They Will Leave Office," *Chattanooga Times*, July 7, 1943
475 "Benton Folk Say Shootin' Law Gave Richards Boy 'Raw Deal,'" *Knoxville News-Sentinel*, June 5, 1943

476 Ibid
477 Ibid; Everett Richards vs. Burch E. Biggs, et al, No. 606, Eastern District of Tennessee, Southern Division (1943)
478 Ibid
479 Ibid
480 "Benton Folk Say Shootin' Law Gave Richards Boy 'Raw Deal'"
481 Ibid
482 Ibid
483 "'Speed Trap' at Ocoee Rapped by Knoxvillian," *Knoxville Journal*, January 16, 1943
484 "Ocoee 'Speed Trap' Catches Jefferson County Driver," *Knoxville Journal*, January 21, 1943
485 "Maryville Victims Asks Probe Of Speed Traps," *Knoxville Journal*, January 19, 1943
486 "'Speed Trap' at Ocoee Rapped by Knoxvillian"
487 Ibid
488 "Victim of Speed Trap Was Pacing School Bus," *Knoxville Journal*, January 29, 1943
489 "Tom Anderson: From Up Close," *Knoxville Journal*, January 29, 1943
490 "'Speed Trap' in Polk Is Reported by Truck Men," *Knoxville News-Sentinel*, July 12, 1943
491 "Polk County Politics"
492 "Burch Biggs, Dictator of Polk County, Says He Provides 'Clean Government,'"; "Ocoee 'Speed Trap' Is One Thing Sheriff Biggs Can't Quite Laugh Off," *Knoxville News-Sentinel*, June 22, 1943; "Biggs Machine Beats GOP By Seeing That All Democrats Qualify To Vote," *Knoxville News-Sentinel*, June 23, 1943; "'Ripper Bills' in Neighbor Counties Promoted by Biggs' Polk Machine," *Knoxville News-Sentinel*, June 24, 1943; "Burch Biggs Looks Like a Farmer, Not the Powerful Politician He Is; "Times Reporter Spends Day With Sheriff Burch E. Biggs."
493 Talley interview
494 "Burch Biggs' Way," *Chattanooga Daily Times*, May 1, 1943
495 Lillie Biggs, et al vs. B.E. Biggs, et al, No. 1434, Polk County Chancery Court at Benton (1938)
496 Painter interview
497 Watson interview; Wesley J. Lowery, interview with Kristin N. Patterson
498 "Biggs To File Suit On Poll Tax Monday," *Knoxville Journal*, March 21, 1943
499 "Biggs' Bill Names Self on Both Sides of Case," *Knoxville News-Sentinel*, March 25, 1943
500 "Polk Republican Files Answer To Biggs Bill," *Knoxville Journal*, April 2, 1943
501 "State To Answer Biggs' Suit Today," *Chattanooga Times*, April 9, 1943
502 "Answer Filed In Polk To Biggs' Poll Tax Suit," *Knoxville Journal*, April 10, 1943
503 "Poll Tax Suit Opens Tuesday In Polk Court," *Chattanooga Times*, April 26, 1943
504 "Court Battle Over Poll Tax Opens In Polk," *Chattanooga Times*, April 28, 1943

505 Ibid
506 "Biggs, Beeler Are Friendly Opponents," *Knoxville Journal*, April 28, 1943; "Judge Stewart Hears Tenn. Poll Tax Case," *Copper City Advance*, April 30, 1943
507 "Poll Tax Bill Held Invalid; State Will Appeal Decision," *Chattanooga Times*, May 8, 1943
508 "Poll Tax Brief Filed by State," *Chattanooga Times*, May 29, 1943
509 "High Tribunal Gets Tax Fight," *Chattanooga Times*, June 4, 1943
510 Ibid
511 "Tax Issue May Go To U.S. High Court," *Chattanooga Times*, June 7, 1943
512 Biggs vs. Beeler, 180 Tenn. 198 (1943)
513 "Politics and Poll Tax," *Knoxville News-Sentinel*, July 7, 1943
514 "Next To The News," *Chattanooga Times*, July 4, 1943
515 "Sheriff Biggs Pleased By Decision Of Court," *Chattanooga Times*, July 4, 1943
516 "Support of M'Cord Pledged By Biggs," *Chattanooga Times*, April 6, 1944
517 "Sheriff Biggs May Offer Son In Senate Race," *Chattanooga Times*, July 26, 1943
518 Van Devander, Charles. "Mailed Fist in Tennessee." *American Mercury*, May 1944.
519 Ibid
520 Ibid
521 "Know The Facts," *Chattanooga Daily Times*, July 26, 1944
522 "Sheriff Biggs Pleased By Decision Of Court," *Chattanooga Times*, July 4, 1943
523 "Polk County GOP Indorsed Dewey," *Chattanooga Times*, April 30, 1944
524 "Jennings Starts Re-Election Fight," *Chattanooga Times,* June 7, 1944
525 "Polk Barbecue To Open Drive By Democrats," *Chattanooga Times*, July 8, 1944
526 "Biggs To Support Shelby Candidate," *Chattanooga Times*, January 14, 1944
527 "2,000 Democrats Attend Rally, Hear M'Cord and F.D.R. Lauded," *Chattanooga Times*, July 9, 1944
528 Ibid
529 "Letters: Biggs' Barbecue," *Chattanooga Times*, July 11, 1944
530 Ibid
531 "Biggs' Machine Hasn't Any Designs on Knox, Says Son," *Knoxville News-Sentinel*, July 14, 1944
532 "Vote Thieves Draw Wrath Of Jennings," *Knoxville Journal*, July 22, 1944
533 "Burch E. Biggs Faces Suit for $25,000 Damages," *Knoxville News-Sentinel*, July 22, 1944; "Benton Officers Sued For Damages," *Chattanooga Times*, July 22, 1944
534 "Sheriff Biggs Has No Intention Of Resigning Despite Request," *Knoxville Journal*, June 12, 1943
535 Ibid
536 Polk County Quarterly Court Minutes (October 1944)

537 Anonymous source #2
538 "Jennings Supporter 'Knows Biggs Clan,'" *Knoxville Journal*, August 13, 1944
539 "Politics Must Be Served?" *Bristol Herald Courier*, July 25, 1943
540 "Biggs Political Machine Is Gunning For Knox GOP Scalp, Parks Charges"
541 "Jennings Blames Biggs-Cantrell Machine In Undermining Ballot Rule," *Knoxville Journal*, September 16, 1944
542 "Athens Voter Tells Story Of Elections," *Knoxville Journal*, September 17, 1944
543 Ibid
544 "Polk Group Warns Of Biggs Peril," *Knoxville Journal*, October 18, 1944
545 "Nominees Hammer At Biggs Clique," *Knoxville Journal*, October 22, 1944
546 "Jennings Sees Victory For Entire GOP Ticket," *Knoxville Journal*, November 2, 1944
547 "Jennings' Reports: 'Ripper' Woods Is Accused Of Ballot Fraud," *Knoxville Journal*, November 4, 1944
548 "Says Absentee Voter List Denied Crumbliss," *Knoxville News-Sentinel*, November 5, 1944
549 "Polk County Politics;" Henry Crox Aff., November 10, 1944, John Jennings Papers, MPA.113. University of Tennessee Libraries, Knoxville, Special Collections.
550 "Sheriff Biggs Quits Election Hot Spot," *Knoxville News-Sentinel*, November 7, 1944
551 Wm. Prince Aff., November 10, 1944, Jennings Papers
552 W.C. Dalton Aff., November 9, 1944, Jennings Papers
553 Shillings Aff., November 9, 1944, Jennings Papers
554 "Biggs Runs Behind In Senate Contest," *Chattanooga Times*, November 8, 1944
555 "GOP Has Clean Sweep Unless Upset By Polk," *Knoxville News-Sentinel*, November 8, 1944
556 Ibid
557 "Biggs Runs Behind In Senate Contest," *Chattanooga Times*, November 8, 1944
558 "Biggs, Citadel of Polk Still Silent; Crumbliss Lead 6707," *Knoxville News-Sentinel*, November 9, 1944
559 "Crumbliss Holds Lead Of 6600 Over Biggs," *Knoxville Journal*, November 9, 1944
560 "Polk Vote Key To Sixth Race," *Chattanooga Times*, November 9, 1944
561 "Crumbliss Unworried Over Race With Biggs," *Knoxville News-Sentinel*, November 10, 1944
562 "'Just Waiting' Sheriff Biggs Says Conceding Son's Defeat," *Knoxville Journal*, November 11, 1944
563 "Biggs Beaten, Returns Show," *Chattanooga Times*, November 11, 1944
564 Blair, Reuben Moore. "Development of Education in Polk County, Tennessee," p. 83
565 "Politics," *Nashville Tennessean*, December 29, 1944
566 Anonymous source #3

567 "Polk County Man Killed By Jailer," *Chattanooga Times*, December 19, 1944; Mary Ann Lockaby, Facebook message to the author, June 15, 2022
568 "Reporters Find 'Everything Greased' For Gerber Show," *Nashville Tennessean*, January 10, 1945
569 "Biggs Redistrict Bill Irks Chattanooga Folk," *Knoxville Journal*, February 15, 1945
570 "Biggs Plan Defeat Seen By Kefauver," *Chattanooga Times*, February 15, 1945
571 "Fraud Bugs Seen in New Vote Bill," *Knoxville News-Sentinel*, February 9, 1945
572 "Biggs & Cantrell Plan County 'Swap,'" *Knoxville News-Sentinel*, February 7, 1945
573 "The Sweetwater Lions Club Condemns The Ripper Bill," *Sweetwater Valley News*, February 9, 1945
574 "Biggs Will Resign, Give Post To Son," *Chattanooga Times*, March 27, 1945
575 "Sheriff Biggs May Leave Job To Burch Jr.," *Knoxville Journal*, March 28, 1945
576 "Sheriff Biggs Resigns Office," *Polk County News*, June 7, 1945
577 "Biggs Doesn't Want Prison Warden Job," *Knoxville News-Sentinel*, April 2, 1945
578 "Biggs Resigns as Sheriff; To Support Rep. Kefauver," *Knoxville News-Sentinel*, June 10, 1945
579 Anonymous source #3
580 "Locals," *Polk County News*, August 9, 1945
581 "Broughton Biggs Recovering," *Chattanooga Times*, January 27, 1946
582 Letter, Estes Kefauver to E.H. Crump, March 29, 1944, Kefauver Papers
583 "Biggs Reaffirms M'Kellar Backing," *Chattanooga Times*, July 6, 1945
584 "Couch, Biggs Bury Hatchet; To Back McKellar, McCord," *Chattanooga Times*, April 14, 1946
585 "Kefauver Bolts McKellar In Demo Primary," *Knoxville Journal*, May 2, 1946
586 "M'Minn Group For Kefauver," *Chattanooga Times*, May 15, 1946
587 "M'Whorter Claims Kefauver-Red Tie," *Chattanooga Times*, July 31, 1946
588 Gregory interview
589 Letter, John C. Prince to R.E. Barclay, April 14, 1946, Robert Edward Barclay Papers, 1854-1977, TSLA.
590 Blair, "Development of Education in Polk County, Tennessee," p. 78-79, 86
591 Letter, R.R. Vance to Sam E. Sharp, October 3, 1950, Barclay Papers
592 "Teachers In Polk County Schools Required To Post Bonds Of $250," *Chattanooga Times*, August 22, 1943; GGL Executive Committee Resolution adopted on November 26, 1946, Barclay Papers
593 Anonymous source #1
594 "Post-Election Thoughts," *Chattanooga Times*, August 14, 1938
595 "Copperhill Man Shot in Quarrel," *Chattanooga Times*, April 5, 1946
596 "Funeral is Held for R.W. Brown Jr.," *Copper City Advance*, May 2, 1946
597 Robert E. Barclay Jr., interview with Kristin N. Patterson
598 "The Streets of Ducktown"
599 Ibid; State vs. James Boggs, No. 675, Polk County Criminal Court at Ducktown (1946)

600   Witt interview
601   "Bradley GI Ticket Denounced By GOP," *Chattanooga Times*, May 12, 1946
602   "Bradley Veteran Denies Biggs Ties," *Chattanooga Times*, July 17, 1946
603   "GOP In M'Minn Quits, Blesses All-GI Ticket," *Chattanooga Times,* May 12, 1946
604   "Kefauver Wins Polk Support; Purge Dropped," *Chattanooga Times*, May 19, 1946
605   Anonymous Source #11
606   "Kefauver Wins Polk Support; Purge Dropped"
607   "Carmack Divides Polk Democrats," *Chattanooga Times*, June 28, 1946
608   "Carmack Sees M'Minn 'Steal,'" *Chattanooga Times*, July 21, 1946
609   "Carmack Lashes At Vote Stealing In Biggs Fortress," *Nashville Tennessean*, July 24, 1946
610   "GI Ticket Dubs Cantrell $100,000 Sheriff Of McMinn County In Race," *Knoxville Journal*, July 26, 1946
611   "Five Former GIs Quietly Campaign Against Biggs Machine In Monroe," *Knoxville Journal*, July 28, 1946
612   Ibid
613   "FBI Asked To Aid," *Nashville Tennessean*, July 24, 1946
614   For an accurate and thorough account of the McMinn County election of August 1, 1946 and the subsequent "Battle of Athens," read *The Fighting Bunch* by Chris DeRose.
615   R.E. Barclay Journal, August 2, 1946, Barclay Papers
616   "Cantrell Men Leave M'Minn," *Chattanooga Times*, August 3, 1946
617   "Jennings Blames Justice Department For Riots After Athens Election," *Knoxville Journal*, August 3, 1946
618   "Bullet-Battered McMinn Smiles As Embers of Machine Rule Die," *Nashville Tennessean*, August 4, 1946
619   "Calm Reigns In Athens Battle Scene," *Knoxville Journal*, August 5, 1946
620   "Rumor Of Raid Alerts M'Minn; GIs Are Ready," *Chattanooga Times*, August 4, 1946; "GIs Set Up Road Block To Prevent Rumored Invasion," *Knoxville Journal*, August 4, 1946
621   "Athens Citizens Worship In Sunday Calm After Riots," *Nashville Tennessean*, August 5, 1946
622   "Inside Kefauver's Backyard"
623   "100 Copper Basin Veterans Unite, Plan to Fight Biggs,'" *Chattanooga Times*, August 20, 1946
624   Ibid
625   Ibid
626   "Democrats, GOP To Canvass Vote In Session Today," *Nashville Tennessean*, August 21, 1946
627   "Polk Veterans Set Up League, Call Meeting," *Chattanooga Times*, August 24, 1946
628   Ibid
629   Ibid
630   Ibid

631 "Cartwright Vows He's 'After Biggs,'" *Chattanooga Times*, August 30, 1946
632 "Stuart To Ask Seat In Senate: Announces as Nonpartisan, Opposes Cartwright, Who Was Leader in Revolt," *Chattanooga Times*, August 30, 1946
633 "GIs Of Polk Face Long, Tough Fight," *Chattanooga Times*, August 25, 1946
634 Ibid
635 "Polk Veterans Set Up League, Call Meeting"
636 "The Streets of Ducktown"
637 Gregory interview
638 "GI's Pick Slate To Fight Biggs," *Chattanooga Times*, September 1, 1946; "Polk Veterans Form League," *Nashville Tennessean*, September 1, 1946
639 "GI's Pick Slate To Fight Biggs"
640 Ibid
641 "Inside Kefauver's Backyard"
642 Witt interview
643 Talley interview
644 "The Polk County Tennessee Election War of 1948"
645 William Frank Lowery, interview with the author
646 "GI's Pick Slate To Fight Biggs"
647 Ibid
648 "Polk Veterans Form League"
649 "GGL, Meetings and Broadsides, 1946-1948," Barclay Papers
650 Lowery interview
651 "Conspiracy Charged Against 2 Benton Men," *Chattanooga Times*, September 6, 1946
652 "Polk Native Sues Biggs Over Arrest," *Knoxville Journal*, September 8, 1946
653 "The Sheriff's Boarders," *Chattanooga Times*, September 11, 1946
654 Walker vs. Biggs (1946)
655 "Darr Adjourns Biggs Hearing Until Monday"
656 Walker vs. Biggs (1946)
657 Ibid; "Broughton Biggs Loses In False Arrest Suit," *Knoxville Journal*, September 10, 1946
658 Richards vs. Biggs (1943); "Suit Against Biggs To Continue Today," *Chattanooga Times*, September 27, 1946; "$5,000 Judgment Won By Richards," *Chattanooga Times*, September 29, 1946
659 "Crying On Paper," *Copper City Advance*, September 26, 1946
660 GGL campaign advertisement, "GGL Meetings and Broadsides, 1946-1948," Barclay Papers
661 "Anti-Biggs League Plans Discussed," *Chattanooga Times*, October 2, 1946; "League Urges Election Of Lowery, Cartwright," *Copper City Advance*, October 3, 1946
662 Watson interview
663 Lewis interview
664 Rice interview
665 Lillard, "Some Aspects of Polk County Politics," p. 27
666 Resolution by Men's Community Club of Ducktown, June 17, 1939, Cooper Papers

667 "League Urges Election Of Lowery, Cartwright"
668 Anonymous source #12
669 "Second GI League Is Formed In Polk," *Chattanooga Times*, October 4, 1946
670 Letter, Ralph Duggan to R.E. Barclay, September 27, 1946, Barclay Papers
671 "R.E. Barclay," *Copper City Advance*, October 17, 1946; "Any Voter May See Ballot Count, League Chairman in Polk Assured," *Chattanooga Times*, October 23, 1946
672 Ibid
673 Letter, Thomas H. Malone to R.E. Barclay, October 14, 1946, Barclay Papers
674 Ibid
675 "Next to the News," *Chattanooga Times*, October 27, 1946
676 "McCord Explains to Party Rally Why Troops Not Sent to Athens," *Chattanooga Times*, October 22, 1946
677 Ibid
678 "Lowe Says State Machine Stole Name of Democrats," *Nashville Tennessean*, September 22, 1946
679 "Benton GGL Rally Draws Large Crowd," *Copper City Advance*, October 17, 1946
680 Lemond, "The Good Government League and Polk County (Tennessee) Politics, 1946-1965," p. 35
681 "Benton GGL Rally Draws Large Crowd"
682 "GGL Meeting Held Here Tuesday Night," *Copper City Advance*, October 24, 1946; "Biggs Dominates Polk, Barclay Tells League," *Chattanooga Times*, October 23, 1946
683 Watson interview
684 "Next to the News," *Chattanooga Times*, October 31, 1946
685 "Cartwright Given GOP Indorsement," *Chattanooga Times*, October 20, 1946
686 Letter, Burch Glenn Biggs to Gov. Jim McCord, November 1, 1946, Governor Jim Nance McCord (1879-1968) Papers 1945-1949, GP 45, TSLA
687 Letter, Roy H. Beeler to Gov. Jim McCord, November 4, 1946, McCord Papers
688 Letter, Hoyt Lillard to Teachers and Employees of Polk County Schools, October 28, 1946, "GGL Meetings and Broadsides, 1946-1948," Barclay Papers
689 Painter interview
690 "Explosive Ballot Race Seen In Polk," *Knoxville Journal*, October 25, 1946
691 "Polk Officials Are Directed To Follow Laws on Election," *Chattanooga Times*, November 2, 1946
692 "Tension Grips Polk As Vote Battle Looms," *Nashville Tennessean*, November 5, 1946; "Benton Tense; Ex GIs Ready," *Chattanooga Times*, November 5, 1946
693 "Polk Officials Are Directed To Follow Laws on Election"
694 "Polk War Veterans Smash Biggs Machine," *Nashville Tennessean*, November 6, 1946
695 "Tension Grips Polk As Vote Battle Looms" ; "Benton Tense; Ex GIs Ready"

696 "Ladd, Lowe – GOP Candidates – Wage Vigorous Campaigns," *Knoxville Journal*, November 3, 1946
697 "Biggs Machine Slated For Defeat by GOP," *Nashville Tennessean*, November 4, 1946
698 Ibid
699 "Election 'Apprehension' Prevalent In Benton," *Knoxville Journal*, November 4, 1946; "Overseers Expect Trouble In Polk Balloting," *Kingsport News*, November 4, 1946
700 "Tension Grips Polk As Vote Battle Looms"
701 "Mr. Biggs Defended," *Chattanooga Times*, November 4, 1946
702 "Tension Grips Polk As Vote Battle Looms"
703 Ibid
704 Bill Rose, "To the People of Polk County," "GGL Meetings and Broadsides, 1946-1948," Barclay Papers
705 GGL Campaign Ad, *Copper City Advance,* October 31, 1946
706 "Tension Grips Polk As Vote Battle Looms"
707 "Burch Biggs Given Beating; Cartwright Defeats Stuart," *Chattanooga Times*, November 6, 1946; "GI Candidates Defeat Biggs Men," *Knoxville News-Sentinel*, November 6, 1946
708 Ibid
709 "Polk War Veterans Smash Biggs Machine," *Nashville Tennessean*, November 6, 1946; "Burch Biggs Given Beating,"; "GI Candidates Defeat Biggs Men"
710 "Lowery, Cartwright Are Elected Tuesday"
711 Ibid; "Polk War Veterans Smash Biggs Machine"
712 "Wrinkle Praises Election In Polk," *Chattanooga Times*, November 6, 1946
713 "From Mr. Barclay," *Chattanooga Times*, November 9, 1946
714 "Thanks," *Copper City Advance*, November 7, 1946
715 "The Election," *Copper City Advance*, November 14, 1946
716 Ibid; "'Clean Slate in '48' Is GIs' Cry in Polk," *Knoxville News-Sentinel*, November 17, 1946
717 "Deputy's Home Dynamited In Polk County," *Knoxville Journal*, November 20, 1946
718 "J.P. Cartwright Denies Would Curtail Biggs," *Polk County News*, November 28, 1946
719 "Want Mayor-Council Rule, Citizens Say," *Copper City Advance*, November 21, 1946
720 Lemond, "The Good Government League and Polk County (Tennessee) Politics, 1946-1965," p. 33
721 "Give School Teachers More Pay, GGL Asks," *Copper City Advance*, December 5, 1946
722 Letter, John Shamblin to R.E. Barclay, October 2, 1946, Barclay Papers
723 "State Auditor John E. Bacon Praises Polk County Officials," *Polk County News*, January 16, 1947
724 Lowery interview
725 "Biggs, Gerber 'Just Looking,' Shun Newsmen," *Nashville Tennessean*, January 6, 1947

726 "4 Bills Aimed At Burch Biggs," *Chattanooga Times*, January 8, 1947; "Bills Designed to Break Biggs' Grip Will Reach Legislative Hopper Today," *Chattanooga Daly Times*, January 9, 1947
727 "Bills Introduced To End Biggs Rule," *Chattanooga Times*, January 10, 1947
728 Ibid; "Assembly Gets Measure Aimed At 'Boss' Biggs," *Nashville Tennessean*, January 10, 1947
729 "Next to the News," *Chattanooga Times*, January 12, 1947
730 "Biggs Says 3 Bills Aren't Necessary," *Chattanooga Times*, January 13, 1947
731 Tennessee Private Acts (1947) p. 271-273
732 Letter, R.E. Barclay to Frank D. Lowery, January 19, 1947, Barclay Papers; "City Clerk is Held on Embezzlement Charge," *Copper City Advance*, January 2, 1947
733 "Bill Revives Aldermanic Rule, Names Mayor and Aldermen for Copperhill," *Chattanooga Times*, January 25, 1947; Tennessee Private Acts (1947) p. 582-584
734 "M'Cord To Ask For Enactment Of Funds Bill," *Chattanooga Times*, February 21, 1947
735 Letter, R.E. Barclay to Frank D. Lowery, January 19, 1947, Barclay Papers
736 "Bill Would Form Polk Commission," *Chattanooga Times*, February 5, 1947; Tennessee Private Acts (1947) p. 1474-1492
737 Ibid
738 "Councilmen Takes Reigns in M'Minn; Commission Given Polk Authority," *Chattanooga Times*, March 2, 1947
739 "Polk County High To Be Repaired," *Polk County News*, April 17, 1947
740 "Chancery Bill Filed To Void Commission," *Polk County News*, May 22, 1947
741 "Polk County Court To Fight Commission; Attorneys Employed," *Polk County News*, June 12, 1947
742 "County Commission Ruled Constitutional," *Copper City Advance*, June 26, 1947
743 Letter, R.E. Barclay to Joe C. Carr, April 3, 1947, Barclay Papers
744 "Organization Here Tries Comeback, As Does Biggs, Before State Board," *Chattanooga Times*, April 8, 1947; "Polk Election Row Marks State Hearing," *Nashville Banner*, April 7, 1947
745 "Polk Election Row Marks State Hearing"
746 Ibid, "Organization Here Tries Comeback, As Does Biggs, Before State Board"
747 "Tennessee Affairs," *Chattanooga Times*, May 4, 1947
748 Witt interview, Sartin family interview
749 "Gas Funds In Polk Used Irregularly," *Chattanooga Times*, July 18, 1947
750 Ibid
751 Ibid
752 Ibid
753 "Polk Official Affirms Stand," *Chattanooga Times*, July 19, 1947
754 Ibid
755 Ibid
756 "Polk Politics Boiling Again," *Chattanooga Times*, July 20, 1947

757 "Lowery Claims 4 Draw Illegal Pay," *Chattanooga Times*, July 21, 1947
758 Ibid
759 Ibid
760 Ibid
761 "Polk Orders Shift in Funds," *Nashville Tennessean*, July 29, 1947; "Lowery Says Biggs Squires Shifted School Funds, Added to Jail Money," *Chattanooga Times*, July 30, 1947
762 "R.E. Barclay," *Copper City Advance*, August 7, 1947
763 "Anti-Biggs Faction Goes to Nashville In Fight for Polk County Road Funds," *Chattanooga Times*, August 1, 1947; "It's Polk County's Affair," *Chattanooga Times*, August 2, 1947
764 Lemond, "The Good Government League and Polk County (Tennessee) Politics, 1946-1965," p. 35; "Lowery Says Biggs Squires Shifted School Funds, Added to Jail Money"
765 "Next to the News," *Chattanooga Times*, August 3, 1947
766 "A Review: Part 1," *Copper City Advance*, April 10, 1947
767 "A Review: Part 2," *Copper City Advance*, April 17, 1947
768 "A Review: Part 3," *Copper City Advance*, April 24, 1947
769 "A Review: Part 4," *Copper City Advance*, May 1, 1947
770 Ibid
771 Posey interview
772 Watson interview
773 "Basin's Schools Set To Open Monday," *Copper City Advance*, August 28, 1947
774 "A Review: Part 5," *Copper City Advance*, May 8, 1947
775 "A Review: Final," *Copper City Advance*, May 15, 1947
776 "Broughton Biggs Dies Here; Blow to Polk Organization," *Chattanooga Times*, August 9, 1947
777 "Funeral For Biggs To Be Held Today," *Chattanooga Times*, August 10, 1947; "Last Rites Held Sunday For Broughton E. Biggs," *Copper City Advance*, August 14, 1947
778 "Broughton Biggs," *Polk County News*, September 11, 1947
779 "Next to the News," *Chattanooga Times*, August 25, 1947
780 "Anvils In The Wind," *Copper City Advance*, November 27, 1947
781 "The Grand Jury Reports," *Polk County News*, November 20, 1947
782 Ibid
783 Anonymous source #3
784 Talley interview; Watson interview
785 "Auditor Report Questions Items In Polk Expense," *Chattanooga Times*, November 9, 1947
786 Ibid; "Terror In Tennessee"
787 Talley interview
788 "Auditor Report Questions Items In Polk Expense,"
789 "Sheriff in Denial Took Excess Fees," *Chattanooga Times*, November 9, 1947; "Biggs Blames Audit In Polk on 'Politics,'" *Chattanooga Times*, November 10, 1947

790 Ibid
791 Ibid
792 Ibid
793 "$47,000 Shortage Report Branded Lie by Biggs," *Nashville Tennessean*, November 11, 1947
794 Polk County Quarterly Court Minutes (1936, 1941)
795 "Sheriff in Denial Took Excess Fees," *Chattanooga Times*, November 9, 1947
796 Ibid; "Biggs Blames Audit In Polk on 'Politics,'" *Chattanooga Times*, November 10, 1947
797 Ibid
798 State of Tennessee Ex Rel Burch G. Biggs, Sheriff of Polk County, Tennessee vs. R.E. Barclay, Commissioner of Finance and Chairman of the Board of County Commissioners of Polk County, Tennessee et als, Polk Equity (1948)
799 Code of Tennessee, Sections 12060 and 12221, Chapter 367, Private Acts of 1947, Vol. 1, p. 1474, Secs. 5 and 13.
800 Polk County Tax Books (1948)
801 "GGL To Offer Full GI Ticket Next August," *Copper City Advance*, November 6, 1947
802 "Biggs Forces Face Crucial 1948 Test," *Chattanooga Times*, July 24, 1947
803 "Battle Lines Drawn In Polk," *Chattanooga Times*, August 3, 1948
804 "Biggs Will Try Political Comeback," *Knoxville News-Sentinel*, February 22, 1948
805 "Fair Elections Named GGL First Objective," *Copper City Advance*, February 19, 1948
806 Ibid
807 "Polk County Court Wins Tax Rate Fight," *Polk County News*, April 1, 1948
808 "The Polk County Financial Crisis," *Chattanooga Times*, April 10, 1948
809 "Jake Higgins Says," *Polk County News*, April 8, 1948
810 Polk County Quarterly Court Minutes (January 1948)
811 "Hickey, Secretary Good Government League, Resigns," *Polk County News*, April 15, 1948
812 "Candidates Named By GGL At Benton," *Copper City Advance*, April 22, 1948; "Polk Reform Body Names Candidates," *Chattanooga Times*, April 18, 1948
813 "Terror In Tennessee"
814 "Candidates Named By GGL At Benton" ; "Polk Reform Body Names Candidates"
815 "Polk Reform Body Names Candidates"
816 Painter interview; Talley interview; Wilma Edwards Jones, phone interview with the author; Anonymous source #4
817 "Pair Join Contest Against Biggs Men," *Chattanooga Times*, May 4, 1948
818 "Biggs Machine Denying Republicans Right to Pay Poll Tax, Says Jennings," *Chattanooga Times*, May 1, 1948
819 "State GOP Raps Civil Rights Bill, Food Sales Tax," *Nashville Tennessean*, May 1, 1948
820 Lemond, "The Good Government League and Polk County (Tennessee) Politics, 1946-1965," p. 4

821 "Seeks To Oust Polk Officials," *Chattanooga Times*, May 4, 1948
822 "Polk Courthouse Invaded In Protest Against Biggs," *Knoxville Journal*, May 5, 1948; "400 Polk Countians Are Unsuccessful In March on Courthouse for Poll Tax," *Chattanooga Times*, May 5, 1948
823 "Polk Courthouse Invaded In Protest Against Biggs"
824 Ibid
825 "Polk Voters Refused Poll Tax Receipts," *Nashville Tennessean*, May 5, 1948
826 "Polk Courthouse Invaded In Protest Against Biggs"
827 "Polk Upheaval Averted, Attorney General Avers," *Knoxville Journal*, May 6, 1948; "Polk Countians Set May 15 As Poll Tax Issue Deadline," *Chattanooga Times*, May 6, 1948
828 Ibid
829 Ibid
830 "Polk Countians Set May 15 As Poll Tax Issue Deadline"
831 "Ex-McMinn Deputy Accused In Blackjacking of Polk Man," *Chattanooga Times*, May 9, 1948; "Former McMinn Deputy In Custody For 'Own Safety' In Blackjack Case," *Knoxville Journal*, May 9, 1948
832 Ibid
833 R.E. Barclay Journal, May 8, 1948, Barclay Papers
834 Ibid; "Ex-McMinn Deputy Accused In Blackjacking of Polk Man';"Former McMinn Deputy In Custody For 'Own Safety' In Blackjack Case"
835 "Wilburn, of Athens, Free of Charge Of Blackjacking Polk GGL Leader," *Chattanooga Times*, May 11, 1948; "Says Wilburn Forces To Go Back Into Jail," *Chattanooga Times*, May 11, 1948
836 "Two Candidates Demand Secret Ballot When Biggs Ticket Is Named Saturday," *Chattanooga Times*, May 13, 1948
837 "No Biggs Name On Polk Slate," *Chattanooga Times*, May 16, 1948
838 Painter interview
839 "No Biggs Name On Polk Slate"
840 "Biggs Steps Aside, Polk Seen Happy," *Knoxville Journal*, May 16, 1948
841 "No Biggs Name On Polk Slate"; "Williams Is Nominated As Sheriff Candidate," *Copper City Advance*, May 20, 1948
842 "No Biggs Name On Polk Slate"
843 Ibid
844 "Biggs Steps Aside, Polk Seen Happy"
845 "Young Biggs Quits As Polk Candidate," *Nashville Tennessean*, May 16, 1948
846 "To The Voters Of Polk County," *Polk County News*, June 3, 1948
847 "Terror in Tennessee"
848 "GGL Pledges Honest Vote; Asks For Same," *Copper City Advance*, June 24, 1948
849 Ibid
850 "Large Crowd Attends Demo Rally Saturday," *Copper City Advance*, July 1, 1948
851 Ibid
852 "Burch Biggs Jr. Is Ill In Hospital At Athens," *Chattanooga Times*, July 3, 1948; "Sheriff Biggs Improved," *Chattanooga Times*, July 13, 1948

853 "Battle Lines Drawn In Polk," *Chattanooga Times*, August 3, 1948
854 "Mitchell Asks Vets' Support," *Chattanooga Times*, July 11, 1948
855 Ibid, "Deals Again Prove Estes Product Of Biggs Gang" *Knoxville Journal*, July 2, 1948
856 "Kefauver Admits Biggs Backs Him," *Knoxville Journal*, July 20, 1948
857 "Rep. Kefauver Reminds Barley Growers of Aid," *Knoxville News-Sentinel*, July 25, 1948
858 GGL political advertisement, *Copper City Advance*, July 29, 1948; "GGL Meetings and Broadsides, 1948-1950," Barclay Papers
859 "'Biggs To Lose,' Says Polk GGL," *Chattanooga Times*, August 1, 1948
860 Anonymous source #1
861 Lemond, "The Good Government League and Polk County (Tennessee) Politics, 1946-1965," p. 4; "'Goo-Goo' Barclay Spouts," *Polk County News*, August 5, 1948
862 "Burch Biggs' Democratic Machine In Polk Blasted," *Knoxville Journal*, August 1, 1948
863 Ibid
864 Ibid
865 "'Polk GGL Holds Meeting As 'Last Show of Strength," *Nashville Tennessean*, August 2, 1948
866 R.E. Barclay Journal, July 31, 1948, Barclay Papers
867 "Polk County Biggs Machine Faces Finish Fight With GGL," *Knoxville News-Sentinel*, August 4, 1948
868 "Lowery Charges, Hoyt Lillard Denies Polk County to Vote 1,800 Absentees," *Chattanooga Times*, July 30, 1948
869 "Polk GGL Gets Absentee Voters List With Injunction From 12th Chancery," *Chattanooga Times*, August 4, 1948
870 Passmore interview
871 R.E. Barclay Journal, July 31, 1948, Barclay Papers
872 "'Biggs To Lose,' Says Polk GGL"
873 "'Illegal' List Raised Polk Political Tension," *Nashville Tennessean*, July 31, 1948
874 "Battle Lines Drawn In Polk"
875 Lake Ledford, Aff., August 2, 1948, Barclay Papers
876 Painter interview; "Jailed," *Knoxville News-Sentinel*, August 6, 1948
877 "2 Dead, 5 Hurt After 'Hotbed' Election Activity," *Knoxville News-Sentinel*, August 6, 1948
878 Gregory interview
879 "Reporter Freed In Polk County; 2 Men Killed," *Nashville Tennessean*, August 6, 1948"; "2 Dead, 5 Hurt After 'Hotbed' Election Activity"
880 "2 Dead, 5 Hurt After 'Hotbed' Election Activity"
881 "Two Biggs Men Shot At Polls," *Chattanooga Times*, August 6, 1948
882 Ibid; "3 Dead, Four Hurt in Polk; Biggs Machine Beaten," *Chattanooga News-Free Press*, August 6, 1948
883 "2 Dead, 5 Hurt After 'Hotbed' Election Activity"

884 "The Streets of Ducktown;" "The Polk County Tennessee Election War of 1948"; Shirley Watkins Hamby, phone interview with Katherine Goodman Smith
885 "2 Dead, 5 Hurt After 'Hotbed' Election Activity"; "Reporter Freed In Polk County; 2 Men Killed;" Talley interview, Passmore interview
886 Watson interview
887 "The Streets of Ducktown"
888 "2 Dead, 5 Hurt After 'Hotbed' Election Activity"
889 Passmore interview
890 Oliver interview
891 "2 Dead, 5 Hurt After 'Hotbed' Election Activity"
892 Watson interview
893 Oliver interview
894 "Inside Kefauver's Backyard"
895 "2 Dead, 5 Hurt After 'Hotbed' Election Activity"
896 "3 Dead, Four Hurt in Polk; Biggs Machine Beaten"; "Reporter Freed In Polk County; 2 Men Killed"
897 "3 Dead, Four Hurt in Polk; Biggs Machine Beaten"
898 "Two Biggs Men Shot At Polls;" Anonymous source #1
899 "2 Dead, 5 Hurt After 'Hotbed' Election Activity"
900 Ibid; "3 Dead, Four Hurt in Polk; Biggs Machine Beaten"; "GGL Wins Control Of County; 3 Men Die As Violence Flairs," *Copper City Advance*, August 12, 1948; "The Streets of Ducktown"; R.E. Barclay Journal, August 5, 1948, Barclay Papers
901 Cheryl Loudermilk Kear, phone interview with the author
902 "The Streets of Ducktown"
903 Ibid
904 Ibid; R.E. Barclay Journal, August 5, 1948, Barclay Papers; "Violence Flairs as Polk County Casts Its Votes," *Cleveland Daily Banner*, August 6, 1948
905 Oliver interview; Watson interview
906 R.E. Barclay Journal, August 5, 1948, Barclay Papers
907 "Two Biggs Men Shot At Polls"
908 R.E. Barclay Journal, August 6, 1948, Barclay Papers
909 Ibid; "Kefauver, Browning Foes Concedes Defeat; 2 Killed, Guard Is Ordered To Polk," *Chattanooga Times*, August 7, 1948
910 Ibid; "Guard Halts Polk Disorders", *Nashville Tennessean*, August 7, 1948; "Polk County Quiet As National Guardsmen Patrol In Three Towns," *Chattanooga News-Free Press*, August 7, 1948
911 "Hidden 'Grenades,' Weapons Confiscated," *Knoxville News-Sentinel*, August 7, 1948
912 "Guard Halts Polk Disorders;" "Biggs Makes Radio Report Here," *Cleveland Daily Banner*, August 8, 1948; "Guard, Troopers Ordered To Polk; Biggs Yells 'Help' Says Mobs Forming," *Daily Post Athenian*, August 6, 1948
913 "Hidden 'Grenades,' Weapons Confiscated;" "Biggs Makes Radio Report Here"
914 Passmore interview; "Guard Halts Polk Disorders"

915 "Guard Halts Polk Disorders" ; "Kefauver, Browning Foes Concedes Defeat; 2 Killed, Guard Is Ordered To Polk"
916 "Reporter Freed In Polk County; 2 Men Killed"
917 Oliver interview
918 "Violence Flairs As Crump Ring Is Defeated," *Charlotte News*, August 6, 1948
919 "Good Government League Says Burch Biggs Rule Has Ended," *Cleveland Daily Banner*, August 6, 1948
920 Stewart, Billy, "278th Regimental Combat Team Sent to Polk County," n.d.
921 "Good Government League Says Burch Biggs Rule Has Ended"
922 "Benton Remains Quiet As Guard Continues Watch," *Cleveland Daily Banner*, August 8, 1948
923 "Hidden 'Grenades,' Weapons Confiscated;" "Guard Halts Polk Disorders" ; "278th Regimental Combat Team Sent to Polk County"
924 "Hidden 'Grenades,' Weapons Confiscated;" "Guard Halts Polk Disorders"
925 "Hidden 'Grenades,' Weapons Confiscated"
926 "Guard Halts Polk Disorders"
927 R.E. Barclay Journal, August 7, 1948, Barclay Papers
928 Anonymous source #1
929 Smith interview
930 Lillard II interview
931 "Guard Halts Polk Disorders";" Polk County Quiet As National Guardsmen Patrol In Three Towns"
932 "Hidden 'Grenades,' Weapons Confiscated"
933 "Guard To Leave Town Cleaner Than It Was," *Knoxville Journal*, August 8, 1948
934 "National Guardsmen's Shots Halt Cars In 'Occupied' Polk," *Knoxville Journal*, August 9, 1948
935 Anonymous source #1
936 "Polk County Politics"
937 "Hidden 'Grenades,' Weapons Confiscated"
938 "Guard Halts Polk Disorders"
939 "Benton Gets Real 'Clean-up,'" *Columbus Ledger*, August 8, 1948
940 "Etowah Company Is 'Law' for 6 Days as Violence Feared," *Etowah Enterprise*, August 12, 1948
941 "278th Regimental Combat Team Sent to Polk County"
942 "The Polk County Tennessee Election War of 1948"
943 "The Streets of Ducktown"
944 "Guard Halts Polk Disorders"
945 "Polk County Quiet As National Guardsmen Patrol In Three Towns"
946 "Tennessee Men Held for Murders," *Columbus Ledger*, August 8, 1948
947 "Polk County Quiet As National Guardsmen Patrol In Three Towns"
948 Witt interview
949 "The Streets of Ducktown"
950 "The Polk County Tennessee Election War of 1948"
951 "Hidden 'Grenades,' Weapons Confiscated"

952 "Benton Remains Quiet As Guard Continues Watch"
953 "Guard Continues Watch In Polk" *Nashville Tennessean* August 8, 1948
954 Ibid; "2 Major Boxes Challenged In Board Session," *Chattanooga News-Free Press*, August 9, 1948; R.E. Barclay Journal, August 7, 1948, Barclay Papers
955 "Rep. Lowery, Polk, Claims Biggs Rout," *Chattanooga Times*, August 8, 1948
956 "Tenn. Trouble Spot Quiet After Flareup," *Atlanta Constitution,* August 8, 1948
957 Ibid
958 "National Guardsmen's Shots Halt Cars In 'Occupied' Polk;" Anonymous source #1
959 "National Guardsmen's Shots Halt Cars In 'Occupied' Polk"
960 "Polk Ballot Boxes Have Mark Of Political Blast," *Cleveland Daily Banner*, August 9, 1948
961 "Polk Canvass Set, Guard Is On Alert," *Chattanooga Times*, August 9, 1948
962 R.E. Barclay Journal, August 8, 1948, Barclay Papers
963 "Polk Ballot Boxes Have Mark Of Political Blast"
964 2 Major Boxes Challenged In Board Session"
965 Ibid; "Machine Guns Protect Polk Official Counting," *Knoxville Journal*, August 10, 1948
966 "Polk Vote Count Certified; Benton Quiet; GGL Wins," *Cleveland Daily Banner*, August 10, 1948; "278th Regimental Combat Team Sent to Polk County"
967 Ibid
968 "Machine Guns Protect Polk Official Counting"
969 "Polk Vote Count Certified; Benton Quiet; GGL Wins"
970 Ibid
971 Ibid
972 Ibid; Painter interview
973 "Polk Vote Count Certified; Benton Quiet; GGL Wins"
974 "Benton Quiet After Guard Leaves Polk," *Knoxville Journal*, August 12, 1948
975 R.E. Barclay Journal, August 11, 1948, Barclay Papers
976 Guy, Joe. *Hidden History of East Tennessee*, p. 52
977 "Barclay Thanks Supporters; Asks That Strife Ends," *Copper City Advance*, August 12, 1948
978 "Dewey Campaign Manager Says Biggs' Influence Broken," *Knoxville News-Sentinel*, August 8, 1948
979 "Breaking Under The Strain," *Chattanooga Times*, August 11, 1950
980 "Suit Names Biggs, Claiming $25,000," *Chattanooga Times*, February 2, 1951
981 Richard Jones, Facebook message to the author, December 26, 2020
982 Polk County Tax Books (1953)
983 "Biggs Trial Jury Again Deadlocks," *Chattanooga Times*, February 3, 1951; "Ex-Sheriff Biggs and Deputies Face $25,000 Damage Suit for Third Time," *Chattanooga Times*, October 8, 1952
984 "Grim GGL Members In Polk County Block Court Session For Fourth Time," *Chattanooga Daily Times*, April 17, 1951
985 "Polk May Vote Its Own Death By Absorption," *Chattanooga Times*, May 22, 1951

986 "Barclay and Biggs Answer Collier's," *Chattanooga Times*, September 3, 1951
987 "Ex-Sheriff Biggs and Deputies Face $25,000 Damage Suit for Third Time"; "Polk Sheriff Given Alibi By Patrolman," *Knoxville Journal*, October 9, 1952
988 "Biggs Hearing Starts Again," *Chattanooga News-Free Press*, October 7, 1952
989 "Ex-Sheriff Biggs and Deputies Face $25,000 Damage Suit for Third Time"
990 "Richards Gets $2,000 Damage," *Chattanooga News-Free Press*, October 10, 1952
991 Ibid
992 "Ex-Sheriff Biggs and Deputies Face $25,000 Damage Suit for Third Time" ; "Polk Sheriff Given Alibi By Patrolman"
993 "Ex-Sheriff Biggs and Deputies Face $25,000 Damage Suit for Third Time"
994 Ibid
995 "Ex-Sheriff Biggs, 2 Aides Assessed $2,000 Damages in '43 Shooting Suit," *Chattanooga Times*, October 10, 1952
996 "Next to the News," *Chattanooga Times*, July 5, 1952
997 Lillard, "Some Aspects of Polk County Politics," p. 18
998 "Jake Higgins Says," *Polk County News*, September 16, 1954

INDEX

A

Adams, Ed 88, 93
Adams, H.A. 198
Adams, J.E. 44, 134, 137
Addington, T.J. 24, 156
Allen, James 24-26, 29, 149
Aluminum Company of America 152
American Federation of Labor (AFL) 122, 125, 127-129
Anderson, Carl 307
Anderson County, Tennessee 202, 206
Anderson, Homer 295
Anderson, Mitchell 122-123, 125, 127, 131, 133, 141-142, 169
Anderson, Mote 92
Anderson, Wade 127, 129
Andrews, North Carolina 293, 304
Archville, Tennessee 23, 70, 119, 303
Arp, Alfred R. (Buck) 34, 38, 41-42, 44-45, 105, 109, 152-153, 156, 181, 257
Arp Jr., Alfred R. (Little Buck) 150, 228, 230, 243-244, 255
Athens, Tennessee 218-219, 221-226, 286, 299
Atlanta Constitution 299, 305
Avery, Anna Lee Ledford 98
Aytes, Glenn R. 299, 302-303, 305

B

Bachman, Nathan 67
Bacon, Will 199, 201
Bagwell, George 248
Baker, E.B. 133, 141-142
Baker Sr., Howard 315
Ballew, Amos 44, 78, 152, 290
Ballew, Charles 299
Ballew, Robert Lee 131, 133, 142
Bandy, Arthur 89
Bankhead, William 65-66
Barclay, Gus 27-28, 30, 34, 212
Barclay Jr., Robert E. 215, 307
Barclay, R.E. (Bob) 21, 29-30, 34, 108, 123, 137, 208-209, 212-213, 218-219, 223, 226, 229-232, 237-242, 245-246, 248-249, 251, 253, 255-262, 264-265, 267-268, 272-276, 278-281, 283-284, 288-290, 297, 299-301, 303-304, 307-309, 312-314, 317
Barker, John 97
Barker, Wesley 302
Barnes, Bill 292
Barnes, Charles 24, 26
Barry, William 184, 185
Bates, Amos 148
Bates, Andrew 85
Bates, Andrew Sr. 119, 275
Bates, Charles 36
Bates, Charlie 181
Bates, Everett (Eb) 279, 290
Bates, F.E. 148-149
Bates, Flavis 39, 43, 79, 173, 175, 193, 198, 235, 270, 290, 315, 317, 319
Bates, Noah 89, 146-148
Bates, P.R. 39-40
Bates, W.I. 276
Battle of Athens 222-223, 228, 243, 280, 304
Bearden, Arthur 89-90
Beaty, Jim 164
Beeler, Roy 159-160, 162, 183, 185, 239, 241, 257, 280
Benson, W.G. 104
Benton Banking Company 24, 53, 87, 114, 118, 137, 145
Benton, Tennessee 20-21, 23, 25, 35, 58, 65-66, 69, 71-73, 76-77, 79-81, 97, 100, 103-104, 112, 125, 127, 135, 137, 143, 145, 148, 151, 178, 184, 198-201, 209, 216, 219, 227, 238, 243, 246-247, 249, 253, 256, 260, 264, 273, 280, 285-287, 290, 292, 295, 297-299, 301, 303-305, 307-309, 311, 314, 316, 319
Bibb, James L. 266
Biddle, Francis 197
Big Bosses, The 188
Biggs, Broughton Euclid 23, 40, 43, 58, 71, 74, 80, 85-88, 94, 96-97, 99-101, 106-109, 111, 115, 118, 122-124, 127-128, 130-131, 133-135, 137, 139, 141-149, 151-152, 156, 159-166, 168, 175, 183, 187, 189-191, 193-194, 196-202, 204-209, 216, 233-236, 242, 247, 252-253, 258, 266, 270, 318
Biggs, Burch Euclid 20-21, 23-37, 39-43, 44-46, 49-50, 52-54, 56, 58, 61, 63-64, 66-70, 74, 76-77, 79-84, 86-88, 91, 94-96, 98-100, 102-109, 111-114, 116-121, 123, 130, 134-137, 139-141, 147-148, 150-153, 155-156, 158-164, 166-167, 169, 171-176, 178-184, 186-191, 193-194, 198-199, 201-205, 207-208, 210-213, 216-221, 224-225, 227-228, 231, 233-236, 241-245, 247-248, 251-253, 255-256, 258-259, 263-264, 266, 268-278, 280-284, 286-287, 290-291, 297-298, 300, 305, 311, 313-321
Biggs, Burch Glen 31, 104, 118, 122, 135, 137, 144, 160, 207-209, 215-217, 223, 225, 228, 231, 241, 243, 246, 253, 260, 266, 268-272, 274-277, 281-282, 286, 298, 300, 307, 315, 320
Biggs, Charles (Charlie) 148, 180, 320
Biggs, Coop 21, 23
Biggs, Della Lillard 23, 31, 112-113, 193, 266, 283-284, 286, 320
Biggs, Della Etholeen 23, 31, 266, 320
Biggs, Duke 23, 320
Biggs, Eunice Attaline Kimbrough (Attie) 20, 32, 182
Biggs, Gus 320
Biggs, Joann 85, 266, 283, 320
Biggs, John 20
Biggs, Lillie 180
Biggs, Louise Higgins 85, 100, 139, 266
Biggs Machine 39, 72, 74, 86, 98, 100, 111, 114, 118-119, 128, 139, 142, 144-145, 151, 156-157, 159, 189, 194-196, 198, 202, 204, 206, 209, 212-213, 216, 217, 219, 221, 224-226,

229, 231, 236-238, 240-243, 245, 247-252, 256, 258, 259, 260, 262-264, 266, 268, 281, 284, 287, 304, 307, 309, 311, 316-317
Biggs, Mary Temple 139, 266, 320
Biggs, Robert 195
Biggs, Temp 21, 39, 44, 72, 79
Biggs, Thomas Temple (Tom, Uncle Tom) 20, 23, 26, 320
Biggs, Tom Henry 100, 118, 181, 266, 319
Biggs, William McClure 20, 180
Bingham, Octavius 127
Bishop Sr., G.W. 112
Bishop, Will 97
Black, Esco 77
Blackwell, John 44, 64, 85
Blackwell, Noah 75, 77
Blair, John J. 33, 44, 66-67, 88
Blair, Reuben M. 213
Blue Ridge Dam 130-131
Blue Ridge, Georgia 90, 100, 127
Boggess, J.B. 276, 307
Boggs, Jim 216, 296, 303-304
Bomar, Lynn 298, 302-304, 307
Boring, Jessie 127, 129
Boyd, Erby 207
Bradley County, Tennessee 33, 46, 52, 87, 99, 109, 117, 121, 134, 138, 140, 152, 156-157, 159, 163-166, 171-172, 179, 194, 199, 201-202, 206, 208, 217, 225, 229, 241, 247-248, 316-317, 320
Brakebill, W.O. 138, 151, 155-156, 162, 188-189, 193, 205, 220
Bratton, Frank 88, 93, 143, 210-211
Breeden, Floyd 146-147
Breeden, Lawrence 146-147
Bridges, Newman 91
Brock, J. Creed 38, 218, 261-267
Brock, Lon 171-172
Brock, Maude 171
Brock, Tom 102
Brooks, Clarence 63, 65, 67, 88, 90-93, 95, 102
Brookshire, Riley 97
Broome, James 159, 161
Brown, Bethel 164
Brown, Burton 42, 81, 215-216, 296-297, 303-304

Browning, Gordon 80, 83, 87, 105, 107, 109, 219, 225, 240, 286, 304, 313, 317, 319
Brown, John 145
Brown, Richard Whitfield (Junior) 215-216, 304
Brushy Mountain State Penitentiary 24, 71, 83, 146, 151
Bryant, Becky 319
Bryant, Carol 319
Bryant, Everett 193, 319
Bryant, L'Ene Biggs 31, 134, 193, 209, 266, 298, 319, 320
Bryant, Nancy 319
Burchfield, Horace 78
Burn, Harry T. 313, 316
Burns, Frank 317
Burris, Hugh 31
Butler, Hilton 305
Buttram, Jim 224

C

Caldwell, Nat 158-159, 166
Calhoun, Virgil 281
Callaway, Hugh 134-136, 139, 141, 154, 156, 158, 161-162, 166-168, 187, 202
Callaway, James 291-292, 298
Campbell, Broughton 309
Campbell, Charlie 23, 36, 108
Campbell, C.L. (Roxy) 36, 38, 40, 53-54, 58, 68, 69-70, 72, 80, 106, 108-109, 111-112, 117-118, 134-135, 137, 143, 151, 153, 217, 225, 233-234, 253, 261-262, 269, 282, 290
Campbell, Elbert 146, 147
Campbell, Porter 34, 53, 100, 106, 180
Campbell, Walter 303
Cantrell Machine 109, 138, 140, 157, 169, 187, 189, 202, 211, 218, 221, 225, 231
Cantrell, Paul 32, 81, 134, 140-141, 151, 156, 158, 161-165, 179, 184, 187-190, 202, 204-206, 208, 217, 219, 220-224, 227, 317
Cardon, Lloyd 48
Carey, Hobart 117-118, 134-136, 139
Carmack Jr., Edward W. 153-154, 210, 219
Carmichael, Earl 299
Carmichael, Frank 218
Carpenter, Wayne 302

Carr, Joe C. 258
Carter, Dewey 152
Carter, Tom 26, 27
Cartwright, James P. (Jobo) 228, 231, 237, 240-241, 243, 245, 247, 250-254, 256, 313
Cartwright, W.B. 194
Carver, James 57
Casada, Roy 260
Cecil, Perry 165
Center Furniture Store 115
Chambliss, Alexander 85, 186, 210
Chancey, Claude 130
Chastain, J.P. 89
Chastain, J.W. 79, 99, 256
Chastain, Traynor 78, 105
Chatsworth, Georgia 32, 290
Chattanooga News 51, 61, 63-64, 70-71, 81-82, 84, 95
Chattanooga News-Free Press 292, 295
Chattanooga, Tennessee 36, 50, 102-103, 154, 165-166, 246, 266, 277, 291, 303, 305
Chattanooga Times 21, 27, 54, 58, 63-64, 66, 70-71, 74, 76, 79-80, 83, 89, 95-97, 106-107, 109, 120, 135, 148, 152, 154, 157-158, 162, 164, 166-170, 172, 177-178, 186, 191, 196, 204-205, 207-208, 217, 228-230, 234, 244, 246-250, 253, 259, 262, 268, 270, 272, 274, 278, 281, 292, 298, 304, 321
Cherokee County, North Carolina 42-43, 48, 87, 127, 138, 201, 249, 308
Cherokee Hotel 50, 60
Cherokee National Forest 22, 23, 130
Chilhowee Gliderport 113, 316
Chilhowee Mountains 20, 321
Civil Works Administration 71, 111
Civilian Conservation Corps 111
Clark, E.A. 24, 39, 40, 156
Clark, Tom 220
Clark, Virgil 148
Clayton, Frank 43-44, 72-74, 76, 79, 85-86, 99, 115-116, 127, 135, 137, 146, 156, 167, 198, 199, 215-216, 228, 296
Clement, Frank 319
Clements, Hal H. 119
Clemmer, J.D. 214
Clemmer, M.E. 233-234

361

Clemmer Motor Company 143
Clemmer, R.W. 209
Cleveland Daily Banner 73, 164, 304, 308
Cleveland Herald 164
Cleveland, Tennessee 21, 50, 60, 143, 145, 159, 163-164, 175, 241, 298-299, 319, 320
Cochran, C.J. 141
Cody, Bill 24
Coffee, Joe 199, 243
Collier's 317
Collins, H.C. 141
Collins, R.M. (Meigs) 131, 142
Colonial Hotel 30
Conasauga River Lumber Company 112
Conasauga Schoolhouse 73, 76-77
Conasauga, Tennessee 21, 35-36, 72, 76, 97, 99, 180, 243, 247, 285, 287
Congress of Industrial Organizations (CIO) 122-123, 125, 127-128, 130-131
Cook, L.L. 131
Cooke, Robert Fielding 121
Cooper, Harry 88, 94
Cooper, Prentice 31, 109, 117, 118, 121, 127, 134-139, 141, 144, 153-154, 156-158, 160-162, 164-165, 168, 177, 187, 191, 240
Cooper, William Prentice 31
Copeland, Flint 36
Copper City Advance 38, 44, 95, 100, 109, 123-124, 129, 135, 146, 153, 200, 208, 212-213, 225-226, 231, 245-247, 249, 251, 256, 268, 283, 286, 304, 311
Copperhill High School 114, 213, 265
Copperhill Kiwanis Club 218
Copperhill Ripper Bill 212, 238, 245, 250, 253, 264, 290
Copperhill, Tennessee 23, 24, 29-30, 35-37, 44, 52, 56, 58, 64, 68, 72, 78, 82, 88, 114, 122-123, 127-130, 131, 133, 137, 145, 153, 159, 166-168, 188, 198-199, 212, 215, 226-227, 238, 240, 243, 246-247, 250, 256, 264, 269, 284, 290, 292, 296-298, 300, 307-311
Copperhill YMCA 131, 133
Corn, James F. 42, 46-47, 69, 76, 266

Corn, Terrell 164
Corn, W.T. 165
Corner Lunch Restaurant 238
Couch, W.B. 137
Couch, Wiley 152, 162, 187, 204-205, 210-211, 225, 286
Craig, Luther 78
Crawford, Frank 72, 78-79, 85, 100, 115-116, 124, 127, 249
Crawford, George 36, 40, 57, 61, 72, 79, 85, 92, 320
Crawford, Irving 145
Crewse, John W. 257
Crippen Construction Company 48
Crippen, D.A. 48-50
Crippen, J.D. 103
Cronan, Rex 281
Cross, Benjamin 141
Cross, Long 291
Crowe, Pryor 127, 137, 145, 156, 223, 235, 266, 270, 290, 292, 320
Crox, Henry 42-44, 105, 110, 150, 154, 181, 183-185, 196-200, 241, 243, 257, 259, 277, 300, 302, 308-310, 312
Crox, Ruth 44, 302
Crox, William H. 42
Crumbliss, James G. 194-201, 205
Crumley, Albert 30
Crumley, James 260
Crump, Edward H. (Boss) 30, 46, 83, 105, 109, 117-118, 136, 139, 151, 154, 158-161, 168, 178, 186-188, 190, 196, 204, 210, 218, 252, 273, 287, 291, 319, 321
Crump, T. Sherman 75, 77, 82-83, 99
Crye, Warren 230, 238
Culbertson, Clarence 78
Culpepper, Charles 98
Cummings, Homer 67

D

Dale, Clyde 127, 131, 142, 156, 216, 228, 243, 277
Dalton, Arthur 59, 68-69, 80, 85, 87, 153, 275, 310
Dalton, Charles 105
Dalton, Floyd (Bad Eye) 64, 76, 79, 297
Dalton, Georgia 193
Dalton, Hal 238
Dalton, T.W. 98
Dalton, W.C. 44, 199-200, 203, 290, 297

Darr, Leslie 128, 141-142, 169, 191, 233-236, 315
Darwin, Frank 211
Daugherty, Gordon 137
Davidson County, Tennessee 201, 290
Davis, Claude 58, 74, 97, 194
Davis, Eldon Lee (El) 76, 99
Davis, Homer 80
Davis, "Little Vance" 76, 230, 243, 273
Davis, Mildred 194
Davis, R.A. 184-186, 257
Davis, Vance 33-34, 36, 38, 40, 42, 46-47, 53-54, 58, 68, 74-76, 87, 106, 118, 151, 153, 179, 183, 194, 219, 256, 269-271, 273, 294
Davis, W.G. 85, 262, 270, 293
Davis, W.I. (Buster) 76
Deal, Jesse 128
Deal, John 44
Dean, Bill 81
Delano, Tennessee 21, 35, 53, 72, 79, 96, 135, 200
Dempster, George 189
Denver Post 299
Derryberry, Carl 303
Dethero, H.L. 164
Dewey, Thomas 201
Doak, Lester 120
Dodson, Casto 121
Donner, Lester 148-149
Doogan, Sam 97
Dossett, Burgin 80, 83
Draewell, O.T. 268-270
Ducktown Back In Raht's Time 218, 267
Ducktown Banking Company 273
Ducktown High School 228, 230, 285
Ducktown Hotel 88, 126-127
Ducktown Law Court 88, 90, 128, 216, 256, 295-296
Ducktown, Tennessee 21-23, 35, 44, 46-48, 60, 67-68, 71-72, 78, 85-86, 90, 94, 100, 103, 108, 115-116, 122, 124-126, 129-130, 145, 148, 198-199, 213, 231, 237, 243, 247, 252-253, 274, 284, 287, 290, 293, 295-298, 300, 303, 307-309, 311, 315
Duffy, Will 30
Duggan, D.C. 81
Duggan, Ralph 223, 231, 238, 240, 242, 248, 313
Duncan, A.C. 137, 138

E

Earley, George 125
Edwards, John 89, 275-279, 283, 298, 308-309, 311-312, 321
Eldridge, Nat 163
Eller, Leroy 215, 297
Ellis, Jim 228, 270, 298, 302
Ellis, Marion 130-131, 142
Ellis, W.G. 76
Elrod, Charlie 91
Ensley, Ottis (Shorty) 215-216, 296, 304
Epperson, Bill 292, 300
Etowah Enterprise 303
Etowah Police Department 32
Etowah, Tennessee 29, 31-34, 145, 191, 195, 280, 299, 318

F

Fair, B.H. 164, 165
Faircloth, Rudy 295
Fannin County, Georgia 48, 57, 87, 125, 127, 130-131, 138, 145, 162, 201, 258
Farner, Tennessee 23, 85, 303
FBI 125, 131, 133, 141-143, 149, 169-170, 220
Fetzer, Herman 30
Fifth Congressional District 187
First Civil District 21, 272
Fite, B.W. 73, 76
Fitzgerald Jr., R.H. 178
Ford, Earl 221
Four Mile Creek 173-174
Fourth Civil District 38
Foust, J. Lon 53, 165
Frankfurter, Felix 170
Franklin, Walter (Tino) 164
Frazier Jr., James B. 64, 119, 142, 187, 313
Frazier Sr., James B. 187
Freeman, James 297, 303-304
Frye, Robert 61, 64-65
Fulbright, H.M. 164

G

Gaddis, A.J. 65
Gaddis, Andrew Jackson 94
Gaddis, Anna 93
Gaddis, Emmett 44, 48-51, 56, 61, 63-67, 72, 78-79, 88-96, 99, 102-104, 111, 115-116, 148-149, 216, 318
Gaddis, Olen 90, 94
Gaddis, Windom 56, 72, 78, 91
Gailor, Justice 186
Ganues, L.C. 297, 311

Gardener, Earl 85
Geer, Cas 216, 252, 257-259, 283, 286, 292, 297, 300, 308-309, 312
Geisler, Alfred 89
Gerber, Will 190, 252
Giles, Lt. Col. 307
Gillespie, Tom 222
Gilliland, Bill 39
Gilliland, Farrell 292
Gilliland, George 34, 39, 53, 100, 105-106, 109, 151, 180, 253, 262
Gilliland, John K. (Chet) 38
Goforth, Alvin 303
Goforth, John 295
Goforth, Julius 146-149, 170
Good County League 261
Good Government League (GGL) 227-232, 237-238, 240-246, 248-250, 254-258, 260, 262, 264-268, 273-279, 283-285, 287-290, 292, 294-295, 297-298, 300, 303-304-305, 307-308, 310-311, 314, 316-317
Goode, Chester 295
Gore Sr., Albert 319
Goss, Leonard C. 167, 254
Gowan, Arlene Dillard 146-148
Gowan, Stephen 146
Grady, Lake 76
Grassy Creek, Tennessee 150, 267
Gray, George (Mutt) 189, 193, 217, 225, 261-262, 269
Greasy Creek, Tennessee 23, 44, 70, 72, 128, 146, 285
Green, Abraham B. (Abie) 36, 40, 53-54, 58, 68, 80, 85, 99, 134-135, 189, 193, 225
Green, George 292
Green, Grafton 186
Green, Leslie Bryant 131, 141
Green, Newt 292
Green, Tate C. 141
Green, Willie 291
Greene, Emil 254, 307
Greene, Mark 109
Gregory, Joseph Milburn 194, 196, 255
Gregory, Joseph N. 255-256
Gregory, Sally Hutchins 45, 56, 84, 98, 112, 114, 213, 229, 291
Gregory, Watson 255-256, 275, 295, 305, 309
Griffith, Oscar 216
Grooms, Bill 107
Grooms, Johnnie 107
Grooms, Ralph 107
Grubb, Mrs. Fenton 103
Grubb, W. French 159

Grundy County, Tennessee 138
Guinn, Abbie McCay 24, 26
Guinn, A.J. 115, 137, 145
Guinn, Charles 38, 41, 43, 57, 64, 67, 69, 88, 93, 97, 107, 135, 145, 148-149, 156, 184-186, 315, 317
Guinn Jr., Charles (Charlie) 84, 145
Guinn, H. 266
Guinn, John M. 195
Guinn, W.A. 24, 26

H

Haddock, Bill 73
Haddock, Jack 73, 318
Haddock, Mattie 73, 318
Haddock, Walter 73-74
Hall, John 76
Hallbrook, Blanche 144
Hallbrook, Ted 144
Hamby, Bill 218
Hamby, Cecil 300
Hamby, David 300
Hamby, Reuben 135
Hamby, Shirley 300
Hamilton County Herald 266
Hamilton County, Tennessee 50, 53, 134-135, 157, 168, 204-205, 208, 318
Hamilton National Bank 123, 128
Hamilton, William 23
Hammer, John 313
Hammons, Benson 44, 85, 137, 159, 282, 309
Hammons, Carl 277, 281-282
Hammons, Harvey 97, 148, 278-279, 282, 285, 291-292, 308-309
Hampton, Bernie 224
Harbison, George 30
Harbison, Hattie Crowe 57
Harbison Hotel 57
Harbison, Joe 261
Harbison, John 42, 57-58, 68, 71, 80-82, 85, 99-100, 105-106, 109, 151-153, 189
Harbison, Thomas N. 72, 75, 89
Harbuck Roller Mountain 91
Hardwick, C.L. 164
Hardwick, George L. 164-165
Haren, Frank 300
Hargis Lumber Company 177
Harper, Clyde 105
Harrill, Bob 222, 280
Harrison, Claude 309
Harrison, Mrs. Ethie 173
Harrison, Walter 29
Harrison, William Oliver (Ol) 33-36, 69, 80, 246, 290
Haskins, Dave 58

Haskins, Pearl 238
Haskins, Ruth 214
Hatcher, Joe 81, 184, 190
Hawkins, Jim 39
Headrick, George 65, 91
Headrick, John 43
Headrick, Travis 80
Hedden, Bill 98, 137, 146-149, 170
Hedden, Ernest 146
Hedden, Garrett 27-28, 147, 318
Hedden, James (Jack) 98, 146-149
Hedden, Lecia 146, 148
Hedden, Mary 170
Hedden, Millie 149
Hedden, Riley 27, 147
Helton, Wes 125
Henry, Knox 218, 220, 317
Henry, Thomas Wayne 131, 142
Henslee, J.J. 141
Henson, Everett 275
Hermitage Hotel 187, 227
Herrell, J.C.F. 187
Hickey, Thomas R. 275
Hicks, Sue K. 88-90, 92-95, 97, 109, 128, 145, 153, 156, 216
Hicks, Thomas J. 115, 297
Higdon, W. Q. 250, 256
Higgins, F.D. (Dyke) 30
Higgins, F.W. 281
Higgins, Jake 41, 76, 99, 112, 274, 283, 287, 308, 321
Higgins, J.C. 281
Higgins, Walter 189
Higgins, Wayne 99, 243
Higgins, W.C. 243
Hildebrand, Michael 207
Hill, Felix 43
Hitener, Tom W. 89
Hiwassee River 20, 27, 32, 102, 112
Hixon, Fred 152, 259, 260
Hofferbert, Louis 178, 187
Holder, Wilburn 78
Hood, Frank 83, 107
Hood, George 27, 30, 63
Hood, Oliver 63-64, 81
Hood, R.G. 38, 58, 68, 80, 83, 85, 99-100
Hoover, Herbert 34
Hotel Farragut 199
Howard, Neil 236
Howell, Leon 72, 141, 264
Hubbard, Earl 131, 133, 141-142
Huffman, Clint 131, 141
Huffman, Clyde 125, 141
Hughes, Jim 91
Hughes, John Horace 203, 318

Humphries, Brownell 103
Hunt, Ernest 228, 250, 275, 293-294, 298, 311
Hunter, George 128-129
Hutchins, John S. 39
Hutchins, P.R. 39-40, 45, 77, 79, 159
Hyatt, G. Parks 88, 94, 137
Hyatt, H.H. 93, 115, 145, 266
Hyde, Fred 125
Hyde, H.P. 65, 89, 100, 141

I

Ingle, C.A. 85
International Union of Mine, Mill, and Smelter Workers 122, 124
Isabella, Tennessee 23, 48, 60, 63, 85, 122, 125, 264, 285
Ivins, Burkett 32

J

Jacks, Richard 295
James, Eddie 104
Jenkins, Charles 76
Jennings Jr., John J. 134, 138, 155-157, 169, 189-191, 194-197, 199-200, 202-205, 224, 277, 315
Jett, John Q. 72
Johnson, Hub 221
Johnson, Lee 297
Johnson, Wayne 89
Johnston, Thomas Lynn 316
Joins, Fred 220
Jones, Don 86
Jones, Jerry 89
Jones, Richard 315
Jones, Van D. 133, 141
Jones, Wilma Edwards 276
Jordan, Paul 305

K

Kefauver, Estes 53, 119-121, 134-136, 138, 141, 153, 155, 159, 169, 182, 190-191, 194, 201, 204-205, 207-208, 210-211, 218-219, 225, 227, 248, 273, 286-287, 291, 311
Kell, Cecil 167
Kelley, Euclid 76
Kelly, Alan 257, 267, 277
Kelly, Tom 320
Kemp, Ted 76
Kennedy, Bull 295, 305
Kennedy, Otto 280, 295
Kerr, James 277, 281-282, 292
Kerr, W.A. 33, 85, 176, 208, 270, 281
Kilpatrick, Wendell 256
Kimbrough, Brad 151

Kimbrough, Dorothy Trevena 136
Kimbrough, Eliza Cooke 121
Kimbrough, John 72
Kimbrough, Tate 270
Kimsey Junior College 47, 230
Kimsey, L.E. 46-47
Kimsey, Lester 275, 309
Kimsey, Parks 105
Kimsey, Wayne 295
Kincaid, T.J. 261
Kirkpatrick, R.L. 106
Knox County, Tennessee 117, 154-155, 187, 189, 191, 194-196, 199, 201, 203, 206
Knoxville Journal 118, 135, 136, 139, 140, 155, 160, 161, 163, 165, 167, 176, 177, 187, 196, 197, 200, 204, 227, 286-287, 314
Knoxville Journal and Tribune 32
Knoxville News-Sentinel 88, 139, 153-156, 164, 175, 178, 186-187, 198, 200, 202, 206, 208, 224, 253, 291, 295, 314
Knoxville, Tennessee 60, 123, 128, 157, 189, 196, 199, 246, 287, 291, 315, 317
Kramer, Russell 65, 88-90, 92, 94-95, 97, 100, 102-103, 234-236, 315, 318

L

Ladd, William 243, 248
Land, Donald 293-294, 307
Landon, Alf 87
Lanning, L.B. 33
Larkin, Frank 291, 295
Lawson, O.J. 50
Ledford, Anna Lee 96
Ledford, Cornelia 96-97
Ledford, George 53, 58, 82, 96-97, 100, 310, 318
Ledford, Lake 290
Ledford, M.C. 152-153
Ledford, Melvin 59, 146
Ledford, Sonny 293, 298
Ledford, Troy 96
Lee, Jim 135
Lee, Toy 276, 310
Lewis, August 69, 72, 78, 99, 106, 135, 173, 224, 236, 257, 273, 275-276, 291, 300, 305, 309, 316, 318
Lewis, Austin 302
Lewis, A.W. 78
Lewis, Clifford 148
Lewis, G.C. 76
Lewis, Mary Lethco 145, 150, 237
Lewis, Mrs. Joe 173, 175

Lillard, Abraham 23, 207
Lillard Auto 72
Lillard, Cecil 137, 225
Lillard, Frank 152, 173, 175, 181, 200, 224, 236, 314, 316, 318
Lillard, Garfield 77
Lillard, George 260
Lillard, Grace 44
Lillard Hardware 314
Lillard, Herb 224, 302
Lillard, Howard 97
Lillard, Hoyt 36-38, 40, 43-44, 53-55, 65, 67, 71-72, 75, 79, 87, 100, 106, 111, 114, 118-119, 130, 134, 137, 150, 183, 197, 199, 208, 213-214, 217, 242, 244, 247-248, 252, 258-259, 265, 269, 281-282, 285, 289, 300, 307-309, 312
Lillard III, Abraham (Abe) 31, 77, 103, 106, 152, 237
Lillard, John 144, 232
Lillard, John Haskell (Cap) 103, 225
Lillard, John M. 103, 105-106, 109, 152, 181, 224
Lillard, Roy G. 237, 292
Lillard, Sue Biggs 26
Lillard, T. Blair 302
Linder, Chester 148
Lindsay, Robert 140, 155, 163
Linsdale, Tennessee 35, 237, 287
Little, M.W. 283
Littleton, Carlyle 185-186, 234-235, 315, 317
Lockaby, Lucian 78
Locke, James O. (Red) 150
London Observer 287
Long, Freed 131, 141-142
Lost Creek 27-28
Loudermilk, Ernest 295-296, 298, 307
Loudermilk, Hardy (Cobby) 296-297
Loudermilk, J.E. 303
Loudermilk, Luther 127
Loudon County, Tennessee 46, 87, 109, 117, 138, 155, 157, 187, 196, 199, 201-202, 206, 225, 248
Love, Fount 72, 75
Love, H.M. 230, 246, 276-278, 280, 304, 310
Love Jr., H.M. 256
Lowe, W.O. (Chink) 240 247-248
Lowery, Frank 136, 144, 231-232, 237-238, 240-241, 243, 245, 247, 250-256, 258-261, 263, 282,

289-290, 297-298, 300, 304, 308, 312, 316
Lowery Jr., W.M. 281
Lowery, Mabel 136
Lowery, Marshall 150
Lowery, Marvin 36, 38, 40, 42, 54, 58, 105, 136, 231, 252
Lowery, Sam 80
Lowery, Wesley 181
Lowery, William Frank 231
Lusk, Bill 217
Lyle, Elmo 282
Lyle, Isham 275, 277
Lyle, O.K. 167

M

Mabry, Mrs. Joe H. 137
Mackey, Afton 171-172
Mansfield, Pat 151, 184, 217, 222-225
Manu, R.T. 131
Marion County, Tennessee 201
Marler, T.J. 164-165
Mason, Boyd 38, 59, 68, 80
Massengale, Wayne 199, 297
Massengill, John 78
Maxwell, Blan 118, 139-140
Mayfield, Joe Ben 275, 278, 309
Mayfield Jr., Charles S. 267, 305, 308, 312
Mayfield Sr., Charles S. 99, 143, 164, 166, 194, 267
Maynor, Broughton 159
Maynor, Burch E. 111, 137,158-159, 290
McAlister, Hill 40, 44, 46, 49-50, 61, 66, 83
McAmis, J.C. 53, 71
McCabe, N.H. 142
McCay, Buck 254
McCay, Harbert T. 24, 29
McCaysville, Georgia 25, 277, 297
McClary, Ben Franklin 110
McClary, Boyd 150
McClary, Jr., J. Lake 152
McClary, Mrs. Parnick 173, 174, 236, 317
McClary, Paul 256, 276, 278
McClary, Robert E. (Bob) 58, 105-106, 109, 111, 134-135, 151, 183, 189, 257
McClary, R.W. 44
McClary, Stella 173-174, 236, 317
McClure, J.L. 228
McCord, Jim 187, 190, 194, 201, 204-207, 210, 219, 225, 239, 241-242, 247-249, 252-253, 255, 258, 259, 266, 286, 289, 298, 300, 304, 313

McDaris, L.D. 164
McDonald, Claude 89
McDonald, Henry 78
McDonald, Luther 89
McDonald, Walter 148
McFadden, David S. 63-64, 67, 84, 104
McFadden, David W. 48-53, 60-66, 81, 88-94, 103-104, 115, 135, 318
McFadden, Frank W. 63, 84
McFadden, Rozelle 61, 64, 89, 91, 95, 102-104
McFadden, Thelma 61, 95
McGee, Bill 295-296, 303
McGee, Ernest 39-40, 43, 48, 56, 78-80, 91, 100, 103-104, 109, 115, 181
McGee, Jack 261
McGee, John 131, 142
McGee, Lake 231, 261, 281, 307
McGee, Wade 228-230, 261, 275
McGee, W.P. 255, 261
McKellar, Kenneth 46, 83, 117, 121, 135, 136, 153, 158, 187, 210, 219, 225, 239, 248, 258, 287, 319
McKenzie, Jim 308
McMahan, Raymond 238
McMillan, James 57, 129
McMinn County, Tennessee 29, 46, 87, 97, 109, 117, 134, 138, 140-141, 151, 155-157, 162-163, 169, 179, 187-189, 194-196, 200-206, 208, 218-225, 228-229, 237, 239, 247-250, 280, 283, 313, 317, 322
McNeel Jr., M.L. 176
McReynolds, Dwight 299, 302, 305, 309
McReynolds, Samuel D. 34, 46, 58, 65-67, 71, 80, 83, 87, 105, 107, 117, 119, 152, 182
McWhorter, William F. 211
Mee, Columbus 157, 164
Meigs County, Tennessee 46, 87, 117, 138, 157, 202, 225, 248
Melton, William 293
Memphis, Tennessee 30, 46, 154, 178, 190, 287
Merrill, Arthur 89
Michael, W.E. 156
Middleton, E. A. 250
Middleton, Frank 200
Middleton, Virginia 261
Miller, L.C. 143-144, 234
Miller, L.D. 52, 85, 119, 120
Million, John 171, 172
Mitchell, John 273, 286

Mitchell, J. Ridley 153-154
Moats, Bill 281
Monroe County, Tennessee
  46, 87, 109, 117, 138,
  155-157, 189, 196, 199,
  201-202, 204, 205-206,
  208, 210-211, 220, 225,
  229, 247-250, 317
Moon, John A. 34
Moore, Bill 32
Moore, Carl 76
Moore, P.H. 119
Morgan County, Tennessee
  24, 71, 204
Morris, Tom 134
Moses, Freddie 159
Moss, James Hugh 32
Mt. Harmony Baptist Church
  60, 63
Murphy, North Carolina 60
Murray County, Georgia 32,
  202
Mynders, Alfred 205, 208,
  244, 249, 256, 263, 274,
  317, 319

N
Nancy Ward Grammar School
  71
Nashville Banner 161
Nashville Tennessean 81,
  139, 154, 156, 158-159,
  161, 166, 172, 183-184,
  190, 202, 204, 206, 208,
  218, 225, 227, 242, 245,
  247, 252, 259, 283, 298,
  300, 302, 314
Nashville, Tennessee 87,
  105-106, 118, 139, 149,
  157, 159-160, 175, 187,
  202, 205, 227, 246, 252-
  253, 259, 273, 279, 316
National Guard 36, 61, 153,
  241, 298, 300-301, 303-
  304, 307, 312-313
Neil, A.B. 186
Nevin, Robert 102-104
New York Hotel 88, 103, 131
New York Post 188
New York Times 299
Newman, John V. (Chili) 275,
  310
Nichols, Claude 97
Norton, George 112

O
Ocoee Baptist Church 266,
  283, 320
Ocoee Dam #1 132
Ocoee Lake 132
Ocoee River 20, 29, 112,
  131, 151
Ocoee River Gorge 21, 132,
  273

Ocoee Speed Trap 176, 177
Ocoee, Tennessee 21, 35, 43,
  72, 76, 80, 136, 175, 198,
  237, 247, 256, 275, 287,
  291, 293
O'Connor, John 157
Old Fort, Tennessee 21, 35,
  43, 96, 119, 265
Oliver, Earl 39, 116, 122-123,
  181, 293-294, 297, 298
Olympian, The 299
O'Neal, Daniel B. 72-73
Osborn, Coleman 32
Owens, Albert 303

P
Padgett, Burl 78
Painter, Doris 242
Painter, George 144, 218, 224
Painter, Ralph 107, 111-112,
  137, 180, 242, 282, 309
Panter, Carl E. 254
Panter, Cliff 152
Paris, Clifford 97
Park, Bertha 54
Park, Grover 39, 40, 43
Park, J.M. (Jim) 80, 87, 145,
  311
Park Jr., J. Franklin 18, 45
Park, Kirby 58, 76
Park, Leach 33, 42-45, 53,
  54, 77, 80, 85, 87, 100,
  106, 109-111, 114, 130,
  137, 145, 151, 198, 217,
  225, 243, 246, 256, 261-
  262, 269, 277-278, 280,
  282, 289-291, 295, 311,
  320
Park, Willis 240
Parkey, Wayne 285
Parks, Ben 217, 225, 282,
  304, 308-309
Parks, W.B. 164, 195, 217
Parksville Dam 130-131
Parksville Lake 81, 132, 305
Parksville, Tennessee 21, 66,
  67, 71, 115, 287, 297
Parr, James Gordon 131, 141
Parton, Lloyd 63, 67, 88, 90-
  93, 95, 102, 104
Passmore, G.W. 34, 38, 105,
  273
Passmore, James Lucius
  (Red) 38-39, 134, 137,
  150, 214, 241, 289, 292-
  293, 295, 298
Passmore, Paul 150
Passmore, Ruth Haskins 288
Patterson, Malcom 26, 29
Patterson, Rockford 123
Patton, E.E. 189, 194
Payne, Bob 65
Payne, Bud 276, 310
Payne, Carl 293

Payne, Inez 91
Payne, Marion 152
Peck, John 249
Phillips, Harry 184
Pickel, Charlie 218
Pierce, Wes 39-40, 44, 56, 61
Pike, Jim 36, 78
Pilgrim, William 143-144,
  233-234
Plaxico, H.E. 131
Polk County Commission Act
  255, 257, 262, 272, 277
Polk County Democratic Party
  20, 31, 33, 41-42, 58, 75,
  87, 105, 107, 134, 193,
  217-218, 282-285, 291, 306
Polk County Department of
  Education 118
Polk County High School 31,
  213, 256, 265, 268, 319
Polk County News 34, 53-54,
  59, 71, 86-87, 96, 115, 129,
  134, 136, 144-145, 148,
  151, 207, 212, 224, 251,
  257, 261, 274, 283, 285,
  288, 304, 321
Polk County Republican Party
  42, 57-59, 105, 134, 152,
  188, 217
Polk County Sheriff's
  Department 40, 116, 131,
  143, 170
Polk County, Tennessee 20-
  21, 23, 26, 33, 44, 46, 52,
  55, 60, 66, 87, 99, 105,
  109, 117, 130, 135-136,
  138-139, 152-153, 155-158,
  164-165, 169, 177-178,
  184, 188-191, 194-196,
  198-203, 206-208, 210,
  213-215, 219-220, 224-227,
  229-230, 233, 237, 239-
  240, 242, 245-249, 252-
  253, 258-260, 262, 264,
  270, 280, 286-291, 298,
  302, 304-305, 313-314,
  318, 321
Polk County Veterans League
  283
Polk, James K. 20
Pope, Lewis 267, 279
Posey, Lowell 39, 112, 265
Postelle, R.S. (Oris) 131, 133
Poston, Bill 105
Potato Creek 21
Prendergast Cotton Mills 53
Presswood, B.F. (Banjo) 79,
  86, 245, 284, 295-296,
  303-304
Prewitt, Justice 186
Price, Fannie 42
Price, Manuel 72, 85, 96-98,
  149, 310
Price, R.N. 134, 188, 217

Prince, John 75, 188, 197, 213, 243, 248, 262, 267, 277, 308, 312
Prince, Raymond 39
Prince, William M. 198
Prince, Winston 40-41, 46, 58, 69, 75, 82, 99, 107-109, 145, 313

Q

Queen, G.M. 125
Queen, John David 131, 133, 142
Quinn, Jack 56
Quinn, Pat 33, 37, 44, 71, 85, 97-98, 100, 107, 143, 148-149, 153, 262, 268
Quinn Springs 109, 153, 190, 192, 285, 287, 321

R

Radcliffe, Granville 167, 254, 264, 290, 297
Radford, Raymond 297, 303-304
Raht, Julius E. 21
Ray, C.C.L. 308
Ray, Harve 127
Read House 51, 103-104, 266
Reece, W.L. 97
Reece, Woodrow 173-175, 235-236, 316, 318
Reed, Will 130
Reedy, J.M. 265
Reliance, TN 23, 27
Reynolds, Horace 195
Reynolds, Robert 65, 67
Rhea County, Tennessee 201
Rhodes, Robert Lee 131, 133, 142
Rhodes, W.C. 141
Rice, Billy 84, 237
Rice, C.C. 260
Rice, Oliver W. 136
Richards, Everett (Shorty) 173-175, 178, 193, 234-236, 315, 317-318, 319
Richmond Times Dispatch 299
Ringgold, Georgia 212
Ritchie, W.H. 258-259
Roach, John 131
Roach, Reg 130
Roane County, Tennessee 202, 206
Robinson, Reid 124
Rodgers, Will 164
Rogers, Clyde 219
Rogers, George O. 151, 282, 300, 309
Rogers, Leslie 39-40, 42-43
Roosevelt, Franklin D. 40, 69, 87, 137-138, 149, 201, 209, 235

Rose, Jim 78
Rose, William C. (Bill) 72, 78, 89, 135, 137, 142, 144, 146-147, 151, 153, 189, 194, 199, 201-202, 205, 215-217, 225, 229, 238, 242, 244-245, 248, 250, 254, 256, 274, 282-283, 309
Rucker, James 275
Rucker, Will 187
Runion, Elias 44, 77, 79, 119, 198, 290
Runion, G. Scott 69, 72, 79, 106, 119, 318
Runion, John 44, 77-79, 119, 290
Russell, Herbert 83
Russell, William F. 31, 53, 83
Rymer, Bob 109
Rymer, C.C. 89
Rymer, Dave 146
Rymer, E.M. 270
Rymer, Frank 256, 276
Rymer, Jess 43, 87, 157, 163, 165-166, 179
Rymer, Jim 89, 148-149
Rymer Jr., Robert (Little Bob) 282
Rymer, Noah J. 89
Rymer, Wilbur 148

S

Sartin, Bob 228
Sartin, Hubert C. (Buck) 114, 231, 259, 275, 309
Scarbrough, George 97, 109, 214
Scarbrough, William Oscar 97
Schaffer, Harry 118, 184
Scott County, Tennessee 204
Scott, Shy 222
Second Civil District 23
Second Congressional District 190, 204, 250
Sengebusch, G.A. 176
Servilla, Tennessee 23, 44, 70
Seventh Senatorial District 202, 206, 217
Shamblin, John 251
Sharp, Sam 256, 274, 276
Sharp, S.E. 264
Shearer, Edwin 293-294, 304, 308
Shearer, James M. (Jim) 34, 44, 78, 85, 293-294, 310
Shearer, Morris 293
Shelby County, Tennessee 46, 155-156, 158, 160, 168, 178, 184, 190, 220
Shelton, Jim 97
Sherrill, Zeb 302, 304
Shillings, Arthur 131, 133

Shillings, Theodore 199, 203
Shoemaker, James (Newt) 228, 230-231, 255-256, 259-260, 275, 277-278, 309
Simonds, John Edward 131, 133, 142
Simonds, Martin 131, 142
Simpson, P.C. 49
Simpson, W.D. 98
Sims, E.M. 176
Singleton, F.P. 58
Sixth Senatorial District 187, 200-201, 206
Smith, Al 34
Smith, Ben 43, 111, 137, 146, 156, 173, 175-176, 193, 235, 270, 315, 319
Smith, Edward B. 156
Smith, Margaret Evelyn 283
Smith, Mitchell 152, 193
Smith, Tommie 97
Smith, William Ran 133, 142
Snell, Bertrand 66
Sosebee, George 276
Sparks, Owen 104
Spiker, Curley 176
Spradling, Herbert 103-104
Springtown, Tennessee 23, 69-70, 72, 78, 99, 135, 246, 287, 291, 293
Spurling, George 221
Spurling, James 31, 318
Spurling, Jim 228
Standridge, John 72, 80, 87, 137, 155, 158-159, 209, 227, 243, 251, 257, 261-262, 269, 274, 292
Standridge, Robert John 191
Standrige, Gena 269
Stansberry, Bill 224
State Highway Patrol 241, 254, 298, 300, 307
Stephenson, G.E. 33, 43, 203
Stewart, Billy 299-300, 303, 308, 311
Stewart, Grady 278, 281
Stewart, Jack 281
Stewart, John 97
Stewart, T.L. 47, 53, 58, 68, 100, 166, 171, 183-184, 190, 262, 267
Stewart, Tom 117, 153, 157, 211, 273
Stillwell, Roy 58, 108-109
Stone, Charles 89
Stone, Spence 281
Stoval, Hugh 305
Strader, C.W. 254
Stuart, Hardwick 134, 137-139, 151, 228, 231, 241, 247
Styles, Fred 42
Styles, Louise 254
Styles, M.T. 105

Summers, Sandy 58
Super Sod 113, 316
Sutton, Clarence (Red) 128-129
Swan, Gus 79
Sweetwater Lions Club 206
Sweetwater Valley News 206, 211
Syfan, Dorothy 89-90, 93
Syfan, Manning 89

T

Tallant, William G. 250, 254
Tallant, W.O. 250
Talley, Arthur Harold (Chuck) 39, 86, 109, 115-116, 226-228, 231-232, 296, 303
Talley, David 39, 86-87, 116, 125, 180, 229, 231, 268-269, 303-304
Talley, Florene 303
Talley, Marion 89
Tate, Frank 38
Taylor, Alf 20
Taylor, B.L. 188
Taylor, Bob 20
Taylor, Charles E. 137, 273
Taylor, Dayo 78
Taylor, George 317-318
Taylor, Hoyt 290
Taylor, J.J. 85, 176, 181, 270
Taylor, J. Tom 109, 221
Taylor, J. Will 117
Taylor, Luther 275, 309
Taylor, Robert 315
Taylor, R.P. 57-58, 167, 254, 290
Taylor, Thurston 119
Taylor's School 23
Tennessee Copper Company (TCC) 29-30, 69-70, 122-123, 125, 127-131, 142, 212-213, 289
Tennessee Power Company 115, 130
Tennessee Rural Electric Company 132
Tennessee Supreme Court 37, 47, 107, 144, 160, 170, 185, 194, 233, 262, 277
Tennessee Valley Authority (TVA) 111, 130-131, 138, 141, 150, 202, 277
Terry, Pat 250, 254, 264, 274, 304
Third Civil District 23
Third Congressional District 119-121, 134, 152, 190, 204, 208, 227, 248, 311
Thompson, Clifford 32
Thompson, Eula 32
Tilson, Clifford 276
Townsend, J.M.C. 142
Townsend, John B. 180
Trevena, W.A. 46, 56, 74, 85, 135, 146
Trotter, A.J. 230, 238
Trotter, Frank 261
Turner, Julius 44, 78, 100
Turtletown, Tennessee 23, 35, 44, 74, 77, 108, 119, 127, 135, 198, 275, 290, 293-294, 297, 303, 308, 311

U

Underhill, Patsy Crox 39, 42, 44-45, 86, 150, 154, 177
Underwood, E. Marvin 57
United States Supreme Court 170
United States Surplus Commodities Program 125

V

Van Devander, Charles 188
Vann, E.J. 44
Vaughn, Sarah 27
Verner, Bessie 78
Verner, Pearl 78
Vestal, Ed 222
Veterans League of Polk County 238
Voiles, Carl 221

W

Waldrop, M.N. 39, 40
Walker, Herbert 143-144, 233-234
Ward, Frank 129
Ware, H.M. (Gid) 167, 254, 273, 279
Warren County, Tennessee 138, 201
Washington, D.C. 121, 130, 134, 157, 200
Watson, Bertie 173, 317
Watson, Henry 74, 116, 145, 151, 181, 237, 241, 265, 269, 293-294, 297
Watson, Pryor 27
Watters, Newman 76
Webb, Charles 302
Webb, C.R. 89
Webb, Reuel 102, 148, 184
Westerberg, George 166, 195
Westmoreland, Ed 297
Wetmore, Tennessee 20
White, Bill 222
White County, Tennessee 138, 201
White, Dud 44, 79, 198
White, Grant 275
Wilburn, Minus 221-223, 280
Williams, Charles 53-54, 106, 114, 189, 193, 217, 225, 256, 262, 269, 277-283, 298, 308-309, 311
Williams, George 34, 42, 44, 54, 58, 77, 82, 105, 275, 279
Williams, H.E. 195
Williams, J.E. 40
Williams, Joe 24, 156
Williams, Joe V. 68, 99, 128, 233
Williams, Sam 148
Williamson, W.H. 31
Willkie, Wendell 138
Wimberly, M.B. 80, 176, 270
Wise, Windy 222
Witt, Ben 238, 251, 257, 282
Witt, Matt 44, 83, 86, 112, 114, 123, 216, 231, 259, 304
Witt, R. Beecher 39, 44, 63-64, 67, 88-89, 92, 94-95, 97, 125, 148-149, 153, 155, 177, 216, 280
Witt, Traynor 43, 290, 308
Woodlee, Glenn 268, 274, 281, 289
Woods, George 139, 156, 161, 184, 187, 189, 198, 204-206, 217, 223
Woodward, Felton 128-129, 131, 133, 141-142
Woodward, Theodore 141
Woody, Ben 276
Woody, Dutch 57, 87, 101, 105, 117, 119, 137, 152, 188, 199, 201
Woody, Robert N. 119
Works Progress Administration (WPA) 48, 72-73, 111
Wright, Herman 36, 40, 43, 44, 64, 72, 77, 85, 87, 91, 111, 137, 144, 146, 156, 183, 228, 235, 238, 270, 320
Wright, I.J. 144, 238, 243
Wright, Louis 43, 72, 137, 144, 198-199, 228, 238, 270, 284
Wrinkle, John S. 49-50, 52-53, 60-61, 63-65, 67, 88, 93, 102-104, 106, 119-120, 128, 134-135, 227-228, 233, 248, 317

Y

Yarnell, Oscar 36

www.ingramcontent.com/pod-product-compliance
Lightning Source LLC
Chambersburg PA
CBHW050159240426
43671CB00013B/2186